Fodor's

Madrid & Barcelona

D0104297

The complete guide, thoroughly up-to-date

Packed with details that will make your trip

The must-see sights, off and on the beaten path

What to see, what to skip

Mix-and-match vacation itineraries

City strolls, countryside adventures

Smart lodging and dining options

Essential local do's and taboos

Transportation tips, distances and directions

Key contacts, savvy travel tips

When to go, what to pack

Clear, accurate, easy-to-use maps

Books to read, films to watch, background essays

Excerpted from *Fodor's Spain*

Fodor's Travel Publications, Inc.
New York • Toronto • London • Sydney • Auckland
www.fodors.com

Fodor's Madrid & Barcelona

EDITOR: Christine Cipriani

Editorial Contributors: David Brown, Michael Jacobs, Helayne Schiff, M. T. Schwartzman (Gold Guide editor), George Semler, Katherine Semler, Annie Ward

Editorial Production: Melissa Klurman

Maps: David Lindroth, *cartographer*; Steven Amsterdam, *map editor*

Design: Fabrizio La Rocca, *creative director*; Guido Caroti, *associate art director*; Jolie Novak, *photo editor*

Production/Manufacturing: Rebecca Zeiler

Cover Photograph: Owen Franken

Copyright

Special Sales

CONTENTS

Maps

ON THE ROAD WITH FODOR'S

WHEN I PLAN A VACATION, the first thing I do is cast around among my friends and colleagues to find someone who's just been where I'm going. That's because there's no substitute for a recommendation from a good friend who knows your tastes, your budget, and your circumstances, someone who's just been there. Unfortunately, such friends are few and far between. So it's nice to know that there's *Fodor's Madrid & Barcelona.*

In the first place, this book won't stay home when you hit the road. It will accompany you every step of the way, steering you away from wrong turns and wrong choices and never expecting a thing in return. It includes a wonderful, full-color map from Rand McNally, the world's largest commercial mapmaker. Most important of all, it's written and assiduously updated by the kind of people you *would* hit up for travel tips if you knew them. They're as choosy as your pickiest friend, except they've probably seen a lot more of Spain. In these pages, they don't send you chasing down every sight in Madrid and Barcelona, but have instead selected the best ones, the ones that are worthy of your time and money. To make it easy for you to put it all together in the time you have, they've created short, medium, and long itineraries and, in cities, neighborhood walks that you can mix and match in a snap. Will this be the vacation of your dreams? We hope so.

About Our Writers

Our success in helping to make your trip the best of all possible vacations is a credit to the hard work of our extraordinary writers and editors.

Californian journalist **Deborah Luhrman** has visited many parts of the globe both as a travel writer and as press attaché for the Madrid-based World Tourism Organization, where she helps other journalists write about tourism and assists tourism ministries in dealing with the media. She has called Spain home for the past nine years and loves it, but still finds time for adventures in the likes of Egypt, China, and Germany.

Born and educated in the United States, writer, journalist, and translator **George Semler** has lived in Spain for the last 25 years. During that time he has published works on Spain, Catalonia, the Pyrenees, France, North Africa, and the Mediterranean region for the *International Herald Tribune,* the *Los Angeles Times, Forbes,* and *Saveur,* among other publications. When not hiking, skiing, playing hockey, or fly-fishing in the streams of the Pyrenees, he finds time to contribute to Fodor's guides, write poetry, and work on a magnum opus about the Pyrenees. He is also the author of books on Madrid and Barcelona.

Raised in Madrid, San Sebastián, and Barcelona, **Katherine Semler** attended preschool in Euskera (the Basque language), kindergarten in Spanish, elementary school in French, and secondary school in the United States in English. She went on to earn a B.A. in French and Russian literature at Vassar and an M.A. in French and Catalan literature at Dartmouth. (We are not making this up.) Married to singer-songwriter Sam Lardner, she now lives in Barcelona.

A native of Kansas City, **Annie Ward** holds a B.A. in English literature from the University of California–Los Angeles and an M.F.A. in screenwriting from the American Film Institute. Her first short film, *Strange Habit,* was the grand jury's selection for Best Film at the 1996 Aspen Film Festival. She lived in Spain for several years, where she taught screenwriting at the American Center of Barcelona, and now lives in Sofia, Bulgaria, where she is a reporter for the Bulgarian English-language newspaper *The Sofia Independent.* She has edited English translations of Bulgarian children's books, and is completing a novel set in both Spain and Bulgaria.

We'd also like to thank Pilar Vico and Natalia Zapatero at the Tourist Office of Spain, New York, for their kind assistance.

Connections

We're pleased that the American Society of Travel Agents continues to endorse Fodor's as its guidebook of choice. ASTA is the world's largest and most influential travel trade association, operating in more than 170 countries, with 27,000 members pledged to adhere to a strict code of ethics reflecting the Society's motto, "Integrity in Travel." ASTA shares Fodor's devotion to providing smart, honest travel information and advice to travelers, and we've long recommended that our readers—even those who have guidebooks and traveling friends—consult ASTA member agents for the experience and professionalism they bring to your vacation planning.

On Fodor's Web site (www.fodors.com), check out the new Resource Center, an online companion to the Gold Guide chapter of this book, complete with useful hot links to related sites. In our forums, you can also get lively advice from other travelers and more great tips from Fodor's experts worldwide.

How to Use This Book

Organization

Up front is the **Gold Guide,** an easy-to-use section arranged alphabetically by topic. Under each listing you'll find tips and information that will help you accomplish what you need to in Spain. You'll also find addresses and telephone numbers of organizations and companies that offer destination-related services and detailed information and publications.

The first chapter in the guide, Destination: Madrid and Barcelona helps get you in the mood for your trip. New and Noteworthy cues you in on trends and happenings, What's Where gets you oriented, Pleasures and Pastimes describes the activities and sights that make Spain unique, Fodor's Choice showcases our top picks, and Festivals and Seasonal Events alerts you to special events you'll want to seek out.

Chapters in *Fodor's Madrid & Barcelona* are arranged by city or by grouping several provinces into a distinct entity (Around Madrid). Each city chapter begins with Exploring information, which is divided into neighborhood sections; each recommends a walking or driving tour and lists sights in alphabetical order. Each regional chapter is divided by geographical area; within each area, towns are covered in logical geographical order, and attractive stretches of road and minor points of interest between them are indicated by the designation *En Route.* And within town sections, all restaurants and lodgings are grouped.

To help you decide what to visit in the time you have, all chapters begin with our recommended itineraries. The A to Z section that ends all chapters covers getting there and getting around. It also provides helpful contacts and resources.

At the end of the book you'll find a Portrait of Madrid and Barcelona—an appetizing profile of Spanish food and wine.

Icons and Symbols

★	Our special recommendations
✕	Restaurant
🏨	Lodging establishment
✕🏨	Lodging establishment whose restaurant warrants a special trip
♨	Good for kids (rubber duck)
☞	Sends you to another section of the guide for more information
✉	Address
☎	Telephone number
☉	Opening and closing times
💷	Admission prices (those we give apply to adults; substantially reduced fees are almost always available for children, students, and senior citizens)

Numbers in white and black circles ③ ❸ that appear on the maps, in the margins, and within the tours correspond to one another.

Dining and Lodging

The restaurants and lodgings we list are the cream of the crop in each price range. Price charts appear in the Pleasures and Pastimes section that follows each chapter introduction.

Hotel Facilities

We always list the facilities that are available—but we don't specify whether you'll be charged extra to use them: When pricing accommodations, always ask what's included. In addition, assume that all rooms have private baths unless noted otherwise. In addition, when you book a room, be sure to mention if you have a disability or are traveling with children, if you prefer a private bath or a certain type of bed, or if you have specific dietary needs or other concerns.

Assume that hotels operate on the **European Plan** (EP, with no meals) unless we specify that they use the **Continental Plan** (CP, with a Continental breakfast daily), **Modified American Plan** (MAP, with breakfast and dinner daily), or the **Full American Plan** (FAP, with all meals).

Restaurant Reservations and Dress Codes

Reservations are always a good idea; we mention them only when they're essential or are not accepted. Book as far ahead as you can, and reconfirm as soon as you arrive. Unless otherwise noted, the restaurants listed are open daily for lunch and dinner. We mention dress only when men are required to wear a jacket or a jacket and tie. Look for an overview of local dining-out habits in the Gold Guide and in the Pleasures and Pastimes section that follows each chapter introduction.

Credit Cards

The following abbreviations are used: **AE,** American Express; **DC,** Diners Club; **MC,** MasterCard; and **V,** Visa.

Don't Forget to Write

You can use this book in the confidence that all prices and opening times are based on information supplied to us at press time; Fodor's cannot accept responsibility for any errors. Time inevitably brings changes, so always confirm information when it matters—especially if you're making a detour to visit a specific place.

Were the restaurants we recommended as described? Did our hotel picks exceed your expectations? Did you find a museum we recommended a waste of time? Keeping a travel guide fresh and up-to-date is a big job, and we welcome your feedback, positive *and* negative. If you have complaints, we'll look into them and revise our entries when the facts warrant it. If you've discovered a special place that we haven't included, we'll pass the information along to our correspondents and have them check it out. So send us your thoughts via e-mail at editors@fodors.com (specifying the name of the book on the subject line) or on paper in care of the Spain editor at Fodor's, 201 East 50th Street, New York, New York 10022. In the meantime, have a wonderful trip!

Karen Cure

Karen Cure
Editorial Director

FRANCE

San
Sebastián Fuenterrabia
Roncesvalles
Vitoria Pamplona
Jaca P Y R E N E E S ANDORRA
roño Tudela Huesca Seu d'Urgell Figueres/
Soria Barbastro Figueras
Ebro Manresa Vich/Vic Girona/Gerona
Zaragoza Lérida Montserrat COSTA
Calatayud Barcelona BRAVA
Medinaceli Daroca Alcañiz Tarragona COSTA DORADA
ara Tajo Caminreal Tortosa
Monreal
del Campo La Jana Vinaròs Balearic TO
Teruel Sea MENORCA
Cuenca Castellón COSTA DEL AZAHAR
rancón de la Plana
Sagunto Golfo de Palma
Requena Valencia Valencia Majorca
Jucar Ibiza BALEARIC
Albacete ISLANDS
Alcaraz Eivissa
Hellín Alicante Formentera
Elche COSTA BLANCA
Orihuela Menorca
da Murcia Ciudadela Mahón
Cazorla Lorca Manga del
Mar Menor
NEVADA Cartagena
COSTA
CALIDA Mediterranean
Sea
Almería
COSTA DE ALMERIA

ALGERIA

N

0   100 miles
0   150 km

SMART TRAVEL TIPS A TO Z

Basic Information on Traveling in Madrid and Barcelona, Savvy Tips to Make Your Trip a Breeze, and Companies and Organizations to Contact

AIR TRAVEL

MAJOR AIRLINE OR LOW-COST CARRIER?

Most people choose a flight based on price, but there are other issues to consider. Major airlines offer the greatest number of departures; smaller airlines—including regional, low-cost, and no-frill airlines—usually have a more limited number of flights daily. Major airlines have frequent-flyer partners, which allow you to credit mileage earned on one airline to your account with another. Low-cost airlines offer a definite price advantage and fewer restrictions, such as advance-purchase requirements. Safety-wise, low-cost carriers as a group have a good history, but **check the safety record before booking** any low-cost carrier; call the Federal Aviation Administration's Consumer Hotline (☞ Airline Complaints, *below*).

American, US Airways, and Air Europa travel to Madrid; Continental, Delta, Iberia, and TWA travel to Madrid and Barcelona.

➤ AIRLINES: **Air Europa** (☎ 888/238–7672). **American** (☎ 800/433–7300). **Continental** (☎ 800/231–0856). **Delta** (☎ 800/241–4141). **Iberia** (☎ 800/772–4642). **TWA** (☎ 800/892–4141). **US Airways** (☎ 800/428–4322).

➤ NONSTOP FROM NORTH AMERICA: **AeroMexico** (☎ 800/237–6639). **American** (☎ 800/433–7300). **Continental** (☎ 800/231–0856). **Delta** (☎ 800/221–1212). **Iberia** (☎ 800/772–4642). **TWA** (☎ 800/892–4141).

➤ FROM THE U.K.: **British Airways** (☎ 0345/222–111). **Iberia** (☎ 0171/830–0011).

GET THE LOWEST FARE

The least-expensive airfares to Barcelona and Madrid are priced for round-trip travel. Major airlines usually require that you **book far in advance and stay at least seven days** and no more than 30 to get the lowest fares. Ask about "ultrasaver" fares, which are the cheapest; they must be booked 90 days in advance and are nonrefundable. A little more expensive are "supersaver" fares, which require only a 30-day advance purchase. Remember that penalties for refunds or scheduling changes are stiffer for international tickets, usually about $150. International flights are also sensitive to the season: **plan to fly in the off season** for the cheapest fares. If your destination or home city has more than one gateway, **compare prices to and from different airports.** Also price flights scheduled for off-peak hours, which may be significantly less expensive.

To save money on flights from the United Kingdom and back, **look into an APEX or Super-PEX ticket.** APEX tickets must be booked in advance and have certain restrictions. Super-PEX tickets can be purchased at the airport on the day of departure—subject to availability.

DISCOUNT PASSES

If you buy a round-trip transatlantic ticket on **Iberia** (☞ *above*), you might want to purchase a Visit Spain pass, good for four domestic flights during your trip. It must be purchased before you arrive in Spain, all flights must be booked in advance, and the cost is $260, or $350 if you want to include flights to the Canary Islands (prices are $20 to $50 less if you travel during the low season, between October 1 and June 14).

On certain days of the week, Iberia also offers minifares, which can save you 40% on domestic flights. Tickets must be purchased in advance, and you must stay over Saturday night (☞ Discounts, *below*).

USE AN AGENT

Travel agents, especially those who specialize in finding the lowest fares (☞ Discounts & Deals, *below*), can be especially helpful when booking a plane ticket. When you're quoted a price, **ask your agent if the price is likely to get any lower.** Good agents know the seasonal fluctuations of airfares and can usually anticipate a sale or fare war. However, waiting can be risky: the fare might go *up* as seats become scarce, and you may wait so long that your preferred flight sells out. A wait-and-see strategy works best if your plans are flexible, but if you must arrive and depart on certain dates, don't delay.

CHECK WITH CONSOLIDATORS

Consolidators buy tickets for scheduled flights at reduced rates from the airlines, then sell them at prices that beat the best fare available directly from the airlines, usually without advance restrictions. Sometimes you can even get your money back if you need to return the ticket. Carefully read the fine print detailing penalties for changes and cancellations, and **confirm your consolidator reservation with the airline.**

➤ CHARTERS: **Air Comet** (☎ 615/373–7904 or 800/234–1700). **Air Europa** (contact Spanish Heritage, ☎ 718/244–6017, 718/544–2752, or 800/221–2580). **Oasis International** (Club Vacations, ☎ 615/373–7904 or 800/234–1700). **Toto Tours International** (☎ 718/237–2312 or 800/676–7843).

➤ CONSOLIDATORS: **United States Air Consolidators Association** (✉ 925 L St., Suite 220, Sacramento, CA 95814, ☎ 916/441–4166, ℻ 916/441–3520).

ENJOY THE FLIGHT

For better service, **fly smaller or regional carriers,** which often have higher passenger-satisfaction ratings. Sometimes you'll find leather seats, more legroom, and better food.

For more legroom, **request an emergency-aisle seat.** Don't, however, sit in the row in front of the emergency aisle or in front of a bulkhead, where seats may not recline.

If you have specific dietary needs, such as vegetarian, low-cholesterol, or kosher food, **ask for special meals when booking.**

To avoid jet lag, try to maintain a normal routine while traveling. At night, **get some sleep.** By day, **eat light meals, drink water (not alcohol), and move around the cabin** to stretch your legs.

Some carriers have prohibited smoking throughout their systems; others allow smoking only on certain routes or even certain departures from that route. **Contact your carrier regarding its smoking policy.**

Always **bring a photo ID to the airport.** You may be asked to show it before you're allowed to check in.

COMPLAIN IF NECESSARY

If your baggage goes astray or your flight goes awry, complain right away. Most carriers require that you file a claim immediately.

➤ AIRLINE COMPLAINTS: **U.S. Department of Transportation, Aviation Consumer Protection Division** (✉ C-75, Washington, DC 20590, ☎ 202/366–2220). **Federal Aviation Administration (FAA) Consumer Hotline** (☎ 800/322–7873).

WITHIN SPAIN

Iberia and its sister carrier, Aviaco, are the main airlines offering domestic service. Two independent airlines, Air Europa and Spanair, offer a number of domestic routes at lower prices.

➤ CARRIERS: **Iberia** (☎ 91/329–4353). **Aviaco** (☎ 91/554–3600). **Air Europa** (☎ 91/540–6000 or 91/305–8159). **Spanair** (☎ 91/393–6740).

AIRPORTS

All transatlantic flights arriving in Spain from the United States and Canada pass through Madrid's Barajas airport. The country's other major gateway is Barcelona's El Prat de Llobregat.

Flying time is seven hours from New York and 14½ hours from Los Angeles.

➤ AIRPORT INFORMATION: Madrid: **Barajas airport** (☎ 91/305–8343). Barcelona: **El Prat de Llobregat** (☎ 93/298–3838).

THE GOLD GUIDE / SMART TRAVEL TIPS

BUS TRAVEL

An array of private companies operate Spain's buses, providing service that ranges from knee-crunchingly basic to luxurious. Some buses have televisions and free drinks, and many offer tours (easily arranged through your hotel) in English. Fares are lower than the corresponding train fares. There are depots in Madrid, but some of the companies are expected to move to a new terminal. Call ahead.

➤ FROM THE U.K.: Eurolines/National Express (☎ 0171/730–0202).

➤ TOURS WITHIN SPAIN: **Julià Tours** (✉ Gran Vía 68, Madrid, ☎ 91/571–5300). **Pullmantur** (✉ Plaza de Oriente 8, Madrid, ☎ 91/541–1805). **Marsans** (✉ Gran Vía 59, Madrid, ☎ 91/547–7300).

➤ COMMUTER BUS SERVICE WITHIN SPAIN: **Enatcar** (✉ C/ Canarias 17, Madrid, ☎ 91/527–9927. **Autored** (✉ C/ Fernandez Shaw 1, Madrid, ☎ 91/551–7200. **Continental Auto** (✉ C/ Alenza 20, Madrid, ☎ 91/533–0400. **Sepulvedana** (✉ C/ Palos de la Frontera 16, Madrid, ☎ 91/530–4800).

BUSINESS HOURS

Banks are generally open weekdays 8:30–2, Saturday 8:30–1, but in the summer most banks close at 1 PM weekdays and do not open on Saturday. Currency exchanges at airports and train stations stay open later. Traveler's checks can also be cashed at El Corte Inglés department stores until 9 PM.

Most museums are open from 9:30 to 2 and from 4 to 7 and are closed one day a week, usually Monday; but opening hours vary widely, so check before you set off. A few large museums, such as Madrid's Prado and Reina Sofía and Barcelona's Picasso Museum, stay open all day.

When planning a shopping day, **keep in mind that almost all shops close at midday** for at least three hours, except for the department-store chain El Corte Inglés. Stores are generally open from 10 to 1:30 and from 5 to 8. Shops are closed all day Sunday, and in Madrid they are also closed Saturday afternoon.

CAMERAS, CAMCORDERS, & COMPUTERS

Always **keep your film, tape, or computer disks out of the sun.** Carry an extra supply of batteries, and **be prepared to turn on your camera, camcorder, or laptop** to prove to security personnel that the device is real. Always **ask for hand inspection of film,** which becomes clouded after successive exposure to airport x-ray machines, and **keep videotapes and computer disks away from metal detectors.**

CUSTOMS

Before departing, **register your foreign-made camera or laptop with U.S. Customs** (☞ Customs & Duties, *below*). If your equipment is U.S.-made, call the consulates of the countries you'll be visiting to find out whether the device should be registered with local customs upon arrival.

➤ PHOTO HELP: **Kodak Information Center** (☎ 800/242–2424). *Kodak Guide to Shooting Great Travel Pictures,* available in bookstores or from Fodor's Travel Publications (☎ 800/533–6478), $16.50 plus $4 shipping.

CAR RENTAL

Rates in Madrid begin at $38 a day and $132 a week for an economy car with air conditioning, a manual transmission, and unlimited mileage. This does not include the tax on car rentals, which is 16%.

➤ MAJOR AGENCIES: **Budget** (☎ 800/527–0700; 0800/181181 in the U.K.). **Dollar** (☎ 800/800–4000; 0990/565656 in the U.K., where it's known as Eurodollar). **Hertz** (☎ 800/654–3001; 800/263–0600 in Canada; 0345/555888 in the U.K.). **National InterRent** (Europcar InterRent, ☎ 800/227–3876; 0345/222525 in the U.K.).

➤ LOCAL AGENCIES: **ATESA** (✉ Infante Mercedes 90, Madrid, ☎ 91/571–1931; ✉ Plaza Carmen Benítez 7, Seville, ☎ 95/441–9712).

CUT COSTS

To get the best deal, **book through a travel agent who is willing to shop around.**

Also **ask your travel agent about a company's customer-service record.** How has it responded to late plane arrivals and vehicle mishaps? Are there often lines at the rental counter, and, if you're traveling during a holiday period, does a confirmed reservation guarantee you a car?

Be sure to **look into wholesalers,** companies that do not own fleets but rent in bulk from those that do and often offer better rates than traditional car-rental operations. Prices are best during off-peak periods. Rentals booked through wholesalers must be paid for before you leave the United States.

➤ RENTAL WHOLESALERS: **Auto Europe** (☎ 207/842–2000 or 800/223–5555, FAX 800–235–6321). **Europe by Car** (☎ 212/581–3040 or 800/223–1516, FAX 212/246–1458). **DER Travel Services** (✉ 9501 W. Devon Ave., Rosemont, IL 60018, ☎ 800/782–2424; FAX 800/282–7474 for information, 800/860–9944 for brochures). The **Kemwel Group** (☎ 914/835–5555 or 800/678–0678, FAX 914/835–5126).

NEED INSURANCE?

When driving a rented car you are generally responsible for any damage to or loss of the vehicle. Before you rent, **see what coverage you already have** under the terms of your personal auto-insurance policy and credit cards.

Collision policies that car-rental companies sell for European rentals typically do not cover stolen vehicles. Before you buy additional coverage for theft, find out if your credit card or personal auto insurance will cover the loss.

BEWARE SURCHARGES

Before you pick up a car in one city and leave it in another, **ask about drop-off charges or one-way service fees,** which can be substantial. Note, too, that some rental agencies charge extra if you return the car before the time specified on your contract. To avoid a hefty refueling fee, **fill the tank just before you turn in the car,** but be aware that gas stations near the rental outlet may overcharge.

MEET THE REQUIREMENTS

Your own driver's license is valid in Spain, but you may want to get an International Driver's Permit for extra assurance; it's available from the American or Canadian automobile association, or, in the United Kingdom, from the Automobile Association or Royal Automobile Club.

CAR TRAVEL

Driving is the best way to get outside the cities and off the beaten track. Roads are classified as follows: A for *autopista* (toll road or *peaje*); N for *nacional* (main roads that are either divided highways or two lanes); and C for *comarcal* (local roads that crisscross the countryside).

Spain's highway system now includes some 6,000 km (3,600 mi) of superhighways. Still, you'll find some stretches of major national highways that are two lanes wide, where traffic often backs up behind heavy trucks. Autopista tolls are steep.

Barcelona and Madrid have notoriously long morning and evening rush hours that can try any driver's patience. If possible, it's best to **avoid the morning rush hour, which can last until noon, and the evening rush hour, which runs from 7 PM to 9 PM.**

Driving is on the right, and horns are banned in cities, but that doesn't keep Spaniards from blasting away. Children under 10 may not ride in the front seat, and seat belts are compulsory everywhere. Speed limits are 60 kph (37 mph) in cities, 100 kph (62 mph) on N roads, 120 kph (74 mph) on the autopista, and 90 kph (56 mph) unless otherwise signposted on other roads.

Gas stations are plentiful. Prices, decontrolled in 1993, were 112 ptas. a liter for *normal* (regular; 92 octane) and 117 ptas. a liter for *super* (97 octane) at press time. Credit cards are widely accepted, especially along main routes.

The large car-rental companies, Hertz and Avis, have 24-hour breakdown service. If you belong to an automobile club (AAA, CAA, or AA), you can get help from the Spanish auto club, RACE.

THE GOLD GUIDE / SMART TRAVEL TIPS

THE GOLD GUIDE / SMART TRAVEL TIPS

➤ AUTO CLUBS: In the United States: **American Automobile Association** (☎ 800/564–6222). In the United Kingdom: **Automobile Association** (AA, ☎ 0990/500–600), **Royal Automobile Club** (RAC, ☎ 0990/722–722 membership; 0345/121–345 insurance). In Spain: **RACE** (✉ José Abascal 10, Madrid, ☎ 91/447–3200; 91/593–3333 for emergency assistance).

CHILDREN & TRAVEL

CHILDREN IN MADRID AND BARCELONA

Spaniards love children. You'll see children accompanying their parents everywhere, including bars and restaurants, so bringing yours along on your trip should not be a problem. Shopkeepers will shower your child with *caramelos* (sweets), and even the coldest waiters tend to be friendlier when you have a youngster with you. But although you won't be shunted into a remote corner when you bring kids into a Spanish restaurant, **you won't find high chairs or special children's menus.** Children are expected to eat what their parents do, and it is perfectly acceptable to ask for an extra plate and share your food. Museum admissions and bus and metro rides are generally free for children up to age five. Be prepared for late bedtimes—especially in summer; it's surprisingly common to see under-fives playing cheerfully outdoors until midnight. Disposable diapers (*pañales*), formula (*papillas*), and bottled baby foods are readily available at supermarkets and pharmacies.

Be sure to plan ahead and **involve your youngsters** as you outline your trip. When packing, include things to keep them busy en route. Try to schedule sightseeing activities of special interest to the children. If you're renting a car, don't forget to **arrange for a car seat** when you reserve. Most hotels allow children under a certain age to stay in their parents' room at no extra charge, but others charge them as extra adults; be sure to **ask about the cutoff age for children's discounts.**

FLYING

As a general rule, infants under age two not occupying a seat fly at greatly reduced fares and occasionally for free. If your child is two or older, **ask about children's airfares.**

The adult baggage allowance generally applies to children paying half or more of the adult fare. When booking, **ask about carry-on allowances for those traveling with infants.** In general, for babies charged 10% of the adult fare you are allowed one carry-on bag and a collapsible stroller, which may have to be checked; you may be limited to less if the flight is full.

The FAA recommends using safety seats aloft for children weighing less than 40 pounds. Airlines, however, can set their own policies: U.S. carriers allow FAA-approved models but usually require that you buy a ticket, even if your child would otherwise ride free, since the safety seats must be strapped into regular seats. Airline rules vary regarding their use, so it's important to **check your airline's policy about using safety seats during takeoff and landing.** Safety seats cannot obstruct any of the other passengers in the row, so get an appropriate seat assignment as early as possible.

When making your reservation, **request children's meals or a free-standing bassinet** if you need them; the latter are available only to those seated at the bulkhead, where there's enough legroom. Remember, however, that bulkhead seats may not have their own overhead bins, and there's no storage space in front of you—a major inconvenience.

GROUP TRAVEL

If you're planning to take your kids (or grandkids) on a tour, look for companies that specialize in family travel.

➤ FAMILY-FRIENDLY TOUR OPERATORS: **Grandtravel** (✉ 6900 Wisconsin Ave., Suite 706, Chevy Chase, MD 20815, ☎ 301/986–0790 or 800/247–7651).

CONSUMER PROTECTION TIPS

Whenever possible, **pay with a major credit card** so you can cancel payment if there's a problem, as long as you can provide documentation. This is a good practice whether you're buying travel arrangements before your trip or shopping in your destination.

If you're doing business with a particular company for the first time, **contact your local Better Business Bureau and the attorney general's offices** in your state and the company's home state, as well. Have any complaints been filed?

Finally, if you're buying a package or tour, always **consider travel insurance** that includes default coverage (☞ Insurance, *above*).

➤ LOCAL BBBs: **Council of Better Business Bureaus** (✉ 4200 Wilson Blvd., Suite 800, Arlington, VA 22203, ☎ 703/276–0100, FAX 703/525–8277).

CUSTOMS & DUTIES

When shopping, **keep receipts** for all of your purchases. Upon reentering the country, **be ready to show customs officials what you've bought.** If you feel a duty is incorrect, appeal the assessment. If you object to the way your clearance was handled, get the inspector's badge number. In either case, first ask to see a supervisor, then write to the port director at the address listed on your receipt. Send a copy of the receipt and other appropriate documentation. If you still don't get satisfaction you can take your case to customs headquarters in Washington.

ENTERING SPAIN

From countries that are not part of the European Union, visitors age 15 and over are permitted to bring into Spain up to 200 cigarettes or 50 cigars, up to one liter of alcohol over 22 proof, and up to two liters of wine. Dogs and cats are admitted, as long as they have up-to-date vaccination records from their home country.

BACK IN THE U.S.

You may bring home $400 worth of foreign goods duty-free if you've been out of the country for at least 48 hours and haven't already used the $400 allowance or any part of it in the past 30 days.

Travelers 21 and older may bring back one liter of alcohol duty-free. In addition, regardless of your age, you are allowed 200 cigarettes and 100 non-Cuban cigars. (At press time, a federal rule restricting tobacco access to persons 18 years and older did not apply to importation.) Antiques, which the U.S. Customs Service defines as objects more than 100 years old, enter duty-free, as do original works of art done entirely by hand, including paintings, drawings, and sculptures.

You may also send packages home duty-free: up to $200 worth of goods for personal use, with a limit of one parcel per addressee per day (and no alcohol or tobacco products or perfume worth more than $5); label the package PERSONAL USE, and attach a list of its contents and their retail value. Do not label the package UNSOLICITED GIFT, or your duty-free exemption will drop to $100. Mailed items do not affect your duty-free allowance on your return.

➤ INFORMATION: **U.S. Customs Service** (Inquiries: ✉ Box 7407, Washington, DC 20044, ☎ 202/927–6724; complaints: ✉ Commissioner's Office, 1301 Constitution Ave. NW, Washington, DC 20229; registration of equipment, ✉ Resource Management, 1301 Constitution Ave. NW, Washington, DC, 20229, ☎ 202/927–0540).

BACK IN CANADA

If you've been out of Canada for at least seven days you may bring in C$500 worth of goods duty-free. If you've been away for fewer than seven days but more than 48 hours, the duty-free allowance drops to C$200; if your trip lasts 24–48 hours, the allowance is C$50.

Alcohol and tobacco products may be included in the seven-day and 48-hour exemptions but not in the 24-hour exemption. If you meet the age requirements of the province or territory through which you reenter Canada you may bring in, duty-free, 1.14 liters (40 imperial ounces) of wine or liquor *or* 24 12-ounce cans or bottles of beer or ale. If you are 16 or older you may bring in, duty-free,

THE GOLD GUIDE / SMART TRAVEL TIPS

200 cigarettes and 50 cigars; these items must accompany you.

You may send an unlimited number of gifts worth up to C$60 each duty-free to Canada. Label the package UNSOLICITED GIFT—VALUE UNDER $60. Alcohol and tobacco are excluded.

➤ INFORMATION: **Revenue Canada** (✉ 2265 St. Laurent Blvd. S, Ottawa, Ontario K1G 4K3, ☎ 613/993–0534; 800/461–9999 in Canada).

BACK IN THE U.K.

If your travels fall entirely within EU countries, you needn't pass through customs when you return to the United Kingdom. If you plan to bring back large quantities of alcohol or tobacco, check on EU limits before-hand.

➤ INFORMATION: **HM Customs and Excise** (✉ Dorset House, Stamford St., London SE1 9NG, ☎ 0171/202–4227).

DISABILITIES & ACCESSIBILITY

ACCESS IN MADRID AND BARCELONA

Spain has done little overall to make traveling easy for visitors with disabil-ities, but most public buildings built within the last five years are accessi-ble, so **it's advisable to stay in newer lodgings.** Only the Prado and newer museums, such as the Reina Sofía and the Thyssen-Bornemisza museum in Madrid, have wheelchair-accessible entrances or elevators. Most of the churches, castles, and monasteries on a tourist's itinerary involve quite a bit of walking, often on uneven terrain.

TIPS & HINTS

When discussing accessibility with an operator or reservationist, **ask hard questions.** Are there any stairs, inside *or* out? Are there grab bars next to the toilet *and* in the shower/tub? How wide is the doorway to the room? To the bathroom? For the most extensive facilities meeting the latest legal specifications, **opt for newer accom-modations,** which are more likely to have been designed with access in mind. Older buildings or ships may have more limited facilities. Be sure to **discuss your needs before booking.**

➤ COMPLAINTS: **Disability Rights Section** (✉ U.S. Dept. of Justice, Box 66738, Washington, DC 20035-6738, ☎ 202/514–0301 or 800/514–0301, TTY 202/514–0383 or 800/514–0383; FAX 202/307–1198). **Aviation Consumer Protection Division** (☞ Air Travel, *above*) for airline-related problems. **Civil Rights Office** (✉ U.S. Dept. of Transportation, Departmen-tal Office of Civil Rights, S-30, 400 7th St. SW, Room 10215, Washington, DC 20590, ☎ 202/366–4648) for problems with surface transportation.

TRAVEL AGENCIES & TOUR OPERATORS

The Americans with Disabilities Act requires that travel firms serve the needs of all travelers. That said, you should note that some agencies and operators specialize in making travel arrangements for individuals and groups with disabilities.

➤ TRAVELERS WITH MOBILITY PROB-LEMS: **Access Adventures** (✉ 206 Chestnut Ridge Rd., Rochester, NY 14624, ☎ 716/889–9096). **Flying Wheels Travel** (✉ 143 W. Bridge St., Box 382, Owatonna, MN 55060, ☎ 507/451–5005 or 800/535–6790) for European cruises and tours. **Hins-dale Travel Service** (✉ 201 E. Ogden Ave., Suite 100, Hinsdale, IL 60521, ☎ 630/325–1335). **Wheelchair Journeys** (✉ 16979 Redmond Way, Redmond, WA 98052, ☎ 206/885–2210 or 800/313–4751).

DISCOUNTS & DEALS

Be a smart shopper—**compare all your options before making a choice.** A plane ticket bought with a promo-tional coupon may not be cheaper than the least expensive fare from a discount ticket agency. For high-price travel purchases, such as packages or tours, keep in mind that what you get for the money is just as important as what you save. Just because some-thing is cheap doesn't mean it's a bargain.

LOOK IN YOUR WALLET

When you use your credit card to make travel purchases, you may get free travel-accident insurance, collision-damage insurance, and medical or legal assistance, depending on the card and the bank that issued it. American Express, MasterCard, and Visa provide one or more of these services, so **get a copy of your credit card's travel-benefits policy.** If you belong to the American Automobile Association (AAA) or an oil-company–sponsored road-assistance plan, always **ask hotel or car-rental reservationists about auto-club discounts.** Some clubs offer additional discounts on tours, cruises, or admission to attractions. And don't forget that auto-club membership entitles you to free maps and trip-planning services.

DIAL FOR DOLLARS

To save money, **look into "1-800" discount reservations services,** which use their buying power to get better prices on hotels, airline tickets, and even car rentals. When reserving a room, always **call the hotel's local toll-free number** (if one is available) rather than the central reservations number—you'll often get a better price. Always ask about special packages or, if applicable, corporate rates.

When shopping for the best deals on hotels and car rentals **look for guaranteed exchange rates,** which protect you against a falling dollar. With your rate locked in you won't pay more even if the price goes up in the local currency.

➤ AIRLINE TICKETS: **800/FLY–4–LESS.**

➤ HOTEL ROOMS: **Hotels Plus** (☎ 800/235–0909). **International Marketing & Travel Concepts** (☎ 800/790–4682).

JOIN A CLUB?

Many companies sell discounts in the form of travel clubs and coupon books, but these cost money. You must use participating advertisers to get a deal, and only after you recoup the initial membership cost or book price do you begin to save. If you plan to use the club or coupons frequently, you may save considerably. Before signing up, find out what discounts you get for free.

➤ DISCOUNT CLUBS: **Entertainment Travel Editions** (✉ Box 1068, Trumbull, CT 06611, ☎ 800/445–4137),

$28–$53, depending on destination. **Great American Traveler** (✉ Box 27965, Salt Lake City, UT 84127, ☎ 800/548–2812), $49.95 per year. **Moment's Notice Discount Travel Club** (✉ 7301 New Utrecht Ave., Brooklyn, NY 11204, ☎ 718/234–6295), $25 per year, single or family. **Privilege Card International** (✉ 201 E. Commerce St., Suite 198, Youngstown, OH 44503, ☎ 330/746–5211 or 800/236–9732), $74.95 per year. **Sears's Mature Outlook** (✉ Box 9390, Des Moines, IA 50306, ☎ 800/336–6330), $14.95 per year. **Travelers Advantage** (✉ CUC Travel Service, 3033 S. Parker Rd., Suite 1000, Aurora, CO 80014, ☎ 800/548–1116 or 800/648–4037), $49 per year, single or family. **Worldwide Discount Travel Club** (✉ 1674 Meridian Ave., Miami Beach, FL 33139, ☎ 305/534–2082), $50 per year family, $40 single.

SAVE ON COMBOS

Packages and guided tours can both save you money, but don't confuse the two. When you buy a package your travel remains independent, just as though you had planned and booked the trip yourself. Fly-drive packages, which combine airfare and car rental, are often a good deal. If you **buy a rail/drive pass** you'll save on train tickets and car rentals. All Eurail- and Europass holders get a discount on Eurostar fares through the Channel Tunnel.

ELECTRICITY

To use your U.S.-purchased electric-powered equipment, **bring a converter and adapter.** The electrical current in Spain is 220 volts, 50 cycles alternating current (AC); wall outlets take Continental-type plugs, with two round prongs.

If your appliances are dual-voltage, you'll need only an adapter. Don't use 110-volt outlets, marked FOR SHAVERS ONLY, for high-wattage appliances such as blow-dryers. Most laptops operate equally well on 110 and 220 volts, so they require only an adapter.

FERRY TRAVEL

➤ FROM THE U.K.: **Brittany Ferries** (☎ 0752/221–321). Hover-Speed

(☎ 0171/554–7061). **P&O European Ferries** (☎ 0181/575–8555). **Sealink** (☎ 0223/47047). **SNCF** (☎ 0171/409–3518 for Motorail).

GAY & LESBIAN TRAVEL

Since the end of Franco's dictatorship, the situation for gays and lesbians in Spain has improved dramatically: the paragraph in the Spanish civil code that made homosexuality a crime was repealed in 1978. Violence against gays does occur, but it's generally restricted to the rougher areas of very large cities.

In the summer, the beaches of the Costa Brava (Sitges and Lloret del Mar) are gay and lesbian hot spots.

➤ LOCAL RESOURCES: **Gai Inform** (✉ C. Carretas 12, 3-2a, 28012 Madrid, ☎ 91/523–0070). **Teléfono Rosa** (✉ C. Carolinas 13, 08012 Barcelona, ☎ 93/234–7070).

➤ TOUR OPERATORS: **Olivia** (✉ 4400 Market St., Oakland, CA 94608, ☎ 510/655–0364 or 800/631–6277).

➤ GAY- AND LESBIAN-FRIENDLY TRAVEL AGENCIES: **Advance Damron** (✉ 1 Greenway Plaza, Suite 800, Houston, TX 77046, ☎ 713/682–2002 or 800/695–0880, FAX 713/888–1010). **Club Travel** (✉ 8739 Santa Monica Blvd., West Hollywood, CA 90069, ☎ 310/358–2200 or 800/429–8747, FAX 310/358–2222). **Islanders/Kennedy Travel** (✉ 183 W. 10th St., New York, NY 10014, ☎ 212/242–3222 or 800/988–1181, FAX 212/929–8530). **Now Voyager** (✉ 4406 18th St., San Francisco, CA 94114, ☎ 415/626–1169 or 800/255–6951, FAX 415/626–8626). **Yellowbrick Road** (✉ 1500 W. Balmoral Ave., Chicago, IL 60640, ☎ 773/561–1800 or 800/642–2488, FAX 773/561–4497). **Skylink Women's Travel** (✉ 3577 Moorland Ave., Santa Rosa, CA 95407, ☎ 707/585–8355 or 800/225–5759, FAX 707/584–5637), serving lesbian travelers.

HEALTH

Two problems frequently encountered during Spanish summers are sunburn and sunstroke. On hot, sunny days, even people who are not normally bothered by strong sun should cover themselves with a long-sleeve shirt, a hat, and long pants or a beach wrap. These are essential for a day at the beach, but they're also advisable for a long day of touring. Carry sunblock lotion for your nose, ears, and other sensitive areas, such as eyelids or ankles. Be sure to drink enough liquids. Above all, limit your sun time for the first few days until you get accustomed to the heat.

Spain was recently found to have the highest number of AIDS cases in Europe. Those applying for work permits will be asked for proof of HIV-negative status.

MEDICAL PLANS

No one plans to get sick while traveling, but it happens, so **consider signing up with a medical-assistance company.** Members get doctor referrals, emergency evacuation or repatriation, 24-hour telephone hot lines for medical consultation, cash for emergencies, and other personal and legal assistance. Coverage varies by plan, so **review the benefits carefully.**

➤ MEDICAL-ASSISTANCE COMPANIES: **International SOS Assistance** (✉ Box 11568, Philadelphia, PA 19116, ☎ 215/244–1500 or 800/523–8930; ✉ Box 466, pl. Bonaventure, Montréal, Québec H5A 1C1, ☎ 514/874–7674 or 800/363–0263; ✉ 7 Old Lodge Pl., St. Margarets, Twickenham TW1 1RQ, England, ☎ 0181/744–0033). **MEDEX Assistance Corporation** (✉ Box 5375, Timonium, MD 21094, ☎ 410/453–6300 or 800/537–2029). **Traveler's Emergency Network** (✉ 3100 Tower Blvd., Suite 1000B, Durham, NC 27707, ☎ 919/490–6055 or 800/275–4836, FAX 919/493–8262). **TravMed** (✉ Box 5375, Timonium, MD 21094, ☎ 410/453–6380 or 800/732–5309). **Worldwide Assistance Services** (✉ 1133 15th St. NW, Suite 400, Washington, DC 20005, ☎ 202/331–1609 or 800/821–2828, FAX 202/828–5896).

HOLIDAYS

In 1999, Spain's national holidays include: January 1, January 6 (Epiphany), March 19 (St. Joseph), April 2 (Good Friday), April 5 (Easter Monday), May 1 (May Day), August 15 (Assumption), October 12 (National Day), November 1 (All Saints), December 6 (Constitution), December 8 (Immaculate Conception), December 25, and December 26 (Boxing Day).

In addition, each city and town has its own holidays honoring political events and patron saints. Madrid holidays include May 2 (Madrid Day), May 15 (St. Isidro), and November 9 (Almudena). Barcelona celebrates April 23 (St. George), September 11 (Catalonia Day), and September 24 (Merced).

If a public holiday falls on a Tuesday or Thursday, **remember that many businesses also close on the nearest Monday or Friday** for a long weekend called a *puente* (bridge).

INSURANCE

Travel insurance is the best way to **protect yourself against financial loss.** The most useful policies are trip-cancellation-and-interruption, default, medical, and comprehensive insurance.

Without insurance you will lose all or most of your money if you cancel your trip, regardless of the reason. It's essential that you **buy trip-cancellation-and-interruption insurance,** particularly if your airline ticket, cruise, or package tour is nonrefundable and cannot be changed. When considering how much coverage you need, look for a policy that will cover the cost of your trip plus the nondiscounted price of a one-way airline ticket, should you need to return home early. Also **consider default or bankruptcy insurance,** which protects you against a supplier's failure to deliver.

Medicare generally does not cover health-care costs outside the United States, nor do many privately issued policies. If your own policy does not cover you outside the United States, **consider buying supplemental medical coverage.** Remember that travel health insurance is different from a medical-assistance plan (☞ Health, *above*).

Citizens of the United Kingdom can buy an annual travel-insurance policy valid for most vacations during the year in which it's purchased. Make sure you're covered if you're preg-

nant or have a preexisting medical condition.

If you've purchased an expensive vacation, comprehensive insurance is a must. It's important to **look for comprehensive policies that include trip-delay insurance,** which will protect you in the event that weather problems cause you to miss your flight, tour, or cruise. A few insurers sell waivers for preexisting medical conditions. Companies that offer both features include Access America, Carefree Travel, Travel Guard, and Travel Insured International (☞ *below*).

Always **buy travel insurance directly from the insurance company.** If you buy it from a travel agency or tour operator that goes out of business, you will probably not be covered for the agency or operator's default, a major risk. Before you make any purchase, **review your existing health and home-owner's policies** to see whether they cover expenses incurred while traveling.

➤ TRAVEL INSURERS: In the United States: **Access America** (✉ 6600 W. Broad St., Richmond, VA 23230, ☎ 804/285–3300 or 800/284–8300). **Carefree Travel Insurance** (✉ Box 9366, 100 Garden City Plaza, Garden City, NY 11530, ☎ 516/294–0220 or 800/323–3149). **Near Travel Services** (✉ Box 1339, Calumet City, IL 60409, ☎ 708/868–6700 or 800/654–6700). **Travel Guard International** (✉ 1145 Clark St., Stevens Point, WI 54481, ☎ 715/345–0505 or 800/826–1300). **Travel Insured International** (✉ Box 280568, East Hartford, CT 06128-0568, ☎ 860/528–7663 or 800/243–3174). **Travelex Insurance Services** (✉ 11717 Burt St., Suite 202, Omaha, NE 68154-1500, ☎ 402/445–8637 or 800/228–9792, ℻ 800/867–9531). **Wallach & Company** (✉ 107 W. Federal St., Box 480, Middleburg, VA 20118, ☎ 540/687–3166 or 800/237–6615). In Canada: **Mutual of Omaha** (✉ Travel Division, 500 University Ave., Toronto, Ontario M5G 1V8, ☎ 416/598–4083; 800/268–8825 in Canada). In the United Kingdom: **Association of British Insurers** (✉ 51 Gresham St., London EC2V 7HQ, ☎ 0171/600–3333).

SMART TRAVEL TIPS / THE GOLD GUIDE

LANGUAGE

Although the Spaniards exported their language to all Central and South America, you may be surprised to find that Spanish is not the principal language in all of Spain: among other dissenters, the Catalonians speak Catalan. While almost everyone also speaks and understands Spanish, in Catalonia **some local radio and television stations broadcast in Catalan. Road signs may be in Catalan or bilingual.** Spanish is referred to as Castellano, or Castilian.

Fortunately, Spanish is fairly easy to pick up, and your efforts to speak the local tongue will be graciously received. Learn at least the following basic phrases: *buenos días* (hello—until 2 PM), *buenas tardes* (good afternoon—until 8 PM), *buenas noches* (hello—after dark), *por favor* (please), *gracias* (thank you), *adiós* (good-bye), *sí* (yes), *no* (no), *los servicios* (the toilets), *la cuenta* (bill/check), *habla inglés?* (do you speak English?), *no comprendo* (I don't understand).

If your Spanish breaks down, you should have no trouble finding people who speak English in Madrid and Barcelona or coastal resorts, but you won't necessarily be able to count on the bus driver or the passerby on the street. Those who do speak English may speak the British variety, so don't be surprised if you're told to queue (line up) or take the lift (elevator) to the loo (toilet). Many guided tours offered at museums and historic sites are in Spanish; ask about the language that will be spoken before signing up.

LODGING

The Spanish government has spent decades buying up old castles and historic buildings and converting them into outstanding lodgings for its parador hotel chain. The rest of Spain's hotels tend to be relatively new high-rises, although there is a growing trend toward the restoration of historic buildings. By law, prices must be posted at the reception desk and should indicate whether tax is included. Breakfast is not usually included in the room price.

For information on hotel consolidators, *see* Discounts, *above*.

APARTMENT & VILLA RENTALS

If you want a home base that's roomy enough for a family and comes with cooking facilities, **consider a furnished rental.** These can save you money, although some are luxury properties, economical only when your party is large. Home-exchange directories list rentals (often second homes owned by prospective house swappers), and some services search for a house or apartment for you (even a castle if that's your fancy) and handle the paperwork. Some send an illustrated catalog; others send photographs only of specific properties, sometimes for a fee. Up-front registration fees may apply.

➤ RENTAL AGENTS: **At Home Abroad** (⊠ 405 E. 56th St., Suite 6H, New York, NY 10022, ☎ 212/421–9165, FAX 212/752–1591). **Europa-Let/ Tropical Inn-Let** (⊠ 92 N. Main St., Ashland, OR 97520, ☎ 541/482–5806 or 800/462–4486, FAX 541/482–0660). **Hometours International** (⊠ Box 11503, Knoxville, TN 37939, ☎ 423/690–8484 or 800/367–4668). **Interhome** (⊠ 124 Little Falls Rd., Fairfield, NJ 07004, ☎ 201/882–6864, FAX 201/808–1742). **Property Rentals International** (⊠ 1008 Mansfield Crossing Rd., Richmond, VA 23236, ☎ 804/378–6054 or 800/220–3332, FAX 804/379–2073). **Rental Directories International** (⊠ 2044 Rittenhouse Sq., Philadelphia, PA 19103, ☎ 215/985–4001, FAX 215/985–0323). **Rent-a-Home International** (⊠ 7200 34th Ave. NW, Seattle, WA 98117, ☎ 206/789–9377 or 800/488–7368, FAX 206/789–9379). **Villas and Apartments Abroad** (⊠ 420 Madison Ave., Suite 1003, New York, NY 10017, ☎ 212/759–1025 or 800/433–3020, FAX 212/755–8316). **Villas International** (⊠ 605 Market St., Suite 510, San Francisco, CA 94105, ☎ 415/281–0910 or 800/221–2260, FAX 415/281–0919). **Hideaways International** (⊠ 767 Islington St., Portsmouth, NH 03801, ☎ 603/430–4433 or 800/843–4433, FAX 603/430–4444); for $99 a year members arrange rentals among themselves.

HOME EXCHANGES

If you would like to exchange your home for someone else's, **join a home-exchange organization** (for about $83 a year), which will send you its updated listings of available exchanges for a year and will include your own listing in at least one of them. Making the arrangements is up to you.

➤ EXCHANGE CLUBS: **HomeLink International** (✉ Box 650, Key West, FL 33041, ☎ 305/294–7766 or 800/638–3841, FAX 305/294–1148).

HOTELS

Hotels are rated by the government with one to five stars. While quality is a factor, **the rating is technically only an indication of how many facilities the hotel offers.** For example, you may find a three-star hotel just as comfortable as a four-star hotel, but lacking a swimming pool.

The major, private hotel groups in Spain include the upscale Meliá chain and the moderately priced Tryp and Sol chains. Dozens of reasonably priced beachside high-rises along the coast cater to package tours.

High-season rates prevail not only in summer but also during Holy Week and local fiestas.

Estancias de España is an association of 20 independently owned hotels in restored palaces, monasteries, mills, and post houses, generally in rural Spain; a free directory is available.

➤ SMALL HOTELS: **Estancias de España** (✉ Menéndez Pidal 31-bajo izq., 28036 Madrid, ☎ 91/345–4141, FAX 91/345–5174).

PARADORS

Spain has about 100 paradors—none within the city limits of Madrid or Barcelona, but several within day-tripping distance. Some are in castles on a hill with sweeping views; others are in historic monasteries or convents filled with art treasures; still others are in modern buildings on Spain's choicest beachfront property. Prices are reasonable, considering that most paradors are four- and five-star hotels. Paradors are immaculate and tastefully furnished, often with antiques or reproductions. All have restaurants that serve some regional specialties, and you can stop in for a meal or a drink without spending the night. Breakfast, however, is an expensive buffet; you'll do better to go down the street for a cup of coffee and a roll.

Because paradors are extremely popular with foreigners and Spaniards alike, **make reservations well in advance.**

➤ INFORMATION: In Spain: **Paradores de España** (✉ Central de Reservas, Requena 3, Madrid 28013, ☎ 91/516–6666, FAX 91/516–6657). In the United States: **Marketing Ahead** (✉ 433 5th Ave., New York, NY 10016, ☎ 212/686–9213 or 800/223–1356). In the United Kingdom: **Keytel International** (✉ 402 Edgeware Rd., London W2 1ED, ☎ 0171/402–8182).

MAIL

RATES

Airmail letters to the United States and Canada cost 94 ptas. up to 15 grams. Letters to the United Kingdom and other EU countries cost 65 ptas. up to 20 grams. Letters within Spain are 32 ptas. Postcards are charged the same rate as letters. Letters and postcards mailed within the same city are 21 ptas. You can buy stamps at post offices and at government-run tobacco shops.

RECEIVING MAIL

Because mail delivery in Spain can often be slow and unreliable, it's best to have your mail sent to American Express. An alternative is to have mail held at a Spanish post office; have it addressed to **Lista de Correos** (general delivery) in the city you'll be visiting.

You can pick up mail at **American Express** (☎ 800/528–4800 for a list of foreign American Express offices).

MONEY

The peseta (pta.) is Spain's unit of currency. Bills are 10,000, 5,000, 2,000, and 1,000 ptas. Coins are 500, 200, 100, 50, 25, 10, 5, and 1 pta. Be careful not to confuse the 100- and 500-pta. coins—they're the same color and almost the same size. Five-pta. coins are called *duros*. At press

THE GOLD GUIDE / SMART TRAVEL TIPS

time European currency markets were highly unstable, with exchange rates of 145 ptas. to the U.S. dollar, 106 ptas. per Canadian dollar, and 232 ptas. to the pound sterling.

ATMS

Before leaving home, **make sure that your credit cards have been programmed for ATM use in Madrid and Barcelona.** Note that Discover is accepted mainly in the United States. Local bank cards often do not work overseas or may access only your checking account; **ask your bank about a MasterCard/Cirrus or Visa debit card,** which works like a bank card but can be used at any ATM displaying a MasterCard/Cirrus or Visa logo. These cards, too, may tap only your checking account; check with your bank about their policy.

➤ ATM LOCATIONS: **Cirrus** (☎ 800/424–7787).

COSTS

Coffee in a bar: 125 ptas. (standing), 150 ptas. (seated). Beer in a bar: 125 ptas. (standing), 150 ptas. (seated). Small glass of wine in a bar: 100 ptas. Soft drink: 150–200 ptas. a bottle. Ham-and-cheese sandwich: 300–450 ptas. One-mile taxi ride: 400 ptas., but the meter keeps ticking in traffic jams. Local bus or subway ride: 125–150 ptas. Movie ticket: 500–600 ptas. Foreign newspaper: 225 ptas.

CURRENCY EXCHANGE

For the most favorable rates, **change money at banks.** Although fees charged for ATM transactions may be higher abroad than at home, Cirrus and Plus exchange rates are excellent, because they're based on wholesale rates offered only by major banks. You won't do as well at exchange booths in airports or rail and bus stations, in hotels, in restaurants, or in stores, although you may find their hours more convenient. To avoid lines at airport exchange booths, **get some Spanish currency before you leave home.**

➤ EXCHANGE SERVICES: **International Currency Express** (☎ 888/842–0880 on the East Coast; 888/278–6628 on the West Coast for telephone orders). **Thomas Cook Currency Services** (☎

800/287–7362 for telephone orders and retail locations).

TRAVELER'S CHECKS

Traveler's checks are fine in cities, but **take cash as well if your trip includes small towns** or rural areas. If your checks are lost or stolen, they can usually be replaced within 24 hours. To ensure a speedy refund, buy your checks yourself (don't ask someone else to make the purchase). When making a claim for stolen or lost checks, the person who bought the checks should make the call.

PACKING FOR MADRID AND BARCELONA

Pack light. Although baggage carts are free and plentiful in most Spanish airports, they're rare in train and bus stations.

On the whole, Spaniards dress up more than Americans or the British. What you bring should depend on the season. Summer will be hot nearly everywhere, but **don't forget a rain-coat or an umbrella.** Visits in winter, fall, and spring call for warm clothing and boots.

It's sensible to wear casual, comfortable clothing and shoes when sightseeing, but you'll want to **dress up a bit when visiting the cities, especially if you'll be going to fine restaurants and nightclubs.** American tourists are easily spotted in Madrid and Barcelona because they're the ones wearing sneakers—if you want to blend in, wear leather shoes.

On the beach, anything goes; it's common to see females of all ages wearing only bikini bottoms, and many of the more remote beaches allow nude sunbathing. Regardless of your style, **bring a cover-up** to wear over your bathing suit when you leave the beach.

Bring an extra pair of eyeglasses or contact lenses in your carry-on luggage. If you have a health problem, **pack enough medication** to last the entire trip or have your doctor write you a prescription using the drug's generic name, as brand names vary from country to country. It's important that you **don't put prescription** drugs or valuables in luggage to be checked: it might go astray. To avoid problems with customs officials, carry medications in the original packaging. And don't forget to pack the addresses of offices that handle refunds of lost traveler's checks.

LUGGAGE

In general, you're entitled to check two bags on flights within the United States and on international flights leaving the United States.

If you're flying between two foreign destinations, note that baggage allowances may be determined not by piece but by weight—generally 88 pounds (40 kilograms) in first class, 66 pounds (30 kilograms) in business class, and 44 pounds (20 kilograms) in economy. If your flight between two cities abroad *connects* with your transatlantic or transpacific flight, the piece method still applies.

Airline liability for baggage is limited to $1,250 per person on flights within the United States. On international flights it amounts to $9.07 per pound or $20 per kilogram for checked baggage (roughly $640 per 70-pound bag) and $400 per passenger for unchecked baggage. Insurance for losses exceeding these amounts can be bought from the airline at check-in for about $10 per $1,000 of coverage; note that this coverage excludes a rather extensive list of items, which is shown on your airline ticket.

PASSPORTS & VISAS

Once your travel plans are confirmed, check the expiration date of your passport. It's also a good idea to make photocopies of the data page; leave one copy with someone at home and keep another with you, separated from your passport. If you lose your passport, promptly call the nearest embassy or consulate and the local police. Having a copy of the data page can speed replacement.

U.S. CITIZENS

All U.S. citizens, including infants, need only a valid passport to enter Spain for stays of up to 90 days.

➤ INFORMATION: **Office of Passport Services** (☎ 202/647–0518).

CANADIANS

You need only a valid passport to enter Spain for stays of up to 90 days.

➤ INFORMATION: **Passport Office** (☎ 819/994–3500 or 800/567–6868).

U.K. CITIZENS

As members of the European Union, citizens of the United Kingdom need only valid identification to enter Spain.

➤ INFORMATION: **London Passport Office** (☎ 0990/21010).

SENIOR-CITIZEN TRAVEL

While there are few early-bird specials or movie discounts, senior citizens generally enjoy discounts at museums in Spain. Spanish social life encompasses all ages—it's very common to see senior citizens having coffee next to young couples or families at late-night cafés.

To qualify for age-related discounts, mention your senior-citizen status up front when booking hotel reservations (not when checking out) and before you're seated in restaurants (not when paying the bill). Note that discounts may be limited to certain menus, days, or hours. When renting a car, ask about promotional car-rental discounts, which can be cheaper than senior-citizen rates.

➤ EDUCATIONAL TRAVEL PROGRAMS: **Elderhostel** (✉ 75 Federal St., 3rd floor, Boston, MA 02110, ☎ 617/426–7788). **Interhostel** (✉ University of New Hampshire, 6 Garrison Ave., Durham, NH 03824, ☎ 603/862–1147 or 800/733–9753, 🖷 603/862–1113).

SPORTS

Spain's sports-specific agencies can provide listings to help you choose your court, course, mooring, and more. The local tourist offices (☞ Visitor Information, *below*) can also be very helpful.

➤ BOATING CHARTERS: **Federación Española de Motonautica** (✉ Spanish Motorboat Federation, Avda. de América 33, 4-B, 28002 Madrid, ☎ 91/415–3769).

➤ BOATING MARINAS: **Federación Española de Vela** (✉ Spanish Sailing Federation, Luís de Salazar 12,

28002, Madrid, ☎ 91/519–5008).
Federación de Actividades Subacuáti-cas (✉ Spanish Underwater Activities
Federation, Santaló 15, 08021 Bar-
celona, ☎ 93/200–6769). **Federación
Española de Esquí Nautico** (✉ Span-
ish Waterskiing Federation, Sabiano
Aran 30, 08028 Barcelona, ☎ 93/
330–8903).

➤ CYCLING TOURS: **Bicibus** (✉ Puerta
del Sol 14, 2nd floor, Madrid, ☎ 91/
522–4501).

➤ EQUESTRIAN: **Federación Española
de Polo** (✉ Spanish Polo Federation,
Comandante Zorita 13, 28020
Madrid, ☎ 91/533–7569). **Federa-
ción Hípica Española** (✉ Spanish
Horseracing Federation, Monte
Esquinza 8, 28010 Madrid, ☎ 91/
319–0233).

➤ FISHING PERMITS: **ICONA** (✉
Environmental Institute, Princesa 3,
Madrid, ☎ 91/580–1653). **Federación Española de Pesca** (✉ Navas
de Tolosa 3, 28013 Madrid, ☎ 91/
532–8353).

➤ FLYING INFORMATION: **Federación
Nacional de Deporte Aéreo** (✉ Spanish Flying Federation, Ferraz 16,
28008 Madrid, ☎ 91/547–5922).

➤ GOLF: **Real Federación Española de
Golf** (✉ Capitán Haya 9, 28020
Madrid, ☎ 91/555–2757).

➤ HIKING: **Federación Española de
Montañismo** (✉ Alberto Aguilera 3,
28015 Madrid, ☎ 91/445–1382).

➤ SKIING INFORMATION: **Federación
Española de Deportes de Invierno**
(✉ Infanta María Teresa 14, 28016
Madrid, ☎ 91/344–0944). **Tourism
and Ski-run Information Line** (☎ 91/
359–1557).

➤ SPAS LISTINGS: **La Asociación
Nacional de Estaciones Termales**
(✉ National Health Spa Association,
Rodrígues San Pedro 56-3, 28015
Madrid, ☎ 91/549–0300).

➤ TENNIS: **Real Federación Española
de Tenis** (✉ Spanish Tennis Federation, Diagonal 618, 01028 Barcelona,
☎ 93/201–0844).

STUDENTS

➤ STUDENT IDS AND SERVICES: In the
United States: **Council on Interna-**
tional Educational Exchange (✉
CIEE, 205 E. 42nd St., 14th floor,
New York, NY 10017, ☎ 212/822–
2600 or 888/268–6245, FAX 212/
822–2699), for mail orders only. In
Canada: **Travel Cuts** (✉ 187 College
St., Toronto, Ontario M5T 1P7, ☎
416/979–2406 or 800/667–2887).

➤ HOSTELING: **Hostelling International—American Youth Hostels**
(✉ 733 15th St. NW, Suite 840,
Washington, DC 20005, ☎ 202/783–
6161, FAX 202/783–6171). **Hostelling
International—Canada** (✉ 400-205
Catherine St., Ottawa, Ontario K2P
1C3, ☎ 613/237–7884, FAX 613/
237–7868). **Youth Hostel Association
of England and Wales** (✉ Trevelyan
House, 8 St. Stephen's Hill, St. Al-
bans, Hertfordshire AL1 2DY, ☎
01727/855215 or 01727/845047,
FAX 01727/844126). Membership in
the United States, $25; in Canada,
C$26.75; in the United Kingdom,
£9.30.

➤ STUDENT TOURS: **Contiki Holidays**
(✉ 300 Plaza Alicante, Suite 900,
Garden Grove, CA 92840, ☎ 714/
740–0800 or 800/266–8454, FAX
714/740–0818). **AESU Travel** (✉
2 Hamill Rd., Suite 248, Baltimore,
MD 21210-1807, ☎ 410/323–4416
or 800/638–7640, FAX 410/323–
4498).

TAXES

VALUE-ADDED TAX (VAT)

Value-added tax (or sales tax) is
called IVA in Spain. It is levied on
services, such as hotels and restaurants, and on many categories of
consumer products. When in doubt
about whether tax is included, ask,
Está incluido el IVA (ee-vah)?

The IVA rate (7%) is the same for all
categories of hotels and restaurants,
regardless of their number of stars or
forks. A special tax law for the Canary Islands allows all hotels and
restaurants there to charge 4% IVA.
Menus will generally say at the bottom whether tax is included (*IVA
incluido*) or not (*más 7% IVA*).

A number of shops, particularly large
stores and boutiques in holiday
resorts, offer a refund of 16% IVA
sales tax on purchases of more than

15,000 ptas. You **show your passport and fill out a form, and the store mails the refund to your home.** The receipt must detail the purchase and IVA paid, be signed by vendor and customer, and be sealed.

You can also **present your original receipt in the VAT office at the airport** (the airports in both Barcelona and Madrid have IVA booths near their duty-free shops). Customs signs the original and gives it back to the customer, who mails it to the vendor. The vendor then mails the refund to the customer.

TELEPHONES

The country code for Spain is 34.

All provincial codes begin with a 9. To call within Spain—even locally—dial the area code first. Large cities such as Madrid (91), Barcelona (93), Bilbao (94), Sevilla (95), and Valencia (96) have a two-digit area code followed by a seven-digit local number; less populous regions have a three-digit area code followed by a six-digit local number.

CALLING HOME

International calls are awkward from public pay phones because of the enormous number of coins needed, and they can be expensive from hotels, which often add a surcharge. The best way to phone home is to go to the local telephone office. Every town has one, and major cities have several. When the call is connected, you'll be sent to a quiet cubicle, and charged according to the meter. If the price is 500 ptas. or more, you can pay with Visa or MasterCard.

To make an international call yourself, dial 07 and wait for a loud tone. Then dial the country code (1 for the United States, 01 for Canada, 44 for the United Kingdom), followed by the area code and number.

In Madrid the main telephone office is at Gran Vía 28. There is another at the main post office, and a third at Paseo Recoletos 43, just off Plaza Colón. In Barcelona you can phone overseas from the office at Carrer de Fontanella 4, off Plaça de Catalunya.

Before you go, **find out the local long-distance access codes** for your desti-

nations. AT&T, MCI, and Sprint long-distance services make calling home relatively convenient, but you may find the local access code blocked in many hotel rooms. First ask the hotel operator to connect you. If the hotel operator balks, ask for an international operator, or dial the international operator yourself. One way to improve your odds of getting connected to your long-distance carrier is to travel with more than one company's calling card (a hotel may block Sprint, for example, but not MCI). If all else fails, **call your phone company collect in the United States** or call from a pay phone in the hotel lobby.

➤ To OBTAIN ACCESS CODES: AT&T USADirect (☎ 800/874–4000). MCI Call USA (☎ 800/444–4444). Sprint Express (☎ 800/793–1153).

OPERATORS & INFORMATION

For general information in Spain, dial 003. The operator for international information and assistance is at 025 (some operators speak English).

PUBLIC PHONES

There are three types of pay phones in Spain, all of them bright green or dull blue. The most common kind has a digital readout, so you can see your money ticking away. You need at least 25 ptas. for a local call, 75 ptas. to call another province. Simply insert coins and wait for a dial tone. (At older models, you line coins up in a groove on top of the dial, and they drop down as needed.)

Newer pay phones work on special phone cards, which you can buy at any tobacco shop for 1,000 or 2,000 ptas.

TIPPING

Pride keeps Spaniards from acknowledging tips, but waiters and other service people are poorly paid, and you can be sure that your contribution will be appreciated. On the other hand, if you run into some bad or surly service, don't feel obligated to leave a tip.

Restaurant checks may or may not include service, but **do not tip more than 10% of the bill in any case,** and leave less if you eat tapas or sandwiches at a bar—just enough to round out the bill to the nearest 100. Tip cocktail servers 50–75 ptas. a drink, depending on the bar.

Tip taxi drivers about 10% of the total fare, but more for long rides or extra help with luggage. Note, though, that there is an official surcharge for airport runs and baggage.

Tip hotel porters 50–100 ptas. a bag, and the bearer of room service 50–100 ptas. A doorman who calls a taxi for you gets 100 ptas. If you stay in a hotel for more than two nights, tip the maid about 100 ptas. per night. A concierge should receive a tip for any additional help he or she provides.

Tour guides should be tipped about 300 ptas., ushers in theaters or at bullfights 25–50 ptas., barbers 100 ptas., and ladies' hairdressers at least 200 ptas. for a wash and style. Restroom attendants are tipped 10–25 ptas.

TOUR OPERATORS

Buying a package tour or independent vacation can make your trip to Madrid and Barcelona less expensive and more hassle-free. Because everything is prearranged, you'll spend less time planning.

Operators that handle several hundred thousand travelers per year can use their purchasing power to give you a good price. Their high volume may also indicate financial stability. But some small companies provide more personalized service, and because they tend to specialize, they may also be more knowledgeable about a given area.

A GOOD DEAL?

The more your package or tour includes, the better you can predict the ultimate cost of your vacation. Make sure you know exactly what's covered, and **beware of hidden costs.** Are taxes, tips, and service charges included? Transfers and baggage handling? Entertainment and excursions? These can add up.

If the price of the package or tour you're considering is lower than in your wildest dreams, **be skeptical.** Also, **make sure your travel agent**

knows the accommodations and other services. Ask about the hotel's location, room size, beds, and whether it has a pool, room service, or programs for children, if you care about these. Has your agent been there in person or sent others you can contact?

BUYER BEWARE

Each year consumers are stranded or lose their money when tour operators—even very large ones with excellent reputations—go out of business. So **check out the operator.** Find out how long the company has been in business, and ask several agents about its reputation. Unless the firm has a consumer-protection program, **don't book through it.**

Members of the National Tour Association and United States Tour Operators Association are required to set aside funds to cover your payments and travel arrangements in case the company defaults. Nonmembers may carry insurance instead. Look for the details, and for the name of an underwriter with a solid reputation, in the operator's brochure. Note: when it comes to tour operators, **don't trust escrow accounts.** Although there are laws governing charter-flight operators, no governmental body prevents tour operators from raiding the till. For more information, *see* Consumer Protection, *above.*

➤ TOUR-OPERATOR RECOMMENDATIONS: **National Tour Association** (✉ NTA, 546 E. Main St., Lexington, KY 40508, ☎ 606/226–4444 or 800/755–8687). **United States Tour Operators Association** (✉ USTOA, 342 Madison Ave., Suite 1522, New York, NY 10173, ☎ 212/599–6599, FAX 212/599–6744).

USING AN AGENT

Travel agents are excellent resources. When shopping for an agent, however, you should **collect brochures from several sources;** some agents' suggestions may be skewed by promotional relationships with tour and package firms that reward them for volume sales. If you have a special interest, **find an agent with expertise in that area** (☞ Travel Agents, *below*). Don't rely solely on your agent, who may be unaware of niche operators. Note that some special-interest travel companies only sell directly to the public, and that some large operators only accept bookings made through travel agents.

SINGLE TRAVELERS

Prices for packages and tours are usually quoted per person, based on two sharing a room. If you're traveling solo, you may be required to pay the full double-occupancy rate. Some operators eliminate this surcharge if you agree to be matched with a roommate of the same sex, even if one is not found by departure time.

GROUP TOURS

Among companies that sell tours to Madrid and Barcelona, the following are nationally known, have a proven reputation, and offer plenty of options. The classifications used below represent different price categories, and you'll probably encounter these terms when talking to a travel agent or tour operator. The key difference is usually in accommodations, which run from budget to better, and better yet to best.

➤ FIRST CLASS: **Odysseys Adventures** (✉ 537 Chestnut St., BOX 305, Cedarhurst, NY 11516-2223, ☎ 516/569-2812 or 800/344-0013, FAX 516/569-2998). **Spain Tours and Beyond** (✉ 261 W. 70th St., New York, NY 10023, ☎ 212/595-2400, FAX 212/580-8935). **Viajes Corte Inglés** (✉ 500 5th Ave., Suite 1044, New York, NY 10110, ☎ 212/944-9400 or 800/333-2469).

PACKAGES

Like group tours, independent vacation packages are available from major tour operators and airlines. The companies listed below offer vacation packages in a broad price range.

➤ AIR/HOTEL: **Delta Vacations** (☎ 800/872-7786). **DER Tours** (✉ 9501 W. Devon St., Rosemont, IL 60018, ☎ 800/937-1235, FAX 847/692-4141 or 800/282-7474, 800/860-9944 for brochures). **4th Dimension Tours** (✉ 7101 S.W. 99th Ave., No. 105, Miami, FL 33173, ☎ 305/279-0014 or 800/644-0438, FAX 305/273-9777). **Odysseys Adven-**tures (☞ Group Tours, *above*). **Spain Tours and Beyond** (☞ Group Tours, *above*). **TWA Getaway Vacations** (☎ 800/438-2929). **VE Tours** (✉ 7270 N.W. 12th St., Suite 210, Miami, FL 33126, ☎ 305/477-5161 or 800/222-8383).**US Airways Vacations** (☎ 800/455-0123). **Viajes Corte Inglés** (☞ Group Tours, *above*).

➤ FROM THE U.K.: **British Airways Holidays** (✉ Astral Towers, Betts Way, London Rd., Crawley, West Sussex RH10 2XA, ☎ 01293/722-727, FAX 01293/722-624). **Mundi Color** (✉ 276 Vauxhall Bridge Rd., London SW1V 1BE, ☎ 0171/828-6021). **Page & Moy Ltd.** (✉ 136-140 London Rd., Leicester LE2 1EN, ☎ 0116/250-7676). **Magic of Spain** (✉ 227 Shepherds Bush Rd., London W6 7AS, ☎ 0181/748-4220).

THEME TRIPS

➤ ART AND ARCHITECTURE: **4th Dimension Tours** (☞ Packages, *above*).

➤ FOOD AND WINE: **Odysseys Adventures** (☞ Group Tours, *above*).

➤ SPAS: **Spa-Finders** (✉ 91 5th Ave., No. 301, New York, NY 10003-3039, ☎ 212/924-6800 or 800/255-7727).

TRAIN TRAVEL

International overnight trains run from Madrid to Lisbon and Barcelona to Paris (both 11½ hours). A daytime trip runs from Barcelona to Grenoble and Geneva (10 hours).

If you purchase a same-day round-trip ticket while in Spain, a 20% discount applies; if you purchase a different-day round-trip ticket, you'll get a 10% discount.

Spain's high-speed train, the AVE, travels between Madrid and Seville (with a stop in Córdoba) in less than three hours. However, the rest of the government-run railroad, RENFE, remains below par by European standards. Train travel can be tediously slow, and most long-distance trips run at night. While overnight trains have comfortable sleeper cars, first-class fares that include a sleeping compartment are comparable to airfares.

THE GOLD GUIDE / SMART TRAVEL TIPS

For most journeys, however, trains are the most economical way to go. First- and second-class seats are reasonably priced, and you can get a bunk in a compartment with five other people for a supplement of about $25. The most comfortable train, TALGO, has a special inverted suspension system designed to give a faster and smoother ride on winding rails. Food in the dining cars and bars is overpriced and uninspired.

Most Spaniards buy train tickets in advance by standing in long lines at the station. The overworked clerks rarely speak English, however, so if you don't speak Spanish, you're better off going to a travel agency that displays the blue-and-yellow RENFE sign. The price is the same.

To save money, **look into rail passes,** but be aware that unless you plan to cover many miles, you may come out ahead by sticking to individual tickets.

DISCOUNT PASSES

If Spain is your only destination in Europe, **consider purchasing a Spain Flexipass.** Prices begin at $144 for three days of second-class travel within a two-month period and $180 for first class. Other passes cover more days and longer periods.

Spain is one of 17 countries in which you can **use EurailPasses,** which provide unlimited first-class rail travel in all of the participating countries, for the duration of the pass. If you plan to rack up the miles, get a standard pass. These are available for 15 days ($522), 21 days ($678), one month ($838), two months ($1,148), and three months ($1,468). If your plans call for only limited train travel, **look into a Europass,** which costs less money than a EurailPass but allows a limited number of travel days, in a limited number of countries, during a specified time period. For example, a two-month pass ($316) allows between 5 and 15 days of rail travel but costs $200 less than the least expensive EurailPass. Keep in mind, however, that the Europass is good only in France, Germany, Italy, Spain, and Switzerland, and the number of countries you can visit is further limited by the type of pass you buy.

For example, the basic two-month pass allows you to visit only three of the five participating countries.

In addition to standard EurailPasses, **ask about special rail-pass plans.** Among these are the Eurail Youthpass (for those under age 26), the Eurail Saverpass (which gives a discount for two or more people traveling together), a Eurail Flexipass (which allows a certain number of travel days within a set period), the Euraildrive Pass and the Europass Drive (which combines travel by train and rental car). Whichever pass you choose, remember that you must **purchase your pass before you leave** for Europe.

Many travelers assume that rail passes guarantee them seats on the trains they wish to ride. Not so: you need to **reserve seats in advance even if you're using a rail pass.** Seat reservations are required on some European trains, particularly high-speed trains, and are a good idea on trains that may be crowded—particularly in summer on popular routes. You'll also need a reservation if you purchase sleeping accommodations.

➤ INFORMATION AND PASSES: **Rail Europe** (✉ 226–230 Westchester Ave., White Plains, NY 10604, ☎ 914/682–5172 or 800/438–7245; ✉ 2087 Dundas E, Suite 105, Mississauga, Ontario L4X 1M2, ☎ 416/602–4195). **DER Tours** (✉ Box 1606, Des Plaines, IL 60017, ☎ 800/782–2424, FAX 800/282–7474). **CIT Tours Corp.** (✉ 342 Madison Ave., Suite 207, New York, NY 10173, ☎ 212/697–2100 or 800/248–8687; 800/248–7245 in western U.S.).

FROM THE U.K.

Train services to Spain are not as frequent, fast, or inexpensive as airplane travel. To reach Spain from Britain, you have to change trains (and rail stations) in Paris. It's worth paying extra for a Talgo express or for the Puerta del Sol express to avoid having to change trains again at the Spanish border. Journey time to Paris is around six hours; from Paris to Madrid, an additional 13 hours. Allow at least two hours in Paris for changing trains. If you're under 26 years old, Eurotrain has excellent deals.

➤ FROM THE U.K.: **British Rail Travel Centers** (☎ 0171/834–2345). **Eurotrain** (✉ 52 Grosvenor Gardens, London SW1W OAG, ☎ 0171/730–3402). **Transalpino** (✉ 71–75 Buckingham Palace Rd., London SW1W 0RE, ☎ 0171/834–9656).

TRAVEL AGENCIES

A good travel agent puts your needs first. It's important to **look for an agency that specializes in your destination, has been in business at least five years, and emphasizes customer service.** If you're looking for an agency-organized package or tour, your best bet is an agency that's a member of the National Tour Association or the United States Tour Operator's Association (☞ Tour Operators, *above*).

➤ LOCAL AGENT REFERRALS: **American Society of Travel Agents** (✉ ASTA, 1101 King St., Suite 200, Alexandria, VA 22314, ☎ 703/739–2782, FAX 703/684–8319). **Alliance of Canadian Travel Associations** (✉ 1729 Bank St., Suite 201, Ottawa, Ontario K1V 7Z5, ☎ 613/521–0474, FAX 613/521–0805). **Association of British Travel Agents** (✉ 55–57 Newman St., London W1P 4AH, ☎ 0171/637–2444, FAX 0171/637–0713).

TRAVEL GEAR

Travel catalogs specialize in useful items, such as compact alarm clocks and travel irons, that can **save space when packing.** They also offer dual-voltage appliances, currency converters, and foreign-language phrase books.

➤ MAIL-ORDER CATALOGS: **Magellan's** (☎ 800/962–4943, FAX 805/568–5406). **Orvis Travel** (☎ 800/541–3541, FAX 540/343–7053). **TravelSmith** (☎ 800/950–1600, FAX 800/950–1656).

U.S. GOVERNMENT

The U.S. government can be an excellent source of inexpensive travel information. When planning your trip, **find out what government materials are available.**

➤ ADVISORIES: **U.S. Department of State American Citizens Services**

Office (✉ Room 4811; Washington, DC 20520), enclose a self-addressed, stamped envelope. **Interactive hotline** (☎ 202/647–5225, FAX 202/647–3000). **Computer bulletin board** (☎ 202/647–9225).

➤ PAMPHLETS: **Consumer Information Center** (✉ Consumer Information Catalogue, Pueblo, CO 81009, ☎ 719/948–3334).

VISITOR INFORMATION

For general information, contact the tourism offices below. If calling the brochure line in the United Kingdom, remember it costs 50p per minute peak rate, 45p per minute cheap rate.

➤ TOURIST OFFICE OF SPAIN: **U.S. Nationwide** (✉ 666 5th Ave., 35th floor, New York, NY 10103, ☎ 212/265–8822, FAX 212/265–8864). **Chicago** (✉ 845 N. Michigan Ave., Chicago, IL 60611, ☎ 312/642–1992, FAX 312/642–9817). **Los Angeles** (✉ 8383 Wilshire Blvd., Suite 960, Beverly Hills, CA 90211, ☎ 213/658–7188, FAX 213/658–1061). **Miami** (✉ 1221 Brickell Ave., Suite 1850, Miami, FL 33131, ☎ 305/358–1992, FAX 305/358–8223). **Canada** (✉ 2 Bloor St. W, 34th floor, Toronto, Ontario M4W 3E2, ☎ 416/961–3131, FAX 416/961–1992). **United Kingdom** (✉ 57–58 St. James's St., London SW1A 1LD, ☎ 0171/499–0901; 0891/669–920 for brochures; FAX 0171/629–4257).

WEB SITES

Do check out the World Wide Web when you're planning. You'll find everything from up-to-date weather forecasts to virtual tours of famous cities. Fodor's Web site, www.fodors.com, is a great place to start your online travels. For more information specifically on Spain, visit www.okspain.org and www.tourspain.es.

WHEN TO GO

May and October, when the weather is generally warm and dry, are considered the best months for travel to Madrid and Barcelona. May gives you more hours of daylight for sightseeing, while October offers a chance to enjoy the harvest season.

THE GOLD GUIDE / SMART TRAVEL TIPS

In April you can catch some of Spain's most spectacular fiestas, in honor of *Semana Santa* (Holy Week).

Spain is the number-one destination for European tourists, so **if you want to avoid crowds, don't go in June, July, August, or September.** It's crowded and more expensive then, especially along the coasts. However, most people find the waters of the Mediterranean too cold for swimming the rest of the year, and beach season on the Atlantic coast is slightly shorter. Spaniards themselves vacation in August, and their annual migration to the beach causes huge traffic jams on August 1 and 31. Madrid and Barcelona can be delightfully relaxed and empty for the duration; small shops and some restaurants shut down for the entire month, but museums remain open.

Summers are hot; temperatures frequently hit 100°F (38°C), and air conditioning is not widespread. Try to **limit your touring to the morning hours and take a siesta in the afternoon.** Warm summer nights are among Spain's most pleasant experiences.

Winters are mild and rainy along the coasts; elsewhere winter blows bitterly cold. Snow is infrequent except in the mountains, where you can ski from December through March at resorts near Madrid.

CLIMATE

➤ FORECASTS: **Weather Channel Connection** (☎ 900/932–8437), 95¢ per minute from a Touch-Tone phone.

The following are average daily maximum and minimum temperatures for Madrid and Barcelona.

Climate

MADRID

Jan.	48F	9C	May	70F	21C	Sept.	77F	25C
	36	2		50	10		57	14
Feb.	52F	11C	June	81F	27C	Oct.	66F	19C
	36	2		59	15		50	10
Mar.	59F	15C	July	88F	31C	Nov.	55F	13C
	41	5		63	17		41	5
Apr.	64F	18C	Aug.	86F	30C	Dec.	48F	9C
	45	7		63	17		36	2

BARCELONA

Jan.	55F	13C	May	70F	21C	Sept.	77F	25C
	43	6		57	14		66	19
Feb.	57F	14C	June	77F	25C	Oct.	70F	21C
	45	7		64	18		59	15
Mar.	61F	16C	July	82F	28C	Nov.	61F	16C
	48	9		70	21		52	11
Apr.	64F	18C	Aug.	82F	28C	Dec.	55F	13C
	52	11		70	21		46	8

THE GOLD GUIDE / SMART TRAVEL TIPS

1 Destination: Madrid and Barcelona

A TALE OF TWO CITIES

THE ETERNAL RIVALRY between Barcelona, medieval capital of an opulent Mediterranean empire, and Madrid, once the nerve center of one of the greatest global empires ever assembled, may be a driving force behind Spain's current vitality. The two cities debate every national issue from politics to sports to the economy, even as three domestic airlines shuttle thousands of businesspeople daily between the two.

How to get a Catalan to speak Spanish? Misunderstand the price by a peseta. Madrid bureaucrats don't work after lunch? No, that's in the morning; after lunch they don't even show up.

Catalan avarice, Madrid sloth: old standbys in the arsenal of barbs that citizens of Spain's two largest cities routinely toss at each other.

Beneath the humor lies a well-aged and historically rooted bitterness combining elements of the world's great internecine tensions—Québec and the rest of Canada, Milan and Rome, even the United States' North–South divide more than a century after the American Civil War.

Though largely undetectable to a visitor, traces of this rivalry crop up everywhere. Cars with Madrid license plates may encounter extra discourtesies in Catalonia. Madrileños are not known for their patience with the Catalan language and are apt to insist upon being addressed in Castilian Spanish; Catalans, in turn, seem to "forget" their Castilian, or deliberately lapse into bizarre grammatical distortions. A foolproof way to ruin a social gathering in Madrid is to proselytize the Catalan point of view vis à vis Catalonian history and culture. Meanwhile, in Barcelona, the "language of Cervantes" can be a surefire soporific at dinner parties that would crackle with humor and innuendo in Catalan.

This mutual antipathy has been centuries in the making and will not go away anytime soon, even if feelings have cooled considerably since the 1714 siege and conquest of Barcelona by Spain's first Bourbon monarch, Felipe V. Armed conflict between the two is no longer a threat. Catalans are a pragmatic people who have always managed to prosper no matter whose army was manning the cannon over Barcelona; and the cities are now so intertwined and interdependent that a Catalan, Narcis Serra, was a recent Spanish Minister of Defense. Spain's conservative government, elected in 1997, is able to govern only with the support of Catalonian President Jordi Pujol's Catalan nationalist party.

The dramatic changes of the last 25 years—the end of Franco, the establishment of the constitutional monarch—have actually reversed some of the qualities that have traditionally characterized the two cities. Thus, whereas Barcelona was always considered Spain's most European city up to 1975, Catalonia's zealous restoration of its long-suppressed language and culture has made it somewhat self-absorbed and cost it a few points in cosmopolitanism. Madrid, on the other hand, has burst back onto the world stage with a vigor and energy unimaginable when it was the seat of Franco's reactionary and repressive regime. The capital's legendary bureaucratic indolence has been replaced by a frenzy of activity in the arts and business and a powerful international orientation and appeal.

But some things don't change. Madrid remains open; Barcelona, despite its seaport, is less so. Even the topography reinforces this fact: Madrid stands on a promontory at the center of Spain's central steppe, Barcelona nestles in a crease between the hills and the sea. Barcelona is moist, pungent, even fetid, slippery. Madrid is high, arid, brittle. Madrid's streets are broader and seem to embrace the sky, while Barcelona's are predominantly darker and narrower, leafier and more intimate, older: tunnels to the city's medieval past. Barcelona is, after all, 2,000 years old, to Madrid's mere millennium.

Even—maybe especially—the air is different. Barcelona's steamy and passionate Mediterranean breath is a far cry from

Madrid's legendary highland air, with its sharp and icy lightness.

Catalans are more private and self-contained, feline, Gallic. Madrileños are a little of everything, coming as they do from all corners of the peninsula and the world, but they are known for a more gregarious, accessible, open, generous spirit. In Madrid they *give* you things—tapas, hot broth, the time of day. In Barcelona, trade is absolutely fundamental to every nuance of social contact.

Catalonia's *fets diferencials,* or "differentiating facts," are based on linguistic and historical realities often dismissed as fantasy by non-Catalans educated during the unity-oriented Franco regime. Barcelona is geographically closer to Marseilles than to Madrid, and medieval Catalonia included much of what is today southern France. The Roussillon, or French Catalonia, stretched as far north as Avignon and Nîmes, where the Catalan language is still spoken. Grammatically closer to Provençal French than to Castilian Spanish, Catalan lacks the fricative phonemes and nearly all of the Arabic-rooted vocabulary that modern Spanish inherited from 700 years of Moorish occupation. Sacked but never colonized by the Moors, Catalonia was the border zone for Charlemagne's Frankish empire, finally gaining independence from the Carolingians in 988, only a few years after Madrid was made a military outpost by the Moorish command defending regional headquarters at Toledo. When Catalonia became, through royal marriage, part of the House of Aragon in 1137, Barcelona's commercial and maritime power made it the kingdom's nerve center and royal court. But in 1469, when Isabella of Castile married Ferdinand of Aragon, Barcelona found itself left dangling on the eastern edge of an Iberian power about to turn its attention west, across the Atlantic.

The "discovery" of the New World and the great enterprise of exploiting its riches definitively sealed Catalonia's fate as a declining power within the new, unified Spain. Legally excluded from participation in Castile's colonization and plunder of the Americas, Catalonia did manage to retain a measure of home rule and cultural identity until 1714, when, as a reprisal for having supported Archduke Carlos of Austria in the War of the Spanish Succession, Felipe V stripped Catalonia of all of its institutions and privileges.

Deprived of the loot pouring in from the colonies, Barcelona developed an industrial power base that led to a resurgence of Catalan nationalism—*la Renaixença*—in the latter half of the 19th century. Limited home rule returned from 1914 to 1924 and, later, during the Second Republic, from 1931 to 1936; but after the Spanish Civil War, 1936–1939, the Franco regime's "National Movement" endeavored to eradicate all traces of the Catalan language and culture, along with any political parties that might threaten the national fabric of church, state, oligarchy, and the army. Officially suppressed but never abandoned, Catalan language and culture have returned more powerfully than ever since Franco's death in 1975.

Madrid's history, shorter but less checkered, took the city from military observation post to provincial town to world capital in just over 500 years. When the previously itinerant royal court was permanently established there in 1561, riches were already pouring in from the Spanish empire's far-flung colonies. Soon Madrid was a teeming boom town, with a burgeoning population and government subsidies promoting architecture, theater, and, especially, painting. Rubens and Velázquez shared a studio; Cervantes and Lope de Vega (the "Spanish Shakespeare") exchanged acerbic sonnets; and the city's literary quarter was a crush of poets, actors, composers, and playwrights. The lavish cultural spending of Spain's Golden Age left a legacy of artistic masterpieces that today fill the Prado and other museums, as well as convents, churches, foundations, and over a hundred art galleries.

Madrid, from the twisting streets of its early Moorish and Jewish quarter, through the stately and austere Habsburg architecture of the 16th and 17th centuries and the broad avenues of the 18th- and 19th-century Bourbon monarchy, has grown into a sprawling industrial and cultural giant of (like Barcelona) more than four million people.

Comparing the pros and cons and respective assets of these two cities—an endless exchange of proposals and rebuttals—may only be valuable as a means of better defining and characterizing each of the two. Certainly, they seem perfectly organized for debate. Madrid's landlocked, highland monochrome, for example, contrasts with Barcelona's vivid and varied palette, a rich mixture of the Pyrenees, the Mediterranean, and metropolitan hues. Madrid offers convenient access to all of the Iberian Peninsula, whereas Barcelona is nearly equidistant from Rome and London, as close to Geneva as it is to Madrid. Madrid is most appealing in winter, when the hearty Castilian cuisine of roasts and thick stews makes the most sense, where Barcelona's sweetest season is springtime, between the lovers' fiesta of Sant Jordi, in late April, and the all-night bonfires of Sant Joan, on Midsummer's Eve. Madrid's treasury of paintings is countered by Barcelona's relentless innovation in art, architecture, and design and by the legacies of Picasso, Miró, Dalí, and Gaudí. Barcelona has delicious markets such as the central Boqueria; Madrid has its Sunday flea market, the Rastro, and bookstall browsing along the Cuesta de Moyanes. Madrid's superb day trips—Toledo, Segovia, El Escorial—are balanced by Barcelona's excellent beaches on the Costa Brava, to the north, and the Delta del Ebro, to the south. Madrid is centered around its peerless and peaceful Plaza Mayor, whereas Barcelona has the meandering Rambla. Madrid has a midtown forest in the stately Retiro, while Gaudí's Güell Park hovers on a hill above Barcelona. Madrid's oldest quarters are a jumble of red, clay-tiled rooftops, while Barcelona's are Roman, Romanesque, and Gothic stone.Ultimately, Barcelona's Mediterranean vitality draws heavily on its rich triangle of mountains, sea, and city life, whereas modern Madrid, brisk and lively, is broader and more universal, the melting pot of the many Spains.

Today, both cities are riding a wave of excitement that even terrorism and political scandals can't seem to discourage. Barcelona continues to generate energy in the afterglow of the 1992 Olympic Games, Catalonia's greatest domestic and international triumph since the glory days of its medieval Mediterranean prominence. Madrid, meanwhile, has reassumed an energy and outlook comparable only to that of its own 16th-century Golden Age.

–George Semler

NEW AND NOTEWORTHY

A general travel trend throughout Madrid and Barcelona is to depart from the usual full-service lodging and spend the night in a more rustic and romantic setting, such as a farmhouse, manor house, or restored noble home.

Madrid

With Madrid increasingly recognized as one of Europe's great cultural centers, Madrileños are prouder than ever of their beautiful and historic buildings, ancient landmarks, and urban showpieces. The city is constantly investing in renovations, restorations, and beautification projects, most recently that of the opera house, legendary for its disastrous history of fire, bombs, and structural problems. Overhauled at a staggering expense of $150 million, the gilded and gleaming Teatro Real reopened to much fanfare in October 1997.

Barcelona

Barcelona will be more musical than ever when its fabled Liceu Opera House reopens, in early 1999. Check out the new, computerized Catalonian tourist office in the Palau Robert (at Passeig de Gràcia and Diagonal) and the Espai Gaudí, the best Gaudí composite ever assembled, atop La Pedrera. Meanwhile, FC (Futbol Club) Barcelona will be playing in the European Champions League in early 1999, possibly sending the city into a soccer frenzy.

WHAT'S WHERE

Madrid

Madrid, smack in the middle of Spain, is one of Europe's most vibrant cities. Madrileños are a vigorous, joyful lot, famous for their apparent ability to defy the need for sleep; they embrace their city's cultural offerings and make enthusiastic use of its cafés and bars. If you can match this energy, you'll take in Madrid's museum mile, with more masterpieces per yard than anywhere else in the world; the palaces and boutiques of regal Madrid; the dark, narrow lanes of medieval Madrid; and Madrid post-midnight, where today's action is.

Around Madrid

Castilla (Castile), the area surrounding Madrid, is a vast, windswept plateau with clear skies and endless vistas. An outstanding Roman aqueduct and a fairy-tale castle and cathedral make Segovia one of the most popular excursions from Madrid. The walled city of Ávila was the home of St. Teresa, Spain's female patron saint, and the university town of Salamanca is a flourish of golden sandstone. Aranjuez tempts with the French-style elegance of a Bourbon palace, while enigmatic Toledo is dramatic and austere, with rich legacies from three religions.

Barcelona

Barcelona is one of Europe's most dynamic and artistic cities. From the medieval atmosphere of the Gothic Quarter's narrow alleys to the elegance of the Moderniste Eixample or the action-packed modern Olympic Village, Barcelona is on the move. Picasso, Miró, and Dalí have links to this vibrant city with its ever-stronger Catalan identity. After 40 years of repression through post–civil-war Franco dictatorship, Catalan language and culture have flourished since home rule was granted in 1975. Now this ancient romance language is heard in every street and is, along with Castilian Spanish, Barcelona's co-official language.

PLEASURES AND PASTIMES

Bullfighting

Bullfighting is a form of ritualized slaughter: The bull never wins, and gorings are unusual. Those who can conceive of the bull as a symbol rather than as an animal, who can remain undisturbed by the blood, and who can appreciate the drama and the fanfare will get the most out of a bullfight. For Spaniards, it's an art form and a national passion.

Bullfights start with a procession of banderilleros, picadors, and matadors. First, the matador waves capes to encourage the bull's charges. Then a picador, on horseback, stabs the bull's neck and shoulder area. Next, banderilleros plant darts in the bull's back. After more cape taunting, the matador kills the bull with a sword: He or she (some matadors are female) may receive the bull's ears and/or tail for a job well done. Six bulls are killed per day, by several different matadors.

Corridas (bullfights), are normally held around 5 PM on Sundays, from April to early November. Hemingway made famous **Pamplona**'s running of the bulls and bullfighting during the feast of San Fermín, in the second week of July, but nowhere is bullfighting better than at **Madrid**'s Las Ventas, where three weeks of daily *corridas* in May mark the festival of San Isidro.

Dining

Seafood and roast meats are Spain's national specialties. Foods are lightly seasoned, although garlic is considered a basic ingredient. Salads are delicious and fundamental, especially in the heat of summer. *Ensalada mixta* includes canned tuna, asparagus, olives, tomatoes, onions, and egg. *Ensalada verde* is simpler, usually limited to lettuce, tomato, and onion.

Breakfast in Spain is usually coffee and a roll; in Madrid, it might be *churros* (strips of fried dough) and *chocolate* (thick, hot cocoa). Spanish coffee is strong espresso taken straight (*café solo*) or with hot milk (*café con leche*). If you prefer weaker coffee, ask for *café américano*.

Spaniards generally eat paella, the delicious seafood and saffron-spiced rice dish, at midday, preferably at a beachside restaurant or around a campfire at a country picnic.

Lunch usually consists of a first plate, which is a salad, soup, vegetable, or smoked fish or cured meat; a second plate, almost always meat or fish; and dessert, which can be ice cream, yogurt, or flan but is more often a piece of fresh fruit, which natives peel deftly with a knife and fork. All this is accompanied by bread (no butter) and washed down with a bottle of wine. In big cities, some workers now grab a quick sandwich instead of stopping for the traditional three-course lunch.

Restaurants are required by law to offer for lunch a *menú del día,* which includes all the above for 80% of what the courses would cost à la carte. Restaurants that specialize in a *menú del día* post it at the door; in others, you have to inquire, and the *menú del día* may be only a couple of unappetizing choices designed to get you to order from the regular menu.

Supper is three courses, sometimes with lighter fare replacing the meat course. Some restaurants may offer a *menú del día,* but it's usually leftover lunch.

Shopping

Clothing is expensive in Spain: World-famous Spanish **leather** jackets and shoes are beautiful, if pricey. Madrid has the best selection of leather clothing, purses, and shoes; shoes are generally made in Alicante and the Balearic Islands. Distinctive, country-style **ceramics** are in ready supply throughout the country; most are made in Talavera, Puente del Arzobispo (Toledo), and Seville.

In any **stationery** shop you'll find unusual pen and pencil boxes.

Other shopping in Spain will probably have something to do with **alcohol.** Each region produces its own wine, with the sherries of Jerez, the Riojas of the north, and the sparkling wines (*cavas*) of Catalonia famous around the world.

Sports

Sailing, boating, and other **water sports** are popular along the Mediterranean coast and in the Balearic Islands. The **golf** course at El Saler, south of Valencia, is considered one of the best in Continental Europe. Marbella has 14 excellent courses, and the Costa Brava and Costa Blanca also have commendable courses. **Hiking** is excellent in the interior of Spain, and the numerous national parks, from the marshy Doñana to the mountainous Picos de Europa. Spain has excellent **skiing and winter sports** facilities, with major resorts including Navacerrada, Valcoto, and Valdesqui, near Madrid. Spain is renowned for its horses: **polo** is played at the magnificent Puerta de Hierro Country Club, in Madrid, and the Royal Polo Club, in

Barcelona. Thousands of pedal-pushers turn out in early summer, when the roads are closed off for Madrid's annual bicycle day. Otherwise, **bicycling** is impossible in crowded cities, but many coastal resorts rent bikes.

FODOR'S CHOICE

No two people agree on what makes a perfect trip, but it can be helpful to know what others have experienced. For more details on these suggestions, see their individual entries in the relevant chapters.

Castles and Palaces

★ **Alarcón, Cuenca.** Crossing the narrow bridge into the walled city and castle of Alarcón—a parador with a memorable restaurant—will catapult you into medieval times. Throw open the shutters of the turret's bedroom window and cry, "The legions are approaching!"

★ **Castle, Sigüenza.** At the very top of the beautiful town of Sigüenza, this mighty, crenellated parador has hosted royalty over the centuries, from Ferdinand and Isabella to Juan Carlos.

★ **Palacio Real, Aranjuez.** Surrounded by extensive gardens and woods, this palace reflects a French grandeur. The high point of the sumptuous interior is a room covered entirely with porcelain.

Churches and Monasteries

★ **El Escorial, Madrid.** This great, granite monastery holds the bodies of many a Spanish king as well as priceless tapestries, paintings by Velázquez and El Greco, a lavish library with rare works, and a basilica with a Titian fresco.

★ **Temple Expiatori de la Sagrada Família, Barcelona.** Unfinished at the time of Antoni Gaudí's death in 1926, this surreal cathedral has been amended by other architects, who have themselves not shied away from controversy. Take an elevator to one of the spires for a magnificent view of the city.

Museums

★ **Museu Picasso, Barcelona.** You rather expect to see Juliet leaning over the courtyard balcony of this 15th-century palace, which houses Picasso's childhood sketches and paintings from his Rose and Blue periods. The surrounding cobblestone streets are full of shops and tapas bars.

★ **Prado, Madrid.** One of the world's greatest museums, the Prado has masterpieces by Italian and Flemish painters, but its jewels are the works of Spaniards: Goya, Velázquez, and El Greco.

Other Sights

★ **Roman ruins in Mérida, Segovia, and Tarragona.** Mérida has Spain's largest concentration of Roman monuments, including a 64-arch bridge, a fortress, and a Roman ampitheater that once drew crowds of more than 14,000 to grizzly duels between gladiators and wild beasts. The enchanting city of Segovia, near Madrid, has a nearly 3,000-ft aqueduct that dates from the 1st century AD; and Tarragona, near Barcelona, has many classical remains, the highlight of which is an amphitheater near the sea.

★ **University, Salamanca.** Founded in 1220, Salamanca's university is one of the most prestigious in Europe. The architectural highlight is the Escuelas Mayores, whose ornate eyeful of a frontispiece is surrounded by graceful quadrangles and greens.

FESTIVALS AND SEASONAL EVENTS

From solemn Holy Week processions to hilarious wine and tomato battles, Spain has a fiesta for every occasion. All require hotel reservations far in advance.

WINTER

➤ DEC.: **New Year's Eve** ticks away at Madrid's Puerta del Sol, where crowds gather to eat 12 grapes, one on each stroke of midnight, to guarantee good fortune in the coming year.

➤ JAN.: **Epiphany,** on the 6th, is a Spanish child's Christmas. Youngsters leave their shoes on the doorstep to be filled with gifts from the Three Kings. In towns throughout Spain, the Wise Men arrive by boat, camel, or car and are featured in a parade on the night of January 5.

➤ FEB.: **Carnival** dances through Spain as a final fiesta before Lent. One of the most flamboyant parades take place in Sitges (Barcelona).

SPRING

➤ APR.: **Semana Santa** (Holy Week; March 28– April 4 in 1999), Spain's most spectacular fiesta; some of the most famous processions take place in Valladolid, Toledo, and Cuenca.

➤ MAY: The smells of rosemary and thyme fill Barcelona on **Sant Ponç** (May 11), when farmers come into the city to sell their products (honey, cheeses, herbs, sausages, wooden utensils, artisanal oils). **San Isídro** (May 15) begins two weeks of the best bullfighting in Spain in honor of the patron saint of Madrid.

SUMMER

➤ JUNE: **Corpus Christi** (June 3) is celebrated with processions throughout Spain, but the most mag-

nificent are in Toledo and Sitges (Barcelona).

➤ JULY: **Veranos de la Villa** cools off Madrid's summer nights with a series of outdoor films as well as concerts of everything from flamenco to rock-and-roll all summer long.

➤ AUG.: The end of the month is tinged another color for the **Saffron Rose Festival** in Consuegra (near Toledo), the world's saffron capital. Participants celebrate the harvest of the world's most expensive spice with three days of music, dance, and regional folklore exhibits.

AUTUMN

➤ SEPT.: **La Merch** is celebrated in Barcelona on September 24 with concerts, fireworks, and parades in which people wear giant papier-mâché heads.

2 Madrid

Madrid is one of Europe's most vibrant cities. Madrileños are a vigorous, joyful lot, famous for their apparent ability to defy the need for sleep; they embrace their city's cultural offerings and make enthusiastic use of its cafés and bars. If you can match this energy, you'll take in Madrid's museum mile, with more masterpieces per square foot than anywhere else in the world; the palaces and boutiques of regal Madrid; the dark, narrow lanes of medieval Madrid; and Madrid post-midnight, where today's action is.

By Mark Potok
and Deborah
Luhrman

Updated by
Annie Ward

LIFE IN MADRID is lived in the crowded streets and in the noisy cafés, where talking, toasting, and tapa-tasting last long into the night. Many find the city's endless energy hard to resist, and its social lifestyle makes it especially easy for travelers to get involved.

Madrid's other chief attraction is its unsurpassed collection of paintings by some of the world's great artists, among them Goya, El Greco, Velázquez, Picasso, and Dalí. Nowhere else will you find such a concentration of masterpieces as in the three museums—the Prado, the Reina Sofía, and the Thyssen-Bornemisza—that make up Madrid's so-called Golden Triangle of Art.

The bright blue sky, as immortalized in Velázquez's paintings, is probably the first thing you'll notice about Madrid. Despite 20th-century pollution, that sky is still much in evidence thanks to breezes that sweep down from the Guadarrama mountains, blowing away the urban smog.

The skyline has its share of skyscrapers, but these are far outnumbered by the more typical Madrid towers of red brick crowned by gray slate roofs and spires. Built in the 16th and 17th centuries by the occupying Habsburgs, who made Madrid the capital of the Iberian realm, this architecture gives parts of Madrid a timeless, Old World feel. Monumental neoclassical structures, like the Prado Museum, the Royal Palace, and the Puerta de Alcalá arch—the sights most visited by travelers—make up Madrid's other historic face. Most of these were built in the 18th century, during the reign of Bourbon monarch Charles III; inspired by the enlightened ideas of the age, Charles also created Retiro Park and the broad, leafy boulevard Paseo del Prado.

Modern-day Madrid sprawls northward in block after block of dreary, high-rise brick apartment and office buildings. The swelling population of 3.2 million is also moving into surrounding villages and new suburbs, creating traffic problems in and around the city. Although these new quarters and many of Madrid's crumbling old residential neighborhoods may seem uninviting, don't be put off by first impressions. Much of the city's appeal comes from its vivacious people and the electricity they generate, whether at play in the bars and clubs or at work in Spain's advertising, television, and film industries, all headquartered here.

Poised on a plateau 2,120 ft above sea level, Madrid is the highest capital in Europe. It can be one of the world's hottest cities in summer, and freezing cold in winter. Spring and summer are the most delightful times to visit, when balmy evenings have virtually everyone in town lingering at outdoor cafés, but each season has its own charms; in winter, steamy café windows beckon, and the famous blue skies are especially crisp and bright. That's when Madrid, as the local bumper stickers will tell you, is the next best place to heaven.

The city's sophistication stands in vivid contrast to the ancient ways of the historic villages nearby. Less than an hour away from the downtown skyscrapers are villages where farm fields are still plowed by mules. Like urbanites the world over, Madrileños like to escape to the countryside. Getaways to the dozens of Castilian hamlets nearby and to Toledo, El Escorial, and Segovia are cherished by both locals and travelers.

Pleasures and Pastimes

Art Museums

Madrid's greatest attractions are its three world-class art museums, the Prado, the Reina Sofía, and the Thyssen-Bornemisza, all within 1 km (½ mi) of each other along the leafy Paseo del Prado, sometimes called the Golden Triangle of Art. The Prado houses Spain's old masters, with the world's foremost collections of Goya, El Greco, and Velázquez along with hundreds of other 17th-, 18th-, and 19th-century masterpieces. The Reina Sofía focuses on modern art, especially Dalí, Miró and Picasso, whose famous *Guernica* hangs here; it also shows modern Spanish sculptors, such as Eduardo Chillida, and hosts excellent temporary exhibits. The Thyssen-Bornemisza attempts to trace the entire history of Western art and includes good collections of impressionist and German expressionist works.

Dining

Unlike most other regions of Spain, Madrid does not really have a native cuisine. But as capital of the realm and home of the king, Madrid has attracted generations of courtiers, foreign diplomats, politicians, and tradesmen, all of whom have brought their own culinary styles and tastes, both from other regions of Spain and from abroad.

The roast meats of Castile and the seafoods of the Cantabrian coast are just as at home in Madrid as they are in their native lands. Madrid's best restaurants specialize in Basque cooking, Spain's haute cuisine, and seafood houses take advantage of the capital's abundant supply of fish and shellfish, trucked in nightly from the coast. Spaniards quip that Madrid is Spain's biggest seaport.

The only truly local dishes are *cocido a la Madrileño* (garbanzo-bean stew) and *callos a la Madrileño* (stewed tripe). Given half a chance, Madrileños will wax lyrically over the mouthwatering merits of both. The *cocido* is a delicious and hearty winter meal consisting of garbanzo beans, vegetables, potatoes, sausages, and pork. The best cocidos are slowly simmered in earthenware crocks over open fires and served as a complete meal in several courses: first the broth, which comes with angel-hair pasta, then the beans and vegetables, and finally the meat. You can order cocido in the most elegant restaurants, such as Lhardy and at the Ritz hotel, as well as at the humblest holes-in-the-wall, and it's usually offered as a midday selection on Monday or Wednesday. The *callos* is a much simpler concoction of veal tripe stewed with tomatoes, onions, and garlic. *Jamon serrano* (cured ham), a specialty from the livestock lands of Extremadura and Andalusia, has become a beloved staple in Madrid; travelers can hardly walk a city block without coming upon a *museo del jamon* (ham museum), where endless legs of the dried delicacy dangle in the windows, inviting passersby in for a taste. Busy Madrileños grab a *bocadillo* (sandwich) from a stand for a quick bite; a *bocadillo de calamares* (calamari sandwich), often served with mayonnaise, is a tasty favorite and a meal in itself.

Although the countryside near the capital produces some wines, they are less than exceptional. The house wine in nearly all Madrid restaurants is a sturdy, uncomplicated *Valdepeñas* from La Mancha. A traditional, anise-flavored liqueur called *Anís* is manufactured just outside the village of Chinchón.

CATEGORY	COST*
$$$$	over 6,000 ptas.
$$$	4,000–6,000 ptas.
$$	1,800–4,000 ptas.
$	under 1,800 ptas.

per person for three-course meal, excluding drinks, service, and tax

Lodging

Hotel prices in Madrid have come down significantly since the glory days of the early '90s, especially in the upper price brackets. The Ritz and the Villamagna both once charged upwards of $600 a night, but each now offers a room rate comparable to that in other world capitals—$250 to $300 a night. If that's still too steep, try bargaining—surveys show that only 15% of Madrid's hotel guests pay the posted room rate. As most hotels cater to business travelers, special weekend rates are widely available; you can generally save 50% on a Friday, Saturday, or Sunday night, and many hotels throw in extras, like meals or museum admissions. Business customers can ask for a business or professional discount, which can amount to up to 40% off.

If you're willing to hunt a bit, you can also find *hostels* for 4,000 pesetas or even less. Most of these very cheap rooms are on the upper floors of apartment buildings and have shared baths. They are frequently full, however, and don't take reservations, so we don't list them here; you simply have to go door-to-door and trust your luck. Many such places are concentrated in the old city between the Prado Museum and the Puerta del Sol; start by looking around the Plaza Santa Ana.

CATEGORY	COST*
$$$$	over 25,000 ptas.
$$$	14,000–25,000 ptas.
$$	10,000–14,000 ptas.
$	under 10,000 ptas.

All prices are for a standard double room, excluding tax.

Tapas Bars

Madrid has some of the best tapas bars in Spain. A *tapa* is a bit of food that usually comes free with a drink; it might be a few olives, a mussel in vinaigrette, a sardine, or spicy potatoes. You can also order a larger plate of the same sort of food, called a *ración,* meant to be eaten with toothpicks and shared among friends. Tapas bars are sprinkled throughout the city, but the best place to start a tapa tour is near the Plaza Santa Ana or at the *mésones* built into the wall beneath the Plaza Mayor, along Cava San Miguel. These are some of the oldest buildings in the city, and each bar specializes in a different tapa—for example, potato-and-egg tortillas (a Spanish tortilla is an omelet of sorts, not to be confused with the Mexican tortilla), garlicky mushrooms, or a small wedge of *empañada de atún,* a rich, fried pastry stuffed with tuna, egg, and onions.

EXPLORING MADRID

Madrid is a compact city, and most of the things visitors want to see are concentrated in a downtown area barely a mile across, stretching between the Royal Palace and Retiro Park. Broad *avenidas,* twisting medieval alleys, grand museums, stately gardens, and tiny, tiled taverns are all jumbled together in an area easily covered on foot.

The texture of Madrid is so rich that walking is really the only way to experience those special moments—peeking in on a guitar maker at work or watching a child dip sweet *churros* into a steamy cup of hot chocolate—whose images linger long after the photos have faded.

Numbers in the text correspond to numbers in the margin and on the Madrid, Madrid Excursions, and El Escorial maps.

Great Itineraries

IF YOU HAVE 2 DAYS

On a brief stay, you should limit yourself to only one or two museums, leaving the remainder of your time to soak up the rest of the city. See the works of Spain's great masters at the **Museo del Prado** ⑦; then visit the **Palacio Real** ② for a regal display of art, architecture, and history. The palace tour includes admission to the Royal Library and Royal Armory, both sights in their own right. Stroll along the Paseo de la Castellana to see the fountains **Fuente de la Cibeles** ⑨ and **Fuente de Neptuno** ⑥. Visit the **Puerta del Sol** ⑤, and then relax at an outdoor café on the **Plaza Mayor** ④. Try some of the historic tapas bars along the **Cava de San Miguel** ㉚.

IF YOU HAVE 4 DAYS

Four days will give you time to uncover historic Madrid, visit more museums, and take an excursion outside the city.

Visit the **Centro de Arte Reina Sofía** ⑳ and the **Museo Thyssen-Bornemisza** ⑧. Don't miss the 16th-century **Convento de las Descalzas Reales** ㉒, with a beautiful frescoed staircase, paintings by Zurbarán and Titian, and a hall of sumptuous tapestries. Explore medieval Madrid, beginning on Calle Mayor toward the **Plaza de la Villa** ㉙, to see Spain's Mudéjar architecture and flamboyant plateresque decoration. Turn onto Calle Segovia, a main medieval drag, and make your way to the **Plaza de Paja** ㉛ and the Museo de San Isidro, named for Madrid's patron saint and the site of his most famous miracle. Take an excursion outside of Madrid to **El Escorial** ㊳ and the **Real Monasterio de San Lorenzo de El Escorial,** 50 km (31 mi) from Madrid in the Guadarrama mountains. Here, in the Royal Pantheon, are the bodies of most of Spain's kings since Carlos I. A few miles away is Franco's tomb, **Valle de los Caídos** ㊴, built with the forced labor of Republican prisoners after the civil war.

Central Madrid

Central Madrid stretches between the Royal Palace, to the west, and Retiro Park, to the east—a distance of about 3 km (2 mi) that's loaded with most of the city's museums, monuments, and historic buildings.

A Good Walk

A leisurely walk across town will help you get your bearings while locating many of the major sights. Begin at the **Plaza de Oriente** ①. From your position in the round plaza, you'll see the majestic **Palacio Real** (Royal Palace) ②, a glimpse of the impressive **Catedral de la Almudena** ㉔, on Calle Bailén, the Palacio's **Jardines Sabatini** ㉕, and **Campo del Moro** ㉖. Just east of the Plaza de Oriente is the newly restored **Teatro Real** ③. Walk south on Calle Bailén, then east on Calle Mayor toward the **Plaza Mayor** ④. On the way, walk through the narrow San Ginés passageway, which runs along the 14th-century church of **San Ginés,** one of the oldest in the city; wooden stalls selling used books and prints of old Madrid are built into the church wall. This is one of Madrid's most picturesque corners. Where the passageway jogs to the right is the Chocolatería San Ginés, known for its chocolate and churros, and the final stop on many a wee-hours bar crawl. Leaving the Plaza Mayor, wend your way east among the crowds to the **Puerta del Sol** ⑤.

A little detour to the northwest, on Calle de Arenal, will bring you to the **Convento de las Descalzas Reales** ㉒ and the **Convento de la Encarnación** ㉓. Backtrack to Puerta del Sol and wander along Carrera San Jerónimo, a jumble of shops and cafés. Turn south on Calle de la Cruz for a quick peek into the delicatessen at Lhardy, one of Madrid's oldest and most traditional restaurants. Shoppers stop in here on cold winter mornings for steamy cups of *caldo* (chicken broth). Be sure to look up at the buildings' beautifully tiled and decorated upper floors, especially at the corner of Calle Sevilla. The big, white-granite building on the left with the lions out in front is the Congress, the lower house of Spain's parliament.

You'll reach the wide Paseo del Prado right across from the renowned **Museo del Prado** ⑦, with the **Fuente de Neptuno** ⑥ right in front of you. A left turn will take you past the **Museo Thyssen-Bornemisza** ⑧ and the elegant Ritz Hotel to the plaza with the **Fuente de la Cibeles** ⑨, beautifully framed by the **Palacio de Comunicaciones** ⑩, now the post office; **Banco de España** ⑪; and **Casa de las Américas** ⑫. The grand yellow mansion near the post office (now the Banco Argentaria) was once the home of the Marquis of Salamanca, who at the turn of the 20th century built the exclusive shopping and residential neighborhood that bears his name. Go right at Calle Alcalá and you'll see Madrid's symbol, the **Puerta de Alcalá** ⑬, and the Retiro. Detour north for the **Museo Arqueológico** ⑭ and **Plaza Colón** ⑮.

Back at the Fuente de Neptuno: heading due east, you'll find the **Museo del Ejército** ⑯, the **Casón del Buen Retiro** ⑰, and the **Parque del Retiro** ⑱. Heading south on Paseo del Prado, you'll come to the **Jardín Botánico** ⑲ and eventually the **Atocha** train station, spruced up in 1992. The high-speed train (AVE) to Córdoba and Seville leaves from here, as do regular trains to other points south and local trains to Toledo and Segovia. Across the traffic circle, the immense pile of painted tiles and winged statues houses the Ministerio de Agricultura (Agriculture Ministry). The **Centro de Arte Reina Sofía** ⑳, home to Picasso's *Guernica,* is in the building with the glass elevators on the front.

If you choose to do this walk in reverse, you can head from the **Palacio Real** ② to the **Parque del Oeste** (West Park; stop first for coffee at the Café de Oriente) to explore the Egyptian **Templo de Debod.** Then visit the **Convento de la Encarnácion** ㉓, **Convento de la Descalzas Reales** ㉒, and **Academia de Bellas Artes de San Fernando** ㉑ on your way east.

TIMING
This walk covers about 3 km (2 mi) and, depending on how often you stop, can be covered in two to three hours.

Set aside an entire morning or afternoon for return visits to each of Madrid's main sights: the Royal Palace, the Prado, the Reina Sofía, and the Thyssen-Bornemisza.

Sights to See
㉑ **Academia de Bellas Artes de San Fernando** (St. Fernando Academy of Fine Arts). Designed by Churriguera in the waning baroque years of the early 18th century, this little-visited museum is a showcase of painting and the other plastic arts. The same building houses the **Instituto de Calcografía** (Prints Institute), which sells limited-edition prints from original plates engraved by Spanish artists, including Goya. ⊠ *Alcalá 13,* ☎ *91/522–1491.* 💷 *300 ptas.* ☉ *Tues.–Fri. 9–7, Sat.–Mon. 9–2.*

⑪ **Banco de España.** Spain's equivalent of the U.S. Federal Reserve, the massive 1884 building takes up an entire city block. It's said that the nation's gold reserves are held in great vaults that stretch under the Plaza de Cibeles traffic circle all the way to the fountain. The bank is not open to visitors, but if you want to risk dodging traffic to reach the median strip in front of it, you can take a fine photo of the fountain and the palaces with the monumental Puerta de Alcalá arch in the background.

㉖ **Campo del Moro** (Moors' Field). Below the Sabatini Gardens, but accessible only by walking around to an entrance on the far side, is the Campo del Moro. This park's clusters of shady trees, winding paths, and long lawn leading up to the Royal Palace make for strategically beautiful photographs. Even without considering the riches inside, the palace's immense size (twice as large as Buckingham Palace) is awe-inspiring.

⑫ **Casa de las Américas** (House of the Americas). A cultural center and art gallery focusing on Latin America, the Casa de las Américas is housed in the allegedly haunted Palacio de Linares, built by a man who made his fortune in the New World and returned to a life of incestuous love and strange deaths. ⊠ *Paseo Recoletos 2,* ☎ *91/595–4800.* ◰ *Palace tour 300 ptas., art gallery free.* ◷ *Palace tour Tues.–Fri. 9:30–11:30, weekends 10–1:30; art gallery Tues.–Sat. 11–7, Sun. 11–2.*

⑰ **Casón del Buen Retiro.** This Prado annex is just a five-minute walk from the museum and can be entered on the same ticket. The building, once a ballroom, and the formal gardens in the Retiro are all that remain of Madrid's second royal complex, which filled the entire neighborhood until the early 19th century. On display here are 19th-century Spanish paintings and sculpture, including works by Sorolla and Rusiñol. ⊠ *C. Alfonso XII s/n,* ☎ *91/330–2867.* ◷ *Tues.–Sat. 9–7, Sun. 9–2.*

㉔ **Catedral de la Almudena.** The first stone of the cathedral (which adjoins the Royal Palace to the south) was laid in 1883 by King Alfonso XII; the whole was consecrated by Pope John Paul II in 1993. The building was intended to be Gothic-style, with needles and spires, but as time ran long and money ran short, the design was simplified by Fernando Chueca Goltia into the more austere, classical form you see today. The cathedral houses the remains of Madrid's male patron saint, St. Isidro, and a wooden statue of Madrid's female patron saint, the Virgin of Almudena, which is said to have been discovered following the Christian reconquest of Madrid in 1085. Legend has it that a divinely inspired woman named María led authorities to a secret spot in the old wall of the Alcázar (which in Arabic can also be called *almudeyna*), where the statue was found framed by two lighted candles inside a grain storage vault. That wall is part of the cathedral's foundation. ⊠ *C. de Bailén s/n,* ☎ *91/542–2200.* ◰ *Free.* ◷ *Daily 10–1:30 and 6–7:45.*

★ ⑳ **Centro de Arte Reina Sofía** (Queen Sofia Art Center). Madrid's museum of modern art is housed in a converted hospital whose classic, granite austerity is somewhat relieved (or ruined, depending on your point of view) by the two glass elevator shafts on the facade.

The collection focuses on Spain's three great modern masters: Pablo Picasso, Salvador Dalí, and Joan Miró. Take the elevator to the second floor to see the permanent collections; the other floors house visiting exhibits.

The first rooms are dedicated to the beginnings of Spain's modern-art movement and contain paintings from around the turn of the century. The focal point is Picasso's 1901 *Woman in Blue*—hardly beautiful, but surprisingly representational compared to his later works.

Moving on to the **Cubist collection,** which includes nine works by Juan Gris, be sure to see Dalí's splintered, blue-gray *Self-Portrait,* in which the artist painted his favorite things—a morning newspaper and a pack of cigarettes. The other highlight here is Picasso's *Musical Instruments on a Table,* one of many variations on this theme.

16

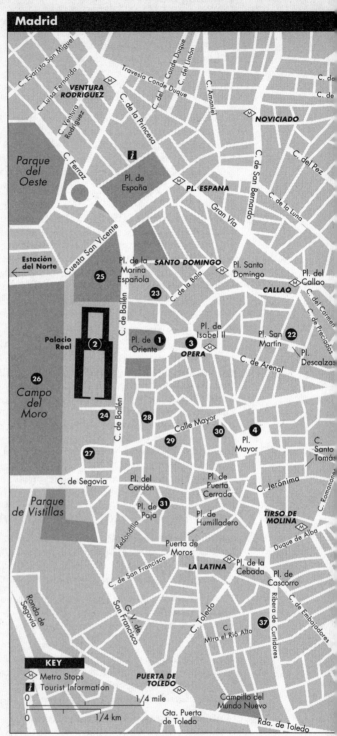

Madrid

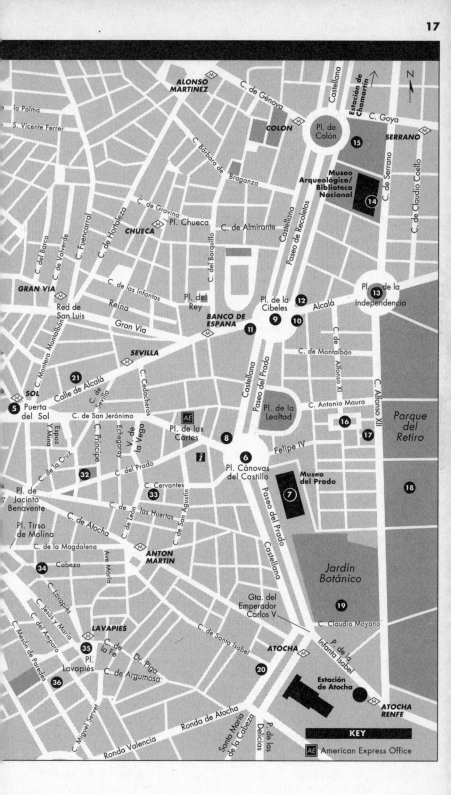

ALONSO MARTINEZ

C. de Génova

Castellana

Estación de Chamartín

C. Goya

N

la Palma

S. Vicente Ferrer

COLON

Pl. de Colón

SERRANO

15

C. de Serrano

C. de Claudio Coello

C. Bárbara de

Braganza

Museo Arqueológico/ Biblioteca Nacional

14

C. del Baño

C. de Valverde

C. Fuencarral

C. de Hortaleza

C. de Gravina

Pl. Chueca

CHUECA

C. de Almirante

Castellana

Paseo de Recoletos

C. del Barquillo

GRAN VIA

C. de las Infantas

Pl. del Rey

Pl. de la Cibeles

12

Alcalá

Pl. de la Independencia

13

Red de San Luis

Reina

Gran Vía

BANCO DE ESPANA

9

10

C. de Montalbán

C. de

Alfonso XI

Gran Vía

11

SEVILLA

Castellana

Paseo del Prado

Pl. de la Lealtad

C. Antonio Maura

C. Alfonso XII

Parque del Retiro

21

Calle de Alcalá

C. de Sevilla

C. Cedaceros

16

17

C. Montera

SOL

5

Puerta del Sol

C. de San Jerónimo

C. de V la Vega

Echegaray

AE

Pl. de las Cortes

8

Felipe IV

Espoz Y Mina

C. de la Cruz

C. Príncipe

C. del Prado

32

i

Pl. Cánovas del Castillo

6

Museo del Prado

7

18

Pl. de Jacinto Benavente

C. Cervantes

33

las Huertas

C. de San Agustín

Paseo del Prado

Pl. Tirso de Molina

C. de León

C. de Atocha

C. de la Magdalena

Ave María

ANTON MARTIN

Castellana

Jardín Botánico

34

Cabeza

C. Lavapiés

C. Jesús y María

C. del Amparo

LAVAPIES

Gta. del Emperador Carlos V

19

C. Claudio Moyano

Mesón de Paredes

35

Pl. Lavapiés

C. de la Fe

Dr. Piga

C. de Argumosa

C. de Santa Isabel

ATOCHA

P. de la Infanta Isabel

36

C. Miguel Servet

Ronda Valencia

Ronda de Atocha

Santa María de la Cabeza

20

Estación de Atocha

P. de las Delicias

ATOCHA RENFE

KEY

AE American Express Office

The museum's showpiece is Picasso's famous *Guernica,* which occupies the center hall and is surrounded by dozens of studies for individual figures within it. The huge painting depicts the horror of the Nazi Condor Legion's bombing of the ancient Basque town of Guernica, in 1937, an act that brought Spanish dictator Francisco Franco to power. The work—in many ways a 20th-century version of Goya's *The 3rd of May*—is something of a national shrine, as evidenced by the solemnity of Spaniards viewing it. The painting was not brought into Spain until 1981; Picasso, an ardent antifascist, refused to allow it to enter the country while Franco was alive.

The room in front of *Guernica* contains a collection of **surrealist works,** including six canvases by Miró, known for his childlike graphicism. Opposite *Guernica* is a hall dedicated to the surrealist Salvador Dalí, with paintings bequeathed to the government in the artist's will. Although Dalí is perhaps best known for works of a somewhat whimsical nature, many of these canvases are dark and haunting and bursting with symbolism. Among the best known are *The Great Masturbator* (1929) and *The Enigma of Hitler* (1939), with its broken, dripping telephone.

The rest of the museum is devoted to more recent art, including the massive, gravity-defying sculpture *Toki Egin,* by Eduardo Chillida, considered Spain's greatest living sculptor, and five textural paintings by Barcelona artist Antoní Tàpies, who incorporates materials such as wrinkled sheets and straw into his works. ⊠ *Santa Isabel 52,* ☎ *91/467–5062.* ⊡ *400 ptas.; free Sat. 2:30–9 and Sun.* ⊙ *Mon. and Wed.–Sat. 10–9, Sun. 10–2:30.*

㉓ **Convento de la Encarnación** (Convent of the Incarnation). Once connected to the Royal Palace by an underground passageway, this Augustinian convent was founded in 1611 by the wife of Felipe III. It has many artistic treasures, but the convent's biggest attraction is the reliquary, which holds among the sacred bones a vial containing the dried blood of St. Pantaléon, which is said to liquify every year on July 27. You can enter Encarnación on the same ticket as the Convent of Descalzas Reales. ⊠ *Plaza de la Encarnación 1,* ☎ *91/547–0510.* ⊡ *400 ptas.* ⊙ *Wed. and Sat. 10:30–1 and 4–5:30, Sun. 11–1:30.*

㉒ **Convento de las Descalzas Reales** (Convent of the Royal Barefoot Nuns). This 16th-century building was restricted for 200 years to women of royal blood. Its plain, brick-and-stone facade hides a treasure trove, including paintings by Zurbarán, Titian, and Breughel the Elder, as well as a hall of sumptuous tapestries crafted from drawings by Rubens. The convent was founded in 1559 by Juana of Austria, whose daughter shut herself up here rather than endure marriage to Felipe II. A handful of nuns (not necessarily royal) still live here, cultivating their own vegetables in the convent's garden. You must visit as part of a guided tour, conducted once a day in English, the rest of the day in Spanish. ⊠ *Plaza de las Descalzas Reales 3,* ☎ *91/542–0059.* ⊡ *650 ptas.* ⊙ *Tues.–Thurs. and Sat. 10:30–12:30 and 4–5:30, Fri. 10:30–12:30, Sun. 11–1:30.*

❾ **Fuente de la Cibeles** (Fountain of Sybil). A landscaped walkway runs down the center of the Paseo del Prado to the Plaza de la Cibeles, where this famous fountain depicts Sybil, the wife of Saturn, driving a chariot drawn by lions. Even more than the officially designated bear and strawberry tree, this monument, beautifully lighted at night, has come to symbolize Madrid—so much so that during the civil war, patriotic Madrileños risked life and limb to sandbag it as Nationalist aircraft bombed the city.

⑥ Fuente de Neptuno (Neptune's Fountain). Just outside the Palace Hotel and the boutiques-filled Galerias del Prado shopping center, on the Plaza Canovas del Castillo, this fountain is at the hub of Madrid's so-called Golden Triangle of Art, made up of the redbrick Prado Museum spreading out along the east side of the boulevard, the Thyssen-Bornemisza Museum across the plaza, and, five blocks to the south, the Reina Sofía art center.

⑲ Jardín Botánico (Botanical Gardens). Just south of the Prado Museum, the gardens provide a pleasant place to stroll or sit under the trees. True to the wishes of King Carlos III, they hold an array of plants, flowers, and cacti from around the world. ✉ *Plaza de Murillo 2,* ☎ *91/585–4700.* 💷 *200 ptas.* ☉ *Summer, daily 10–9; winter, daily 10–6.*

㉕ Jardines Sabatini (Sabatini Gardens). The formal gardens to the north of the Royal Palace are crawling with stray cats, but they're a pleasant place to rest or watch the sun set.

⑭ Museo Arqueológico (Museum of Archaeology). The museum shares its neoclassical building with the **Biblioteca Nacional** (National Library). The biggest attraction here is a replica of the prehistoric cave paintings in Altamira, Cantabria, located underground in the garden. (Only scholars are allowed to see the real thing.) Inside the museum, look for the *Dama de Elche,* a bust of a wealthy, 4th-century Iberian woman, and notice how her headgear is a rough precursor to the mantillas and hair combs still associated with traditional Spanish dress. Be sure to see the ancient Visigothic votive crowns, discovered in 1859 near Toledo and believed to date back to the 8th century. ✉ *C. Serrano 13,* ☎ *91/577–7912.* 💷 *500 ptas.; free Sat. afternoon and Sun. morning.* ☉ *Tues.–Sat. 9:30–8:30, Sun. 9:30–2:30.*

⑯ Museo del Ejército (Army Museum). A real treat for arms-and-armor buffs, this museum is right on the museum mile. Among the 27,000 items on view are a sword which allegedly belonged to the Spanish hero El Cid; suits of armor; bizarre-looking pistols with barrels capable of holding scores of bullets; Moorish tents; and a cross carried by Christopher Columbus. It's an unusually entertaining collection. ✉ *Mendez Nuñez 1,* ☎ *91/522–8977.* 💷 *100 ptas.* ☉ *Tues.–Sun. 10–2.*

★ **⑦ Museo del Prado** (Prado Museum). When the Prado was commissioned by King Carlos III, in 1785, it was meant to be a natural-science museum. The king, popularly remembered as "Madrid's best mayor," wanted the museum, the adjoining botanical gardens, and the elegant Paseo del Prado to serve as a center of scientific enlightenment for his subjects. By the time the building was completed in 1819, its purpose had changed to exhibiting the vast collection of art gathered by Spanish royalty since the time of Ferdinand and Isabella.

Painting is one of Spain's greatest contributions to world culture, and the Prado's jewels are works by the nation's three great masters: Francisco Goya, Diego Velázquez, and El Greco. The museum also contains masterpieces of Flemish and Italian artists, collected when their lands were part of the Spanish Empire. The museum benefited greatly from the anticlerical laws of 1836, which forced monasteries, convents, and churches to turn over much of their art treasures so that the general public could enjoy them.

A visit to the Prado begins on the upper floor (*primera planta*), where you enter through a series of halls dedicated to **Renaissance painters.** Many people hurry through these rooms to get to the Spanish canvases, but it's worth stopping for Titian's *Portrait of Emperor Charles V* and Raphael's exquisite *Portrait of a Cardinal.*

Next comes a hall filled with the passionately spiritual works of **El Greco** (Doménikos Theotokópoulos, 1541–1614), the Greek-born artist who lived and worked in Toledo. El Greco is known for his mystical, elongated faces. His style was quite shocking to a public accustomed to strict, representational realism; and because he wanted his art to provoke emotion, El Greco is sometimes called the world's first "modern" painter. *The Resurrection* and *The Adoration of the Shepherds,* considered two of his greatest paintings, are on view here.

You can see the meticulous brushwork of **Velázquez** (1599–1660) in his numerous portraits of kings and queens. Be sure to look for the magnificent *Las Hilanderas* (*The Spinners*), evidence of the artist's talent for painting light. One hall is reserved exclusively for the Prado's most famous canvas, Velázquez's *Las Meninas* (*The Maids of Honor*), which combines a self-portrait of the artist at work with a mirror reflection of the king and queen in a revolutionary interplay of space and perspectives. Picasso was obsessed with this work and painted several copies of it in his own abstract style, now on display in the Picasso Museum in Barcelona.

The south end of the first floor is reserved for **Goya** (1746–1828), whose works span a staggering range of tone, from bucolic to horrific. Among his early masterpieces are portraits of the family of King Carlos IV, for whom he was court painter—one glance at their unflattering and imbecilic expressions, especially in the painting *The Family of Carlos IV,* reveals the loathing Goya developed for these self-indulgent and reactionary rulers. His famous side-by-side canvases, *The Clothed Maja* and *The Nude Maja,* may represent the young duchess of Alba, whom Goya adored and frequently painted. No one knows whether she ever returned his affection. The adjacent rooms house a series of bucolic scenes of Spaniards at play, painted as designs for tapestries.

Goya's paintings take on political purpose starting in 1808, when the population of Madrid rose up against occupying French troops. *The 2nd of May* portrays the insurrection at the Puerta del Sol, and its even more terrifying companion piece, *The 3rd of May,* depicts the nighttime executions of patriots who had rebelled the day before. The garish light effects in this work typify the romantic style, which favors drama over detail, and make it one of the most powerful indictments of violence ever committed to canvas.

Downstairs you'll find Goya's "black paintings"—dark, disturbing works, completed late in his life, that reflect his inner turmoil after losing his hearing, and his deep embitterment over the bloody War of Independence. The rest of the ground floor is taken up with Flemish paintings, including the bizarre masterpiece *Garden of Earthly Delights,* by Hieronymous Bosch. ⊠ *Paseo del Prado s/n,* ☎ *91/330–2800.* 🖅 *500 ptas.; free Sat. afternoon and Sun. morning.* ☉ *Tues.–Sat. 9–7, Sun. 9–2.*

NEED A
BREAK?   **La Dolores** (⊠ Plaza de Jesús 4) is one of Madrid's most atmospheric old tiled bars, the perfect place for a beer or glass of wine and a plate of olives. It's a great alternative to the Prado's so-so basement cafeteria and is just across the Paseo, then one block up on Calle Lope de Vega to the tiny plaza.

 Museo Thyssen-Bornemisza. Madrid's third and newest art center, elegantly renovated to create lots of space and natural light, opened in 1992 in the Villahermosa Palace. This ambitious collection of 800 paintings traces the history of Western art with examples from all the important movements, beginning with 13th-century Italy.

The artworks were gathered over the past 70 years by industrialist Baron Hans Heinrich Thyssen-Bornemisza and his father. At the urging of his Spanish wife (a former Miss Spain), the baron agreed to donate the collection to Spain. Critics have described the collection as the minor works of major artists and the major works of minor artists, but the museum itself is beautiful, and its impressionist paintings are the only ones on display in the country.

Among the museum's gems are Hans Holbein's *Portrait of Henry VIII* (purchased from the late Princess Diana's grandfather, who used the money to buy a new Bugatti sports car). American artists are also well represented; look for the Gilbert Stuart portrait of George Washington's cook, and note how closely the composition and rendering resembles the artist's famous painting of the Founding Father himself. Two halls are devoted to the impressionists and post-impressionists, including many works by Pissarro and a few each by Renoir, Monet, Degas, Van Gogh, and Cézanne.

Within 20th-century art, the baron shows a proclivity for terror-filled (albeit dynamic and colorful) German expressionism, but there are also some soothing works by Georgia O'Keeffe and Andrew Wyeth. ⊠ *Paseo del Prado 8,* ☎ *91/369–0151.* ▨ *600 ptas.* ⊙ *Tues.–Sun. 10–7.*

⑩ **Palacio de Comunicaciones.** This ornate building on the southeast side of Plaza de Cibeles is otherwise known as the main post office. ⊙ *Stamps weekdays 9* AM*–10* PM*, Sat. 9–8, Sun. 10–1; phone, telex, telegrams, and fax weekdays 8* AM*–midnight, weekends 8* AM*–10* PM*.*

★ ② **Palacio Real** (Royal Palace). The Royal Palace was commissioned in the early 1700s by the first of Spain's Bourbon rulers, Felipe V, on the same strategic spot where Madrid's first Alcázar (Moorish fortress) was built in the 9th century.

Before entering, take time to walk around the graceful **Patio de Armas** and admire the classical French architecture. King Felipe was obviously inspired by his childhood days with his grandfather Louis XIV at Versailles. Look for the stone statues of Inca prince Atahualpa and Aztec king Montezuma, perhaps the only tributes in Spain to these pre-Columbian American rulers. Notice how the steep bluff drops westward to the Manzanares River; on a clear day, this vantage point also commands a good view of the mountain passes leading into Madrid from Old Castile, and it becomes obvious why the Moors picked this particular spot for a fortress.

Inside, the palace's 2,800 rooms compete with each other for over-the-top opulence. A nearly two-hour guided tour in English winds a mile-long path through the palace. Highlights include the **Salón de Gasparini,** King Carlos III's private apartments—a riot of rococo decoration, with swirling, inlaid floors and curlicued, ceramic wall and ceiling decoration, all glistening in the light of a 2-ton crystal chandelier; the **Salón del Trono,** an exceedingly grand throne room with the royal seats of King Juan Carlos and Queen Sofía; and the **banquet hall,** the palace's largest room, which seats up to 140 people for state dinners. No monarch has lived here since 1931, when Alfonso XIII was hounded out of the country by a populace fed up with centuries of royal oppression. The current king and queen live in the far simpler Zarzuela Palace, on the outskirts of Madrid, using this Royal Palace only for state functions and official occasions, such as the first Middle East peace talks, in 1991.

Within the palace, you can also visit the **Biblioteca Real** (Royal Library), which has a first edition of Cervantes's *Don Quixote*; the **Museo de Música** (Music Museum), where five stringed instruments by Stradivarius form the world's largest collection; the **Armería Real** (Royal Armory), with its vast array of historic suits of armor and some frightening medieval torture implements; and the **Real Oficina de Farmacía** (Royal Pharmacy), with an assortment of vials and flasks that were used to mix the king's medicines. ✉ *C. Bailén s/n,* ☎ *91/559–7404.* 💰 *850 ptas.* ☉ *Mon.–Sat. 9:30–6, Sun. 9–3; closed during official receptions.*

★ ⑱ **Parque del Retiro** (literally, The Retreat). Once the private playground of royalty, the park is a vast expanse of green that includes formal gardens, fountains, lakes (complete with rowboats for rent), exhibition halls, children's play areas, and a **Puppet Theater,** featuring slapstick routines that even non–Spanish speakers will enjoy. Shows take place on Saturday at 1 and on Sunday at 1, 6, and 7; admission is free. The park is especially lively on weekends, when it fills with street musicians, jugglers, clowns, gypsy fortune-tellers, and sidewalk painters along with hundreds of Spanish families out for a walk. The park hosts a month-long book fair in May and often flamenco concerts in summer.

From the entrance at the Puerta de Alcalá, head straight toward the center of Retiro and you'll find the **Estanque** (lake), presided over by a grandiose equestrian statue of King Alfonso XII, erected by his mother. Just behind the lake, north of the statue, is one of the best of the many cafés within the park. If you're feeling energetic, you can rent a boat and work up an appetite just rowing around the lake.

The 19th-century **Palacio de Cristal** (Crystal Palace), southeast of the Estanque, was built to house a collection of exotic plants from the Philippines, a Spanish possession at the time. This airy marvel of steel and glass sits on a base of decorative tile. Next door is a small lake with ducks and swans. At the south end of the park, along the Paseo del Uruguay, is the **Rosaleda** (rose garden), an English garden bursting with color and heavy with floral scents for most of the summer. West of the Rosaleda, look for a statue called the **Ángel Caído** (Fallen Angel), which Madrileños claim is the only one in the world depicting the prince of darkness before—during, actually—his fall from grace.

⑮ **Plaza Colón.** The modern plaza is named for Christopher Columbus. A statue of the explorer (identical to one in Barcelona's port) looks west from a high tower in the middle of the square. The airport bus leaves from the station beneath here every 15 minutes. Behind Plaza Colón is **Calle Serrano,** the city's number one shopping street (think Gucci, Prada, and Loewe). Take a stroll in either direction on Serrano for some window-shopping.

NEED A
BREAK?

Decorated in the style of Belle Epoque Paris, **El Espejo** is the ideal place to rest your feet and sip a cup of coffee or a beer. You can pull up a chair on the shady terrace or inside the air-conditioned, stained-glass bar. It's right in the center of the *paseo,* at Plaza Colón. ✉ *Paseo Recoletos 31,* ☎ *91/308-2347.* ☉ *Daily 10 AM–2 AM.*

❶ **Plaza de Oriente.** The stately plaza in front of the Royal Palace is surrounded by massive stone statues of all the Spanish kings from Ataulfo to Fernando VI. These sculptures were meant to be mounted on the railing on top of the palace (where there are now stone urns), but Queen Isabel of Farnesio, one of the first royals to live in the palace, had them taken off because she was afraid their enormous weight would bring the roof down. At least that's what she *said* . . . palace insiders said the queen wanted the statues removed because her own likeness had not been placed front and center.

The statue of King Felipe IV in the center of the plaza was the first equestrian bronze ever to be cast with a horse rearing. The action pose comes from a Velázquez painting of the king with which the monarch was so smitten that in 1641 he commissioned an Italian artist, Pietro de Tacca, to turn it into a sculpture. De Tacca enlisted Galileo's help in configuring the statue's weight so that it wouldn't topple over.

In the minds of most Madrileños, the Plaza de Oriente is forever linked with Francisco Franco. The *generalísimo* liked to make speeches from the roof of the Royal Palace to his thousands of followers, crammed into the plaza below. Even now, on the November anniversary of Franco's death, the plaza fills with supporters, most of whom are old-timers, though lately the occasion has also drawn Nazi flag–waving skinheads from other European countries in a chilling fascist tribute.

❹ Plaza Mayor. Austere, grand, and surprisingly quiet compared to the rest of the city, this arcaded square has seen it all: autos-da-fé (trials of faith, that is, public burnings of heretics); the canonization of saints; criminal executions; royal marriages, such as that of Princess María and the King of Hungary in 1629; bullfights (until 1847); masked balls; fireworks; and all manner of events and celebrations. It still hosts fairs, bazaars, and performances.

Measuring 360 by 300 ft, Madrid's Plaza Mayor is one of the largest and grandest public squares in Europe. It was designed by Juan de Herrera, the architect to Felipe II and designer of the forbidding El Escorial monastery, outside Madrid. Construction of the plaza lasted just two years and was finished in 1620 under Felipe III, whose **equestrian statue** stands in the center. The inauguration ceremonies included the canonization of four Spanish saints: Teresa of Ávila, Ignatius of Loyola, Isidro (Madrid's male patron saint), and Francis Xavier.

Prior to becoming the Plaza Mayor, this space was occupied by a city market, and many of the surrounding streets retain the names of the trades and foodstuffs once headquartered there. Nearby are Calle de Cuchilleros (Knifemakers' Street), Calle de Lechuga (Lettuce Street), Calle de Fresa (Strawberry Street), and Calle de Botoneros (Buttonmakers' Street). The plaza's oldest building is the one with the brightly painted murals and the gray spires, Casa de la Panadería (the bakery) in honor of the bread shop on top of which it was built. Opposite it is the Casa de la Carnicería (the butcher shop), now a police station.

The plaza is closed to motorized traffic, making it a pleasant place to sit in the sun or to while away a warm summer evening at one of the sidewalk cafés, watching alfresco artists, street musicians, and Madrileños from all walks of life. At Christmas the plaza fills with stalls selling trees, ornaments, and nativity scenes, as well as all types of practical jokes and tricks for December 28, *Día de los Inocentes,* a Spanish version of April Fool's Day.

⓭ Puerta de Alcalá. Marking the spot of the ancient city gates, this triumphal arch was built by Carlos III in 1778. You can still see the bomb damage inflicted on the arch during the civil war.

❺ Puerta del Sol. Always crowded with both people and exhaust fumes, Sol is the nerve center of Madrid's traffic. The city's main subway interchange is below, and buses fan out through the city from here. A brass plaque in the sidewalk on the south side of the plaza marks Kilometer 0, the spot from which all distances in Spain are measured. The restored 1756 French neoclassical building near the marker now houses government offices, but during the Franco period it was used as a political prison and is still known as the Casa de los Gritos (House of Screams). Across the square is a bronze statue of Madrid's official symbol, a bear and a *madroño* (strawberry tree).

❸ **Teatro Real** (Royal Theater). This neoclassical theater was built in 1850 and was long a cultural center for Madrileño society. Plagued by disasters more recently, including fires, a bombing, and profound structural problems, the house went dark in 1988. Closed for almost a decade for an indulgent restoration, it reopened to worldwide fanfare in October 1997. Now replete with golden balconies, plush seats, and state-of-the-art stage equipment for operas and ballets, the theater is a modern showpiece with its vintage appeal intact. ✉ *Plaza Isabell II,* ☎ *91/516–0606.*

❁ **Telefèrico** (cable car). Children love this cable car, which takes you from just above the Rosaleda gardens in the Parque del Oeste to the center of Casa de Campo. Be warned, however, that the walk from where the cable car drops you off to the zoo and the amusement park is at least 2 km (1 mi), and you'll have to ask directions. ✉ *Estación Terminal Telefèrico, Jardines Rosaleda,* ☎ *91/541–7440.* 💳 *490 ptas.* ☉ *Apr.–Sept., daily noon–sundown; Oct.–Mar., weekends noon–sundown.*

Templo de Debod (Debod Temple). This authentic 4th-century BC Egyptian temple was donated to Spain in gratitude for its technical assistance with the construction of the Aswan Dam. It's near the site of the former Montaña barracks, where Madrileños bloodily crushed the beginnings of a Francoist uprising in 1936. ✉ *Hill in Parque de la Montaña, near Estación del Norte train station,* ☎ *91/409–6165.* 💳 *300 ptas.* ☉ *Tues.–Fri. 10–1 and 4–7, weekends 10–1.*

Medieval Madrid

The narrow streets of medieval Madrid wind back through the city's history to its beginnings as an Arab fortress. Madrid's historic quarters are not so readily apparent as the ancient neighborhoods of Toledo and Segovia, nor are they so grand. But the traveler who takes time to explore their quiet, winding alleys gets an impression of the city that is light-years away from today's traffic-clogged avenues.

A Good Walk

The walk begins near the Royal Palace, at the 8th-century **Arab Wall** ㉗ on Cuesta de la Vega street. Traveling east on Calle Mayor to **Plaza de la Villa** ㉙, you'll find Spanish Mudéjar architecture and old family crests carved above doorways. Off Calle Mayor to the left is the church of **San Nicolás de Servitas** ㉘, whose tower is one of the oldest structures in Madrid. Below the Plaza Mayor on **Cava de San Miguel** ㉚ are Madrid's oldest tapas bars, taverns, and restaurants.

From the Puerta Cerrada, Calle Segovia guides you to ramped alleyways that lead to the **Plaza de Paja** ㉛, the heart of the old city, where peasants would deposit their crops as tithes to the church in the Middle Ages. Here you can visit the **Museo de San Isidro,** the site where Madrid's patron saint performed his most famous miracle.

Walk west from the Plaza de Paja on Calle de la Redondilla for one block to the **Plaza Morería,** which is really no more than a wide spot in the street. This neighborhood once housed Moors who chose to stay in Madrid after the Christian Reconquest. Although most of the buildings date from the 18th and 19th centuries, the steep, narrow streets and twisting alleyways recall the much older *medina* (old quarter).

Climb the stairway and cross Calle Bailén near the **Viaduct,** a metal bridge that spans a ravine 100 ft above Calle Segovia. The viaduct has grisly fame as Madrid's preferred spot for suicides.

Across the street on Calle Bailén is the neighborhood **Las Vistillas,** named for the pleasant park on the bluffs overlooking Madrid's western edge.

It's a great place to watch the sun go down or catch a cool breeze on a hot summer night; find an outdoor table and order a drink.

TIMING

This three-hour walk covers 2½ km (1½ mi) and requires some short uphill climbs through the winding streets. Give yourself ample time for stops to absorb the Old World charm (especially in summer, when heat will be a factor).

Sights to See

㉗ Arab Wall. The city of Madrid was founded on Calle Cuesta de la Vega at the ruins of this wall, which protected a fortress built here in the 8th century by Emir Mohammed I. In addition to being an excellent defensive position, the site had plentiful water and was called *Mayrit*, which is Arabic for "water source" and the likely origin of the city's name. All that remains of the *medina*—the old Arab city that formed within the walls of the fortress—is the neighborhood's crazy quilt of streets and plazas, which probably follow the same layout they followed more than 1,100 years ago. The park **Emir Mohammed I** (✉ Cuesta de la Vega s/n), alongside the wall, hosts summertime concerts and plays.

★ **㉚ Cava de San Miguel.** The narrow, picturesque streets behind the Plaza de la Villa are well worth exploring. From Calle Mayor, turn onto the Plaza de San Miguel and continue down Cava de San Miguel. With the Plaza Mayor on your left and the glass-and-iron San Miguel market on your right, walk downhill past the row of **ancient tapas bars** built right into the retaining wall of the plaza above. Each one specializes in something different: Mesón de Champiñones has mushrooms; Mesón de Boquerónes serves anchovies; Mesón de Tortilla cooks up excellent Spanish omelets; and so on. Madrileños and tourists alike flock here each evening to sample the food and sing along with raucous musicians, who delight in playing foreign tunes for tourists.

Costanilla de San Andrés. This ramped street leads to the heart of the old city. To find it, follow Calle Segovia from the Plaza Puerta Cerrada until you reach Plaza Cruz Verde; then turn left up the ramped street. Halfway up the hill, look left down the narrow Calle Principe Anglona for a good view of the Mudéjar tower on the church of **San Pedro el Viejo** (St. Peter the Elder), one of the city's oldest. The brick tower is believed to have been built in 1354 following the Christian reconquest of Algeciras, in southern Spain. Notice the tiny defensive slits, designed to accommodate crossbows.

Cuevas de Luis Candelas. The oldest of Madrid's taverns, about halfway down Cava San Miguel, is named for a 19th-century Madrid version of Robin Hood who was famous for his ingenious ways of tricking the rich out of their money and jewels. As Cava San Miguel becomes Calle Cuchilleros, you'll see **Casa Botín** (☞ Dining, *below*) on the left, Madrid's oldest restaurant and a favorite haunt of Ernest Hemingway. The curving Cuchilleros was once a moat just outside the city walls. The plaza with the bright murals at the intersection of Calle Segovia is called the **Puerta Cerrada** (✉ Cava San Miguel and Calle Cuchilleros), or Closed Gate, named for the entrance to the city that once stood here.

Museo de San Isidro. Just behind the church of San Andrés is the site of St. Isidro's most famous miracle, and the new museum houses the original *pozo milagroso* (miracle well). It is said that when Isidro's infant son Illán fell into the well one day, Isidro raised the water level so that his son floated up to the top and could be pulled out. ✉ *Plaza San Isidro s/n,* ☎ *91/522–5732.* ✇ *Free.* ☉ *Aug.–June, Tues.–Sun. 10–2.*

Palacio de la Nunciatura (Palace of the Nunciat). This mansion once housed the Pope's ambassadors to Spain and is now the official residence of the Archbishop of Madrid. It's near the Plaza Puerta Cerrada off Calle Segovia, one of the main streets of Madrid during the Middle Ages. Although it's not open to the public, you can peek inside the Renaissance garden. ⊠ *Costanilla del Nuncio s/n.*

NEED A
BREAK?

The **Café del Nuncio** (⊠ Costanilla del Nuncio s/n), on the corner of Calle Segovia, is a relaxing Old World spot for a coffee or beer. Classical music plays in the background.

㉙ Plaza de la Villa. Madrid's town council has met here since the Middle Ages. A medieval-looking complex, the Plaza is now Madrid's city hall. It's just two blocks west of the Plaza Mayor on Calle Mayor and was once called the Plaza de San Salvador for a church that used to stand here. The **Casa de los Lujanes** is the oldest building in the Plaza—it's the one with the Mudéjar tower, on the plaza's east side. Built as a family home in the late 15th century, it carries the Lujanes crest over the main doorway. On the east side of the Plaza is the brick-and-stone **Casa de la Villa**, built in 1629, a classic example of Madrid design with its clean lines and spire-topped corner towers. Connected by an overhead walkway, the **Casa de Cisneros** was commissioned in 1537 by the nephew of Cardinal Cisneros. It's one of Madrid's rare examples of the flamboyant plateresque style, which has been likened to splashing water—liquid exuberance wrought in stone. ⊠ *C. Mayor.* ☉ *Guided tour in Spanish Mon. at 5.*

㉛ Plaza de Paja. At the top of the hill, on Costanillo San Andrés, this is medieval Madrid's most important square. Although a few upscale restaurants have moved in, the small plaza retains its own atmosphere. The jewel is the **Capilla del Obispo** (Bishop's Chapel), built between 1520 and 1530; this was where peasants deposited their tithes, called *diezmas*—literally, one-tenth of their crop. The stacks of wheat on the chapel's ceramic tiles refer to this tradition. Architecturally, the chapel marks a transition from the blockish Gothic period (which gave this structure its basic shape) to the Renaissance (which provided the decorations). Try to get inside to see the intricately carved polychrome altarpiece by Francisco Giralta, featuring scenes from the life of Christ. Opening hours are erratic; the best time to visit is during mass or on feast days.

The chapel forms part of the complex of the church of **San Andrés**, whose dome was raised to house the remains of Madrid's male patron saint, San Isidro Labrador. Isidro was a peasant who worked fields belonging to the Vargas family. The 16th-century **Vargas palace** (⊠ Plaza de Paja s/n) forms the eastern side of the Plaza de Paja. According to legend, St. Isidro actually worked little but had the best-tended fields thanks to many hours of prayer. When Señor Vargas came out to investigate the phenomenon, Isidro made a spring of sweet water spurt from the ground to quench his master's thirst. Because St. Isidro's power had to do with water, his remains were paraded through the city in times of drought in the hope that he would bring rain, even as recently as the turn of the 20th century.

㉘ San Nicolás de las Servitas (Church of St. Nicholas of the Servitas). The church tower is one of the oldest buildings in Madrid, and there's some debate over whether it once formed part of an Arab mosque. More likely, it was built after the Christian reconquest of Madrid in 1085, but the brickwork and the horseshoe arches are clear evidence that it was crafted by either Moorish workers (Mudéjars) or Spaniards well versed in the style. Inside the church, exhibits detail the Islamic history of early Madrid. ✉ *Near the Plaza de San Nicolás,* ☎ *91/559–4064.* 💵 *100 ptas.* ⏲ *Tues.–Sun. 6:30 AM–8:30 PM or by appointment.*

Castizo Madrid

A Good Walk

The Spanish word *castizo* means "authentic." There are few "sights" in the usual sense on this tour; instead, we wander through some of Madrid's most traditional and lively neighborhoods.

Begin at the **Plaza Santa Ana** ㉜, which was the hub of the theater district in the 17th century and is now known for its lively nightlife. Around the plaza are many noteworthy sights, such as the **Teatro Español** and the tile facade of the **Casa de Guadalajara,** one of the most beautiful buildings in Madrid. Walk east two blocks on Calle del Prado; then turn right on Calle León, named for a lion kept here long ago by a resident Moor. One block on this street brings you to the corner of **Calle Cervantes,** where the author of *Don Quixote* lived in what is now called the **Casa de Cervantes** ㉝.

Continuing down Calle León one block, turn left on Calle de las Huertas, the premier street of bars in bar-speckled Madrid. One block down Huertas turn right onto **Calle Amor de Dios,** the center of the city's flamenco community. Look for the music shops and guitar makers.

Follow Calle Amor de Dios until it ends at the busy Calle Atocha. Across the street you'll see the church of **San Nicolás.** Next door is the **Pasaje Doré,** home to a colorful assortment of market stalls typical of most Madrid neighborhoods.

Cross the street and walk down Calle Isabel until it bisects Calle de la Rosa. Veer right and follow Calle de la Rosa until it jogs to the left and turns into Calle de la Cabeza; at this point, follow the narrow street south. This is the beginning of the **Barrio Lavapiés**—the old *Judería* (Jewish Quarter). Today, Lavapiés remains one of Madrid's most *castizo* working-class neighborhoods, although gentrification is beginning to creep in. Don't be surprised to see graffiti reading "Yuppies No!" The older buildings are currently being reinforced, and heavy construction has torn up some of the most charming alleyways and marred the most picturesque views. Explore side streets off Calle Lavapiés to escape the sound of jackhammers, but continue winding west—passing the **Cárcel de la Inquisición** ㉞—and south until you reach the heart of the neighborhood, **Plaza Lavapiés** ㉟.

Leave the plaza heading southwest on Calle Sombrerete. After two blocks you'll reach the intersection of Calle Mesón de Paredes; on the corner, you'll see a lovingly preserved example of a popular Madrid architecture, called the **Corrala building** ㊱. Life in this type of balconied apartment building is lived very publicly, with laundry flapping in the breeze, babies crying, and old women dressed in black gossiping over the railings. In the past, neighbors shared common kitchen and bathroom facilities in the patio.

Work your way west, crossing Calle de Embajadores into the neighborhood known as **El Rastro** ㊲. This is a shopper's paradise, with streets of small family shops selling furniture, antiques, and a cornucopia of used junk (some of it highly overpriced). On Sunday, El Rastro becomes a flea market, and Calle de Ribera de Curtidores, the main drag, is closed to traffic, jammed with outdoor booths and shoppers.

TIMING

One of this walk's main attractions is simply the atmosphere. Plan to spend at least three hours. A good time to visit is on a weekday morning, when the markets are bustling.

Plaza Santa Ana is interesting at night as well, with some of Madrid's best tapas bars and nightspots lining its side streets. El Rastro can be saved for a Sunday morning if you decide to brave the crowds at the flea market.

Sights to See

Barrio Lavapiés. The Barrio Lavapiés is the old *Judería* (Jewish Quarter). Like Moors, Jews were forced to live outside the city walls after the Christian reconquest hit Madrid in 1085; this was one of the suburbs they founded.

㉞ Cárcel de la Inquisición (Inquisition Jail). For a chilling reminder of the depth of the Catholic Monarchs' intolerance, stop at the southeast corner of Calle Cabeza and Calle Lavapiés. Unmarked by any historical plaque, the former jail is now a lumber warehouse. Here Jews, Moors, and others designated unrepentant heathens or sinners suffered the many tortures devised by the merciless inquisitors.

㉝ Casa de Cervantes. A plaque marks the house where the author of *Don Quixote* lived and died. Miguel de Cervantes's 1605 epic story of the man with the impossible dream is said to be the world's most widely translated and read book after the Bible. ✉ *C. Cervantes and C. León.*

Casa de Lope de Vega. The home of Lope de Vega, a contemporary of Cervantes, has been turned into a museum that shows how a typical home of the period was furnished. Considered the Shakespeare of Spanish literature, Lope de Vega (1562–1635) wrote some 1,800 plays and enjoyed huge success during his lifetime. ✉ *C. Cervantes 11,* ☎ *91/429–9216.* 🎫 *200 ptas.* ⊙ *Weekdays 9:30–3, Sat. 10–2.*

NEED A BREAK?

Taberna de Antonio Sánchez. Drop in at Madrid's oldest bar for a glass of wine and some tapas, or just a peek inside. The dark walls (lined with bullfighting paintings), zinc bar, and pulley system used to lift casks of wine from the cellar look much the same as they did when the place was first opened, in 1830. Meals are also served in a dining room in the back. Specialties include *rabo de buey* (bull's-tail stew) and *morcillo al horno* (a beef stew). ✉ *Mesón de Paredes 13.*

Cine Doré. A rare example of Art Nouveau architecture in Madrid, the Cine Doré shows movies from the Spanish National Film Archives and eclectic foreign films, usually in the original language. Show times are listed in newspapers under FILMOTECA. ✉ *C. Santa Isabel 3,* ☎ *91/369–1125.* ⊙ *Tues.–Sun.; hrs vary depending on show times.*

㊱ Corrala building. This building is not unlike the *corrales* that were used as the city's early theater venues; there is even a plaque here to remind visitors that the setting for the famous 19th-century *zarzuela* (light opera) *La Revoltosa* was a *corrala* like this one. City-sponsored musical-theater events are occasionally held here in summer. The ruins across the street were once the Escalopíos de San Fernando, one of several churches and parochial schools that fell victim to anti-Catholic sentiments in this neighborhood during the civil war. ✉ *C. Mesón de Paredes and C. Sombrerete.*

㊲ El Rastro. Filled with tiny shops selling antiques and all manner of used stuff (some of it junk), the *rastro* becomes an overcrowded flea market on Sunday morning from 10 to 2. The best time to explore is any other morning, when a little browsing and bargaining are likely to turn up such treasures as old iron grillwork, marble tabletops, or gilt picture frames. The main street of the *rastro* is Ribera de Curtidores; the best streets for shopping are the ones to the west.

㉟ Plaza Lavapiés. This is the heart of the historic Jewish *barrio*. To the left is the Calle de la Fe (Street of Faith), which was called Calle Sinagoga until the expulsion of the Jews in 1492. The church of **San Pedro el Real** (Royal St. Peter) was built on the site of the razed synagogue. Legend has it that Jews and Moors who chose baptism over exile were forced to walk up this street barefoot to be baptized as a demonstration of the sincerity of their new faith. ⊠ *Top of C. de la Fe.*

㉜ Plaza Santa Ana. This plaza was the heart of the theater district in the 17th century—the golden age of Spanish literature—and is now the center of Madrid's thriving nightlife. In the plaza is a statue of 15th-century playwright Pedro Calderón de la Barca delivering one of his own lines. Barca's likeness faces the **Teatro Español,** which is adorned with the names of Spain's greatest playwrights. The theater, rebuilt in 1980 following a fire, stands in the same spot where plays were performed as early as the 16th century, at that time in a rowdy outdoor setting called a *corrala*. These makeshift theaters were usually installed in a vacant lot between two apartment buildings, and families with balconies overlooking the action rented out seats to wealthy patrons of the arts. The **Casa de Guadalajara,** with a ceramic-tile facade, is one of the most beautiful buildings in Madrid and currently a popular nightspot. It faces the Teatro Español across the Plaza Santa Ana. The recently refurbished **Hotel Victoria,** on the Plaza Santa Ana, is now an upscale establishment but was once a rundown residence frequented by famous and not-so-famous bullfighters, including Manolete.

To the side of the hotel is the diminutive **Plaza del Ángel,** home of one of Madrid's best jazz clubs, the Café Central. Back on the Plaza Santa Ana is one of Madrid's most famous cafés, the **Cervecería Alemana,** another Hemingway haunt. It still attracts struggling writers, poets, and beer drinkers.

San Nicolás. The predecessor of this plain, modern church was burned in 1936, a story vividly described by writer Arturo Barea in his autobiographical *The Forge*. Little of the original structure remains. Like many other churches during that turbulent period, the original church of St. Nicholas fell to the wrath of working-class crowds who felt that they were the victims of centuries of clerical oppression. ⊠ *C. Atocha and Plaza Anton Martín.*

DINING

Madrileños tend to eat their meals even later than other Spaniards—and that's saying something. Restaurants generally open for lunch at 1:30 and fill up by 3. Dinnertime begins at 9, but reservations for 11 are common. A meal in Madrid is usually a lengthy (up to three hours) and rather formal affair, even at inexpensive places. Restaurants are at their best at midday, when most places offer a *menú del día* (daily special), containing a main course, dessert, wine, and coffee.

Dinner, on the other hand, can present a problem if you don't want to eat such a big meal so late. One solution is to take your evening meal at one of Madrid's many foreign restaurants; good-quality Italian, Mexican, Russian, Argentine, and American places abound and on the whole tend to open earlier and to be less formal. It's worth trying to defy your body clock for at least one evening, though; a late dinner is a far more authentic experience.

What to Wear

Dress in most Madrid restaurants and tapas bars is stylish but casual. The more expensive places tend to be a bit more formal; men generally wear jackets and ties, and women wear skirts.

$$$$ ✕ **Horcher.** Housed in a luxurious mansion at the edge of Retiro, this
★ classic restaurant is renowned for hearty but elegant fare served with impeccable style. Specialties include the types of game dishes traditionally favored by Spanish aristocracy; try the wild boar, venison, or roast wild duck with almond croquettes. The star appetizer is lobster salad with truffles. Dishes like stroganoff with mustard, pork chops with sauerkraut, and *baumkuchen* (a chocolate-covered fruit and cake dessert) reflect the restaurant's Germanic roots. (The Horcher family operated a restaurant in Berlin at the turn of the century.) The intimate dining room is decorated with rust-colored brocade and antique Austrian porcelain. A wide selection of French and German wines rounds out the menu. ⊠ *Alfonso XII 6,* ☎ *91/522–0731. Reservations essential. AE, DC, MC, V. Closed Sun. No lunch Sat.*

$$$$ ✕ **Lhardy.** Serving Madrid specialties in the same central location for more than 150 years, Lhardy looks pretty much the same as it must have on day one, with its dark-wood paneling, brass chandeliers, and red-velvet chairs. The menu offers international fare, but most diners come for the traditional *cocido a la Madrileño* and *callos a la Madrileño.* Sea bass in champagne sauce, game, and dessert soufflés are also finely prepared. The dining rooms are upstairs; the ground-floor entry doubles as a delicatessen and stand-up coffee bar that on chilly winter mornings fills with shivering souls sipping steaming-hot *caldo* (chicken broth) from silver urns. ⊠ *Carrera de San Jerónimo 8,* ☎ *91/522–2207. AE, DC, MC, V. No dinner Sun.*

$$$$ ✕ **Viridiana.** The trendiest of Madrid's gourmet restaurants, Viridiana has a relaxed bistro atmosphere and black-and-white decor punctuated by prints from Luis Buñuel's classic, anticlerical film (for which the place is named). Iconoclast chef Abraham Garcia says "market-based" is too narrow a description for his creative menu, though the list does change every two weeks depending on what's locally available. Offerings include such varied fare as red onions stuffed with *morcilla* (black pudding); soft flour tortillas wrapped around marinated fresh tuna; and filet mignon in white truffle sauce. If it's available, try the superb duck pâté drizzled with sherry and served with Tokay wine. The tangy grapefruit sherbet is a marvel. ⊠ *Juan de Mena 14,* ☎ *91/ 531–5222. Reservations essential. No credit cards. Closed Sun., Holy Wk, and Aug.*

$$$$ ✕ **Zalacaín.** A deep-apricot color scheme, set off by dark wood and gleaming silver, makes this restaurant look like an exclusive villa. Zalacaín introduced nouvelle cuisine to Spain and continues to set the pace after 20 years at the top. Splurge on such dishes as prawn salad in avocado vinaigrette, scallops and leeks in Albariño wine, and roast pheasant with truffles; a prix-fixe tasting menu allows you to sample the restaurant's best for about 6,500 pesetas. Service staff is somewhat stuffy. ⊠ *Alvarez de Baena 4,* ☎ *91/561–5935. Reservations essential. AE, DC, V. Closed Sun., Aug., and Holy Wk. No lunch Sat.*

$$$ ✕ **Ciao.** Always noisy and packed with happy diners, Ciao is Madrid's best Italian restaurant. Homemade pastas, like tagliatelle with wild mushrooms or *panzerotti* stuffed with spinach and ricotta, are popular as inexpensive main courses; but the kitchen also turns out credible versions of osso buco and veal scallopini, accompanied by a good selection of Italian wines. The decor—mirrored walls and sleek black furniture—convincingly evokes fashionable Milan. A second location (⊠ Apodaca 20, ☎ 91/447–0036), run by the owner's sons and daughter, also serves pizza. ⊠ *Argensola 7,* ☎ *91/308–2519. Reservations essential. AE, DC, MC, V. Closed Sun. No lunch Sat.*

$$$ ✕ **El Cenador del Prado.** The Cenador's innovative menu has French
★ and Asian touches, as well as exotic Spanish dishes that you'll rarely find in restaurants. Dine in a baroque salon or a less formal plant-filled conservatory. The house specialty is *patatas a la importancia* (sliced potatoes fried in a sauce of garlic, parsley, and clams); other possibilities include shellfish consommé with ginger ravioli, veal and eggplant in béchamel, or wild boar with prunes. For dessert try the *cañas fritas,* a cream-filled pastry once served only at Spanish weddings. ⊠ *C. del Prado 4,* ☎ *91/429–1561. AE, DC, MC, V. Closed Sun. and Aug. 1– 15. No lunch Sat.*

$$$ ✕ **El Cosaco.** This romantic, candlelit Russian restaurant, tucked away
★ on the ancient Plaza de Paja, is a favorite with young couples in love. While some diners have eyes only for each other, the food here is definitely worth a look—savory blini stuffed with caviar, smoked trout, or salmon, and hearty beef dishes like stroganoff. The dining rooms are decorated with paisley wallpaper and dark-red linens, and if the cheery glow of the crackling fireplace in winter isn't enough to warm you, one of the eight vodkas ought to do the trick. ⊠ *Plaza de Paja 2,* ☎ *91/365–3548. AE, DC.*

$$$ ✕ **El Pescador.** Spaniards swear that the seafood in Madrid is fresher
★ than in the coastal towns where it was caught. That's probably an exaggeration, but El Pescador, one of Madrid's best-loved seafood restaurants, makes it seem plausible. Before sitting down to dinner, stop for a drink at the bar and take in the delicious aromas wafting from the kitchen, where skilled chefs dressed in fishermen's smocks prepare shellfish just behind the counter. Among the tapas available at the bar or as a first course of your meal, the *salpicón de mariscos* (mussels, lobster, shrimp, and onions in vinaigrette) is incredible. The *lenguado Evaristo* (grilled sole), named for the restaurant's owner, is the best dish on the menu. The place is cheerful and noisy, and the decor is dock-side-rustic, with lobster-pot lamps, red-and-white-checked tablecloths, and rough-hewn posts and beams. ⊠ *José Ortega y Gasset 75,* ☎ *91/ 402–1290. MC, V. Closed Sun. and Aug.*

$$$ ✕ **Gure-Etxea.** In the heart of Old Madrid, on the Plaza de Paja, this is one of the capital's most authentic Basque restaurants. The ground-floor dining room is airy, high-ceilinged, and elegant; brick walls line the lower level, giving it a country-farmhouse feel. As in the Basque country, you are waited on only by women. Classic dishes include *bacalao al pil-pil* (spicy cod fried in garlic and oil—making the "pil-pil" sound), *rape en salsa verde* (monkfish in garlic-and-parsley sauce), and for dessert *leche frita* (fried custard). On weekdays, the lunch menu includes a hearty and inexpensive daily special. ⊠ *Plaza de Paja 12,* ☎ *91/365–6149. AE, DC, V. Closed Sun. and Aug. No lunch Mon.*

$$$ ✕ **La Trainera.** La Trainera is all about fresh seafood—the best money can buy. This informal restaurant, with its nautical decor and maze of little dining rooms, has reigned as the queen of Madrid's seafood houses for decades. Crab, lobster, shrimp, mussels, and a dozen other types of shellfish are served by weight in *raciones* (large portions). Although many Spanish diners share several plates of these delicacies as their entire meal, the grilled hake, sole, or turbot makes an unbeatable second course. Skip the listless house wine and go for a bottle of Albariño from the cellar. ⊠ *Lagasca 60,* ☎ *91/576–8035. AE, MC, V. Closed Sun. and Aug.*

$$$ ✕ **Mentidero de la Villa.** The decor of this intimate eatery is a bewitching blend of pastel colors, pale wood, and candlelight, with fanciful, rough-hewn sculptures of rocking horses. The French and Spanish menu is adventuresome—even the chef's salad mixes fresh kelp and lettuce. Spe-

32

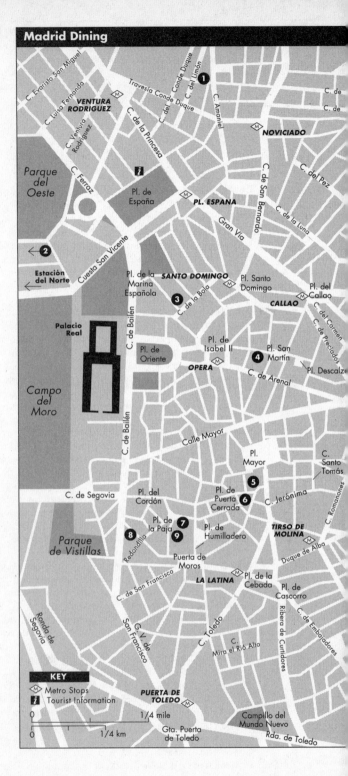

Madrid Dining

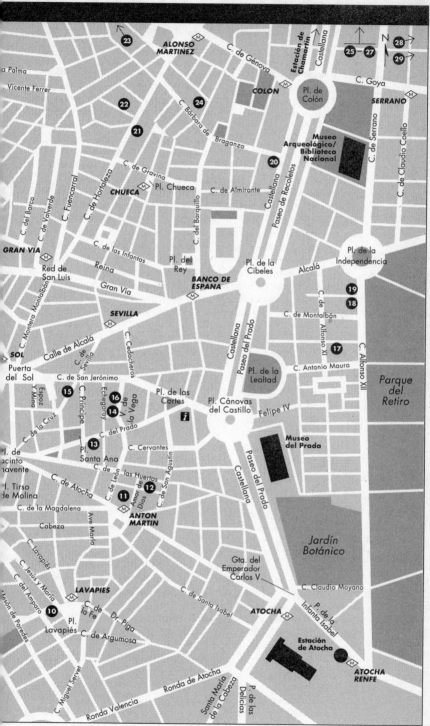

cialties include breast of squab in cherry vinegar, pheasant and chestnuts in wine, and halibut in a black-olive sauce. Apropos of the restaurant's name (which means "gossip shop"), service is informal and chatty. ⊠ *Santo Tomé 6,* ☎ *91/308–1285. AE, MC, V. Closed Sun. and Aug. No lunch Sat.*

$$ ✕ **Brasserie de Lista.** For a gourmet meal in a comfortable, informal setting, this bistro-style spot amid designer boutiques can't be beat. A long, marble bar, lots of brass, and frosted glass create a turn-of-the-century ambience. Waiters in long white aprons serve Spanish specialties with nouvelle touches, such as grilled monkfish with toasted garlic and steak with *cabrales* (blue cheese sauce). The varied menu also includes international fare such as chicken-and-avocado salad with chutney, and beef carpaccio. The weekday lunch special is a good value. ⊠ *José Ortega y Gasset 6,* ☎ *91/435–2818. AE, MC, V.*

$$ ✕ **Café Balear.** Sophisticated yet informal, Café Balear draws creative types from the fashion and advertising worlds and serves them some of the best paella in Madrid. Art prints and potted palms are the only nods to decoration in the stark, white dining room. Specialties include paella *centolla* (with crab) and *arroz negro* (rice with squid in its ink). The perfectly prepared paella *mixta* combines seafood, pork, and vegetables. ⊠ *Sagunto 18,* ☎ *91/447–9115. AE, V. No dinner Sun.–Mon.*

$$ ✕ **Cañas y Barro.** Hidden away on an unspoiled plaza that was the center of Madrid's university in the 19th century, this Valencian restaurant specializes in rice dishes with flair. The most popular is *arroz a la banda* (rice with peeled shrimp cooked in seafood broth). Another good choice is the paella Valenciana, made with chicken, rabbit, and vegetables. The service is friendly and unpretentious, and white-plaster friezes lend the pink dining room a touch of elegance. ⊠ *Amaniel 23,* ☎ *91/ 542–4798. AE, DC, MC, V. Closed Mon. and Aug. No dinner Sun.*

$$ ✕ **Casa Botín.** The *Guinness Book of Records* calls this the world's
★ oldest restaurant (1725), and Hemingway called it the best. The latter claim may be a touch over the top, but the restaurant *is* excellent and extremely charming, despite the hordes of tourists. There are four floors of tiled and wood-beamed dining rooms, and ovens dating back several centuries, which you'll pass if you're seated upstairs. Traditionally garbed musical groups called *tunas* often drop in. Essential specialties are *cochinillo asado* (roast suckling pig) and *cordero asado* (roast lamb). It is said that Francesco Goya was a dishwasher here before he made it as a painter. ⊠ *Cuchilleros 17, off Plaza Mayor,* ☎ *91/366– 4217. AE, DC, MC, V.*

$$ ✕ **Casa Paco.** This popular Castilian tavern wouldn't have looked out
★ of place two or three centuries ago. Squeeze your way past the old, zinc-topped bar, always crowded with Madrileños downing shots of red wine, and into the tiled dining rooms. People come here to feast on thick slabs of red meat, served sizzling on plates so hot that the meat continues to cook at your table. The beef is superb, and the Spanish consider overcooking a sin—so if you ask for your meat well done, be prepared for nasty glares. You order the meat by weight, so remember that a *medio kilo* is more than a pound. Try the *pisto manchego* (the La Mancha version of ratatouille) to start. ⊠ *Puerta Cerrada 11,* ☎ *91/366–3166. DC, V. Closed Sun. and Aug.*

$$ ✕ **Casa Vallejo.** With its homey dining room, friendly staff, creative menu, and reasonable prices, Casa Vallejo is the well-kept secret of Madrid's budget gourmets. Try the tomato, zucchini, and cheese tart or artichokes and clams to start; then follow up with duck breast in prune sauce or meatballs made with lamb, almonds, and pine nuts. The fudge-and-raspberry pie alone makes it worth the trip. ⊠ *San Lorenzo 9,* ☎ *91/308–6158. Reservations essential. MC, V. No dinner Sun.– Mon.*

$$ ✕ **Cornucopia en Descalzas.** Owned by two Americans, a Frenchman, and a Spaniard, this young and friendly restaurant on the first floor of an old mansion (just off the historic Plaza de las Descalzas Reales) serves what it calls Euro-American cuisine. The menu changes with the season; possibilities include grilled entrecote marinated in bourbon and honey, bream on a dill compote, and stewed rabbit with tomatoes, onion, and thyme. In winter, the restaurant becomes a tearoom, Saturday and Sunday from 5 to 8. ⊠ *Flora 1,* ☎ *91/547–6465. AE, MC, V. Closed Mon. and 1 wk in Aug.*

$$ ✕ **La Bola.** First opened as a *botellería* (wine shop) in 1802, La Bola
★ developed slowly into a tapas bar and eventually into a full-fledged restaurant. Tradition is the main draw; blood-red paneling outside beckons you into the original bar and cozy dining nooks decorated with polished wood, Spanish tile, and lace curtains. The restaurant still belongs to the founding family, with the seventh generation currently in training to take over. Dinner is served, but the house specialty is that quintessential Madrid meal *cocido Madrileño,* served only at lunch and accompanied by crusty bread and a hearty red wine. ⊠ *Bola 5,* ☎ *91/ 547–6930. No credit cards. No dinner Sun.*

$$ ✕ **La Cacharrería.** The name of this restaurant means "junkyard," and it's reflected in the funky decor—a mix of dusty calico, old lace, and gilt mirrors, all tucked into the medieval quarter. The cooking, however, is decidedly upscale, with a market-based menu that changes daily and an excellent selection of wines. Venison stew and fresh tuna steaks with *cava* (champagne) and leeks were among the recent specialties. Whatever else you order, save room for the homemade lemon tart. ⊠ *Moreiria 9,* ☎ *91/365–3930. AE, DC, MC, V. Closed Sun.*

$$ ✕ **La Gamella.** American-born chef Dick Stephens has created a new,
★ reasonably priced menu at this perennially popular dinner spot. The sophisticated rust-red dining room, batik tablecloths, oversize plates, and attentive service remain the same, but much of the nouvelle cuisine has been replaced by more traditional fare, such as chicken in garlic, beef bourguignonne, and steak tartare à la Jack Daniels. A few of the old favorite signature dishes, like sausage-and-red-pepper quiche and bittersweet chocolate pâté, remain. The lunchtime *menú del día* is a great value at 1,700 pesetas. ⊠ *Alfonso XII 4,* ☎ *91/532–4509. AE, DC, MC, V. Closed Sun. and Aug. 15–30. No lunch Sat.*

★ ☾ **$$** ✕ **La Pampa de Lavapiés.** This excellent Argentine restaurant is secluded on a side street in Lavapiés. As you enter there's a small eating area to the left, but most people prefer to sit in the rustic dining room to the right. The massive and delicious *bife La Pampa* is the house specialty (enough steak, fried eggs, peas, and tomatoes for two light eaters) and contains enough protein for a week. The pasta dishes, such as cannelloni Rossini, are also good. If you feel like dancing off your dinner, you can tango here on weekends. Sundays—when kids get free pasta—are equally boisterous. ⊠ *Amparo 61,* ☎ *91/528–0449. AE, DC, MC, V. Closed Mon.*

$$ ✕ **Nabucco.** Had enough Spanish food for the moment? With pastel-washed walls and subtle lighting from gigantic, wrought-iron candelabras, this pizzeria and trattoria is a trendy but elegant haven in gritty Chueca. Fresh bread sticks and garlic olive oil show up within minutes of your arrival. The spinach, ricotta, and walnut ravioli is heavenly, and this may be the only Italian restaurant in Madrid where you can order (California-style?) barbecued-chicken pizza. Considering the ambience and quality, the bill is a pleasant surprise. ⊠ *Hortaleza 108,* ☎ *91/310–0611. AE, MC, V.*

$$ ✕ **Sí Señor.** One of Madrid's new crop of entertaining restaurants, Sí Señor specializes in Mexican food and tequila slammers. The big bar in the entryway serves Mexican-style tapas (quesadillas or chips with guacamole). The huge, noisy dining hall is lined with oversize paintings, artfully executed in a unique Mexican pop-art style. The drinks here are far better than the food, but do try the beef enchiladas or *pollo pibil,* a spicy Yucatán-style chicken dish. ✉ *Paseo de la Castellana 128,* ☎ *91/564–0604. AE, DC, MC, V.*

$ ✗ **Casa Mingo.** Resembling an Asturian cider tavern, Casa Mingo is
★ built into a stone wall beneath the Estación del Norte train station, across the street from the hermitage of San Antonio de la Florida. It's a bustling place; you share long plank tables with other diners, and the only things on the menu are succulent roast chicken, salad, and sausages, all to be washed down with numerous bottles of *sidra* (hard cider). Small tables are set up on the sidewalk in summer. Try to get here early (1 for lunch, 8:30 for dinner) to avoid the wait. ✉ *Paseo de la Florida 2,* ☎ *91/547–7918. Reservations not accepted. No credit cards.*

$ ✗ **Inti de Oro.** This Peruvian restaurant on one of Madrid's premier restaurant rows is a big hit, thanks largely to the care the owners put into their native traditional specialties. Try the *ceviche de camarones* (shrimp in lime juice), *conejo con maní* (rabbit in peanut sauce), or *seco de cabrito* (goat-meat stew). The dining room is light, and the walls are adorned with handicrafts. ✉ *Ventura de la Vega 12,* ☎ *91/429–6703. AE, DC, V.*

$ ✗ **La Biotika.** A vegetarian's dream in the heart of the bar district just east of Plaza Santa Ana, this small, cozy restaurant serves macrobiotic vegetarian cuisine every day of the week. Enormous salads, hearty soups, fresh bread, and creative tofu dishes make the meal flavorful as well as healthy. A small market at the entrance sells macrobiotic groceries. ✉ *Amor de Dios 3,* ☎ *91/429–0780. No credit cards.*

$ ✗ **Puebla.** Puebla is always crowded with bankers and congressmen from the nearby Cortés. Although the decor lacks charm (the fake wood beams fool no one), you'd be hard pressed to find better-prepared food at such affordable prices anywhere else in Madrid. There are two price ranges for the *menú del día,* each covering more than a dozen choices. The selection changes frequently, but be sure to try the *berenjenas a la romana* (batter-fried eggplant) if it's offered. The soups are always great; other dishes include roast lamb, trout, and calamari. ✉ *Ventura de la Vega 12,* ☎ *91/429–6713. AE, DC, MC, V. Closed Sun.*

$ ✗ **Sanabresa.** You can tell by the clientele what a find this place is. Professionals who demand quality but don't want to spend too much money come here daily, as does an international assortment of students from the nearby flamenco school. The menu is classic Spanish fare—hearty, wholesome meals like *pechuga villaroy* (breaded and fried chicken breast in béchamel) and paella (for lunch Thursday and Sunday only). The functional, green-tiled dining room is always crowded, so be sure to arrive by 1:30 for lunch or 8:30 for dinner. ✉ *Amor de Dios 12,* ☎ *no phone. Reservations not accepted. No credit cards. Closed Aug. No dinner Sun.*

LODGING

There are booking services at the airport and the Chamartín and Atocha train stations. You can also contact the **La Brujula** agency (✉ Torre de Madrid, 6th floor, Plaza de España, ☎ 91/559–9705); the fee is a modest 250 pesetas. The staff speaks English and can book rooms and tours all over Spain. Unless otherwise indicated, all rooms have private baths.

$$$$ **Palace.** Built in 1912, this enormous, Belle Epoque grand hotel is
★ a creation of Alfonso XIII. At less than two-thirds the price of the nearby

Ritz, the Palace is a pleasure, though its attractions are concentrated in the opulent public areas, including a large cupola with a stained-glass ceiling. The rooms aren't impressive for a hotel of this caliber—they're plain and most are small, with a pronounced 1960s American flavor. Bathrooms are spacious, however, with double sinks, tubs, separate shower stalls, and other welcome touches such as bathrobes and magnifying mirrors. In 1997, *Condé Nast Traveler* readers placed the Palace among the top 25 hotels in Europe. ⊠ *Plaza de las Cortés 7, 28014,* ☎ *91/429–7551,* ㏙ *91/429–8266. 436 rooms, 20 suites. Restaurant, bar, beauty salon, parking. AE, DC, MC, V.*

$$$$
★ 🏨 **Ritz.** When Alfonso XIII was preparing for his marriage to Queen Victoria's granddaughter, he realized to his dismay that Madrid did not have a single hotel up to the exacting standards of his royal guests. Thus was born the Ritz. Opened in 1910 by the king himself, who had personally overseen its construction, the Ritz is a monument to the Belle Epoque, furnished with rare antiques in every public room, hand-embroidered linens from Robinson and Cleaver of London, and all manner of other luxurious details. Guest rooms are carpeted, hung with chandeliers, and decorated in pastels; many have good views of the Prado or the Castellana. The Ritz was named one of Europe's top five hotels by *Condé Nast Traveler* readers in 1997; visit the garden terrace even if you don't stay here. ⊠ *Plaza de Lealtad 5, 28014,* ☎ *91/521–2857,* ㏙ *91/532–8776. 158 rooms. Restaurant, bar, beauty salon, health club, parking. AE, DC, MC, V.*

$$$$ 🏨 **Santo Mauro.** Once the Canadian embassy, this turn-of-the-century mansion was reopened in 1992 as an intimate luxury hotel. The neoclassical architecture is accented by contemporary furniture (such as suede armchairs) in such hues as mustard, teal, and eggplant. Twelve of the rooms are in the main building, which also houses a popular gourmet restaurant; the other rooms are in a new annex and are split-level, with stereos and VCRs. ⊠ *Zurbano 36, 28010,* ☎ *91/319–6900,* ㏙ *91/308–5477. 37 rooms. Restaurant, bar, parking. AE, DC, MC, V.*

$$$$ 🏨 **Villamagna.** Renowned in the early '90s as the favorite of visiting financiers and reclusive rock stars, the Villamagna has been humbled by competition, and its reputation for ultra exclusivity has faded with the decor of its green-and-white lobby. Still, it's one of Madrid's top luxury hotels, its modern facade belying an exquisite interior furnished with 18th-century antiques. It's somewhat overpriced but does have some finishing touches hard to find elsewhere; a pianist provides soothing music in the lounge at lunchtime and during cocktail hour, and rooms all have desks with plenty of working space as well as hidden TVs, VCRs, and plants in the bathrooms. The restaurant, Berceo, has cozy walnut paneling and the feel of an English library; its garden terrace is open for dinner in warm weather. ⊠ *Paseo de la Castellana 22, 28046,* ☎ *91/576–7500,* ㏙ *91/575–9504. 164 rooms, 18 suites. Restaurant, bar, beauty salon, exercise room, parking. AE, DC, MC, V.*

$$$$ 🏨 **Villa Real.** If you fancy a luxury hotel that combines elegance, modern amenities, *and* a great location, this is the ticket. A simulated 19th-century facade gives way to lobbies garnished with potted palms. Each room has a character of its own, albeit with an overall French feel; some suites have both saunas and whirlpool baths. The hotel faces the Cortés and is convenient to almost everything. The staff is very friendly. ⊠ *Plaza de las Cortés 10, 28014,* ☎ *91/420–3767,* ㏙ *91/420–2547. 94 rooms, 20 suites. Restaurant, bar. AE, DC, MC, V.*

$$$ 🏨 **El Prado.** Wedged in between the classic buildings of *castizo* Madrid, this skinny, new hotel is within stumbling distance of the city's best bars and nightclubs and is priced accordingly. Rooms are basic but spacious and virtually immune to street noise thanks to double-paned windows. Decorative touches include pastel floral prints and gleaming marble

38

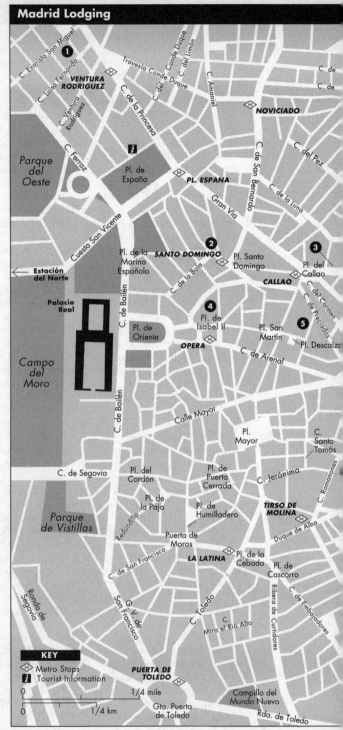

Madrid Lodging

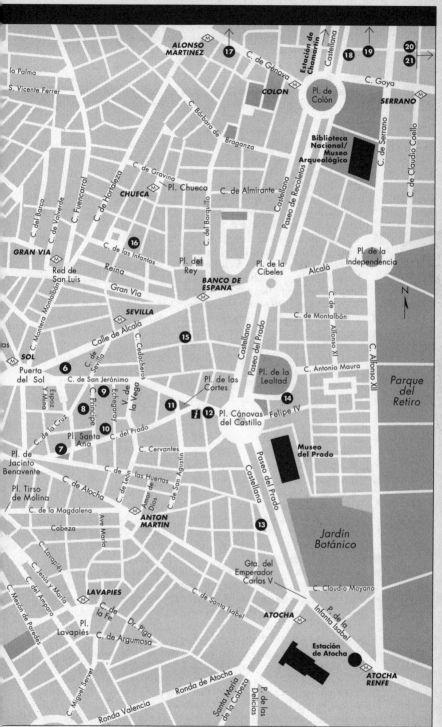

baths. ✉ *C. Prado 11, 28014,* ☎ *91/429–0234,* FAX *91/429–2829. 47 rooms. Cafeteria, parking. AE, DC, MC, V.*

$$$ ☷ **Fenix.** A magnificent marble lobby greets your arrival at this Madrid institution, overlooking Plaza de Colón on the Castellana. The hotel is also just a few steps from the posh shopping street Serrano. Its spacious rooms, decorated in beiges and golds, are carpeted and amply furnished. Flowers abound. ✉ *Hermosilla 2, 28001,* ☎ *91/431–6700,* FAX *91/576–0661. 204 rooms, 12 suites. Bar, café, beauty salon. AE, DC, MC, V.*

$$$ ☷ **Hotel Santo Domingo.** An intimate hotel that artfully blends the best of classical and modern design, the five-year-old Santo Domingo is about 10 minutes' walk from the Puerta del Sol, just off Gran Vía. Rooms are decorated in soft tones of peach and ocher, and all feature telephones with voice mail and double-paned windows for soundproofing. An especially friendly and well-trained staff gives the place a personal feel. ✉ *Plaza Santo Domingo 13, 28013,* ☎ *91/547–9800,* FAX *91/547–5995. 120 rooms. Restaurant, bar, parking. AE, DC, MC, V.*

$$$ ☷ **Lagasca.** In the heart of the elegant Salamanca neighborhood, this newish hotel combines large, brightly decorated rooms with an unbeatable location two blocks from Madrid's main shopping street, Calle Serrano. The marble lobbies border on the coldly functional, but they're fine as a meeting place. ✉ *Lagasca 64, 28001,* ☎ *91/575–4606,* FAX *91/575–1694. 100 rooms. Restaurant, bar, parking. AE, DC, MC, V.*

$$$ ☷ **Reina Victoria.** The Tryp chain recently bought and extensively ren-
★   ovated this grande dame, one of Madrid's most historic and beloved hotels. Now, besides the attractive exterior and great location on one of Madrid's most charming squares, the Victoria draws a far more upscale clientele than its former down-at-the-heels bullfighters and American writers, such as Ernest Hemingway (it now gets well-heeled bullfighters). Beyond the fairly charmless lobby and public rooms, the hotel is quite attractive, with handsome details and an overall stately effect in the hallways and the big, bright, airy guest rooms. The best rooms overlook the Plaza Santa Ana. Reservations are increasingly necessary. ✉ *Plaza del Ángel 7, 28014,* ☎ *91/531–4500,* FAX *91/522–0307. 201 rooms. Restaurant, bar, parking. AE, DC, MC, V.*

$$$ ☷ **Suecia.** The chief attraction of the Suecia is its location, right next to the superchic Círculo de Bellas Artes (an arts society/café/film/theater complex). Though recently remodeled, its lobby is still somewhat soulless. The rooms are trendy, with modern art on the walls and futuristic light fixtures. ✉ *Marqués de Riera 4, 28014,* ☎ *91/531–6900,* FAX *91/521–7141. 119 rooms, 9 suites. 2 restaurants, bar. AE, DC, MC, V.*

$$$ ☷ **Tryp Ambassador.** Ideally located on an old street between Gran Vía
★   and the Royal Palace, this hotel occupies the renovated 19th-century palace of the Dukes of Granada. A magnificent front door and a graceful three-story staircase are legacies of the building's aristocratic past; the rest has been transformed into elegant lodgings favored by executives. Bedrooms are large, with separate sitting areas, and have mahogany furnishings, floral drapes, and bedspreads. The greenhouse bar, filled with plants and songbirds, is especially pleasant on cold days. ✉ *Cuesta Santo Domingo 5 and 7, 28013,* ☎ *91/541–6700,* FAX *91/ 559–1040. 181 rooms. Restaurant, bar, parking. AE, DC, MC, V.*

$$ ☷ **Atlántico.** Don't be put off by the location, on a noisy stretch of Gran Vía, or by the rather shabby third-floor lobby. The Atlántico delivers bright, clean accommodations at good prices. Rooms are small but comfortable, with fabric wall coverings and new furniture. All have tile baths. A member of the Best Western chain, this hotel is a favorite with British travelers and is almost always full, so it's wise to book well in advance. ✉ *Gran Vía 38, 28013,* ☎ *91/522–6480,* FAX *91/531–0210. 80 rooms. Snack bar. AE, MC, V.*

$$ ▥ **Carlos V.** If you like to be in the center of things, hang your hat at this classic hotel on a pedestrian street: it's just a few steps away from the Puerta del Sol, Plaza Mayor, and Descalzas Reales convent, and the price is right. A suit of armor decorates the tiny lobby, while crystal chandeliers add elegance to the second-floor guest lounge. All rooms are bright and carpeted. ✉ *Maestro Victoria 5, 28013,* ☏ *91/531–4100,* FAX *91/531–3761. 67 rooms, 41 with bath. AE, DC, MC, V.*

$$ ▥ **Inglés.** Virginia Woolf was one of the first luminaries to discover this hotel, which is smack in the middle of the old city's bar-and-restaurant district. Since Woolf's time, the Inglés has attracted more than its share of less-celebrated artists and writers. Rather deteriorated and drab now, it's best for those looking for location and value rather than luxury. (Run-down suites cost what you'd normally pay for a standard double.) The balconies overlooking Calle Echegaray give you an unusual view of the medieval quarter from the air, all red Mediterranean tiles and ramshackle gables. ✉ *C. Echegaray 8, 28014,* ☏ *91/429–6551,* FAX *91/420–2423. 58 rooms. Bar, cafeteria, exercise room, parking. AE, DC, MC, V.*

$$ ▥ **Muralto.** Though uninspiring from the outside, the Muralto offers apartments with full kitchens at a price comparable to ordinary doubles in nearby hotels. It's convenient to much of western Madrid—the Royal Palace, Plaza de España, El Corte Ingles department store, and Estación de Norte are all within walking distance. The arrangement buys you convenience and independence to compensate for the drab facade and colorless decor. ✉ *Calle Tutor 37, 28008,* ☏ *91/542–4400. 68 rooms. Restaurant, bar, parking (free). AE, DC, MC, V.*

$$ ▥ **Paris.** You can't get more central than this; for a remarkably fair
★ price, the Paris offers delightful Old World charm right at the corner of the Puerta del Sol and Calle de Alcalá. The odd-shape rooms are clean, spacious, and decorated with orange bedspreads and curtains. The lobby is dark, woody, and somehow redolent of times long past. There's no bar, but three meals are served in the bright second-floor restaurant. All in all, the Paris is an unusual deal. ✉ *Alcalá 2, 28014,* ☏ *91/521–6496,* FAX *91/531–0188. 114 rooms. Restaurant. MC, V.*

$ ▥ **Monaco.** Just a few steps from the tiny Plaza de Chueca, the Monaco is an eccentric delight. The lobby is resplendent with red-carpeted stairs, potted plants, brass rails, and mirrors—and the rooms are similar, with Louis XIV–style furniture and mirrored walls. The Portuguese owner is very gracious. The location is lively but marginal, hence the bargain rates; be aware when coming and going. Bar- and club-heavy Chueca is known for drug traffic and pickpockets. ✉ *Barbieri 5, 28004,* ☏ *91/522–4630,* FAX *91/521–1601. 33 rooms. Restaurant, bar, cafeteria. AE, MC, V.*

$ ▥ **Mora.** Directly across the Paseo del Prado from the Botanical Gar-
★ dens, the Mora welcomes weary travelers with a sparkling, faux-marble lobby and bright, carpeted hallways. The guest rooms are modestly decorated but large and comfortable; those on the street side have great views of the gardens and the Prado. Double-paned windows keep them fairly quiet. ✉ *Paseo del Prado 32, 28014,* ☏ *91/420–1569,* FAX *91/420–0564. 61 rooms. AE, DC, MC, V.*

$ ▥ **Ramón de la Cruz.** If you don't mind a longish metro ride from the city center, this medium-size hotel is a find. The rooms are large, with modern bathrooms, and the stone-floor lobby is spacious. For Madrid, it's a bargain. ✉ *Don Ramón de la Cruz 94, 28006,* ☏ *91/401–7200,* FAX *91/402–2126. 103 rooms. Cafeteria. MC, V.*

$ ▥ **Villar.** All of these rooms are pleasant, clean, and tastefully furnished, with antique beds and armoires, but the real attractions are the eight rooms with balconies. Laden with flowers, the balconies overlook lively Calle Príncipe and have corner views of the Plaza Santa Ana, including the well-heeled crowds arriving at the Teatro Español. The best bargain in the area, Villar is on the second floor of a beautiful old building with a marble foyer and winding staircase. ⊠ *Calle Príncipe 18, 28014,* ☎ *91/531–6600,* 𝔽𝔸𝕏 *91/521–5073. 34 rooms, 18 with bath. AE, DC, MC, V.*

NIGHTLIFE AND THE ARTS

The Arts

Madrid's cultural scene is so lively that it's hard to follow. As the city's reputation as a vibrant and contemporary arts center has grown, artists and performers of all stripes have arrived in droves. The best way to stay abreast of events is through the weekly *Guía de Ocio* (published Monday) or daily listings in the leading newspaper, *El País*. Both sources are relatively easy to comprehend even if you don't read Spanish. Tickets to performances are usually best purchased at the hall itself; in the case of major popular concerts, the Corte Inglés department stores have **Discoplay** outlets for advance sales.

The city throws major arts festivals in each of the four seasons. The most comprehensive is the Festival de Otoño (Autumn Festival), from late September to late November, which blankets the entire city with poetry readings, pop concerts, flamenco, and performances by world-renowned ballet and theater companies. Other annual events include world-class jazz, salsa, African music, and rock; art exhibits; film festivals; and more—all at very reasonable prices. More often than not, the events take place outdoors, in city parks and amphitheaters.

Concerts/Ballet

Opened in 1988, the modern **Auditorio Nacional de Música** (⊠ Príncipe de Vergara 136, ☎ 91/337–0100) is Madrid's main hall for classical music and regularly hosts major orchestras from around the world. The newly reopened **Teatro Real** (⊠ Plaza de Isabell II, ☎ 91/516–0606) is the center for ballet and opera.

Film

Nearly a dozen theaters regularly show undubbed foreign films, the majority of them in English. These are listed in newspapers and in the *Guía de Ocio* under "V.O."—meaning original version. Leading V.O. theaters include the **Alphaville** (⊠ Martín de los Héroes 14, ☎ 91/559–3836) and **Renoir** (⊠ Martín de los Héroes 12, ☎ 91/559–5760), both just off the Plaza de España. Excellent, classic V.O. films change daily at the **Filmoteca Cine Doré** (⊠ Santa Isabel 3, ☎ 91/369–1125).

Theater

English-speaking performances are a rarity, and when they do come to town, they play on any of a dozen Madrid stages; check local newspapers. One theater you won't need Spanish for is the **Teatro de la Zarzuela** (⊠ Jovellanos 4, ☎ 91/524–5400), which puts on the traditional Spanish operettas known as *zarzuela,* a kind of bawdy comedy. The **Teatro Español** (⊠ Príncipe 25, ☎ 91/429–6297) specializes in 17th-century Spanish classics.

Nightlife

Nightlife—or *la marcha,* as the Spanish fondly call it—reaches legendary heights in Spain's capital. It's been said that Madrileños rarely sleep, and that's largely because they spend so much time in bars—not drunk, but socializing in the easy, sophisticated way that is unique to this city. This is true of old as well as young, and it's not uncommon for children to play on the sidewalks past midnight while multigenerational families and friends convene over coffee or cocktails at an outdoor café. The streets most famous for their social scenes, however, do tend to attract a younger clientele; these include Huertas, Moratín, Segovia, Victoria, and the areas around the Plaza Santa Ana and the Plaza de Anton Martín. Adventuresome travelers may want to explore the scruffier bar district around the Plaza Dos de Mayo, in the Malasaña area, where trendy, smoke-filled hangouts line both sides of Calle San Vicente Ferrer. Equally brave souls can venture a few blocks east to the notorious haunts of neighboring Chueca, where tattoo studios and street-chic boutiques break up the endless alleys of techno discos and after-hours clubs.

Bars

There are countless bars in Madrid, and while almost all serve food, many are known more for their atmosphere. Some recommendations:

Cafe Gijón (⊠ Paseo de Recoletos 24, ☎ 91/521–5425) may be Madrid's most famous café-bar. It has hosted the city's most high-falutin *tertulias* (discussion groups that meet regularly to hash out the issues of the day) for more than a century.

Cervantes (⊠ León 8, ☎ 91/429–6093) is a bright, tiled bar where you can also get a pizza or pasta in a small dining room at the back. It caters to a young neighborhood crowd.

Chicote (⊠ Gran Vía 12, ☎ 91/532–6737) was immortalized in several of Hemingway's short stories about the Spanish civil war and still makes an interesting stop.

Hard Rock Cafe (⊠ Paseo Castellana 2, ☎ 91/435–0200) is wildly popular with young Spaniards. Madrid's version of this U.S. classic opened in 1994 and serves up the usual drinks, burgers, and salads with a heavy dose of loud music.

Hermanos Muñiz (⊠ Huertas 29, ☎ 91/429–5452) is the quintessential Spanish neighborhood bar, neither trendy nor touristy. The tapas here are uniformly excellent, and the men who serve them are both friendly and superbly professional.

La Champañería Gala (⊠ Moratín 24, ☎ 91/429–2562) is one of the city's better-known champagne bars, offering especially good Catalan *cavas* (Spanish champagnes).

Los Gabrieles (⊠ Echegaray 17, ☎ 91/429–6261) is featured in most of Madrid's tourist literature for its remarkable tile walls, but the clientele is, actually, mostly fashionable Spaniards.

Oliver (⊠ Almirante 12, ☎ 91/521–7379) is two bars in one. It's open afternoons and evenings for relaxing live piano music in the upstairs lounge; after midnight, the downstairs becomes a full-fledged Chueca disco.

Palacio de Gaviria (⊠ Arenal 9, ☎ 91/526–8089) is an impeccably restored, 19th-century baroque palace hidden away on the upper floors of a tawdry commercial street between Puerta del Sol and the Royal Palace. Allegedly built to house one of Queen Isabel II's lovers, the palace now serves drinks in an elegant setting, with live jazz late at night.

Soho (✉ Jorge Juan 50, ☎ 91/577–8973) is something of a slice of New York in the Salamanca district. Filled with rap and reggae fans, it has an eclectic menu that includes exotic island drinks as well as Spanish variants of Tex-Mex cuisine.

Taberna de Antonio Sanchez (✉ Mesón de Paredes 13, ☎ 91/539–7826) is reputed to be the oldest bar in Madrid—the proprietors claim it's been around since 1830. Order wine and tapas at the old zinc bar in front; head to the back to order a full meal.

Viva Madrid (✉ Manuel Fernández y González 7, ☎ 91/429–3640) is an extremely popular bar with a Brassai motif and serious personality. Packed with both Spaniards and foreigners, it has become something of a singles scene. There are tables and a small selection of bar food in the rear.

Cabaret

Berlin Cabaret (✉ Costanilla de San Pedro 11, ☎ 91/366–2034) professes to provide authentic cabaret as it was performed in Berlin in the '30s. (These days the audience is *much* different.) Combining magic, chorus girls, and ribald comedy, it draws an eccentric crowd for vintage café theater. On weekends, the absurd fun lasts until daybreak.

Discos

Madrid's hippest new club is a three-story bar, disco, and cabaret called **Bagelus** (✉ María de Molina 25, ☎ 91/561–6100). **Joy Eslava** (✉ Arenal 11, ☎ 91/366–3733), a downtown disco in a converted theater, is an old standby. **Pacha** (✉ Barceló 11, ☎ 91/466–0137), one of Spain's infamous chain discos, is always energetic. The well-heeled crowd likes **Archy's** (✉ Marqués de Riscal 11, ☎ 91/308–3162). **Space of Sound** (✉ Plz. Estación de Chamartin [in the train station], ☎ 91/733–3505) almost fails to qualify as a nightclub: it's open Saturday and Sunday mornings from dawn until noon, full of drag queens and club kids who refuse to let the night end. Salsa has become a fixture in Madrid; check out the most spectacular moves at **Azucar** (Sugar; ✉ Paseo Reina Cristina 7, ☎ 91/501–6107).

Flamenco

Madrid is not a great city for flamenco, but if you won't be traveling south, here are a few possibilities:

Café de Chinitas (✉ Torija 7, ☎ 91/559–5135) puts on the city's best-known show, and its patrons have included such diplomatic guests as former Nicaraguan president Daniel Ortega. It's expensive, but the dancing is the best in Madrid. Try to reserve in advance; it often sells out.

Casa Patas (✉ Canizares 10, ☎ 91/369–0496) is one of Madrid's main flamenco spaces. Along with tapas, it offers good, if a little touristy, performances. The prices are more reasonable than elsewhere.

Corral de la Morería (✉ Morería 17, ☎ 91/365–8446) serves dinner à la carte and invites well-known flamenco stars to perform with the resident group. Since Morería opened its doors in 1956, visiting celebrities such as Frank Sinatra and Ava Gardner have left their autographed photos for the walls.

Nightclubs

Jazz, rock, flamenco, and classical music are all popular in Madrid's many small clubs. A few of the more interesting:

Amadis (⊠ Covarrubias 42, underneath the Luchana Cinema, ☎ 91/446–0036) has telephones on every table, encouraging people to call each other with invitations to dance. The scene is sophisticated; you must be over 25 to enter.

Café Central (⊠ Plaza de Ángel 10, ☎ 91/369–4143), the city's best-known jazz venue, is chic and well run, and the musicians are often very good. Performances generally begin at 10 PM.

Cafe del Foro (⊠ San Andrés 38, ☎ 91/448–9464) is a funky, friendly club on the edge of Malasaña, with live music every night at 11:30.

Café Jazz Populart (⊠ Huertas 22, ☎ 91/429–8407) features blues, Brazilian music, reggae, and salsa, starting at 11 PM.

Clamores (⊠ Albuquerque 14, ☎ 91/445–7938), another famous jazz club, serves a wide selection of French and Spanish champagnes.

Maravillas (⊠ San Vicente Ferrer 35, ☎ no phone) draws an indie crowd for live alternative music in a laid-back, inexpensive dive bar.

Siroco (⊠ San Dimas 3, ☎ 91/593–3070) offers two different kinds of music Tuesday through Saturday: live Spanish pop downstairs, '70s disco and acid jazz on the second-story dance floor.

Torero (⊠ Cruz 26, ☎ 91/523–1129), a thoroughly modern club despite its name, is for the beautiful people—quite literally: a bouncer allows only those judged *gente guapa* (beautiful people) to enter. It's one of Madrid's most stylin' spots.

Tapas Bars

The practice of spending one's evening going from bar to bar and eating tapas is so popular that the Spanish have a verb to describe it: *tapear.* The selection is endless; the best-known tapas bars are the *cuevas* clustered around Cava de San Miguel (☞ Medieval Madrid, *above*). Here are a few more suggestions:

Bocaíto (⊠ Libertad 6, ☎ 91/532–1219) is said by some to serve the best tapas in Madrid—a heady claim. You can have a full meal here or just dip into a few tapas before heading on to the many other fine places in the immediate vicinity.

El Rey de Pimiento (⊠ Plaza Puerta Cerrada, ☎ no phone) serves some 40 different kinds of tapas, including, in keeping with its name (The Pepper King), roasted red pimientos as well as the intermittently hot pimientos *de padrón.*

El Rincon de la Alpujara (⊠ Puerto Rico 35, ☎ 91/359–9000) is one of the few tapas bars in Madrid with an outdoor terrace in summer. If you order from the excellent, international wine selection, the first tapa offered will probably be a wedge of *queso manchego,* a sharp regional cheese.

El Ventorrillo (⊠ Bailén 14, ☎ 91/366–3578) is a place to go between May and October, when tables are set up in the shady park of Las Vistillas overlooking the city's western edge. Specialties include croquettes and mushrooms. This is Madrid's premier place to watch the sun set.

La Chuleta (⊠ Echegaray 20, ☎ 91/429–3729) is a cheery corner bar hung with bullfight memorabilia and stocked with a colorful selection of tapas on the bar. Seating is available.

La Dolores (⊠ Plaza de Jesús 4, ☎ 91/429–2243) is a crowded, noisy, and wonderful place that's rightly reputed to serve the best draft beer in Madrid. Located just behind the Palace Hotel, it has a very few tables in back.

La Trucha (⊠ Manuel Fernández y González 3, ☎ 91/532–0890) is hung with hams and garlic and feels like a medieval inn. It's also a restaurant, but the wonderful tapas that line the aging bar are far better.

Las Bravas (⊠ Alvarez Gato 3, ☎ 91/532–2620), hidden away in an alley off the Plaza Santa Ana, isn't much to look at, but it's here that *patatas bravas* (potatoes in a spicy tomato sauce) were invented. They're now classic Spanish tapas.

Mesón Gallego (⊠ León 4, ☎ 91/429–8997) is a hole-in-the-wall that serves wonderfully hearty Galician potato soup (a famous cure for those who've drunk too much) called *caldo gallego*. Not for everyone is the *Ribeiro,* the somewhat acidic white wine made with grapes from Galician riverbanks.

Museo del Jamon (Ham Museum; ⊠ Carrera de San Jeronimo 6, ☎ 91/458–0163) is a Madrid chain of tapas bars that has become an institution. Look for the window full of dangling hams with hoofs. The best tapas here are, of course, the selection of hams from around the country. Don't be daunted by the variety; try the *serrano* or the *iberico* to start.

The Reporter (⊠ Fúcar 6, ☎ 91/429–3922), true to its English name, is hung with great Spanish and world news photos. Its other great attraction is a garden terrace shaded by a grapevine trellis. The *raciones* (entrée-size portions of tapas, intended for sharing) are very good, and the pâté plate is terrific.

Taberna de Cien Vinos (⊠ Nuncio 17, ☎ 91/365–4704) is the latest addition to Madrid's tapas circuit. It's tucked into a charming old house with wooden shutters and stone columns. You can order by the glass from a wide selection of Spanish wines, and the *raciones* border on the gourmet.

OUTDOOR ACTIVITIES AND SPORTS

Participant Sports

Horseback Riding

On the other side of Casa de Campo, **Club El Trébol** (☎ 91/518–1066) rents both animals and equipment at reasonable prices.

Jogging

Your best bet is **Retiro Park,** where one path circles the entire park and numerous others weave their way under trees and through formal gardens. **Casa de Campo** is crisscrossed by numerous, less-shady trails.

Swimming

Madrid has the perfect antidote to the dry, sometimes intense heat of the summer months—a superb system of clean, popular, and well-run municipal swimming pools (admission about 350 pesetas; there are several reduced-price, multiple-ticket options). Most neighborhoods have pools, but the biggest and best—fitted with a comfortable, tree-shaded restaurant—is in the **Casa de Campo** (take the metro to Lago and walk up the hill a few yards; ☎ 91/463–0050). Another good choice in the city center is the ☺ **Piscina Canal Isabel II** (✉ Plaza Juan Zorrila, entrance off Avda. de Filipinas, ☎ no phone), with diving boards and a wading pool for kids.

Tennis

Club de Tenis Chamartín (✉ Federico Salmon 2, ☎ 91/345–2500), with 28 courts, is open to the public. There are also public courts in the **Casa de Campo** and on the Avenida de Vírgen del Puerto, behind the Palacio Real. (Ask for details at the tourist office.)

Spectator Sports

Bullfighting

For better or for worse, bullfighting is a spectacle, not a sport. For those not turned off by the death of six bulls every Sunday afternoon from April to early November, it offers all the excitement of any major stadium event. Nowhere in the world is bullfighting better than at Madrid's **Las Ventas** (✉ C. Alcalá 231, ☎ 91/356–2200; Metro Las Ventas), formally called the Plaza de Toros Monumental. The sophisticated audience, which follows the sport intensely, is more critical in Madrid than anywhere else, and you'll be amazed at how confusing their reactions to the fights are to the uninitiated. Cheers and hoots are difficult at first to distinguish, and it may take years to understand what prompts the wrath of this most difficult-to-please crowd. For a traveler, the bullfight audience can be the most entertaining part of the experience. Tickets may be purchased at the ring or, for a 20% surcharge, at the agencies on Calle Victoria, just off the Puerta del Sol. Most fights start in the late afternoon, and the best of all—the world's top display of bullfighting—come during the three weeks of consecutive daily fights that mark the feast of San Isidro, in May. Tickets can be tough to get through normal channels, but they're always available from scalpers in the Calle Victoria and at the stadium. You can bargain, but even Spaniards pay prices of perhaps 10 times the face value—up to 10,000 pesetas or even more.

Soccer

Spain's number-one sport is soccer, known locally as *fútbol*. Madrid has two teams, Real Madrid and Atlético Madrid, both among Europe's best, and two stadiums to match. The enormous **Santiago Bernabeu Stadium** (✉ Paseo de la Castellana 140, ☎ 91/315–0046), capacity 130,000, is home to the more popular Real Madrid, while the **Vicente Calderón Stadium** (✉ Paseo de Melancólicos s/n, ☎ 91/366–4704), on the outskirts of town, is where Atlético Madrid defends. You'll generally have to stand in line at the stadium to get tickets, but tickets for many major games are available at agencies inside Corte Inglés department stores (☞ Shopping, *below*).

SHOPPING

Beyond the popular Lladró porcelain and bullfighting posters, Madrid has a great selection of gift items and unique souvenirs. In recent years Spain has been recognized as one of the world's top design centers. You'll have no trouble finding traditional crafts in Madrid, such as ceramics, guitars, and leather goods (albeit not at traditional, countryside prices), but don't stop there. Madrid is now more like Rodeo Drive than the bargain bin that it was just a decade ago. Famous for contemporary furniture and decorator items as well as chic clothing, shoes, and jewelry, Spain's capital is stiff competition for Barcelona, a city that now considers itself the fashion capital of Europe. Most shops accept most major credit cards.

Department Stores

El Corte Inglés. The largest of Spain's chain department stores carries the best selection of everything, from auto parts to groceries to designer fashions. ✉ *Goya 76,* ☎ *91/577–7171;* ✉ *Goya 87,* ☎ *91/432–9300;* ✉ *Preciados 3,* ☎ *91/379–8000;* ✉ *Princesa 42,* ☎ *91/542–4800;* ✉ *Serrano 47,* ☎ *432–5490;* ✉ *La Vaguada Mall,* ☎ *91/387–4000;* ✉ *Parquesur Mall,* ☎ *91/558–4400;* ✉ *Raimundo Fernández Villaverde 79,* ☎ *91/556–2300.*

Marks & Spencer. British chain "Marks & Sparks" is best known for its woolens and underwear, but most shoppers head straight for the gourmet-food shop in the basement. ✉ *Serrano 52,* ☎ *91/520–0000.*

Zara. For those with young tastes and slim pocketbooks (picture hip clothes that you'll throw away in about six months), Zara has the latest looks for men, women, and children. ✉ *Carretas 10,* ☎ *91/522–6945;* ✉ *Gran Vía 32,* ☎ *91/522–9727;* ✉ *Narvaez 20,* ☎ *91/575–0424;* ✉ *Preciados 20,* ☎ *91/532–2014;* ✉ *Princesa 45,* ☎ *91/543–2415;* ✉ *Conde de Peñalver 4,* ☎ *91/435–4135.*

Flea Market

El Rastro (☞ Castizo Madrid, *above*). On Sunday, Calle de Ribera de Curtidores, the Rastro market's main thoroughfare, is closed to traffic and jammed with outdoor booths selling everything under the sun. The Sunday crowds grow so thick that it takes a while just to advance a few feet amid the hawkers and the gawkers. A word of warning: hang on to your purse and wallet, and be especially careful if you choose to bring a camera—pickpockets abound. The flea market sprawls into most of the surrounding streets, with certain areas specializing in particular products. Many of the goods sold here are wildly overpriced.

But what goods! You'll find everything from antique furniture to exotic parrots and cuddly puppies; from pirated cassette tapes of flamenco music to key chains emblazoned with symbols of the CNT, Spain's old anarchist trade union. Practice your Spanish by bargaining with the vendors over paintings, colorful Gypsy oxen yokes, heraldic iron gates, new and used clothes, and even hashish pipes. They may not lower their prices, but sometimes they'll throw in a handmade bracelet or a stack of postcards to sweeten the deal.

Off the Ribera are two *galerías,* courtyards where small shops offer higher-quality, higher-priced antiques and other goods. The whole spectacle shuts down around 2 PM.

Shopping Districts

Madrid has two main centers for shopping. The first is in the center of town, around the **Puerta del Sol,** and includes the major department stores (El Corte Inglés, the French music-and-book chain Fnac, etc.) and a large number of midline shops in the streets nearby. The second area, far more elegant and expensive, is in the northwestern **Salamanca** district, bounded roughly by Serrano, Goya, and Conde de Peñalver. These streets, just off the Plaza de Colón (particularly Calle Serrano), have the widest selection of smart boutiques and designer fashions—think Prada, Armani, and Donna Karan New York, as well as renowned Spanish designers such as Sybilla and Josep Font-Luz Diaz. If you're in the market for clothes, you may find that Spaniards, like Italians, favor browns and oranges; cool palettes don't prevail, though of course black is readily available.

South of the city center, an old factory building has been turned into the **Mercado Puerta de Toledo** (⊠ Ronda de Toledo 1), an ultraslick, government-subsidized mall full of upscale shops charging upscale prices. **Galerías del Prado** (⊠ Plaza de las Cortes 7) is another attractive mall, tucked under the Palace Hotel on the Paseo del Prado; shop here for fine books, gourmet foods, clothing, leather goods, art, and more. The newest of them all is a four-decker mall in the beautifully renovated, 19th-century **Centro Comercial ABC** (⊠ Paseo de la Castellana 34), named for the daily newspaper that started there. The building is a Madrid landmark with an ornate tile facade; inside, a large café is surrounded by shops of all kinds, including leather stores and hairdressers. The fourth-floor coffee shop has a rooftop terrace with scenic urban views. For street-chic shopping closer to medieval Madrid, check out the playful window displays at the **Madrid Fusion Centro de Moda** (⊠ Plaza Tirso de Molina 15, ☎ 91/369–0018), where up-and-coming Spanish design houses such as Instinto, Kika, and Extart fill five floors with faux furs, funky jewelry, and Madrid's most eccentric collection of shoes.

Specialty Stores

Ceramics

Antigua Casa Talavera (⊠ Isabel la Católica 2, ☎ 91/547–3417) is the best of Madrid's numerous ceramics shops. Despite the name, the finest ware sold here is from Manises, near Valencia, but the blue-and-yellow Talavera ceramics are also excellent.

Cerámica El Alfar (⊠ Claudio Coello 112, ☎ 91/411–3587) is laden with pottery from all corners of Spain.

Sagardelos (⊠ Zurbano 46, ☎ 91/310–4830) specializes in distinctive, modern Spanish ceramics from Galicia and has excellent selections of breakfast sets, coffee pots, and objets d'art.

Clothing

Adolfo Domínguez (⊠ Serrano 96, ☎ 91/576–7053; ⊠ Serrano 18, ☎ 91/577–8280) is one of many fashion studios in the Salamanca district. Domínguez is one of Spain's best-known designers, with lines for both men and women.

Del Valle (⊠ Conde Xiqueno 2, ☎ 91/531–1587; ⊠ Princesa 47, ☎ 91/547–1216; ⊠ Orense 6, ☎ 91/556–2735; ⊠ Serrano 88, ☎ 91/577–6149) is an upscale women's boutique with a tasteful collection of evening and casual wear and an emphasis on leather.

Seseña (⊠ De la Cruz 23, ☎ 91/531–6840) has outfitted Hollywood stars (and Hillary Rodham Clinton) and famous painters since the turn of the century, with capes in wool or velvet, some lined with red satin.

Sybilla (⊠ Jorge Juan 12, ☎ 91/578–1322) is the studio of Spain's best-known woman designer. Her fluid dresses and hand-knit sweaters, which have made her a favorite with supermodel Helena Christensen, come in natural colors and fabrics.

Crafts

Artespaña (⊠ Hermosilla 14, ☎ 91/435–0221) used to be run by the government to encourage Spanish craftsmanship. The store stylishly displays the best decorative crafts, such as furniture, lamps, and rugs.

El Arco (⊠ Plaza Mayor 9, ☎ 91/365–2680) has a good selection of contemporary handicrafts from all over Spain, including modern ceramics, handblown glassware, jewelry, and leather items as well as a whimsical collection of pendulum clocks.

Fans

Casa Jimenez (✉ Preciados 42, ☎ 91/431–6592) gets a nod from locals as the best place to buy an authentic Spanish fan. The selection ranges from handpainted works of art to cheaper souvenirs. Open since the 1950s, this homey shop is still family-run.

Guitars

Conde Hermanos (✉ Felipe II 2, ☎ 91/547–0612) is a workshop where three generations of the same family have been building and selling professional guitars since 1917.

José Ramirez (✉ Concepción Jerónimo 2, ☎ 91/369–2211) was founded in 1882 and has been exporting guitars to the rest of the world ever since. Prices start at 15,000 pesetas. The shop includes a museum of antique instruments.

Hats

Casa Yustas (✉ Plaza Mayor 30, ☎ 91/366–5084) is a century-old shop featuring every type of headgear, from the old three-cornered, patent-leather hats of the Guardia Civil to the berets worn by the Guardia's frequent enemy, the Basques. These berets are much wider than those worn by the French and make excellent gifts.

Leather Goods

Caligae (✉ Augusto Figueroa 27, ☎ 91/531–5343) is on a street full of bargain shoe stores (*muestrarios*) and is probably the best of the bunch, offering close-out prices on the avant-garde designs of Parisian Stephane Kélian.

Duna (✉ Lagasca 7, ☎ 91/435–2061) has the best prices in town on fine Spanish leather clothing and shoes, but the selection is somewhat limited.

Loewe (✉ Serrano 26, ☎ 91/577–6056; ✉ Gran Vía 8, ☎ 91/522–6815; ✉ Palace Hotel, ☎ 91/429–8530) features ultra-high-quality designer purses, accessories, and clothing made of buttery-soft leather in dyed, jewellike colors. Prices often hit the stratosphere.

Tenorio (✉ Plaza de la Provincia 6, ☎ no phone) is where you'll find those fine old boots of Spanish leather, made to order with workmanship that should last a lifetime.

SIDE TRIPS

El Escorial

③⑧ *50 km (31 mi) northwest of Madrid.*

Felipe II was one of history's most deeply religious and forbidding monarchs—not to mention one of its most powerful—and the great granite monastery that he had constructed in a remarkable 21 years (1563–84) is an enduring testimony to his austere character. Severe, rectilinear, and unforgiving, the Real Monasterio de San Lorenzo de El Escorial (El Escorial Monastery) is 50 km (31 mi) outside Madrid on the slopes of the Guadarrama Mountains and is one of the most massive yet simple architectural monuments on the Iberian Peninsula.

Felipe built the monastery in the village of San Lorenzo de El Escorial to commemorate Spain's crushing victory over the French at Saint-Quentin on August 10, 1557, and as a final resting place for his all-powerful father, the emperor Carlos V. The vast rectangle it traces, encompassing 16 courts, is modeled on the red-hot grille upon which San Lorenzo was martyred—appropriate enough, since August 10 was

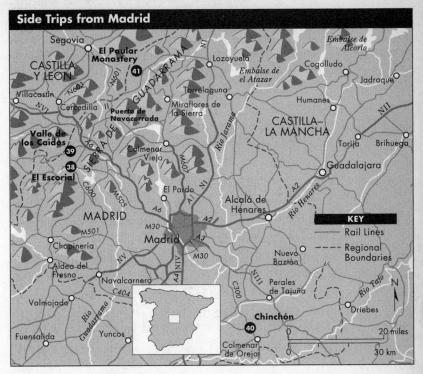

Side Trips from Madrid

that saint's day. (It's also said that Felipe's troops accidentally destroyed a church dedicated to San Lorenzo during the battle, and he sought to make amends.) A Spanish psychohistorian recently theorized that the building is shaped like a prone woman and is thus an unintended emblem of Felipe's sexual repression. Lo and behold, this thesis provoked several newspaper articles and a rash of other commentary.

El Escorial is easily reached by car, train, bus, or organized tour; simply inquire at a travel agency or the appropriate station. Although the building and its adjuncts—a palace, museum, church, and more—can take hours or even days to tour, you should be able to include a day trip to the Valley of the Fallen, an underground basilica where General Franco is buried. Be prepared for the mobs of tourists who visit El Escorial daily, especially during the summer.

The monastery was begun by Juan Bautista de Toledo but finished in 1584 by Juan de Herrera, who would eventually give his name to a major Spanish architectural school. It was completed just in time for Felipe to die here—gangrenous and tortured by the gout that had plagued him for years—in the tiny, sparsely furnished bedroom that resembled a monk's cell more than the resting place of a great monarch. It is in this bedroom—which looks out, through a private entrance, into the royal chapel—that one most appreciates the man's spartan nature. Spain's later, Bourbon kings, such as Carlos III and Carlos IV, had clearly different tastes, and their apartments, connected to Felipe's by the Hall of Battles, are far more luxurious.

Perhaps the most interesting place in the entire Escorial is the **Royal Pantheon**, which contains the body of every king since Carlos I save three—Felipe V (buried at La Granja), Ferdinand VI (in Madrid), and Amadeus of Savoy (in Italy). The body of Alfonso XIII, who died in

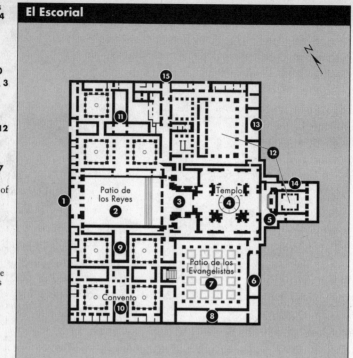

El Escorial

Rome in 1941, was brought to El Escorial in January 1980. The rulers' bodies lie in 26 sumptuous marble and bronze sarcophagi that line the walls (three of which are empty, awaiting future rulers). Only those queens who bore sons later crowned lie in the same crypt; the others, along with royal sons and daughters who never ruled, lie nearby, in the **Pantheon of the Infants.** Many of the royal children are in a single, circular tomb made of Carrara marble.

Another highlight is the monastery's uncharacteristically lavish and beautiful **library,** with 50,000 rare manuscripts, codices, and ancient books, including the diary of St. Teresa of Ávila and the gold-lettered, illuminated *Codex Aureus.* Tapestries, woven from cartoons by Goya, Rubens, and El Greco, cover almost every inch of wall space in huge sections of the building, and extraordinary canvases by Velázquez, El Greco, David, Ribera, Tintoretto, Rubens, and other masters have been collected from around the monastery and are now displayed in the New Museums. In the **basilica,** don't miss the fresco above the choir, depicting heaven, or Titian's fresco, *The Martyrdom of St. Lawrence,* which shows the saint being roasted alive. ⊠ *San Lorenzo de El Escorial,* ☎ *91/890–5905.* 🎫 *800 ptas.* ☉ *Apr.–Sept., Tues.–Sun. 10–6; Oct.–Mar., Tues.–Sun. 10–5.*

NEED A BREAK?

Many Madrileños consider El Escorial the perfect place for an enormous weekend lunch. Topping the list of favorite eating spots is the outdoor terrace of **Charoles** (⊠ Floridablanca 24, ☎ 91/890–5975), where imaginative seasonal specialties round out a menu of Spanish favorites, such as *bacalao al pil-pil* (a fried, salted cod, served still sizzling) and grilled *chuletón* (steak).

Valle de los Caídos (Valley of the Fallen)

39 *13 km (8 mi) north of El Escorial on the C600.*

Just a few minutes north of El Escorial is the Valle de los Caídos (Valley of the Fallen). You drive through a pine-studded state park to this massive basilica, which is carved out inside a hill of solid granite and commands magnificent views to the east. Topped with a cross nearly 500 ft high, the basilica holds the tombs of both Franco and José Antonio Primo de Rivera, founder of the Spanish Falange. It was built with the forced labor of Republican prisoners after the civil war and dedicated, rather disingenuously, to all who died in the three-year conflict. The inside recalls *The Wizard of Oz* more than anything else, with every footstep resounding loudly off its stone walls. Tapestries of the Apocalypse add to the generally terrifying air. ☎ *91/890–5611.* ✆ *Basilica 600 ptas., funicular 300 ptas.* ☉ *Apr.–Sept., Tues.–Sun. 10–7; Oct.–Mar., Tues.–Sun. 10–6.*

Chinchón

40 *54 km (28 mi) southeast of Madrid, off the N III highway to Valencia on the C300 local road.*

The picturesque village of Chinchón, a true Castilian town, seems a good four centuries removed. It makes an ideal day trip, especially if you take time for lunch at one of its many rustic restaurants. The only problem is that swarms of Madrileños have the same idea, so it's often difficult to get a table at lunchtime on weekends.

The high point of Chinchón is its charming Plaza Mayor, an uneven circle of ancient three- and four-story houses embellished with wooden balconies resting on granite columns. It's something like an open-air Elizabethan theater, but with a Spanish flavor. In fact, the entire plaza is converted to a bullring from time to time, with temporary bleachers erected in the center and seats on the privately owned balconies rented out for splendid views of the festivities. (These fights are rare and tickets hard to come by, as they're snatched up by Spanish tourists as soon as they go on sale.) The commanding **Iglesia de la Asunción** (Church of the Assumption) overlooks the plaza; it's known for its Goya mural, *The Assumption of the Virgin.*

NEED A
BREAK?

Two of the best and most popular restaurants on Chinchón's arcaded plaza are **Mesón de la Virreina** (✉ Plaza Mayor 21, ☎ 91/894–0015) and **Café de la Iberia** (✉ Plaza Mayor 17, ☎ 91/894–0998).

Both have balconies for outdoor dining; it's wise to reserve in advance for an outdoor table. The food in each is hearty Castilian fare, such as roast lamb and suckling pig or thick steaks. Be sure to try the locally made *anís* (anise), a licorice-flavored spirit—Chinchón is so famous for its anís that Spaniards converge here every April for the annual Fiesta del Anís y del Vino (Anise and Wine Festival).

On the way back to Madrid, where C300 joins the main highway, you'll pass through the Jarama Valley. This was the scene of one of the bloodiest battles in which the Abraham Lincoln Brigade (American volunteers fighting with the Republicans against Franco in the Spanish civil war) played a major role. The fight was immortalized by folk singer Pete Seeger, who sang, "There's a valley in Spain called Jarama . . .". Until just a few years ago, you could find bones and rusty military hardware in the fields here; today, there are still a number of clearly discernible trenches.

El Paular Monastery and the Lozoya Valley

④ *100 km (62 mi) north of Madrid.*

Behind the great *meseta* on which Madrid sits, the Sierra de Guadarrama rises like a dark, jagged shield separating Old and New Castile. Snowcapped for much of the year, the mountains are indeed rough-hewn in many spots, particularly on their northern face, but there is a dramatic exception—the Lozoya Valley.

About 100 km (62 mi) north of the capital, this valley of pines, poplars, and babbling brooks is a cool, green retreat from the often searing heat of the plain. Madrileños often repair here for a picnic or a simple drive, rarely joined by foreign travelers, to whom the area is virtually unknown.

You'll need a car to make this trip, and the drive is a pleasant one. Take the A6 motorway northwest from the city and exit at signs for the Navacerrada Pass on the N601. As you climb toward the 6,100-ft mountain pass, you'll come to a road bearing off to the left toward Cercedilla. This little village is also accessible by train from Madrid; it's a popular base for hikes. Just above Cercedilla, an old Roman road leads up to the ridge of the Guadarrama, where an ancient fountain, known as Fuenfría, long provided the spring water that fed the Roman aqueduct of Segovia (☞ Chapter 3). The path traced by this cobble road is very close to the route Hemingway had his hero Robert Jordan take in *For Whom the Bell Tolls*; eventually it takes you near the bridge that Jordan blew up in the novel.

If you continue past the Cercedilla road, you'll come to a ski resort at the highest point of the Navacerrada Pass. Take a right here on the C604 and you'll follow the ridge of the mountains for a few miles before descending into the **Lozoya Valley**.

The monastery of **El Paular** (☎ 91/869–1425) will loom on your left as you approach the valley floor. This was the first Carthusian monastery in Castile, built by King Juan I in 1390, but it has been badly neglected since the Disentailment of 1836, when religious organizations gave their artistic treasures to the state. Fewer than a dozen Benedictine monks still live here, eating and praying exactly as their predecessors did centuries ago. One of them gives daily tours—and perhaps advice on the state of your soul—at noon, 1, and 5.

The monastery is physically attached to the hotel **Santa María del Paular** (☎ 91/869–1011, ℻ 91/869–1006), most of whose rooms were tastefully refurbished in 1996. The hotel is charming but not as grand as similarly priced paradors.

The valley is filled with picnic spots along the Lozoya River, including several campgrounds. Afterward, take the C604 north a few kilometers to Rascafria, and then turn right on a smaller road marked for Miraflores de la Sierra. In that town you'll turn right again, following signs for Colmenar Viejo, and then pick up a short expressway back to Madrid.

MADRID A TO Z

Arriving and Departing

By Bus

Madrid has no central bus station; buses are generally less popular than trains (though they can be faster). Most of southern Spain is served by the **Estación del Sur** (✉ Canarias 17, ☎ 91/468–4200), while buses for much of the rest of the peninsula, including Cuenca, Extremadura,

Salamanca, and Valencia, depart from the **Auto Res Station** (✉ Plaza Conde de Casal 6, ☎ 91/551–7200).There are several other, smaller stations, however, so inquire at travel agencies for the one serving your destination.

Bus companies of interest include **La Sepulvedana** (✉ Paseo de la Florida 11, near Estación de Norte, ☎ 91/530–4800), serving Segovia, Ávila, and La Granja; **Herranz** (departures from Fernández de los Ríos s/n, ☎ 91/543–8167; Metro Moncloa), for El Escorial and the Valley of the Fallen; **Continental Auto** (✉ Alenza 20, ☎ 91/533–0400; Metro Ríos Rosas), serving Cantabria and the Basque region; and **La Veloz** (✉ Mediterraneo 49, ☎ 91/409–7602; Metro Conde de Casal), with service to Chinchón.

By Car

Felipe II made Madrid the capital of Spain because it was at the geographic center of his peninsular domains, and today many of the nation's highways radiate from Madrid like the spokes of a wheel. Originating at Kilometer 0 (marked by a brass plaque on the sidewalk of the Puerta del Sol), these highways include A6 (Segovia, Salamanca, Galicia); A1 (Burgos and the Basque Country); the N II (Guadalajara, Barcelona, France); the N III (Cuenca, Valencia, the Mediterranean coast); the A4 (Aranjuez, La Mancha, Granada, Seville); N401 (Toledo); and the N V (Talavera de la Reina, Portugal). The city is surrounded by M30 (the inner ring road) and M40 (the outer ring road), from which most of these highways are easily picked up.

By Plane

Madrid is served by **Barajas Airport**, 12 km (7 mi) east of the city. It's a rather grim-looking facility, and the national terminal is still undergoing renovations. Major carriers, including American, Delta, TWA, US Airways, Iberia, and United, provide regular service to the United States. Most connections go through New York, Washington, or Miami, but American has daily direct flights to and from Dallas–Fort Worth, and US Airways flies into Philadelphia (reserve well in advance). Many carriers serve London and other European capitals daily, but if you shop around at Madrid travel agencies, you'll probably find better deals than those available abroad (especially to and from Great Britain). For more information on flying to Madrid, *see* Air Travel *in* The Gold Guide. For general information and information on flight delays, call the airport (☎ 91/305–8343, 91/305–8344, or 91/305–8345).

BETWEEN THE AIRPORT AND DOWNTOWN

For a mere 450 pesetas there's a convenient **bus** to the central Plaza Colón, where taxis can take you to your hotel. The buses leave every 15 minutes between 5:40 AM and 2 AM (albeit slightly less often very early or late in the day). Be sure to watch your belongings, as the underground Plaza Colón bus station is a favorite haunt of purse snatchers and con artists. **Taxis** are normally waiting outside the airport terminal near the clearly marked bus stop; expect to pay up to 2,000 pesetas, more in heavy traffic, plus small holiday, late-night, and/or luggage surcharges. Make sure the driver works on the meter; off-the-meter "deals" almost always cost more.

By Train

Madrid has three train stations: Chamartín, Atocha, and Norte. Generally speaking, **Chamartín,** near the northern tip of the Paseo Castellana, serves trains heading for points north and west, including Barcelona, San Sebastián, Burgos, León, Oviedo, La Coruña, Segovia, Salamanca, as well as France and Portugal. **Atocha,** at the southern end of the Paseo del Prado, was spiffily renovated for the inauguration of

AVE (high-speed) train service in 1992 and serves points south and east, including Seville, Málaga, Córdoba, Valencia, Castellón, and Toledo. The Estación de **Norte** station is primarily for local trains serving Madrid's western suburbs, including El Escorial. For schedules and reservations call RENFE (☎ 91/563–0202), or go to the information counter in any of the train stations. You can make reservations by phone, charge your tickets to a credit card, and even have them delivered to your hotel. Most major travel agencies can also provide information and tickets.

Getting Around

Madrid has a distinctly different feel depending on the neighborhood. You'll probably want to start out in the old city, where the majority of attractions are clustered, but the spirit of adventure is bound to call you to other parts of town.

By Bus

Red city buses run between 6 AM and midnight and cost 130 pesetas per ride. Signs listing stops by street name are located at every stop, but they're hard to comprehend if you don't know the city well. Pick up a free route map from EMT kiosks on the Plaza de Cibeles or the Puerta del Sol, where you can also buy a 10-ride ticket (*bonobus*, 645 pesetas). If you speak Spanish, you can call for information (☎ 91/401–9900).

Drivers will make change for you, generally up to a 2,000-peseta note. If you've bought a 10-ride ticket, step up just behind the driver and insert it in the ticket-punching machine until the mechanism makes a "ding."

By Car

Driving in Madrid is best avoided by all but the bravest souls. Parking is nightmarish, traffic is extremely heavy almost all the time, and the city's daredevil drivers can be frightening. August may be an exception; the streets are then largely emptied by the mass exodus of Madrileños on vacation.

By Metro

The metro is quick, frequent, and, at 130 pesetas no matter how far you travel, cheap. Even cheaper is the 10-ride *billete de diez,* which costs 645 pesetas and has the added advantage of being accepted by automatic turnstiles (lines at ticket booths can be long). The system is open from 6 AM to 1:30 AM, though a few entrances close earlier. There are 10 metro lines, and system maps in every station detail their routes. Note the end station of the line you need, and just follow the signs to the correct corridor. Exits are marked SALIDA. Crime is rare.

By Motorbike

You can rent motorbikes, scooters, and motorcycles by the day or week at **Moto Alquiler** (✉ Conde Duque 13, ☎ 91/542–0657). If you're up to battling Madrid's traffic, this is a fast and pleasant way to see the city. You'll need your passport, your driver's license, and either a cash deposit or a credit card.

By Taxi

Taxis are one of Madrid's few truly good deals. Meters start at 170 pesetas and add 70 pesetas per kilometer (½ mile) thereafter. Numerous supplemental charges, however, mean that your total cost often bears little resemblance to what you see on the meter. There's a 150-peseta supplement on Sundays and holidays and between 11 PM and 6 AM; 150 pesetas to sports stadiums or the bullring; and 350 pesetas to or from the airport, plus 150 pesetas per suitcase.

Madrid Metro

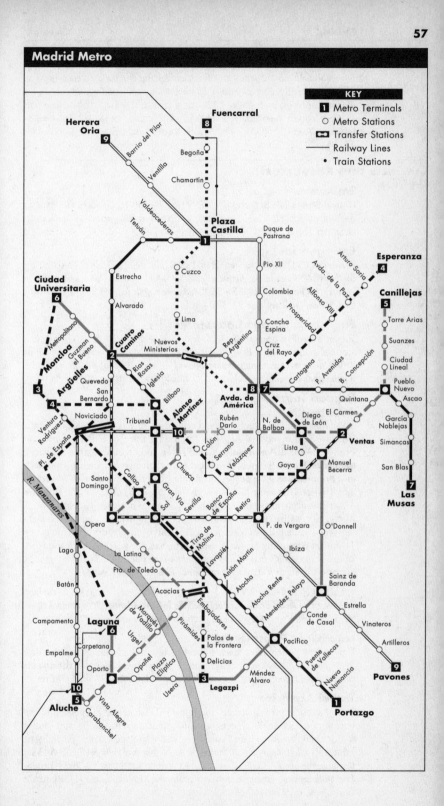

KEY
- **1** Metro Terminals
- ○ Metro Stations
- ⊟ Transfer Stations
- — Railway Lines
- • Train Stations

Taxi stands are numerous, and taxis are easily hailed in the street—
except when it rains, at which point they're exceedingly hard to come
by. Available cabs display a LIBRE sign during the day, a green light at
night. Generally, a tip of about 25 pesetas is right for shorter rides; you
may want to go as high as 10% for a trip to the airport. You can call
a cab through **Tele-Taxi** (☎ 91/445–9008 or 91/448–4259), **Radio-
teléfono Taxi** (☎ 91/547–8200), or **Radio Taxi Gremial** (☎ 91/447–
5180).

Contacts and Resources

Embassies
United States (✉ Serrano 75, ☎ 91/577–4000), **Canada** (✉ Nuñez
de Balboa 35, ☎ 91/431–4300), and **United Kingdom** (✉ Fernando
el Santo 16, ☎ 91/319–0200).

Emergencies
Police (☎ 091). **Ambulance** (☎ 061 or 91/522–2222). English-speaking
doctors (✉ Conde de Aranda 7, ☎ 91/435–1823). Major **hospitals**
include **La Paz** (☎ 91/358–2600), **Ramon y Cajal** (☎ 91/336–8000),
and **12 de Octubre** (☎ 91/390–8000).

English-Language Bookstores
Turner's English Bookshop (✉ Génova 3, ☎ 91/319–0926) has a substantial collection of English-language books and throws in a useful
bulletin-board exchange. **Booksellers** (✉ José Abascal 48, ☎ 91/442–
8104) also has a large selection of books in English.

Guided Tours
ORIENTATION

Your hotel can arrange standard city tours in either English or Spanish; most offer **Madrid Artístico** (including the Royal Palace and the
Prado), **Madrid Panorámico** (a half-day tour for first-time visitors),
Madrid de Noche (combinations include a flamenco or a nightclub show),
and **Panorámico y Toros** (on Sunday, a brief city overview followed by
a bullfight). **Trapsatur** (✉ San Bernardo 23, ☎ 91/302–6039) runs the
Madridvision tourist bus, which makes a 1½-hour sightseeing circuit
of the city with recorded commentary in English. No advance reservation is needed. Buses leave from the front of the Prado Museum every
1½ hours beginning at 12:30 Monday–Saturday, 10:30 on Sunday. A
round-trip ticket costs 1,500 pesetas; a day pass, which allows you to
get on and off at various attractions, is 2,000 pesetas.

PERSONAL GUIDES

Contact the **Asociación Profesional de Informadores** (✉ Ferraz 82, ☎
91/542–1214 or 91/541–1221) to hire a personal guide.

Late-Night Pharmacies
Emergency pharmacies are required by law to be open 24 hours a day
on a rotating basis. All major daily newspapers publish the list of
pharmacies open round-the-clock on any given day.

Travel Agencies
Travel agencies are scattered throughout Madrid and are generally the
best way to get deals, tickets, and information without hassles. Some
major agencies: **American Express,** next door to the Cortés (parliament
building) on Génova (✉ Plaza de las Cortés 2, ☎ 91/322–5445);
Carlson Wagons-Lits (✉ Paseo de la Castellana 96, ☎ 91/563–1202);
and **Pullmantur,** across the street from the Royal Palace (✉ Plaza de
Oriente 8, ☎ 91/541–1807).

Visitor Information

There are four provincial tourist offices in Madrid, but the best is on the ground floor of the Torre Madrid building, on the **Plaza España** (⊠ Princesa 1, ☎ 91/541–2325), ⊘ open weekdays 9–7, Saturday 9:30–1:30. Others are at **Barajas Airport** (☎ 91/305–8656), ⊘ open weekdays 8–8, Saturday 9–1; the **Chamartín** train station (☎ 91/315–9976), ⊘ open weekdays 8–8, Saturday 9–1; and **Duque de Medinaceli** (☎ 91/429–4951), ⊘ open weekdays 9–7, Saturday 9–1. The city tourism office on the **Plaza Mayor** (☎ 91/366–5477), ⊘ open weekdays 10–8 and Saturday 10–2, is good for little save a few pamphlets.

3 Around Madrid

Castilla (Castile), the area surrounding Madrid, is a vast, windswept plateau with clear skies and endless vistas. An outstanding Roman aqueduct and a fairy-tale castle and cathedral make Segovia one of the most popular excursions from Madrid. The walled city of Ávila was the home of St. Teresa, Spain's female patron saint, and the university town of Salamanca is a flourish of golden sandstone. Aranjuez tempts with the French-style elegance of a Bourbon palace, while enigmatic Toledo is dramatic and austere, with rich legacies from three religions.

By Michael Jacobs

Updated by Katherine Semler

FOR ALL THE VARIETY in the towns and countryside outside Madrid, there is an underlying unity. Castile is essentially an endless plain—gray, bronze, green, and severe. Over the centuries, poets and others have characterized it as austere and melancholy, most notably Antonio Machado, whose experiences at Soria in the early 20th century inspired his memorable and haunting *Campos de Castilla* (*Fields of Castile*).

Stone is a dominant element in the Castilian countryside, and it plays a large part in the region's character. Gaunt mountain ranges frame the horizons; gorges and rocky outcrops break up flat expanses; and the fields around Ávila and Segovia are littered with giant boulders. The villages are built predominantly of granite, and their solid, formidable look contrasts markedly with the whitewashed walls of most of southern Spain. The presence of so much stone may help to explain the region's rich tradition of sculpture—Castile has one of Europe's most significant stashes of sculptural treasures, many on display in the unrivaled National Museum of Sculpture, in Valladolid.

Castile is more accurately labeled Old and New Castile, the former north of Madrid, the latter south—known as "New" because it was captured from the Moors at a slightly later date. Whereas southern Spaniards are traditionally passive and peace-loving, Castilians have been a race of soldiers. The very name of the region (in effect, *la región castilla,* the region of castles) refers to the great line of castles and fortified towns built in the 12th century between Salamanca, in the west, and Soria, in the east. Segovia's Alcázar, Ávila's fully intact city walls, and countless other military installations are among Castile's greatest monuments, and some of them—the castles at Sigüenza and Ciudad Rodrigo, for instance—are also splendid hotels.

Faced with the austerity of the Castilian environment, many have taken refuge in the worlds of the spirit and the imagination. Ávila is closely associated with two of Europe's most renowned mystics, St. Teresa and her disciple St. John of the Cross, and Toledo was the main home of one of the most spiritual of all western painters, El Greco. As for escape into fantasy, this is best illustrated by Cervantes' hero Don Quixote, in whose formidable imagination even the dreary expanse of La Mancha—one of the bleakest parts of Spain—became something magical. Many of the region's architects were similarly fanciful: Castile in the 15th and 16th centuries was the center of the plateresque, an ornamental style of extraordinary intricacy and fantasy, suggestive of silverwork. Developed in Toledo and Valladolid, it reached its exuberant climax in the university town of Salamanca.

Pleasures and Pastimes

Dining

The classic dishes of Castile are *cordero* (lamb) and *cochinillo* (suckling pig), the latter roasted in a wood oven. These are specialties of Segovia, widely regarded as Castile's gastronomic capital thanks largely to such long-established restaurants as the Mesón de Cándido and the Mesón Duque. In the Segovian village of Pedraza, superb roast lamb is served with hearty red wine.

The mountainous districts of Salamanca, particularly the villages of Guijuelo and Candelario, are renowned for their hams and sausages. Bean dishes are a specialty of the villages El Barco (Ávila) and La Granja (Segovia), while *trucha* (trout) and *cangrejos de río* (river crab) are common to Guadalajara. Game is abundant throughout Castile, two famous dishes being *perdiz en escabeche* (the marinated partridge of Soria) and *perdiz estofada a la Toledana* (the stewed partridge of Toledo). The most exotic and complex cuisine in Castile is perhaps that of Cuenca, with two outstanding restaurants, Figon de Pedro and Los Claveles. Here a Moorish influence appears in such dishes as *gazpacho pastor* (a hot terrine made with a variety of game, topped with grapes).

Among the region's sweets are the *yemas* (sugared egg yolks) of Ávila, *almendras garrapiñadas* (candied almonds) of Alcalá de Henares, *mazapán* (marzipans) of Toledo, and *ponche Segovia* (egg toddy) of Segovia. La Mancha is the main area for cheese, while Aranjuez is famous for its strawberries and asparagus.

Much of Spain's cheap wine comes from La Mancha, south of Toledo. Far better in quality, and indeed among the most superior Spanish wines, are those from the Duero Valley, around Valladolid. Look for the Marqués de Riscal whites from Rueda and the Vega Sicilia reds from Valbuena; Peñafiel is the most common of the Duero wines. An excellent, if extremely sweet, Castilian liqueur is Cuenca's *resolí*, made from aquavit, coffee, vanilla, orange peel, and sugar and often sold in bottles in the shape of Cuenca's Casas Colgadas (Hanging Houses).

CATEGORY	COST*
$$$$	over 6,500 ptas.
$$$	4,000–6,500 ptas.
$$	2,500–4,000 ptas.
$	under 2,500 ptas.

per person for a three-course meal, including wine, excluding tax and tip

Lodging

Spain's most stylish hotels are usually the paradors. This holds true in Castile, but the region's oldest and most attractive paradors are generally found in the lesser towns, such as Ciudad Real and Sigüenza, rather than the major tourist centers. The paradors in Salamanca, Toledo, Segovia, and Soria are all in ugly or nondescript modern buildings, albeit with magnificent views. Fortunately, the region has many pleasant alternatives to paradors, such as Segovia's centrally situated Los Linajes, Ávila's Palacio de Valderrábanos (a 15th-century palace next to the cathedral), and Cuenca's Posada San José (a 16th-century convent).

CATEGORY	COST*
$$$$	over 14,000 ptas.
$$$	8,000–14,000 ptas.
$$	4,000–8,000 ptas.
$	under 4,000 ptas.

All prices are for a standard double room, excluding tax.

Exploring Around Madrid

Two main regions surround Madrid—Castile and León to the north and west, and Castile–La Mancha to the south and east. From Segovia south to Toledo, there's plenty to see.

Numbers in the text correspond to numbers in the margin and on the Around Madrid, Segovia, Salamanca, and Toledo maps.

Great Itineraries

You can visit Aranjuez, Ávila, Segovia, and Toledo on day trips from Madrid. Salamanca and other major towns can also be day trips from the capital, but you might find yourself spending more time traveling than actually being there. Ideally, especially if you have a car, take at least a four-day trip around the area, staying in Toledo, Segovia, and Salamanca and passing through Ávila. Both Toledo and Segovia have an extra charm at night, not only because their monuments are so beautifully illuminated, but also because they are free of the crowds of tourists that congest them by day. To visit all of the region's main sights would require at least another three to six days, with overnight stays in Zamora, Soria, Sigüenza, and Cuenca.

IF YOU HAVE 3 DAYS

⊞ **Toledo** ㉚–㉟, which was for many years Spain's intellectual and spiritual capital, is a must-see. Spend a night and visit El Greco's former stomping grounds before moving on to **Aranjuez** ㊾, the summer retreat of the Bourbon monarchy. Next, head north of Madrid to **Segovia** ①–⑫, with its Roman aqueduct, countless Romanesque churches, and inviting side streets. On your last day, try to catch the incredible fountain display in the gardens of **El Palacio de La Granja** ⑭ before heading back to Madrid.

IF YOU HAVE 4 DAYS

Visit **El Palacio de La Granja** ⑭ on the way to ⊞ **Segovia** ①–⑫. After viewing the Roman aqueduct and other attractions, visit the famous medieval **Castillo de Coca** ⑰. From there go to ⊞ **Salamanca** ㉒–㉝ to soak up the university atmosphere and some of Spain's architectural treasures. The following day, spend some time in **Ávila** ⑱, famous for its intact medieval walls and the legacy of St. Teresa, Spain's female patron saint, who lived most of her life here. Finally, wander austere ⊞ **Toledo** ㉚–㉟, once the home of El Greco and full of tiny, hilly, winding lanes.

When to Tour Around Madrid

The best time to tour Madrid's environs is between May and October, when the weather is sunny. Many restaurants and cafés have sidewalk terraces where you can relax and people-watch. Be warned, however, that July and August can be brutally hot at times, especially south of Madrid. If possible, arrange to spend at least one weekend night in Salamanca, where the social atmosphere is something to behold. November through February can be rather cold, especially in the Sierra Guadarrama, north and west of Madrid; if you don't mind touring in a winter coat, however, the Christmas holidays can be a good time to visit, with the streets enlivened by decorative lights and colorful processions. Nota bene: many museums in all of these areas are closed on Monday, so you may want to spend that day in places where museums will not be your main focus.

SEGOVIA AND ITS PROVINCE

Segovia, El Palacio de La Granja, Pedraza, Sepúlveda, and Castillo de Coca

The area north of Madrid is dotted with rich and varied history, from the Roman aqueduct in exquisite Segovia to the small 16th-century village of Pedraza. Either town makes a pleasant place to spend the night. Other towns worth a visit include Sepúlveda and Castillo de Coca, for their medieval monuments, and La Granja, where the impressive gardens become even more spectacular when the fountains are turned on, creating an effect to rival that of Versailles.

Segovia

★ ❶ *87 km (54 mi) west of Madrid.*

Segovia's breathtaking location—on a ridge in the middle of a gorgeously stark, undulating plain—is only enhanced by its outstanding Roman and medieval monuments, its excellent cuisine, its embroideries and textiles, and its general personality. An important military town in Roman times, Segovia was later established by the Arabs as a major textile center. Captured by the Christians in 1085, it was enriched by a royal residence, and in 1474 the half sister of Henry IV, Isabella the Catholic (Isabel la Católica, of Castile, married to Ferdinand of Aragon), was crowned queen of Castile here. By that time Segovia was a bustling city of about 60,000 (there are 54,000 today), but its importance soon diminished as a result of its taking the (losing) side of the Comuneros in the popular revolt against the emperor Charles V. Though the construction in the 18th century of a royal palace in nearby La Granja helped revive the town's fortunes somewhat, it never recovered its former vitality. Early in the 20th century, Segovia's sleepy charm came to be appreciated by numerous artists and writers, among them painter Ignacio Zuloaga and poet Antonio Machado. Today it swarms with tourists and day-trippers from Madrid, and you may want to avoid it in the summer, especially on weekends or public holidays. On weekdays in the winter, you can fully appreciate its haunting peace.

When you approach Segovia driving west from Madrid along N603, the first building you see is the cathedral, which seems to rise directly from the fields. Between you and Segovia lies, in fact, a steep and narrow valley, which shields the old town from view. Only when you descend into the valley do you begin to see the old town's spectacular position, rising on top of a narrow rock ledge shaped like a ship. As soon as you reach the modern outskirts, turn left onto the Paseo E. González and follow the road marked "**Ruta Panorámica**"; you'll soon find yourself descending on the narrow and winding Cuesta de los Hoyos, which takes you to the bottom of the wooded valley that dips to the south of the old town. Above, you can see the Romanesque church of San Martín to the right; the cathedral in the middle; and, on the far left, where the rock ledge tapers, the turrets, spires, and battlements of Segovia's castle, known as the Alcázar.

A Good Walk

Driving and parking are problems on the narrow streets of old Segovia, so it's best to leave the car and explore on foot. In short, start in front of the Roman aqueduct in the Plaza de la Artillería, and then walk northwest to the Plaza Mayor on Calle Cervantes, ending your excursion at the Alcázar.

Beginning at the church of **San Millán** ②, go up Avenida de Fernández Ladreda until you come to the **Acueducto Romano** ③. Pass under the arches to the Plaza del Azoguejo, which was once the marketplace and center of the town's activity. Head up Calle Cervantes and look to the left—in the distance is the Sierra de Guadarrama.

Continue up the same pedestrian shopping street, now called Calle de Juan Bravo, and veer off to the right onto Herrería for a look at the late-Gothic **Palacio de los Condes de Alpuente** ④, covered with *esgrafiado* plasterwork. Back on Calle Juan Bravo, and further ahead, you'll come to the small, delightful Plaza Martín, on which rises another Romanesque church, **San Martín** ⑤.

Off to the left of Juan Bravo, across from the Plaza Martín, is the refreshing **Paseo de Salón** ⑥, a small promenade at the foot of the town's southern walls. This walk was very popular with Spain's 19th-century queen, Isabel II; it offers good views over the wooded valley to the south and toward the Sierra de Guadarrama.

At the Plaza del Corpus, where Juan Bravo splits into Calle de La Judería Vieja and Isabel la Católica, head left up Calle de La Judería Vieja into the former Jewish Quarter, where Segovia's Jews lived as early as the 13th century. At Calle de San Frutos, turn right and step into the lively Plaza Mayor. The plaza is lined with bars and terraces, making it an ideal place for a lunch break or early-evening drink. Along the *paseo* of the arcaded main square stand the 17th-century **ayuntamiento** ⑦ and the **cathedral** ⑧. From the *paseo* pick up Calle de Valdeláguila to **San Estéban** ⑨. Calle de Los Leones, lined with tourist shops, slopes gently down from the cathedral toward the western extremity of the old town's ridge. From the partially shaded Plaza del Alcázar, you have excellent views to the north and south. At the western end of the square is the famous **Alcázar** ⑩.

From the Alcázar, you can see the church of **Vera Cruz** ⑪ and the **Casa de la Moneda** (former Mint) ⑫. A walk along the city's peripheral road, Paseo de Santo Domingo de Guzmán, leads to the **Convento de la Santa Cruz** ⑬.

TIMING
This walk can be covered in a few hours, depending on how long you stop at each sight.

Sights to See

❸ **Acueducto Romano** (Roman aqueduct). Segovia's leading monument, the aqueduct ranks with the Pont du Gard in France as one of the greatest surviving examples of Roman engineering. Spanning the dip that stretches from the walls of the old town to the lower slopes of the Sierra de Guadarrama, it is about 2,952 ft long, and rises in two tiers—above the Plaza del Azoguejo—to a height of 115 ft. The raised section of stonework in the center originally carried an inscription, of which only the holes for the bronze letters remain. The massive, granite blocks are held together by neither mortar nor clamps, but the aqueduct has been standing since the end of the first century AD. The only damage it has suffered is the demolition of 35 of its arches by the Moors, and these were later replaced on the orders of Ferdinand and Isabella. Steps at the side of the aqueduct lead up to the walls of the old town, offering at the top an amazing side view of the structure. ⊠ *Plaza de Azoguerjo ("highest point" of Aqueduct).*

❿ **Alcázar.** Possibly dating from Roman times, this castle was considerably expanded in the 14th century, remodeled in the 15th, altered again toward the end of the 16th century, and completely redone after being gutted by a fire in 1862, when it was used as an artillery school. The exterior, especially when seen from the Ruta Panorámica, is certainly imposing, but the castle is little more than a medieval sham, with the exception of the keep through which you enter, the last remnant of the original structure. Crowned by crenellated towers that seem to have been carved out of icing, the keep can be climbed for superb views. The rest of the interior is a bit disappointing. ☎ *921/460759.* 🏷 *375 ptas.* ☉ *May–Sept., daily 10–7; Oct.–Apr., daily 10–6.*

❼ **Ayuntamiento.** The 17th-century town hall stands on the active **Plaza Mayor.** It's closed to the public, but it's a great place to sit and watch the world go by. ⊠ *Plaza Mayor.*

⑫ **Casa de la Moneda** (Mint). All Spanish coinage was struck here from 1455 to 1730. The building is closed for reconstruction, but it's worth a look. ⊠ *C. de la Moneda s/n, just south of River Eresma.*

Around Madrid

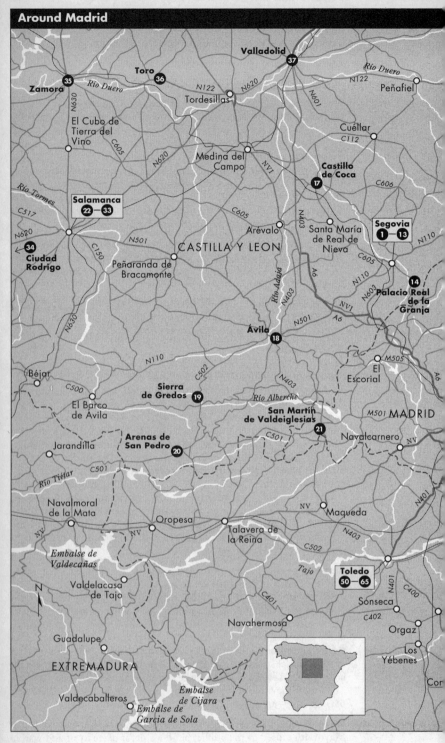

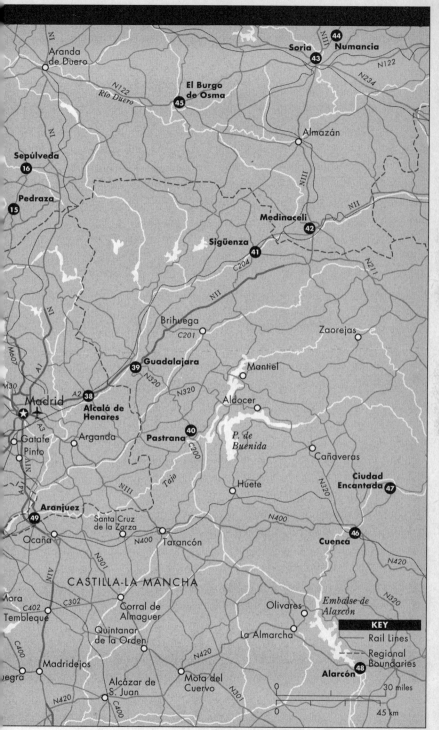

Aranda
de Duero

N1

N122

Río Duero

El Burgo
de Osma

45

Soria **43**

44 Numancia

N1II

N122

N234

Almazán

N1

Sepúlveda

16

Pedraza

15

NIII

Medinaceli

42

NII

Sigüenza

41

C204

N211

NII

Brihuega

C201

Zaorejas

Mo07

A1

Madrid

A2 **38**

39 Guadalajara

N320

N320

Mantiel

Aldocer

M30

Alcalá de
Henares

A3

Arganda

Gatafe
Pinto

Pastrana **40**

C200

P. de
Buenida

Cañaveras

NIV

Tajo

NIII

Húete

N320

Ciudad
Encantada **47**

Aranjuez

49

Santa Cruz
de la Zarza

Ocaña

N400

Tarancón

N400

Cuenca **46**

N420

A41

NIV

N301

CASTILLA-LA MANCHA

Mora

C402

C302

Tembleque

Corral de
Almaguer

Olivares

Embalse de
Alarcón

N320

Quintanar
de la Orden

La Almarcha

C400

Madridejos

uegra

C400

N420

Alcázar de
S. Juan

Mota del
Cuervo

N420

N301

C400

Alarcón **48**

KEY

Rail Lines

Regional
Boundaries

0   30 miles

0   45 km

Segovia

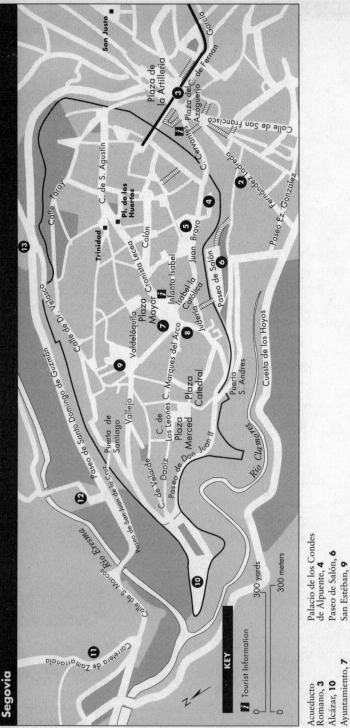

KEY

Z Tourist Information

0 ——— 300 yards
0 ——— 300 meters

Acueducto
Romano, **3**
Alcázar, **10**
Ayuntamiento, **7**
Casa de la
Moneda, **12**
Cathedral, **8**
Convento de la
Santa Cruz, **13**

Palacio de los Condes
de Alpuente, **4**
Paseo de Salón, **6**
San Estéban, **9**
San Martín, **5**
San Millán, **2**
Vera Cruz, **11**

⑧ Cathedral. Begun in 1525 and completed 65 years later, the cathedral was intended to replace an earlier one near the Alcázar, destroyed during the revolt of the Comuneros against Charles V. It's one of the most harmonious in Spain, and one of the country's last great examples of the Gothic style. The designs were drawn up by the leading late-Gothicist Juan Gil de Hontañón but executed by his son Rodrigo, in whose work can be seen a transition from the Gothic to the Renaissance style. The tall proportions and buttressing are pure Gothic, but much of the detailing—on the crossing tower, for instance—is classical. The golden interior, illuminated by 16th-century Flemish windows, is remarkably light and uncluttered, the one distracting detail being the wooden, neoclassical choir. You enter through the north transept, which is marked MUSEO; turn right, and the first chapel on your right has a lamentation group in wood by the baroque sculptor Gregorio Fernández.

Across from the entrance, on the southern transept, is a door opening into the late-Gothic cloister; this and the elaborate door leading into it were transported from the old cathedral and are the work of Juan Guas, architect of the church of San Juan de Los Reyes, in Toledo. Under the pavement immediately inside the cloisters are the tombs of Juan and Rodrigo Gil de Hontañón; that these two lie in a space designed by Guas is appropriate, for the three men together dominated the last phase of the Gothic style in Spain. Off the cloister, a small museum of religious art, installed partly in the first-floor chapter house, is worth a visit for its 17th-century white-and-gold ceiling, a late and splendid example of Mudéjar *artesonado* work. ☎ 921/435325. 🎟 *Museum 250 ptas.* ⊙ *June–Sept., daily 9–7; Oct.–May, daily 9–6.*

⑬ Convento de la Santa Cruz. This 13th-century church was established by St. Dominick of Guzmán, the founder of the Dominican order, and rebuilt in the 15th century by Ferdinand and Isabella. In 1996 it was turned into a private university, La Universidad Sec. During the academic year, you can catch a view of the attractive interior, Gothic with plateresque and Renaissance touches. ✉ *C. Cardenal Zúñiga s/n,* ☎ 921/471997.

④ Palacio de los Condes de Alpuente (Palace of the Counts of Alpuente). This late-Gothic palace is covered with a type of plasterwork known as *esgrafiado,* incised with regular patterns; the style was most likely introduced by the Moors and is characteristic of Segovian architecture. The building is now used for city administrative offices and is no longer open to the public. ✉ *Plaza del Platero Oquendo s/n,* ☎ *no phone.*

⑨ San Estéban. This porticoed church is the third of Segovia's major Romanesque monuments. Though the interior has a baroque facing, the exterior has kept some splendid capitals, as well as an exceptionally tall and elegant tower. Due east of the attractive square on which the church stands is the **Capilla de San Juan de Dios,** next to which is the former pension where the poet Antonio Machado spent his last years in Spain. The family who looked after Machado still owns the building and will show you on request the poet's room, with its paraffin stove, iron bed, and round table. The church is open for mass only. ✉ *Plaza de San Esteban s/n.* ⊙ *Mass daily 8–10 AM and 7–9 PM.*

⑤ San Martín. This Romanesque church stands in an attractive little plaza by the same name. ✉ *Plaza San Martín s/n,* ☎ 921/443402. ⊙ *Open for mass only.*

② San Millán. This 12th-century church is a perfect example of the Segovian Romanesque and is perhaps the finest church in town apart from the cathedral. The exterior is notable for its arcaded porch, where church meetings were once held. The virtually untouched Romanesque interior is dominated by massive columns, whose capitals carry such carved scenes as the Flight into Egypt and the Adoration of the Magi. The vaulting on the crossing shows the Moorish influence on Spanish medieval architecture. ⊠ *Avda. Fernández Ladreda 26, 5-min walk outside town walls.* ⊙ *Open for mass only, daily 8–10 AM and 7–9 PM.*

⓫ **Vera Cruz.** This isolated Romanesque church, made of the warm orange stone of the area, was built in 1208 for the Knights Templar. Like other buildings associated with this order, it is round, inspired by the Church of the Holy Sepulchre, in Jerusalem. Your trip here pays off in full when you climb the bell tower and see all of Segovia profiled against the Sierra de Guadarrama, which is capped with snow in winter. ⊠ *Carretera de Zamarramala s/n, on northern outskirts of town, off Cuesta de los Hoyos,* ☏ *921/431475.* ⌻ *150 ptas.* ⊙ *May–Sept., Tues.–Sun. 10:30– 1:30 and 3:30–7; Oct.–Apr., Tues.–Sun. 10:30–1:30 and 3:30–6. Closed Nov.*

Dining and Lodging

$$$ ✕ **Casa Duque.** Founded by Dionisio Duque in 1895 and still in the family, Casa Duque is the second-most-famous restaurant in town. The intimate interior, with its homey wood-beam decoration and plethora of fascinating *objets,* is similar to that of Cándido (☞ *below*); but Casa Duque is smaller, and benefits greatly from the charismatic presence of owner Julian Duque. Never still for a moment, Duque attends to all his clients with eccentric charm. Roasts are the specialty, but you should also try the *judiones de La Granja Duque*—the excellent kidney beans from nearby La Granja, served with sausages. ⊠ *Cervantes 12,* ☏ *921/430537. Reservations essential. AE, DC, MC, V.*

$$$ ✕ **Mesón de Cándido.** More than a restaurant, Cándido was declared
★ a national monument in 1941. Tucked cozily under the aqueduct, comprising a quaint medley of small, irregular dining rooms covered with memorabilia, it has served as an inn since at least the 18th century. Señor Cándido took it over in 1931 and, with his energy and flair for publicity, managed to make it the Spanish restaurant best known abroad: amid the dark-wood beams and Castilian knickknacks hang photos of the many celebrities who have dined here, from Ernest Hemingway to Princess Grace of Monaco. Cándido passed away several years ago, and the place is now run by his son. First-time visitors are virtually obliged to eat the *cochinillo,* the delicacy of which used to be attested to by Cándido's slicing it with the edge of a plate. The trout here is also renowned. ⊠ *Plaza de Azoguejo 5,* ☏ *921/425911. Reservations essential. AE, DC, MC, V.*

$$$ ✕ **Mesón de José María.** In this case, the exceptionally lively bar,
★ which you must pass to reach the restaurant, augurs well for the rest of the establishment. Though relatively new in Segovian terms, the Mesón de José María has already surpassed its formidable rivals culinarily and deserves to be considered one of Spain's finest restaurants. The hospitable and passionately dedicated owner is devoted to maintaining traditional Castilian specialties while concocting innovations of his own. The emphasis is on freshness and quality of produce, and the menu changes constantly. The large, old-style, brightly lit dining room is often packed, and the waiters are uncommonly friendly. Although it's a bit touristy, with a set menu in English, this *mesón* is also a favorite of the locals. ⊠ *Cronista Lecea 11,* ☏ *921/461111. AE, DC, MC, V.*

$$$$ ✕⌂ **Parador Nacional de Segovia.** Architecturally one of the most interesting and handsome of the modern paradors, this low building is spaciously arranged amid greenery on a hillside. The rooms are light, with generous amounts of glass. The panorama of Segovia and its aque-

duct is unbeatable, but there are disadvantages in staying so far from the town center. The restaurant serves traditional Segovian and international dishes, such as *lomo de merluza al aroma de estragón* (hake fillet with tarragon and shrimp). ✉ *Carretera de Valladolid s/n, 40003,* ☎ *921/443737,* FAX *921/437362. 113 rooms. Restaurant, pool, meeting room. AE, DC, MC, V.*

$$$ ✕⌘ **Los Arcos.** The comfortable lodgings at this modern hotel, a 5- to 10-minute walk from the Roman aqueduct, are a favorite with business travelers. The staff is friendly and always willing to assist in whatever way it can. The rooms are brightly decorated, and many include a small sitting area. The restaurant is attractive, with hardwood floors and arched redbrick doorways. Specialties include *cochinillo* and *lechazo* (baby lamb). ✉ *Paseo Ezequiel González 26, 40002,* ☎ *921/ 437462,* FAX *921/428161. 59 rooms. Restaurant, bar. AE, DC, MC, V.*

$$$ ⌘ **Infanta Isabel.** This small hotel is in a recently restored building with
★ a Victorian feel. It's right on the Plaza Mayor—with an entrance on the charming, if congested, pedestrian shopping street Infanta Isabel— and has great views of Segovia's cathedral. The rooms are spacious, feminine, and light, with painted white furnishings. ✉ *Plaza Mayor s/n, 40001,* ☎ *921/ 461300 ,* FAX *921/ 462217. 29 rooms. Coffee shop. AE, DC, MC, V.*

Shopping

After Toledo, the province of Segovia is Castile's most important for crafts. **Glass** and **crystal** are specialties of La Granja, while **ironwork, lace,** and **embroidery** are famous in Segovia itself. In search of the old, authentic article, go to San Martín 4 (✉ Plaza San Martín 4), an excellent **antiques** shop. You can buy good **lace** from the Gypsies in Segovia's Plaza del Alcázar, but be prepared for some strenuous bargaining, and never offer more than half the opening price.

Palacio Real (Royal Palace) de La Granja

⑭ *11 km (7 mi) southeast of Segovia on the N601.*

The major attraction in Segovia's immediate vicinity, the palace of La Granja stands in the town of San Ildefonso de la Granja, on the northern slopes of the Guadarrama range. Its site was once occupied by a hunting lodge and a shrine to San Ildefonso, administered by Hieronymite monks from the Segovian monastery of El Parral. Commissioned by the Bourbon king Philip V in 1719, the palace has sometimes been described as the first great building of the Spanish Bourbon dynasty. The 19th-century English writer Richard Ford likened it to "a theatrical French château, the antithesis of the proud, gloomy Escorial, on which it turns its back." The architects who brought it to completion in 1739 and gave it such distinction were, in fact, not French but Italian—Juvarra and Sachetti. They were responsible for the imposing garden facade, a late-baroque masterpiece anchored throughout its length by a giant order of columns. The interior has been badly gutted by fire, and the few undamaged rooms are heavy and monotonous; the highlight of the interior is the collection of 15th- to 18th-century tapestries, gathered together in a special museum. It is the **gardens of La Granja** that you come to see—here, terraces, ornamental ponds, lakes, classical statuary, woods, and late-baroque fountains dot the slopes of the Guadarrama. On Wednesday, Saturday, and Sunday evenings in the summer (6–7 PM, May–Sept.), the fountains are turned on, one by one, creating one of the most exciting spectacles in Europe. The starting time has been known to change on a whim; call to check the time. ☎ *921/470020.* ⬧ *Palace 650 ptas., gardens free.*

🕓 *Palace Oct.–May, Tues.–Sat. 10–1:30 and 3–5, Sun. 10–2 (10–
6 Apr. and May); June–Sept., Tues.–Sun. 10–6. Garden daily 10–sunset.*

Pedraza

⑮ *30 km (19 mi) northeast of Segovia.*

Though it's been commercialized and overprettified in recent years, Pedraza is still a striking 16th-century village. Crowning a rocky outcrop
and completely encircled by its walls, it is perfectly preserved, with wonderful views of the Sierra de Guadarrama. Farther up, at the very top
of the tiny village, is a Renaissance castle that was bought as a private
residence by the painter Ignacio Zuloaga early in the 20th century. Two
sons of the French king Francis I were held hostage here after the Battle of Pavia, together with their majordomo, the father of the Renaissance poet Pierre de Ronsard. In the center of the village is the attractive,
irregularly shaped main square, lined with rustic wooden porticoes and
dominated by a Romanesque bell tower.

Dining and Lodging

$$–$$$ ✕ **El Yantar de Pedraza.** This traditional restaurant, with wooden ta-
bles and beamed ceilings, is famous for roast meats. Right on Pedraza's main square, it's the place to come for that most celebrated of
the town's specialties—*corderito lechal en horno de leña* (baby lamb
roasted in a wood oven). ⊠ *Plaza Mayor,* ☎ *921/509842. AE, DC,
MC, V. Closed Mon. No dinner Sept. 15–July 15.*

$$$ ▥ **La Posada de Don Mariano.** This hotel was originally a farmer's home.
Each room in the picturesque old building is decorated differently, but
all have rustic furniture and antiques. The atmosphere is intimate, though
prices are grand. The restaurant, Enebro, serves a good selection of red
meat. ⊠ *Plaza Mayor, 40172,* ☎ 𝖥𝖠𝖷 *921/509886. 18 rooms. Restau-
rant, bar. AE, DC, MC, V.*

Sepúlveda

⑯ *24 km (15 mi) north of Pedraza, 60 km (37 mi) northeast of Segovia.*

A walled village with a commanding position, Sepúlveda has a charm-
ing main square, but its main attraction is the **11th-century Church of
El Salvador,** the highest monument within the walled perimeter. Older
than any other Romanesque church in the province of Segovia, it has
a crude but amusing example of the porches found in later Segovia build-
ings: the carvings on its oversize capitals, probably the work of a
Moorish convert, are fantastical and have little to do with Christian-
ity.

Castillo de Coca

⑰ *52 km (32 mi) northwest of Segovia.*

Perhaps the most famous medieval sight near Segovia, worth a detour
between Segovia and Ávila or Valladolid, is the Castillo de Coca. Built
in the 15th century for Archbishop Alonso de Fonseca I, the castle is
a turreted structure, in plaster and red brick, surrounded by a deep moat.
It looks like a stage set for a fairy tale, and indeed, it was intended not
as a defense but as a place for the notoriously pleasure-loving Arch-
bishop Fonseca to hold riotous parties. The interior, now occupied by
a forestry school, has been modernized, with only fragments of the orig-
inal decoration preserved.

ÁVILA AND THE SIERRA DE GREDOS

Ávila, Sierra de Gredos, Arenas de San Pedro, San Martín de Valdeiglesias

From the spectacular medieval walls of Ávila to the mountains of the Sierra de Gredos, this area yields more than just spectacular views. In Ávila, you can trace the history of St. Teresa, who lived much of her life here. If you're looking for outdoor diversion, the Sierra de Gredos makes for ideal hiking and skiing. Other sights include the small, attractive villages near Arenas de San Pedro and the ancient stone bulls of San Martín de Valdeiglesias.

Ávila

⑱ *107 km (66 mi) northwest of Madrid.*

In the middle of a windy plateau littered with giant boulders, Ávila can look wild and sinister. Modern development on the outskirts of town partially obscures Ávila's intact surrounding **walls,** which, restored in parts, look exactly as they did in the Middle Ages. Begun in 1090, shortly after the town was reclaimed from the Moors, the walls were completed in only nine years—a feat accomplished by the daily employment of an estimated 1,900 men. Featuring nine gates and 88 cylindrical towers bunched together, they are unique to Spain in form, unlike the Moorish defense architecture that the Christians adapted elsewhere. They're most striking when viewed from outside the town; for the most extensive view on foot, cross the Adaja River, take a right on the Carretera de Salamanca, and walk uphill about 250 yards to a monument consisting of four pilasters surrounding a cross. And when you ultimately leave Ávila, look back on your way out.

The walls clearly reflect Ávila's importance during the Middle Ages. Populated by Alfonso VI mainly with Christians from Asturias, the town came to be known as Ávila of the Knights, on account of the high proportion of nobles. Decline set in at the beginning of the 15th century, with the gradual departure of the nobility to the court of Charles V in Toledo. Ávila's fame later on was due largely to St. Teresa, Spain's female patron saint (St. James the Apostle is her male counterpart). Born here in 1515 to a noble family of Jewish origin, Teresa spent much of her life in Ávila, leaving a legacy of various convents and the ubiquitous *yemas* (candied egg yolks), originally distributed free to the poor but now sold for high prices to tourists. Ávila today is well preserved but with a sad, austere, and slightly desolate atmosphere.

The battlement apse of the **cathedral** forms the most impressive part of the walls. The apse was built mainly in the late 12th century, but the construction of the rest of the cathedral continued until the 18th century. Entering the town gate to the right of the apse, you'll reach the sculpted north portal (originally the west portal, until it was moved in 1455 by the architect Juan Guas) by turning left and walking a few steps. The present west portal, flanked by 18th-century towers, is notable for the crude carvings of hairy male figures on each side; known as "wild men," these figures appear in many Castilian palaces of this period, but their significance is disputed.

The Transitional Gothic interior, with its granite nave, is heavy and severe. The Lisbon earthquake of 1755 deprived the building of its Flemish stained glass, so the main note of color appears in the beautiful mottled stone in the apse, tinted yellow and red. Elaborate, plateresque choir stalls built in 1547 complement the powerful high altar of circa 1504 by painters Juan de Borgoña and Pedro Berruguete. On the wall of the ambulatory, look for the early 16th-century marble sepulchre of Bishop Alonso de Madrigal, a remarkably lifelike representation of the bishop seated at his writing table. Known as "El Tostado" for his swarthy complexion, the bishop was a tiny man of enormous intellect, the author of 54 books. When on one occasion Pope Eugenius IV ordered him to stand—mistakenly thinking him to be still on his knees—the bishop indicated the space between his eyebrows and hairline, retorting, "A man's stature is to be measured from here to here!" ☎ 920/211641. ⌨ 250 ptas. ☉ Daily 10–1:30 and 3:30–6:30.

The 15th-century **Casa de Deanes** (Deans' House) is now a cheerful provincial museum of local archaeology and folklore. It's just a few minutes' walk to the east of the cathedral apse. ☎ 920/211003. ⌨ 200 ptas., weekends free. ☉ Tues.–Sat. 10:30–2 and 5–7:30, Sun. 11–2.

The museum in the **Convento de San José** (or de Las Madres), east of the cathedral, displays the musical instruments used by St. Teresa and her nuns at Christmas. Teresa herself specialized in percussion. ☎ 920/222127. ⌨ 50 ptas. ☉ Spring–fall, daily 10–1:30 and 3–6; summer, daily 9:30–1 and 4–7.

North of Ávila's cathedral, on Plaza de San Vincente, is the much-venerated Romanesque **Basílica de San Vicente** (Basilica of St. Vincent), founded on the supposed site where St. Vincent was martyred in 303, together with his sisters Sts. Sabina and Cristeta. The west front, shielded by a narthex, has damaged but expressive Romanesque carvings depicting the death of Lazarus and the parable of the rich man's table. The sarcophagus of St. Vincent, surrounded with delicate carvings from this period, forms the centerpiece of the basilica's Romanesque interior; the extraordinary, Asian-looking canopy that rises over the sarcophagus is a 15th-century addition paid for by the Knights of Ávila. ☎ 920/255230. ⌨ 100 ptas. ☉ Daily 10–2 and 4–7:30.

On Calle de Lopez Nuñez, the elegant chapel of **Mosen Rubi** (circa 1516) is illuminated by Renaissance stained glass by Nicolás de Holanda. Try to persuade the nuns in the adjoining convent to let you inside.

At the bottom of the town's surrounding walls, just above the river, is the small, Romanesque **Ermita de San Segundo** (Hermitage of St. Secundus). This is an enchanting farmyard, nearly hidden by poplars. Founded on the site where the remains of St. Secundus (a follower of St. Peter) were reputedly discovered, the hermitage houses a realistic marble monument to the saint, carved by Juan de Juni. ⌨ Tip caretaker in adjoining house, where you may have to ask for key. ☉ Spring–fall, daily 4:30–6; summer, daily 4–6.

Inside the south wall on Calle Dama, the **Convento de Santa Teresa** was founded in the 17th century on the site of the saint's birthplace. Her famous written account of an ecstatic vision she had, in which an angel pierced her heart, would influence many baroque artists, most famously the Italian sculptor Giovanni Bernini. The convent has a small museum, with relics including one of Teresa's fingers, and you can also see the small and rather gloomy garden where she played as a child. ☎ 920/211030. ⌨ Free. ☉ Daily 9:30–1:30 and 3:30–7:30.

The **Convento de la Encarnación** is where St. Teresa first took orders and was then based for more than 30 years. Its museum has an interesting drawing of the crucifixion by her disciple St. John of the Cross, as well as a reconstruction of the cell she used when she was a prioress here. The convent is outside the walls in the north part of town, on the Paseo de la Encarnación. ☎ 920/211212. ☒ 150 ptas. ☉ May–Sept., daily 9:30–1 and 4–7; Oct.–Apr., daily 9:30–1:30 and 3:30–6.

The most interesting architectural monument on Ávila's outskirts is the **Monasterio de Santo Tomás.** A good 10-minute walk from the walls among blackened housing projects, it's not where you would expect to find one of the most important religious institutions in Castile. The monastery was founded by Ferdinand and Isabella with the financial assistance of the notorious Inquisitor-General Tomás de Torquemada, who is buried in the sacristy. Further funds were provided by the confiscated property of converted Jews who ran afoul of the Inquisition. Three decorated cloisters lead to the church; inside, a masterly high altar (circa 1506) by Pedro Berruguete overlooks a serene marble tomb by the Italian artist Domenico Fancelli. This influential work, one of the earliest examples of the Italian Renaissance style in Spain, was built for Prince Juan, the only son of Ferdinand and Isabella, who died at 19 while a student at Salamanca University. After Juan's burial here, his heartbroken parents found themselves unable to return to the institution they had founded. In happier times, they had frequently attended mass here, seated in the upper choir behind a balustrade exquisitely carved with their coats of arms; you can reach the choir from the upper part of the Kings' Cloister. The Museum of Eastern Art contains works collected from Dominican missions in Vietnam. ☎ 920/220400. ☒ Cloister 150 ptas., museum 100 ptas. ☉ Cloister daily 10–1 and 4–7, museum daily 11–1 and 4–6 .

Dining and Lodging

$$ ✕ **El Fogón de Santa Teresa.** Despite its English-language menu, this newly decorated restaurant is less touristy than most others in Ávila. It offers a traditional array of meats and fish. Try the house specialty, *truchas al fogón* (fried trout with ham). ☒ Alemania 7, ☎ no phone. AE, DC, MC, V.

$$ ✕ **El Molino de la Losa.** Few restaurants could have a better or more
★ distinctive situation than this one. Standing in the middle of the River Adaja, with one of the best views of the town walls, it occupies a 15th-century mill, the working mechanism of which has been well preserved and provides much distraction for those seated in the animated bar. Lamb is roasted in a medieval wood oven, and fish comes straight from the river; this is also a good place to try the beans from nearby El Barco (*judías de El Barco*). In the refreshing garden outside is a small playground for children. ☒ Bajada de la Losa 12, ☎ 920/211101 or 920/211102. AE, MC, V. Closed Mon. in winter.

$$ ✕ **Mesón del Rastro.** This restaurant occupies a wing of the medieval Abrantes Palace and has an attractive Castilian interior with exposed stone walls and beams, low lighting, and dark-wood furniture. Once again, try the lamb and the El Barco beans; also worthwhile is the *caldereta de cabrito* (goat stew). The place suffers somewhat from its popularity with tour buses, and service is sometimes slow and impersonal. ☒ Plaza Rastro 1, ☎ 920/211218. AE, DC, MC, V.

$$$$ ☷ **Meliá Palacio de los Velada.** Ávila's top hotel opened in April 1995
★ in a beautifully restored 16th-century palace. In the heart of the city, right beside the cathedral, the Meliá is the perfect spot to relax between sightseeing jaunts. The lovely courtyard has become a popular meeting place. Rooms are modern and comfortable. ☒ Plaza de la Catedral 10, 05001, ☎ 920/255100, 🖷 920/254900. 85 rooms. 2 restaurants, bar, meeting rooms. AE, DC, MC, V.

$$$ ☷ **Parador Nacional Raimundo de Borgoña.** A largely rebuilt medieval castle attached to the town walls, Ávila's parador has the advantage of a garden, from which you can sometimes climb up onto the

ramparts. The decor throughout is warm and finely executed, mostly in tawny tones, and the public rooms are convivial. Guest rooms have terra-cotta tile floors and leather chairs, and their bathrooms are spacious, gleamingly modern, and fashionably designed. ⊠ *Marqués de Canales de Chozas 2, 05001,* ☎ *920/211340,* ℻ *920/226166. 61 rooms. Restaurant, bar, café, meeting room. AE, DC, MC, V.*

$$ 🖭 **Hostal Alcántara.** This small hostel has modest, clean rooms and is just a two-minute walk from the cathedral. ⊠ *Esteban Domingo 11, 05001,* ☎ *920/225003 or 920/223804. 9 rooms. MC, V.*

Sierra de Gredos

⑲ *79 km (50 mi) southwest of Ávila.*

The small C502 route from Ávila follows a road dating from Roman times, when it was used for the transport of oil and flour from Ávila in exchange for potatoes and wood. In winter, the Sierra de Gredos, Castile's most dramatic mountain range, gives the region a majestic, snowy backdrop. You can enjoy extensive views from the **Puerto del Pico** (4,435 ft); soon after descending, you'll see below you a perfectly preserved stretch of the Roman road, zigzagging down into the valley and crossing the modern road every now and then. Today it is used by hikers, as well as by shepherds transporting their flocks to lower pastures in early December.

Lodging

$$$ 🖭 **Parador Nacional de Gredos.** Built in 1926 on a site chosen by Alfonso XIII, this was the first parador in Spain. It was enlarged in 1941 and again in 1975. Though modern, the stone architecture has a sturdy, traditional look and blends well with the magnificent surroundings. The rooms are standard parador, with heavy, dark furniture and light walls, and over half have excellent views of the Sierra. The parador is the ideal base for a hiking or climbing jaunt. ⊠ *Carretera Barraco-Béjar, 05132,* ☎ *920/348048,* ℻ *920/348205. 77 rooms. Restaurant, meeting room. AE, DC, MC, V.*

Outdoor Activities and Sports

HIKING AND MOUNTAINEERING

Castile's best area for both hiking and mountaineering is the **Sierra de Gredos.** You can base yourself at the Parador Nacional de Gredos (☞ *above*); the range also has six mountain huts with limited accommodations and facilities. For information on huts and on mountaineering in general, contact the Federación Española de Montañismo (Spanish Mountaineering Federation, ☎ 93/426–4267, in Barcelona).

SKIING

Skiing is popular in the Sierra de Gredos and in the Guadarrama resorts of La Pinilla (Segovia), Navacerrada (Madrid), Valdesqui (Madrid), and Valcotos (Madrid). You can get information on ski conditions from **ATUDEM** (☎ 91/350–2020), but it's better to call the slope you're considering. General information is available from **Federación Madrileña de Deportes de Invierno** (Madrid Federation of Winter Sports, ☎ 91/547–0101).

Arenas de San Pedro

⑳ *143 km (89 mi) west of Madrid.*

This medieval town is surrounded by pretty villages such as Mombeltrán, Guisando, and Candeleda, where wooden balconies are decorated with flowers. A colorful sight in Candeleda are wicker baskets filled with pimientos for sale. Guisando, incidentally, has nothing to do with the famous stone bulls of that name, 60 km (37 mi) to the east.

San Martín de Valdeiglesias

㉑　*73 km (45 mi) west of Madrid.*

The **Toros de Guisando** are stone bulls dating from the 6th century BC, thought to have been used as land markers on the frontier of a Celto-Iberian tribe. Just three of many such bulls once scattered around the Castilian countryside, they take their name from the nearby Cerro Guisando (Guisando Hill) and are now a symbol of the Spanish Tourist Board. To see these taurine effigies, head back east from Arenas on the C501 to this town; it's a pleasant drive through countryside bordered to the north by the Gredos range. Just 6 km (4 mi) before San Martín, on the right side of the road, is a stone inscription in front of a hedge; this marks the site where, in 1468, Isabella the Catholic was acknowledged by the assembled Castilian nobility as rightful successor to Henry IV. On the other side of the hedge stand the forlorn stone bulls, whose rustic setting gives them an undeniable pathos and power.

SALAMANCA AND ITS PROVINCE

Salamanca and Ciudad Rodrigo

Salamanca's radiant sandstone buildings and immense Plaza Mayor make it one of the most attractive cities in Spain. Today, as it did centuries ago, the university predominates and creates a stimulating atmosphere. About an hour from here are the preserved medieval walls of Ciudad Rodrigo, an interesting town with fewer tourists.

Salamanca

★　**㉒**　*205 km (125 mi) northwest of Madrid.*

If you approach from Madrid or Ávila, you'll first see Salamanca rising on the northern banks of the wide and murky River Tormes. In the foreground is its sturdy 15-arch Roman bridge; above this, dominating the view, soars the bulk of the old and new cathedrals. Piercing the skyline to the right is the Renaissance monastery and church of San Esteban, the city's second most prominent ecclesiastical structure. Behind San Esteban and the cathedrals, and largely out of sight from the river, extends a stunning series of palaces, convents, and university buildings that culminates in the Plaza Mayor, one of the most elegant squares in Spain. Despite considerable damage over the centuries, Salamanca remains one of Spain's greatest cities architecturally, a showpiece of the Spanish Renaissance. It is the golden sandstone, which seems to glow throughout the city, that you will remember above all things after leaving.

Already an important settlement in Iberian times, Salamanca was captured by Hannibal in 217 BC and later flourished as a major Roman station on the road between Mérida and Astorga. Converted to Christianity by at least the end of the 6th century, it later passed back and forth between Christians and Moors and began to experience prolonged stability only after the Reconquest of Toledo in 1085. The town's later importance was due largely to its university, which grew out of a college founded around 1220 by Alfonso IV of León.

Salamanca thrived in the 15th and early 16th centuries, and the number of students at its university rose to almost 10,000. Its greatest royal benefactor was Isabella, who generously financed both the magnificent New Cathedral and the rebuilding of the university. A dual portrait of Isabella and Ferdinand is incorporated into the facade of the main university building to commemorate her patronage.

Nearly all of Salamanca's other outstanding Renaissance buildings bear the five-star crest of the all-powerful and ostentatious Fonseca family. The most famous Fonseca, Alonso de Fonseca I, was the archbishop of Santiago and then of Seville; he was also a notorious womanizer and one of the patrons of the Spanish Renaissance.

Both Salamanca and its university began to decline in the early 17th century, corrupted by ultraclericalism and devastated by a flood in 1626. Some of the town's former glory was recovered in the 18th century, with the construction of the Plaza Mayor by the native Churrigueras, who were among the most influential architects of the Spanish baroque. The town suffered in the Peninsular War of the early 19th century and was damaged by ugly, modern development initiated by Franco after the civil war; but the university has revived in recent years and is again one of the most prestigious in Europe.

A Good Walk

A good walk in Salamanca starts at the Puente Romano, goes north to the Plaza Mayor, and finishes at the church of San Estebán.

In terms of both chronology and available parking space, the well-preserved **Puente Romano** ㉓ makes a good starting point for your tour. This is a quiet, evocatively decayed part of town, with a strong rural character. After crossing the bridge, head up the sloping, cobblestone Puerta del Rio and make your way up to the old and new **cathedrals** ㉔, built side by side. Across the Plaza Anaya is the neoclassic Colegio de Anaya, which now houses the university's philosophy department. If you face the New Cathedral from the Plaza, the back of the main building of the **universidad** ㉕ is ahead and to your right, facing the cathedral's west facade. Walk between the two down Calle Cardenal Pla y Deniel, turn right on Calle de Calderón de la Barca, then right again on Calle de Los Libreros, and you'll come into the enchanting quadrangle known as the Patio de Las Escuelas. The main university building (Escuelas Mayores) is to your right, while surrounding the square is the Escuelas Menores, built in the early 16th century as a secondary school preparing candidates for the university proper. In the middle of the square is a modern statue of the 16th-century poet and philosopher Fay Luis de León, one of the greatest teachers in the history of the university. On the far side of the Patio is the entrance to the **Museo de Salamanca.**

If you walk north from the Patio de Las Escuelas on Calle de Los Libreros, then bear right onto Rua Antigua, you can't miss the **Casa de Las Conchas** ㉖. Turn left at Calle de Compañía toward the **Palacio de Monterrey** ㉗. Off to the left of the palace, follow Calle de Ramón y Cajal to the **Colegio Mayor Arzobispo Fonseca** ㉘. Walk back east through the Campo de San Francisco. On the corner of Calle Las Ursulas and Calle Bordadores is the **Convento de Las Ursulas** ㉙. Farther ahead on Calle Bordadores is the bizarre **Casa de Las Muertes** ㉚.

Walk east along Calle del Prior to the **Plaza Mayor** ㉛, the center of town. South of the plaza, on Calle de San Pablo, is the Torre del Clavero, a late-15th-century tower topped by fantastic battlements built for the *clavero* (key warden) of the order of Alcántara. Farther down, the Palacio de La Salina is another Fonseca palace designed by Rodrigo Gil de Hontañón. Try to pop inside for a glimpse of the courtyard, where a projecting gallery is supported by wooden consoles carved with expressive nudes and other dynamic forms.

Walking south on Calle de San Pablo and bearing left, you'll circle the Dominican **Convento de las Dueñas** ㉜. Facing the Dueñas, up a monumental flight of steps, is the **Convento de San Estéban** ㉝.

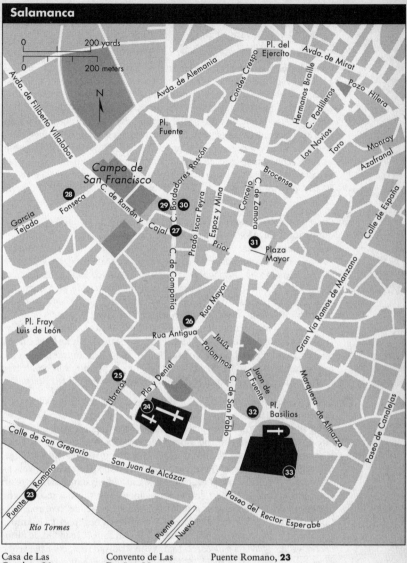

Salamanca

Casa de Las
Conchas, **26**

Casa de Las
Muertes, **30**

Cathedrals, **24**

Colegio Mayor
Arzobispo Fonseca/
Colegio de los
Irlandeses, **28**

Convento de Las
Dueñas, **32**

Convento de Las
Ursulas, **29**

Palacio de
Monterrey, **27**

Plaza Mayor, **31**

Puente Romano, **23**

San Estéban, **33**

Universidad, **25**

TIMING

The length of this walk depends on how much time you spend at each sight, but you'll want to allow at least half a day.

Sights to See

㉖ Casa de Las Conchas (House of Shells). This house was built around 1500 for Dr. Rodrigo Maldonado de Talavera, a professor of medicine at the university and a doctor at the court of Isabella. The scallop motif was a reference to Talavera's status as chancellor of the Order of Santiago, whose symbol is the shell. Among the playful plateresque details are the lions over the main entrance, engaged in a fearful tug-of-war with the Talavera crest. The interior has been converted into a public library. Duck into the charming courtyard, which has an upper balustrade carved with virtuoso intricacy in imitation of basketwork. ⊠ *C. Compañía 2,* ☎ *923/269317.* ⊠ *Free.* ☉ *Weekdays 9–9, weekends 10–2 and 4–7.*

㉚ Casa de Las Muertes (House of the Dead). Built in about 1513 for the majordomo of Alonso de Fonseca II, the house received its name on account of the four tiny skulls that adorn its top two windows. Alonso de Fonseca II commissioned them to commemorate his deceased uncle, the licentious archbishop who lies in the Convento de Las Ursulas, across the street (☞ *below*). For the same reason, the facade also bears the archbishop's portrait. The small square in front of the house was a favorite haunt of the poet, philosopher, and university rector Miguel de Unamuno, whose statue stands here. At the outbreak of the Civil War, Unamuno supported the Nationalists under Franco, but he later turned against them. Placed under virtual house arrest, Unamuno died in the house next door in 1938. During the Franco period, students often daubed his statue red to suggest that his heart still bled for Spain.

㉔ Cathedrals. For a complete tour of the old and new buildings' exterior (an arduous 10-minute walk), circle the complex counterclockwise. Near the river stands the **Catedral Vieja** (Old Cathedral), built in the late 12th century, one of the most interesting examples of the Spanish Romanesque. Because the dome of the crossing tower features strange, plumelike ribbing, it is known as the Torre del Gallo (the rooster's tower). The much larger **Catedral Nueva** (New Cathedral) dates mainly from the 16th century, though some parts, including the dome over the crossing and the bell tower attached to the west facade, had to be rebuilt after the Lisbon earthquake of 1755. Work began in 1513 under the direction of the distinguished late-Gothic architect Juan Gil de Hontañón; as at Segovia's cathedral, Juan's son Rodrigo took over the work after his father's death in 1526. Of the many outstanding architects in 16th-century Salamanca, Rodrigo Gil de Hontañón left the greatest mark, as one of the leading exponents of the classical plateresque. The New Cathedral's north facade (where the main entrance is) is ornamental enough, but the west facade is dazzling in its sculptural complexity. Try to come here in the late afternoon, when the sun shines directly on it.

The interior of the New Cathedral is as light and harmonious as that of Segovia's cathedral, but larger. Here you are treated to a triumphant baroque conception designed by the Churrigueras. The wooden choir seems almost alive with anxiously active cherubim and saints. From a door in the south aisle, steps descend into the Old Cathedral, where boldly carved capitals supporting the vaulting feature a range of foliage, strange animals, and touches of pure fantasy. Then comes the dome, which seems to owe much to Byzantine architecture; it's a remarkably light structure raised on two tiers of arcaded openings. Not the least of the Old Cathedral's attractions are its furnishings, including sepulchres from the 12th and 13th centuries and a magnificent, curved high altar comprising 53 colorful and delicate scenes by the mid-15th-century artist Nicolás Florentino. In the apse above, Florentino painted an astonishingly fresh Last Judgment fresco.

From the south transept of the Old Cathedral, a door leads into the cloister, begun in 1177. From about 1230 until the construction of the main university building in the early 15th century, the chapels around the cloister served as classrooms for the university students. In the chapel of St. Barbara, on the eastern side, theology students answered the grueling questions meted out by their doctoral examiners. The chair in which they sat is still there, in front of a recumbent effigy of Bishop Juan Lucero, on whose head the students would place their feet for inspiration. Also attached to the cloister is a small cathedral museum with a 15th-century triptych of St. Catherine by Salamanca's greatest native artist, Fernando Gallego. ☎ 923/217476. ▣ *New Cathedral free, Old Cathedral 300 ptas.* ◔ *New Cathedral daily 10–1 and 4–6, Old Cathedral daily 10–12:30 and 4–5:30.*

㉘ Colegio Mayor Arzobispo Fonseca/Colegio de Los Irlandeses. (Irish College). This small college was founded by Alonso de Fonseca II in 1521 to train young Irish priests. Today it is a residence hall for guest lecturers at the university. The surroundings are not attractive; this part of town was the most severely damaged during the Peninsular War of the early 19th century, and still has a slightly derelict character. The interior of the building, however, is a treat. Immediately inside to the right is an elegant and spacious late-Gothic chapel, while beyond is one of the most classical and genuinely Italianate of Salamanca's many beautiful courtyards. The architect may have been Diego de Siloe, Spain's answer to Michelangelo. ▢ *C. Fonseca 4,* ☎ *923/294570.* ▣ *100 ptas.* ◔ *Daily 10–2 and 4–6.*

㉜ Convento de Las Dueñas (Convent of the Dames). Founded in 1419, this convent contains a 16th-century cloister that is the most fantastically decorated in Salamanca, if not in the whole of Spain. The capitals of its two superimposed Salamantine arcades are crowded with a baffling profusion of grotesques that could absorb you for hours. There's another good reason to come here: the nuns make and sell excellent sweets and pastries. ▢ *C. Plaza Concilio de Trento s/n,* ☎ *923/ 215442.* ▣ *200 ptas.* ◔ *Daily 10:30–1 and 4:30–7.*

㉙ Convento de Las Ursulas (Convent of the Ursulines). Archbishop Alonso de Fonseca I lies here, in a splendid marble tomb created by Diego de Siloe during the first half of the 16th century. ▢ *C. Las Ursulas 2,* ☎ *923/219877.* ▣ *100 ptas.* ◔ *Daily 10–1 and 4:30–7.*

㉝ Convento de San Estéban (Convent of St. Stephen). The vast size of this building is a measure of its importance in Salamanca's history: its monks, among the most enlightened teachers at the university, were the first to take Columbus's ideas seriously and helped him gain his introduction to Isabella (hence his statue in the nearby Plaza de Colón, back toward Calle de San Pablo). The complex was designed by one of San Estebán's monks, Juan de Alava. The door to the right of the west facade leads you into a gloomy cloister with Gothic arcading, interrupted by tall, spindly columns adorned with classical motifs. From the cloister, you enter the church at its eastern end. The interior is unified and uncluttered, but also dark and severe. The one note of color is provided by the sumptuously ornate and gilded high altar of 1692, a baroque masterpiece by José Churriguera. The most exciting feature of San Estebán, though, is the massive west facade, a thrilling plateresque work in which sculpted figures and ornamentation are piled up to a height of more than 98 ft. ✉ *Plaza de San Estebán s/n,* ☏ *923/215000.* 🎫 *200 ptas.* ☉ *Daily 9–1 and 4–7.*

Museo Art Nouveau y Art Deco. Opened to the public in 1995, the museum is housed in the Casa Lis, a modernist building from the end of the 19th century. On display are 19th-century paintings and glass, as well as French and German china dolls, Viennese bronze statues, furniture, jewelry, enamels, and jars. Note: here and at the university you can buy a 500-pta. *conjunto* (joint ticket) for admission to this museum, the university, the Museum of Salamanca, and the Irish College. ✉ *C. Gibraltar 14,* ☏ *923/121425.* ☉ *Tues.–Fri. 11–2 and 4–7, weekends 11–8.*

Museo de Salamanca (also Museo de Bellas Artes). Consisting mainly of minor 17th- and 18th-century paintings, this museum is also interesting for its 15th-century building, which belonged to Isabella's physician, Alvárez Abarca. ✉ *Patio de Escuelas Menores s/n,* ☏ *923/212235.* 🎫 *200 ptas.* ☉ *Tues.–Fri. 9:30–2 and 5–8, Sat. 10–2 and 4:30–7:30, Sun. 10–2.*

㉗ **Palacio de Monterrey** (Palace of Monterrey). Built after 1538 by Rodrigo Gil de Hontañón, this palace was meant for an illegitimate son of Alonso de Fonseca I. Only one of its four wings was completed, but this one alone makes the palace one of the most imposing in Salamanca. As in Rodrigo's other local palaces, the building is flanked on each side by towers and has an open arcaded gallery running the whole length of the upper level. Such galleries—which in Italy you would expect to see on the ground floor—are common in Spanish Renaissance palaces and were intended as areas where the women of the house could exercise unseen and undisturbed. They also helped to cool the floor below during the summer months. The palace is privately owned and not open to visitors, but you can stroll around the exterior. ✉ *C. de Comañía s/n.*

㉛ **Plaza Mayor.** Built in the 1730s by Alberto and Nicolás Churriguera, Salamanca's Plaza Mayor is one of the largest squares in Spain, and many find it the most beautiful. Its northern side is dominated by the grandly elegant, pinkish **ayuntamiento** (town hall). The square and its arcades are popular gathering spots for most of Salamancan society, and indeed, the many surrounding cafés make this the perfect spot for a coffee break.

㉓ **Puente Romano** (Roman Bridge). Next to the bridge is an Iberian stone bull, and opposite the bull is a statue commemorating Lazarillo de Tormes, the young hero of the eponymous (and anonymous) 16th-century work that is one of the masterpieces of Spanish literature.

㉕ **Universidad** (University). The university's walls, like those of the cathedral and other structures in Salamanca, are covered with large, ocher lettering recording the names of famous university graduates. The earliest names are said to have been written in the blood of the bulls killed to celebrate the successful completion of a doctorate.

The **Escuelas Mayores** (Major Schools) dates to 1415, but it was not until more than 100 years later that an unknown architect provided the building with its gloriously elaborate frontispiece, generally acknowledged as one of the finest works of the classical plateresque. Immediately above the main door is the famous double portrait of Isabella and Ferdinand, surrounded by ornamentation that plays on the yoke-and-arrow heraldic motifs of the two monarchs. The double-eagle crest of Charles V, flanked by portraits of the emperor and empress in classical guise, dominates the middle layer of the frontispiece. On the highest layer is a panel recently identified as representing Pope Martin V (one of the university's greatest benefactors), accompanied by cardinals and university rectors. The whole is crowned by a characteristically elaborate plateresque balustrade.

The interior of the Escuelas Mayores, which has been drastically restored in parts, comes as a slight disappointment after the splendor of the facade. But the *aula* (lecture hall) of Fray Luis de León, where Cervantes, Calderón de la Barca, and numerous other luminaries of Spain's golden age once sat, is of particular interest. Here Fray Luis, returning after five years' imprisonment for having translated the *Song of Solomon* into Spanish, began his lecture, "As I was saying yesterday . . ."

Your ticket to visit the Escuelas Mayores permits entrance to the nearby **Escuelas Menores** (Minor Schools), built in the early 16th century as a secondary school preparing candidates for the university proper. Passing through a gate crowned with the double-eagle crest of Charles V, you'll come to a green, on the other side of which is a modern building housing a fascinating ceiling fresco of the zodiac, originally in the library of the main university building. This painting, a fragment of a much larger whole, is generally attributed to Fernando Gallego. Note: at the university and the Museum of Art Nouveau and Art Deco, you can buy a 500-pta. *conjunto* (joint ticket) for admission to the university, the Museum of Art Nouveau and Art Deco, the Museum of Salamanca, and the Irish College. ☎ 923/294400, ext. 1150. ⌦ 300 ptas. ☉ Weekdays 9:30–1:30 and 4–7:30, Sat. 9:30–1:30 and 4–7, Sun. 10–1.

Dining and Lodging

$$$ ✕ **Chez Victor.** If you're tired of traditional Castilian cuisine, try this chic restaurant. Owner and cook Victoriano Salvador learned his trade in France and adapts French food to Spanish taste, with whimsical touches all his own. Try *patatas rellenas de bacalao* (potatoes stuffed with salt cod) and ravioli *rellenos de marisco* (stuffed with shellfish). Desserts are outstanding, especially the chocolate ones. ⌧ *Espoz y Mina 26*, ☎ 923/213123. AE, DC, MC, V. Closed Sun. July and Aug.

$$–$$$ ✕ **Rio de la Plata.** This tiny basement restaurant, just off Calle de San Pablo, has been in business since 1958 and retains an old-fashioned character. The elegant, gilded decor is a pleasant change of scenery, and the fireplace and local crowd provide warmth. The food is simple but carefully prepared, with good-quality fish and meat. ⌧ *Plaza Peso 1*, ☎ 923/219005. AE, MC, V. Closed Mon. and July.

$$ ✕ **La Aldaba.** This new restaurant is tastefully decorated in a country style, with stone walls, a skylight, and a wood-beamed ceiling. Friendly owners, good food, and a cozy ambience make for a special meal, often centering around the meat from local Cabracho cows. The *carne de Cabracho* is served as *chuletón* (flank steak), *solomillo* (loin), or *carpaccio* (thinly sliced, uncooked, marinated meat). The *alcachofas rellenas* (stuffed artichokes) are also excellent. ⌧ *Felipe Espino 6, 37001*, ☎ 923/212779. AE, MC, V.

$$$$ ⊞ **Gran Hotel.** The grande dame of Salamanca's hotels offers stylishly baroque lounges and refurbished yet old-fashioned oversize rooms, just steps from the Plaza Mayor. ⌧ *Plaza Poeta Iglesias 3, 37001*, ☎ 923/213500, ℻ 923/213501. 140 rooms. Restaurant, bar. AE, DC, MC, V.

$$$$ ⊞ **Palacio del Castellanos.** Opened in 1992 in an immaculately restored 15th-century palace, this hotel is a much-needed alternative to Salamanca's parador (probably the ugliest in the chain). There's an exquisite interior patio and an equally beautiful restaurant, as well as a lovely terrace overlooking San Esteban. ⌧ *San Pablo 58*, ☎ 923/261818, ℻ 923/261819. 69 rooms. Restaurant. AE, DC, MC, V.

$$$$ 🏨 **Rector.** This beautiful hotel is a true European experience, from the elegant front gate to the high-ceilinged rooms. The sitting areas, hallways, and breakfast room are all spotless, spacious, and warm, yet even more remarkable is the service: the owners, clerks, and porters are all incredibly friendly and will devote themselves to your every whim. Take advantage of their willingness to tell you all about Salamanca. You'll feel like you're staying with family—in high places. ✉ *Rector Esperabé 10,* ☎ *923/218482,* FAX *923/214008. 14 rooms. Bar, breakfast room, in-room faxes. AE, DC, MC, V.*

$$ 🏨 **Hostal Plaza Mayor.** You can't beat the location of this great little hostel, just steps from the Plaza Mayor. Completely renovated in 1994, it offers small but modern rooms. Reservations are advisable, as rooms fill up fast. ✉ *Plaza del Corrillo 20, 37008,* ☎ *923/262020,* FAX *923/ 217548. 19 rooms. Restaurant. MC, V.*

Nightlife

The main area for nightclubs is around Calle Bermejeros, but for a fashionable bar-discotheque, try **Camelot,** on Calle Bordadores, or **Abadia,** on Rua Mayor.

Shopping

Salamanca has a reputation for fine **leatherwork**; the most traditional shop in town is **Salón Campero** (✉ Plaza Corrillo 5).

Ciudad Rodrigo

③④   *88 km (54 mi) west of Salamanca.*

Apart from Salamanca itself, Ciudad Rodrigo is the most interesting destination in Salamanca's province. Surveying the fertile valley of the River Agueda, this small town has numerous well-preserved palaces and churches and makes an excellent overnight stop on the way from Spain to Portugal.

The **cathedral** combines the Romanesque and Transitional Gothic styles, and holds a great deal of fine sculpture. Take a close look at the early 16th-century choir stalls, elaborately carved with entertaining grotesques by Rodrigo Alemán. The cloister has carved capitals, and the cypresses in its center lend tranquility. The cathedral's outer walls are still scarred by cannonballs fired during the Peninsular War. 🎫 *Cathedral free, museum 250 ptas.* ⏰ *Daily 10–1 and 4–6.*

The town's other chief monument is its fortified medieval **castle,** part of which has been turned into a parador. From here you can climb onto the town's battlements.

Dining and Lodging

$–$$ ✕ **Mayton.** This restaurant has a most engaging interior, backed with wood beams and bursting with a wonderfully eccentric collection of antiques ranging from mortars and pestles to Portuguese yokes and old typewriters. In contrast to the decor, the cooking is simple; the specialties are fish, seafood, goat, and lamb. ✉ *La Colada 9,* ☎ *923/460720. AE, DC, MC, V.*

$$$–$$$$ 🏨 **Parador Nacional Enrique II.** Occupying part of the magnificent castle built by Enrique II of Trastamara to guard over the Agueda Valley, this parador is a series of small, white rooms along the building's sturdy and gently sloping outer walls. Ask for Room 10 if you want one with original vaulting. A special feature throughout the hotel is the under-floor heating in the bathrooms. Some rooms, as well as the restaurant, overlook a beautiful garden that runs down to the River Agueda; beyond the river, the view surveys fertile plains. ✉ *Plaza Castillo 1, 37500,* ☎ *923/460150,* FAX *923/460404. 27 rooms. Restaurant, bar, meeting room. AE, DC, MC, V.*

PROVINCE OF ZAMORA AND CITY OF VALLADOLID

Zamora, Toro, and Valladolid

Zamora is a densely fertile province divided by the River Duero into two distinct zones: the "land of bread," to the north, and the "land of wine," to the south. The area is most interesting for its Romanesque churches, the finest of which are concentrated in the towns of Zamora and Toro. The city of Valladolid, by contrast, is one of the flattest and dreariest spots in the Castilian countryside, but it has the National Museum of Sculpture and plenty of interesting history.

Zamora

③⑤ *248 km (154 mi) northwest of Madrid.*

Zamora, on a bluff above the Duero, is not conventionally beautiful, as its many interesting monuments are isolated from one another by ramshackle 19th- and 20th-century development. It does have lively, old-fashioned character, making it a pleasant stop for a night or two.

In the medieval center of town, on the south side of the Plaza Mayor, is the Romanesque church of **San Juan** (open for mass only), remarkable for its elaborate rose window. North of the Plaza Mayor, at the end of Calle Reina, is one of the town's surviving medieval gates; near here is the Romanesque church of **Santa María.**

Zamora is famous for its Holy Week celebrations. The **Museo de Semana Santa** (Museum of Holy Week) houses the processional sculptures paraded around the streets during that time. Of relatively recent date, these works have an appealing provincial quality; you'll find, for instance, a Crucifixion group filled with what appears to be the contents of a hardware store, including bales of rope, a saw, a spade, and numerous nails. The museum is located in a hideous modern building next to the church of Santa María. ▣ *300 ptas. ☉ Mon.–Sat. 10–2 and 4–7 (4–8 in summer), Sun. and holidays 10–2.*

Zamora's **cathedral** is in a hauntingly attractive square, situated at the highest and westernmost point of old Zamora. The bulk of the cathedral is Romanesque, and the most remarkable feature of the exterior is its dome, which is flanked by turrets, articulated by spiny ribs, and covered in overlapping stones, like scales. The dark interior is notable for its early 16th-century choir stalls. The austere, late-16th-century cloister has a small museum upstairs, with an intricate *custodia* (monstrance, or receptacle for the Host) by Juan de Arce and some badly displayed but intriguing Flemish tapestries from the 15th and 16th centuries. ▣ *300 ptas. ☉ Mon. 4–6, Tues.–Sat. 11–2 and 4–7 (5–8 in summer), Sun. 11–2.*

Surrounding Zamora's cathedral to the north is an attractive park incorporating the town's heavily restored **castle.** Calle Trascastillo, descending south from the cathedral to the river, affords views of the fertile countryside to the south and the town's **old Roman bridge.**

Lodging

$$$$ ⚏ **Parador Nacional Condes de Alba y Aliste.** This restored Renaissance palace is central yet quiet, in an historic building with a distinctive patio adorned with classical medallions of mythological and historical personages. The views are excellent, and the staff is friendly and resourceful. ✉ *Plaza Viriato 5, 49001, ☎ 980/514497, ℻ 980/530063. 52 rooms. Restaurant, bar, pool. AE, DC, MC, V.*

Toro

36 *33 km (20 mi) east of Zamora, 272 km (169 mi) northwest of Madrid.*

Standing above a loop of the River Duero and commanding extensive views over the vast plain to the south, Toro was also a provincial capital at one time. In 1833, however, it was absorbed into Zamora's province in a loss of status that worked in some ways to its advantage. Zamora developed into a thriving modern town, but Toro slumbered and preserved its old appearance. The town is crowded with Romanesque churches, of which the most important is the **Colegiata,** begun in 1160. The protected west portal, or Portico de La Gloria, has a colorfully painted, perfectly preserved statuary from the early 13th century. The Serbian-Byzantine dome is also prominent. In the sacristy is an anonymous 15th-century painting of the Virgin; this touching work, in the so-called Hispano-Flemish style, is titled *The Virgin of the Fly* because of the fly painted on the Virgin's robe, a rather unusual detail. ✉ *Free.* ⊙ *Summer, Tues.–Sun. 11–1:30 and 5–7:30; winter, Tues.–Sun. 11:30–1:15 and 7:30–8:30; Mon. open for mass only.*

Valladolid

37 *96 km (60 mi) east of Zamora, 193 km (120 mi) northwest of Madrid.*

★ Modern Valladolid is a large, dirty, and singularly ugly modern city in the middle of one of Castile's dullest stretches. It has one outstanding attraction, however—the **Museo Nacional de Escultura** (National Museum of Sculpture)—and many other interesting sights. It is also one of the most important cities in Spain's history. Ferdinand and Isabella were married here, Philip II was born and baptized here, and Philip III made Valladolid the capital of Spain for six years.

To cope with the chaos, take a taxi—from the bus station, train station, or wherever you parked your car—and head for the National Museum of Sculpture, at the northernmost point of the old town. The late-15th-century Colegio de San Gregorio, in which the museum is housed, is a masterpiece of the so-called Isabelline or Gothic plateresque, an ornamental style of exceptional intricacy featuring playful, naturalistic detail. The facade is especially fantastic, with ribs in the form of pollarded trees, sprouting branches, and—to punctuate the forest motif—a row of wild men bearing mighty clubs.

The museum is arranged in rooms off an elaborate, arcaded courtyard. Its collections do for Spanish sculpture what those in the Prado do for Spanish painting; the only difference is that most people have heard of Velázquez, El Greco, Goya, and Murillo, whereas few are familiar with Alonso de Berruguete, Juan de Juni, and Gregorio Fernández, the three great names represented here.

Attendants and directional cues encourage you to tour the museum in chronological order. Begin on the ground floor, with Alonso de Berruguete's remarkable sculptures from the dismantled high altar in the Valladolid church of San Benito (1532). Berruguete, who trained in Italy under Michelangelo, is the most widely appreciated of Spain's postmedieval sculptors. He strove for pathos rather than realism, and his works have an extraordinarily expressive quality. The San Benito altar was the most important commission of his life, and the fragments here allow you to scrutinize his powerfully emotional art. In the museum's elegant chapel (which you normally see at the end of the tour) is a Berruguete retable from 1526, his first known work; on either side kneel gilded bronze figures by the Italian-born Pompeo Leoni, whose polished and highly decorative art is diametrically opposed to that of Berruguete.

Many critics of Spanish sculpture feel that decline set in with the late-16th-century artist Juan de Juni, who used glass for eyes and pearls for tears. Juni's many admirers, however, find his works intensely exciting, and they are in any case the highlights of the museum's upper floor. Many of the 16th-, 17th-, and 18th-century sculptures on this floor were originally paraded around the streets during Valladolid's celebrated Easter processions; should you ever attend one of these thrilling pageants, the power of Spanish baroque sculpture will be instantly clear.

Dominating Castilian sculpture of the 17th century was the Galician-born Gregorio Fernández, in whose works the dividing line between sculpture and theater becomes tenuous. Respect for Fernández has been diminished by the number of vulgar imitators that his work has spawned, even up to the present day, but at Valladolid you can see his art at its best. The enormous, dramatic, and moving sculptural groups that have been assembled in the museum's last series of rooms (on the ground floor near the entrance) form a suitably spectacular climax to this fine collection. ⊠ *C. Cadenas San Gregorio 1,* ☎ *983/250375.* 🎫 *400 ptas., free Sat. afternoon and Sun.* ☉ *Tues.–Sat. 10–2 and 4–6, Sun. 10–2.*

Philip II's birthplace is a brick mansion on the Plaza de San Pablo, at the corner of Calle Angustias. The late-15th-century church of **San Pablo** has another overwhelmingly elaborate facade.The city's **cathedral,** however, is disappointing. Though its foundations were laid in late-Gothic times, the building owes much of its appearance to designs executed in the late 16th century by Juan de Herrera, the architect of the Escorial. Further work was carried out by Alberto de Churriguera in the early 18th century, but the building is still only a fraction of its intended size. The Juni altarpiece is the one bit of color and life in an otherwise visually chilly place. ☎ *983/304362.* 🎫 *Cathedral free, museum 250 ptas.* ☉ *Tues.–Fri. 10–1:30 and 4:30–7, weekends 10–2.*

The main **university** building sits opposite the green space just south of the cathedral. The exuberant and dynamic late-baroque frontispiece is by Narciso Tomé, creator of the remarkable *Transparente* in Toledo's cathedral. Calle Librería leads south from the main university building to the magnificent **Colegio de Santa Cruz,** a large university college begun in 1487 in the Gothic style and completed in 1491 by Lorenzo Vázquez in a tentative and pioneering Renaissance mode. Inside is a harmonious courtyard.

The house where Columbus died, in 1506, has been extensively rebuilt and is open to visitors; inside, the excellent **Museo de Colón** (Columbus Museum) has a well-arranged collection of objects, models, and informational panels illuminating the life and times of the explorer. ⊠ *C. Colón,* ☎ *983/291353.* 🎫 *Free.* ☉ *Tues.–Sat. 10–2 and 4–6 (5–7 in summer), Sun. 10:30–2.*

A more interesting remnant of Spain's golden age is the tiny house where the writer Miguel de Cervantes lived from 1603 to 1606. A haven of peace set back from a noisy thoroughfare, **Casa de Cervantes** (Cervantes' House) is best reached by taxi. Furnished in the early 20th century in a pseudo-Renaissance style by the Marquis of Valle-Inclan—the creator of the El Greco Museum in Toledo—it has a cozy atmosphere. ⊠ *C. Rastro s/n,* ☎ *983/308810.* 🎫 *400 ptas., free on Sun.* ☉ *Tues.–Sat. 10–3:30, Sun. 10–3.*

Dining and Lodging

$$$ ✕ **La Fragua.** In a modern building with a traditional Castilian interior of white walls and wood-beamed ceilings, Valladolid's most famous and stylish restaurant counts members of the Spanish royal family among its guests. Specialties include meat roasted in a wood oven

and such imaginative dishes as *rape Castellano Gran Mesón* (breaded monkfish with clams and peppers) and *lengua empiñonada* (tongue coated in pine nuts). ✉ *Paseo Zorrilla 10,* ☎ *983/337102. AE, DC, MC, V. No dinner Sun. Closed Aug.*

$$$$ 🏨 **Valladolid Meliá.** Despite being in the middle of one of Valladolid's oldest and most attractive districts, this hotel sits on a modern block. The building was erected in the early 1970s and completely redecorated in 1994, with blond-wood furniture and new baths. The ground and first floors have a pristine, marbled elegance. ✉ *Plaza de San Miguel 10, 47003,* ☎ *983/357200,* 📠 *983/336828. 211 rooms. Restaurant, bar, cafeteria, meeting room. AE, DC, MC, V.*

Nightlife

Valladolid has a wide range of nightspots. The Zona Francisco Suarez and the Zona Iglesia La Antigua are two districts popular with students. Livelier and more fashionable are the Zona Cantarranas (in particular, the **Atomium**) and the area around the Plaza Mayor.

NORTHEAST OF MADRID

Alcalá de Henares, Guadalajara, Pastrana, Sigüenza, Medinaceli, Soria, Numancia, and El Burgo de Osma

They're off the main tourist tracks, but the provinces of Guadalajara and Soria have a lot to offer and are—for a change—easily accessible by train. The line from Madrid to Zaragoza passes through all of the towns named above, allowing a manageable and interesting excursion of two to three days. If you have a car, you can extend this trip by detouring into beautiful, unspoiled countryside.

Alcalá de Henares

🔟 *30 km (19 mi) east of Madrid.*

Alcalá's past fame was due largely to its university, founded in 1498 by Cardinal Cisneros. In 1836 the university was moved to Madrid, and Alcalá's decline was hastened. The Civil War destroyed much of the town's artistic and architectural heritage, and in recent years Alcalá has emerged as a dormer town for Madrid. Nevertheless, enough survives of old Alcalá to give a good impression of what it must have been like during its golden age.

The town's main monument is its enormous **Universidad Complutense,** built between 1537 and 1553 by the great Rodrigo Gil de Hontañón. (Complutum was Alcalá's Roman name.) Though this is one of Spain's earliest and most important Italian Renaissance buildings, most Italian architects of the time would probably have shrieked in terror at its principal facade. The use of the classical order is all wrong; the main block is out of line with the two that flank it; and the whole is crowned by a heavy and elaborate gallery. All this is typically Spanish, as is the prominence given to the massive crest of Cardinal Cisneros and to the ironwork, both of which form integral parts of the powerful overall design. Inside are three patios, of which the most impressive is the first, comprising three superimposed arcades. A guided tour of the interior takes you to a delightfully decorated room where exams were once held, and to the chapel of San Ildefonso, with its richly sculpted Renaissance mausoleum of Cardinal Cisneros. ✉ *Plaza San Diego s/n.* 🎟 *250 ptas.* 🕐 *Tues.–Fri. 11:30–1:30 and 5–6, weekends 11–2 and 4–7.*

On one side of the university square is the **Convento de San Diego,** where Clarissan nuns make and sell *almendras garrapiñadas* (candy-coated almonds), a town specialty. The other side adjoins the large and arcaded **Plaza de Cervantes,** Alcalá's animated center. Off the plaza runs the arcaded Calle Mayor, which still looks much as it did in the 16th and 17th centuries.

Miguel de Cervantes was born in a house on this street in 1547; a charming replica, **Casa de Cervantes,** built in 1955, contains a small **Cervantes museum.** ⊠ *Calle Mayor 48,* ☎ *91/889–9654.* ⎯ *Free.* ☉ *Weekdays 10–2 and 4–7, weekends 10–2.*

Dining

$$ ✕ **Hostería del Estudiante.** In one of the first buildings acquired by Spain's parador chain, this restaurant is magnificently set around a 15th-century cloister and features wood-beamed ceilings, a large and splendid fireplace, and glass-and-tin lanterns. Appropriate to the traditional setting is the good and simple Castilian food, with roast lamb a particular specialty. ⊠ *Los Colegios 3,* ☎ *91/888–0330. AE, DC, MC, V.*

Guadalajara

㊴   *17 km (10 mi) east of Alcalá, 55 km (34 mi) northeast of Madrid.*

This provincial capital was severely damaged in the Civil War, but its **Palacio del Infantado** (Palace of the Prince's Territory) still stands and is one of the most important Spanish palaces of its period. Built between 1461 and 1492 by Juan Guas, it's a bizarre and potent mix of Gothic, classical, and Mudéjar influences. The main facade is rich; the lower floors are studded with diamond shapes; and the whole is crowned by a complex Gothic gallery supported on a frieze pitted with intricate Moorish cellular work (the honeycomb motif). Inside is a fanciful and exciting courtyard, though little else; the magnificent Renaissance frescoes that once covered the palace's rooms were largely obliterated in the Civil War. On the ground floor is a modest provincial art gallery. ⊠ *Plaza de los Caídos 1.* ⎯ *200 ptas.* ☉ *Tues.–Sat. 10:30–2 and 4:15–7, Sun. 10:30–2.*

En Route   East of Guadalajara extends the Alcarria, an area of high plateau crossed by rivers forming verdant valleys. It was made famous in the 1950s by one of the great classics of Spanish travel literature, Camilo José Cela's *Journey to the Alcarria,* in which Cela evoked the backwardness and remoteness of an area barely an hour from Madrid. Even today you can feel far removed here from the modern world.

Pastrana

㊵   *42 km (26 mi) southeast of Guadalajara.*

High on a hill, Pastrana's narrow lanes merge into the landscape. This is a pretty village of Roman origin, once the capital of a small duchy. The tiny **museum** attached to Pastrana's **Colegiata** (collegiate church) displays a glorious series of Gothic tapestries. ⎯ *125 ptas.* ☉ *Weekends 1–3 and 4–6.*

Sigüenza

㊶   *86 km (54 mi) northeast of Guadalajara.*

Sigüenza, the next major stop on the journey east from Madrid, is one of the most beautiful towns in Castile. Begun around 1150 and not completed until the early 16th century, Sigüenza's remarkable **cathedral** is an anthology of Spanish architecture from the Romanesque period to the Renaissance. The sturdy western front has a forbidding, fortresslike appearance but contains an inviting wealth of ornamental and artistic masterpieces. Go directly to the sacristan (the sacristy is at the north end of the ambulatory) for an informative guided tour. The sacristy is an outstanding Renaissance structure, covered in a barrel vault designed by the great Alonso de Covarrubias; its coffering is studded with hundreds of sculpted heads, which stare at you disarmingly. The tour then takes you into the late-Gothic cloister, off which is a room lined with 17th-century Flemish tapestries. You will also have illuminated for you (in the north transept) the ornate, late-15th-century sepulchre of Dom Fadrique of Portugal, an early example of the classical plateresque. The cathedral's high point is the Chapel of the Doncel (to the right of the sanctuary), in which you'll see Spain's most celebrated funerary monument, the tomb of Don Martín Vázquez de Arca, commissioned by Isabella, to whom Don Martín served as *doncel* (page) before dying young at the gates of Granada in 1486. The reclining Don Martín is lifelike, an open book in his hands and a wistful melancholy in his eyes. More than a memorial to an individual, this tomb, with its surrounding late-Gothic foliage and tiny mourners, is like an epitaph of the Age of Chivalry, a final flowering of the Gothic spirit. ☒ *300 ptas.* ☉ *Daily 11–1 and 4–6 (until 7 in summer).*

In a refurbished early-19th-century house, next to the cathedral's west facade, the **Museo Diocesano de Arte Sacro** (Diocesan Museum of Sacred Art) contains a prehistoric section and much religious art from the 12th to 18th centuries. ☒ *200 ptas.* ☉ *Tues.–Sun. 11–2 and 4:30–6:30 (4:30–7:30 in summer).*

The south side of the cathedral overlooks the arcaded **Plaza Mayor,** a harmonious Renaissance square commissioned by Cardinal Mendoza. The small palaces and cobbled alleys in the area mark the virtually intact Old Quarter. Along Calle Mayor you'll find the palace that belonged to the *doncel's* family. The enchanting **castle** at the top of the street, overlooking wild, hilly countryside from above Sigüenza, is now a parador (☞ Lodging, *below*). Founded by the Romans but rebuilt at various later periods, most of the present structure was put up in the 14th century, when it was transformed into a residence for the queen of Castile, Doña Blanca de Borbón, who was banished here by her husband, Peter the Cruel.

Lodging

$$$–$$$$ 🏨 **Parador Nacional Castillo de Sigüenza.** Of the many castles in the
★   parador chain, this is one of the most impressive and historically significant. At the very top of the town, this mighty, crenellated structure has hosted royalty over the centuries, from Ferdinand and Isabella right up to the present king, Juan Carlos. Some of the rooms have four-poster beds and balconies overlooking the wild landscape. ☒ *Plaza del Castillo s/n, 19250,* ☎ *949/390100,* 𝔽𝔸𝕏 *949/391364. 81 rooms. Restaurant, meeting room, parking. AE, DC, MC, V.*

Medinaceli

㊷ *32 km (20 mi) northeast of Sigüenza.*

The preserved village of Medinaceli commands an exhilarating position on the top of a long, steep ridge. Dominating the skyline is a Roman triumphal arch from the 2nd or 3rd century AD, the only surviving triple archway of this period in Spain. (The arch's silhouette is now featured in signposts to national monuments throughout the country.) The surrounding village, once the seat of one of Spain's most powerful dukes, had virtually been abandoned by its inhabitants by the end of the 19th century, and if you come here during the week you'll find yourself in a near ghost town. Many Madrileños have weekend houses here, and various Americans are also in part-time residence. The place is undeniably beautiful, with extensive views, picturesquely overgrown houses, and unpaved lanes leading directly into wild countryside. The former palace of the dukes of Medinaceli is currently undergoing restoration, and Roman excavations are also being carried out in one of the squares.

Soria

43 *74 km (46 mi) north of Medinaceli, 234 km (145 mi) northeast of Madrid.*

This provincial capital, which has prospered for centuries as a center of sheep farming, has been spoiled by modern development and is frequently beset by cold, biting winds. Yet its situation in the wooded valley of the Duero is splendid, and it has a number of fascinating Romanesque buildings.

Soria has strong connections with Antonio Machado, Spain's most popular 20th-century poet after García Lorca. The Seville-born poet lived a bohemian life in Paris for many years, but he eventually returned to Spain and taught French in Soria from 1909 to 1911. A large bronze head of Machado is displayed outside the **school** where he taught; and his former classroom (now called the Aula Machado) contains a tiny collection of memorabilia. It was in Soria that Machado fell in love with and married the 16-year-old daughter of his landlady, and when she died only two years later, he felt he could no longer stay in a town so full of her memories. He moved on to Baeza, in his native Andalucía, and then went to Segovia, where he spent his last years in Spain (he died early in the civil war, shortly after escaping to France). His most successful work, the *Campos de Castilla,* was greatly inspired by Soria and by his dead wife, Leonor; the town and the woman both haunted him until his death.

The main roads to Soria converge onto the wide, modern promenade El Espolón, where you'll find the **Museo Numantino** (Museum of Numancia). Founded in 1919, the museum contains a collection of local archaeological finds. Few other museums in Spain are laid out quite as well or as spaciously; the collections are rich in prehistoric and Iberian finds, and one section—on the top floor—is dedicated to the important Iberian-Roman settlement at nearby Numancia (☞ *below*). ✉ *C. Polón 8,* ☎ *975/221397.* ⊡ *200 ptas.* ☉ *May–Sept., Tues.–Sat. 9–2 and 5–9, Sun. 9–2; Oct.–Apr., Tues.–Sat. 9–8:30, Sun. 10–2.*

At the top of **Calle Aduana Vieja** is the late-12th-century church of **San Domingo,** with its richly carved, Romanesque west facade. The imposing, 16th-century palace of the counts of Gomara (now a law court) is on Calle Estudios. Dominating the hill just south of the River Dueron is the Antonio Machado parador (☞ Dining and Lodging, *below*), which shares a park with the ruins of the town's castle. Machado loved the views of the town and valley from this hill. Calle de Santiago, which leads to the parador, passes the church and cemetery of El Espino, where Machado's wife, Leonor, is buried. Just before the river is the **cathedral,** a late-Gothic hall church attached to a large Romanesque cloister.

Across the River Dueron from Soria, in a wooded setting overlooking the river, is the deconsecrated church of **San Juan de Duero,** once the property of the Knights Hospitalers. Outside the church are the curious ruins of a Romanesque cloister, featuring a rare Spanish example of interlaced arching. The church itself, now looked after by the Museo

Numantino, is a small, didactic museum of Romanesque art and architecture. ▨ *100 ptas.* ☉ *Winter, Tues.–Sat. 10–2 and 4–6, Sun. 10–2; summer, Tues.–Sat. 10–2 and 5–9, Sun. 10–2.*

Take an evocative, half-hour walk along the Duero River to the **Ermita (Hermitage) de San Saturio**; you'll follow a path (accessible by car) lined by poplars. The hermitage was built in the 18th century above a cave where the Anchorite St. Saturio fasted and prayed. You can climb up to the building through the cave. ▨ *Free.* ☉ *Winter, daily 10:30–2 and 4–6; summer, daily 10:30–2 and 5–9.*

Dining and Lodging

$$ ✕ **Mesón Castellano.** The most traditional restaurant in town, this cozy establishment has a large, open fire over which succulent *chuletón de ternera* (veal chops) are cooked. Another house specialty is *migas pastoriles* (soaked bread crumbs fried with peppers and bacon), a local dish. ⊠ *Plaza Mayor 2,* ☎ *975/213045. AE, DC, MC, V.*

$$$ 🏨 **Parador Nacional Antonio Machado.** This modern building has a superb hilltop setting, surrounded by trees and parkland, and excellent views of the hilly Duero Valley. The poet came often to this site for inspiration. ⊠ *Parque del Castillo, 42005,* ☎ *975/213445,* ℻ *975/212849. 34 rooms. Restaurant, bar. AE, DC, MC, V.*

Numancia

🟤 *7 km (4 mi) north of Soria.*

The bleak hilltop ruins of Numancia, an important Iberian settlement, are just a few minutes from Soria and accessible only by car. Viciously besieged by the Romans in 135–134 BC, Numancia's inhabitants chose death rather than surrender. Most of the foundations that have been unearthed date from the time of the Roman occupation. ▨ *100 ptas.* ☉ *Winter, Tues.–Sat. 10–2 and 4–6, Sun. 10–2; summer, Tues.–Sat. 10–2 and 5–9, Sun. 10–2.*

El Burgo de Osma

🟤 *56 km (35 mi) west of Soria.*

El Burgo de Osma is an attractive medieval and Renaissance town dominated by a Gothic cathedral and a baroque bell tower.

Dining and Lodging

$$ ✕ **Virrey Palafox.** One of Castile's best-known restaurants, this is a family-run enterprise set in a modern building. Inside, the decor is traditional Castilian, complete with white walls and a wood-beamed ceiling. The long dining room, adorned with old furnishings, is divided into smoking and nonsmoking sections. The emphasis is on fresh, seasonal produce; vegetables are home-grown; and there is excellent local game throughout the year. The house specialty is fish, in particular *merluza Virrey* (hake stuffed with eels and salmon). On February and March weekends a pig is slaughtered, and a marvelous and very popular banquet is held; admission is about 5,000 ptas. ⊠ *Universidad 7,* ☎ *975/340222. AE, DC, MC, V. Closed Sun. and Dec. 22–Jan. 10.*

$$$ 🏨 **Virrey II.** A few hundred yards from the restaurant, and under the same management, the Virrey II offers pleasant accommodations. Situated on the village's main square, it adjoins the 16th-century Convent of San Agustín and appears to form part of it. Though the hotel was only built in 1990, it was made with traditional materials and has an Old-World look. The rooms, most of which overlook the square,

have marble floors, stone walls, and tastefully simple decoration. ✉ *C. Mayor 2, 42300,* ☎ *975/341311,* FAX *975/340855. 52 rooms. Dining room, meeting room. AE, DC, MC, V.*

SOUTHEAST OF MADRID

Cuenca, Ciudad Encantada, Alarcón

Dramatic landscapes are the main attraction here. The rocky countryside and magnificent gorges of the rivers Huécar and Júcar make for spectacular views. Cuenca offers a museum devoted to abstract art, impressive for both its content and its setting. Nearby towns like Ciudad Encantada, with its rock formations, and Alarcón, home to a medieval castle, make pleasant excursions.

Cuenca

46 *167 km (104 mi) southeast of Madrid.*

Built onto a wild and rocky countryside cut with dramatic gorges, Cuenca has a haunting atmosphere and outstanding cuisine. On the north side of the River Huécar, the old town rises steeply, hugging a spine of rock thrust up between the gorges of the Huécar and the Júcar and bordered on two sides by sheer precipices, over which soars the odd hawk or eagle. The lower half of the old town is a maze of tiny streets, any of which will take you up to the Plaza del Carmen. From here the town narrows, and a single street, Calle Alfonso VIII, continues the ascent up to the Plaza Mayor, which you reach after passing under the arch of the town hall.

Just off Calle San Pedro, clinging to the western edge of Cuenca, is the tiny **Plaza San Nicolás,** a picturesquely dilapidated square. Nearby, the unpaved Ronda del Júcar hovers over the Júcar gorge and commands remarkable views over the mountainous landscape. The best views of the mountains are from the square in front of the **castle,** at the very top of Cuenca, where the town tapers out to the narrowest of ledges. Gorges are on either side of you, while directly in front, old houses sweep down toward a distant plateau. The castle itself, which served as the town prison for many years, is now a parador.

The **Museo Diocesano de Arte Sacro** (Diocesan Museum of Sacred Art) is housed in what were once the cellars of the Bishop's Palace. The beautifully clear display features a jewel-encrusted, Byzantine diptych of the 13th century; a Crucifixion by the 15th-century Flemish artist Gerard David; and two small El Grecos. From the Plaza Mayor, take Calle Obispo Valero and follow signs pointing toward the Casas Colgadas. ☎ *969/212011.* 🎫 *200 ptas.* ☉ *Tues.–Fri. 11–2 and 4–6, Sat. 11–2 and 4–8, Sun. 11–2.*

★ Cuenca's most famous buildings, the **Casas Colgadas** (Hanging Houses), form one of the finest and most curious of Spain's museums. This joined group of houses, literally projecting over the town's eastern precipice, originally formed a 15th-century palace; later they served as a town hall before falling into disuse and decay in the 19th century. During the restoration campaign of 1927, the cantilevered balconies that had once hung over the gorge were rebuilt, and finally, in 1966, the painter Fernando Zóbel decided to create inside them the world's first museum devoted exclusively to abstract art. The works he gathered are almost all by the remarkable generation of Spanish artists who grew up in the 1950s and were essentially forced to live abroad during the Franco regime: the major names include Carlos Saura, Eduardo Chillida,

Muñoz, Millares, Antoni Tàpies, and Zóbel. Even if you don't think abstract art is your thing, this museum is likely to win you over with its honeycomb of dazzlingly white rooms and its vistas of sky and gorge. ▨ *500 ptas.* ☉ *Tues.–Fri. 11–2 and 4–6, Sat. 11–2 and 4–8, Sun. 11–2.*

An iron footbridge over the Huécar gorge, the **Puente de San Pablo** was built in 1903 for the convenience of the Dominican monks of San Pablo, who live on the other side. If you've no fear of heights, cross the narrow bridge to take in the vertiginous view of the river below and the equally thrilling panorama of the Casas Colgadas. A path from the bridge descends to the bottom of the gorge, landing you by the bridge that you crossed to enter the old town.

Dining and Lodging

$$$ ✕ **El Figón de Pedro.** This restaurant's owner, Pedro Torres Pacheco,
★ is one of Spain's most famous restaurateurs and has done much to promote the excellence of Cuenca's cuisine. In this pleasantly low-key spot in the lively heart of the modern town, you can try such local specialties as *gazpacho pastor, ajo arriero* (a paste made with pounded salt cod and served with toasted bread), and *alaju* (a Moorish sweet made with honey, bread crumbs, almonds, and orange water). Wash down your meal with *resolí,* Cuenca's liqueur. ⊠ *Cervantes 13,* ☎ *969/ 226821. AE, DC, MC, V. Closed Feb. No dinner Sun.*

$$$ ✕ **Mesón Casas Colgadas.** Run by the same management as El Figón de Pedro (☞ *above*), this *mesón* offers much the same fare, but more pretentiously. The dining room is ultramodern and white and sits next to the Museum of Abstract Art in the spectacularly situated Casas Colgadas. ⊠ *Canónigos s/n,* ☎ *969/223509. Reservations essential. AE, DC, MC, V. No dinner Tues.*

$$ ✕ **Las Brasas.** Meats cooked over wood coals and hearty bean con-
★ coctions characterize this fairly typical Spanish restaurant. Both the cooking and the fire, visible from the bar, make a meal here comforting and festive. The owners use vegetables from their own garden to make a delicious *pucherete* (white bean soup). The decor is Castilian, with wood floors and dark wood furniture. ⊠ *Alfonso VIII 105,* ☎ *969/213821. MC, V. Closed Wed. and July.*

$$$$ 🏨 **Parador de Cuenca.** Spain's newest parador (b. 1993) is in an exquisitely restored 16th-century monastery in the gorge beneath the Casas Colgadas. The guest rooms are furnished in a lighter and more luxurious style than you'd normally find in Castilian houses of this vintage. ⊠ *Paseo Hoz de Huécar s/n, 16001,* ☎ *969/232320,* 🖷 *969/ 232534. 63 rooms. Restaurant, bar, pool, tennis court. AE, DC, MC, V.*

$$$ 🏨 **Cueva del Fraile.** This luxurious hotel, 7 km (4½ mi) out of town on the Buenache road, occupies a 16th-century building in dramatic surroundings. The white rooms have reproduction traditional furniture, stone floors, and in some cases wood ceilings. ⊠ *Ctra. Cuenca-Buenache, 16001,* ☎ *969/211571,* 🖷 *969/256047. 62 rooms. Pool, tennis court, meeting room. AE, MC, V. Closed Jan.–Feb.*

$$–$$$ 🏨 **Posada San José.** This is still the only hotel in the Old Town, and
★ it's just as good as—if somewhat more modest than—the nearby parador. Tastefully installed in a 16th-century convent, the *posada* clings to the top of the Huécar gorge, which most of its rooms overlook. The furnishings are traditional, in the spirit of the building. The atmosphere is friendly and intimate. Reservations are essential and should be made well in advance. ⊠ *Julián Romero 4, 16001,* ☎ *969/211300. 29 rooms, 21 with bath. Bar, cafeteria. AE, DC, MC, V.*

Ciudad Encantada

㊼ *35 km (21 mi) north of Cuenca.*

The "Enchanted City" comprises a series of large and fantastic rock formations erupting in a landscape of pines. If you like to explore on foot, this town is well worth a visit; a footpath can guide you through striking outcrops with names like "El Tobagón" (The Toboggan) and "Mar de Piedras" (Sea of Stones).

Alarcón

㊽ *69 km (43 mi) south of Cuenca.*

This fortified village on the edge of the great plains of La Mancha stands impressively on a high spur of land encircled almost entirely by a bend of the River Júcar. Its **castle** dates to Visigothic times; in the 14th century it came into the hands of the infante Don Juan Manuel, who wrote a collection of moral tales that rank among the great treasures of medieval Spanish literature. Today the castle is one of Spain's finest paradors (☞ Dining and Lodging, *below*).

Dining and Lodging

$$$$ ✕🏨 **Parador Nacional Marqués de Villena.** As a place to indulge in medieval fantasies, this parador, in a 12th-century castle perched above a gorge, can't be beat. There are only 13 rooms here, 12 of them quite small (the turret room is large). Some rooms are in the corner towers and have as windows the narrow slots once used to shoot arrows from; others have window niches where the women of the household sat to do needlework. Dinner is served in a high-arched baronial hall adorned with shields, armor, and a gigantic fireplace recalling medieval banquets. The nearest train connection to Alarcón is Cuenca, 69 km (43 mi) away; a bus to Motilla will leave you a short taxi ride away (call ☎ 969/331797 for a cab). ✉ *Avda. Amigos de los Castillos 3, 16213,* ☎ *969/330315,* ☎ *969/330303. 13 rooms. Restaurant. AE, DC, MC, V.*

SOUTH OF MADRID

Aranjuez and Toledo

The small town of Aranjuez is home to the Palacio Real, a sumptuously decorated French-style palace. Nearby Toledo, on the other hand, is a study in austerity, its introverted, gold-toned houses daring you to know them better. Here you can explore the mighty Gothic cathedral and the Tránsito Synagogue; contemplate El Greco's most famous painting, *The Burial of Count Orgaz*; or just roam the winding lanes.

Aranjuez

㊾ *47 km (29 mi) south of Madrid.*

Once the site of a Habsburg hunting lodge on the banks of the Tajo, Aranjuez became a favorite summer residence of the Bourbons in the 18th century; they built a large palace and other buildings, designed extensive gardens, and planted woods. In the 19th century, Aranjuez developed into a popular retreat for Madrileños. Today, the spaciously and neatly laid-out town that grew up in the vicinity of the palace retains a faded elegance.

Aranjuez's **Palacio Real** (Royal Palace) reflects French grandeur. The high point of the sumptuous interior is a room covered entirely with porcelain; there are also numerous elaborate clocks and a good museum of costumes. Shaded riverside gardens full of statuary and fountains allow pleasant relaxation after the palace tour. ☎ 91/891–1344. 🎫 *Palace 500 ptas., gardens free.* ☉ *Palace May–Sept., Tues.–Sun. 10–6:15; Oct.–Apr., Tues.–Sun. 10–5:15. Gardens May–Sept., daily 8–6:30; Oct.–Apr., daily 8 AM–8:30 PM.*

The charming **Casa del Labrador** (Farmer's Cottage), a small, intimate palace at the eastern end of Aranjuez, was built by Carlos IV in 1804 and has a jewel-like interior bursting with color and crowded with delicate objects. Between the Royal Palace and the Casa del Labrador is the **Casa de Marinos** (Sailors' House), where you'll see a gondola that belonged to Philip V and other decorated pleasure boats that once plied the river. 🎫 *Casa del Labrador 425 ptas., Casa de Marinos 325 ptas.* ☉ *May–Sept., Tues.–Sun. 10–6:30; Oct.–Apr., Tues.–Sun. 10–5:30.*

Toledo

★ ⑤⓿ *35 km (22 mi) southwest of Aranjuez, 71 km (44 mi) southwest of Madrid.*

The contrast between Aranjuez and nearby Toledo could hardly be more marked. From the sensuous surroundings and French-style elegance of the former, you move to a place of drama and austerity, tinged with mysticism, that was long the spiritual and intellectual capital of Spain. No matter which route you take from Madrid, your first glimpse of Toledo will take in its northern gates and battlements rising up on a massive granite escarpment. The flat countryside comes to an end, and a steep range of ocher-colored hills rises on each side of the city.

The rock on which Toledo stands was inhabited in prehistoric times, and there was already an important Iberian settlement here when the Romans came in 192 BC. On the highest point of the rock—on which now stands the Alcázar, the dominant building in Toledo's skyline— the Romans built a large fort; this was later remodeled by the Visigoths, who transformed the town into their capital by the middle of the 6th century AD. In the early 8th century, the Moors arrived.

During their occupation of Toledo, the Moors furthered its reputation as a great center of learning and religion. Unusual tolerance was extended to those who continued to practice Christianity (the so-called Mozarabs), as well as to the town's exceptionally large Jewish population. Today the Moorish legacy is evident in Toledo's strong crafts tradition, in the mazelike arrangement of the streets, and in the predominance of brick rather than stone. To the Moors, beauty was a quality to be savored within rather than displayed on the surface, and it is significant that even Toledo's cathedral—one of the most richly endowed in Spain—is difficult to see from the outside, largely obscured by the warren of houses that surrounds it. Long after the departure of the Moors, Toledo remained secretive, its life and treasures hidden behind closed doors and forbidding facades.

Alfonso VI, aided by El Cid, captured Toledo in 1085 and styled himself Emperor of Toledo. Under the Christians, the town's strong intellectual life was maintained, and Toledo became famous for its school of translators who spread to the West a knowledge of Arab medicine, law, culture, and philosophy. Religious tolerance continued, and during the rule of Peter the Cruel (so named because he allegedly had members of his own family murdered to advance himself), a Jewish banker, Samuel Levi, became the royal treasurer and one of the wealthiest and most important men in town. By the early 15th century, however, hostility toward both Jews and Arabs had grown as Toledo developed more and more into a bastion of the Catholic Church.

As Florence had the Medici and Rome the papacy, so Toledo had its long and distinguished line of cardinals, most notably Mendoza, Tavera, and Cisneros. Under these great patrons of the arts, Renaissance Toledo emerged as a center of humanism. Economically and politically, however, Toledo had already begun to decline in the 16th century. The expulsion of the Jews from Spain in 1492 had particularly serious economic consequences for Toledo; the decision in 1561 to make Madrid the permanent center of the Spanish court led to the town's loss of political importance; and the expulsion from Spain of the converted Arabs (Moriscos) in 1601 resulted in the departure of most of Toledo's celebrated artisan community. The years the painter El Greco spent in Toledo—from 1572 to his death in 1614—were those of the town's decline. Its transformation into a major tourist center began in the late 19th century, when the works of El Greco came to be widely appreciated after years of neglect. Today, Toledo is prosperous and conservative, expensive, silent at night, and closed in atmosphere. Yet Spain has no other town of this size with such a concentration of monuments and works of art.

A Good Walk

The eastern end of the gorge, along Calle de Circunvalación, has a panoramic view of Toledo. Here you can park your car (except in the middle of the day, when buses line up) and look down over almost all of Toledo's main monuments.

Start at the **Puente de Alcántara** ⑤. If you choose to go north, skirting the city walls, you'll come to the **Hospital de Tavera** ㊾. If you enter the city wall, travel west and pass the **Plaza de Zocodover** ㊿, the **Museo de la Santa Cruz** ㊾, and the **Capilla del Cristo de la Luz** ㊿. From opposite the southwestern corner of the **Alcázar** ㊾, a series of alleys descends to the east end of the **cathedral** ㊾, affording good views of the cathedral tower. Make your way around the southern side of the building, passing the mid-15th-century Puerta de los Leones, with detailed and realistic carvings by artists of northern descent. Emerging into the small square in front of the cathedral's west facade, you will see to your right the elegant *ayuntamiento,* begun by the young Juan de Herrera and completed by El Greco's son, Jorge Manuel Theotokópoulos.

Near the Museo de los Concilios, on Calle de San Clemente, take in the richly sculpted portal by Covarrubias on the Convento de San Clemente; across the street is the church of **San Román** ㊽. Almost every wall in this quiet part of town belongs to a convent, and the empty streets make for contemplative walks. This was a district loved by the Romantic poet Gustavo Adolfo Bécquer, author of *Rimas (Rhymes),* the most popular collection of Spanish verse before García Lorca's *Romancero Gitano.* Bécquer's favorite corner was the tiny square in front of the 16th-century convent church of **Santo Domingo** ㊾, a few minutes' walk north of San Román, below the Plazuela de Padilla.

Backtrack following Calle de San Clemente through the Plaza de Valdecaleros to Calle de Santo Tomé to get to the church of **Santo Tomé** ㊿. Down the hill from Santo Tomé, off Calle de San Juan de Díos, is the **Casa de El Greco** ㊽. Next door to the Casa de El Greco is the 14th-century **Sinagoga del Tránsito** ㊾, financed by Samuel Levi, and the accompanying **Museo Sefardi.** Come out of the synagogue and turn right up Calle de Reyes Católicos. A few steps past the town's other synagogue, **Santa María la Blanca** ㊿, is the late-15th-century church of **San Juan de los Reyes** ㊽, the most prominent monument in western Toledo. The walk finishes at the city's western extremity, the **Puente de San Martín** ㊿.

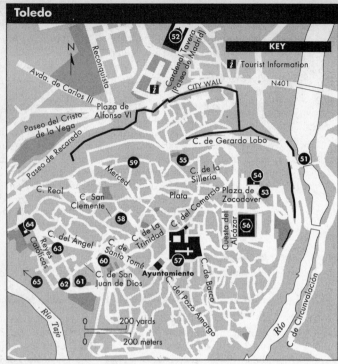

TIMING

Toledo's winding streets and steep hills can be exasperating at times, especially when you're looking for a specific sight; but one of the main attractions of this walk is simply enjoying the medieval atmosphere. Plan to spend the whole day.

Sights to See

56 **Alcázar.** The south facade, the most severe, is the work of Juan de Herrera, of Escorial fame; the east facade gives a good idea of the building's medieval appearance, incorporating a large section of battlements. The finest facade is undoubtedly the northern, one of many Toledan works by Alonso de Covarrubias, who did more than any other architect to introduce the Renaissance style here.

Within the building are a military headquarters and a large military museum—one of Spain's few remaining homages to Francoism, hung with tributes from various right-wing military groups and figures from around the world. The Alcázar's architectural highlight is Covarrubias's harmonious Italianate courtyard, which, like most other parts of the building, was largely rebuilt after the Civil War, when the Alcázar was besieged by the Republicans. Though the Nationalists' ranks were depleted, they managed to hold on to the building. Franco later turned the Alcázar into a monument to Nationalist bravery; the office of the Nationalist general who defended the building, General Moscardó, has been left exactly as it was after the war, complete with peeling ceiling paper and mortar holes. The gloomy tour can continue with a visit to the dark cellars, which evoke living conditions at the time of the siege.

More cheerful is a ground-floor room full of beautifully crafted swords, a Toledan specialty introduced by Moorish silversmiths. At the top of

In case you want to see the world.

At American Express, we're here to make your journey a smooth one. So we have over 1,700 travel service locations in over 120 countries ready to help. What else would you expect from the world's largest travel agency?

do more ®

AMERICAN EXPRESS

Travel

http://www.americanexpress.com/travel

In case you want to be welcomed there.

We're here to see that you're always welcomed at establishments everywhere. That's why millions of people carry the American Express® Card – for peace of mind, confidence, and security, around the world or just around the corner.

do more

AMERICAN EXPRESS

Cards

And just in case.

We're here with American Express® Travelers Cheques and Cheques *for Two*.® They're the safest way to carry money on your vacation and the surest way to get a refund, practically anywhere, anytime.
Another way we help you...

do more®

AMERICAN EXPRESS

Travelers Cheques

the grand staircase, which apparently made even Carlos V "feel like an emperor," are rooms displaying a vast collection of toy soldiers. ☎ *925/223038.* ✉ *125 ptas.* ⊘ *Tues.–Sun. 10–1:30 and 4–5:30 (4–6:30 in summer).*

⑤⑤ Capilla del Cristo de la Luz (Chapel of Christ of the Light). This chapel lies behind railings in a small park above the town's northern ramparts. The gardener will open the gate for you and show you around; if he's not there, inquire at the house opposite. The exposed chapel was originally a tiny Visigothic church, transformed into a mosque during the Moorish occupation; the arches and vaulting of the mosque survive, making this the most important relic of Moorish Toledo. The chapel got its name when the horse of Alfonso VI, who was riding in triumph into Toledo in 1085, knelt in front of the building; it was then discovered that behind the masonry was a candle that had burned continuously throughout the time that the so-called Infidels had been in power. The first Mass of the Reconquest was said here, and later a Mudéjar apse was added (now shielded by glass). After you've looked at the chapel, the gardener will take you across the ramparts to climb to the top of the Puerta del Sol, a 12th-century Mudéjar gatehouse. ✉ *Tip to gardener.* ⊘ *Any reasonable hr.*

⑥① Casa de El Greco (El Greco's House). This tourist magnet is on the property that belonged to Peter the Cruel's Jewish treasurer, Samuel Levi. The artist once lived in a house owned by this man, but it's pure conjecture that he lived in this particular one. The interior, done up in the late 19th century to resemble a "typical" house of El Greco's time, is a pure fake, albeit a pleasant one. The once-drab museum next door is currently being restored and remodeled; one of the few El Grecos currently on display is a large panorama of Toledo, with the Hospital of Tavera in the foreground. ✉ *C. Samuel Levi 3,* ☎ *925/224046.* ✉ *200 ptas.* ⊘ *Tues.–Sat. 10–2 and 4–6, Sun. 10–2.*

⑤⑦ Cathedral. Jorge Manuel Theotokópoulos was responsible for the cathedral's Mozarabic chapel, the elongated dome of which crowns the right-hand side of the west facade. The rest of this facade is mainly early-15th-century and features a depiction of the Virgin presenting her robe to Toledo's patron saint, the Visigothic Ildefonsus.

Enter the cathedral from the 14th-century cloisters to the left of the west facade. The primarily 13th-century architecture was inspired by the great Gothic cathedrals of France, such as Chartres; the squat proportions, however, give it a Spanish feel, as do the wealth and weight of the furnishings and the location of the elaborate choir in the center of the nave. Immediately to your right as you enter the building is a beautifully carved plateresque doorway by Covarrubias, marking the entrance to the Treasury. The latter houses a small Crucifixion by the Italian painter Cimabue and an extraordinarily intricate late-15th-century monstrance by Juan del Arfe, a silversmith of German descent; the ceiling is an excellent example of Mudéjar workmanship.

From here, walk around to the ambulatory, off the right side of which is a chapter house featuring a strange and quintessentially Spanish mixture of Italianate frescoes by Juan de Borgoña. In the middle of the ambulatory is a dazzling and famous example of baroque illusionism by Narciso Tomé, known as the *Transparente,* a blend of painting, stucco, and sculpture.

Finally, off the northern end of the ambulatory, you'll come to the sacristy, where you'll find a number of El Grecos, most notably the work known as *El Espolio* (Christ Being Stripped of his Raiment). One of

El Greco's earliest works in Toledo, it fell afoul of the Inquisition, which accused the artist of putting Christ on a lower level than some of the onlookers. El Greco was thrown into prison, and there his career might have ended had he not by this stage formed friendships with some of Toledo's more moderate clergy. Before leaving the sacristy, look up at the colorful and spirited late-baroque ceiling painting by the Italian Luca Giordano. *500 ptas. Mon.–Sat. 10:30–1 and 3:30–6 (3:30–7 in summer), Sun. 10:30–1:30 and 4–6 (4–7 in summer).*

(52) **Hospital de Tavera.** You'll find this hospital, Covarrubias's last work, outside the walls beyond Covarrubia's imposing Puerta de Bisagra, Toledo's main northern gate. Unlike the former Hospital of Santa Cruz, this complex is unfinished and slightly dilapidated, but it is nonetheless full of character and has an evocatively ramshackle museum in its southern wing, looked after by two exceptionally friendly and eccentric women. The most important work in the museum's miscellaneous collection is a painting by the 17th-century artist José Ribera. In the hospital's monumental chapel are El Greco's *Baptism of Christ* and the exquisitely carved marble tomb of Cardinal Tavera, the last work of Alonso de Berruguete. Descend into the crypt to experience some bizarre acoustical effects. ☎ *925/220451. 500 ptas. Daily 10–1:30 and 3:30–6.*

(54) **Museo de la Santa Cruz.** One of the joys of this museum is its location in a beautiful Renaissance hospital with a stunning classical-plateresque facade. Unlike Toledo's other monuments, the museum is open all day without a break and is delightfully quiet in the early afternoon. The light and elegant interior has changed little since the 16th century, the main difference being that works of art have replaced the hospital beds; among the displays is El Greco's *Assumption* of 1613, the artist's last known work. A small **Museo de Arqueología** (Museum of Archaeology) has been arranged in and around the hospital's delightful cloister, off which you'll also find a beautifully decorated staircase by Alonso de Covarrubias. ⊠ *C. de Cervantes 3,* ☎ *925/221036. 200 ptas. Mon. 10–2 and 4–6:30, Tues.–Sat. 10–6:30, Sun. 10–2.*

(53) **Plaza de Zocodover.** The town's main square was built in the early 17th century as part of an unsuccessful attempt to impose a rigid geometry on the chaotic Moorish ground plan. Nearby, you'll find **Calle del Comercio,** the town's narrow and lively pedestrian thoroughfare, lined with bars and shops and shaded in the summer months by awnings suspended from the roofs of tall houses.

(51) **Puente de Alcántara.** Here is the town's oldest bridge, Roman in origin. Next to the bridge is a heavily restored castle built after the Christian capture of 1085, and above this a vast and depressingly severe military academy, a typical example of Fascist architecture under Franco. The bridge is off the city's eastern peripheral road, just north of the New Bridge.

(65) **Puente de San Martín.** A pedestrian bridge on the western edge of the town, the Puente de San Martín dates from 1203 and features splendid horseshoe arches.

(64) **San Juan de los Reyes.** This convent church in western Toledo was erected by Ferdinand and Isabella to commemorate their victory at the battle of Toro in 1476 and was intended to be their burial place. The building is largely the work of Juan Guas, who considered it his masterpiece and asked to be buried here himself. Guas, one of the greatest exponents of the Gothic, or Isabelline, was an architect of prolific imagination and great decorative exuberance. In true plateresque fash-

ion, the white interior is covered with inscriptions and heraldic motifs. ☎ 925/223802. ☑ *150 ptas.* ☉ *Daily 10–1:45 and 3:30–5:45 (until 6:45 in summer).*

❸ San Román. In a virtually unspoiled part of Toledo is this early 13th-century Mudéjar church, with extensive remains of frescoes inside. It has been deconsecrated and now serves as the **Museo de los Concilios y de la Cultura Visigoda** (Museum of Visigothic Art), featuring statuary, manuscript illustrations, and delicate jewelry. ⊠ *C. de San Clemente s/n,* ☎ *925/227872.* ☑ *100 ptas.* ☉ *Tues.–Sat. 10–2 and 4–6:30, Sun. 10–2.*

❻❸ Santa María la Blanca. Founded in 1203, Toledo's second synagogue is nearly two centuries older than the Tránsito Synagogue. The white interior features a forest of columns supporting capitals of the most enchanting filigree workmanship. Stormed in the early 15th century by a Christian mob led by St. Vincent Ferrer, the synagogue was later put to a variety of uses—as a carpenter's workshop, a store, a barracks, and a refuge for reformed prostitutes. ⊠ *Calle Reyes Católicos 2,* ☎ *925/227257.* ☑ *150 ptas.* ☉ *Daily 10–1:45 and 3:30–5:45 (3:30–7 in summer).*

❺❾ Santo Domingo. A few minutes' walk north of San Román is this 16th-century convent church where you'll find the earliest of El Greco's Toledo paintings as well as the crypt where the artist is believed to be buried. The friendly nuns at the convent will show you around an odd little museum that includes documents bearing El Greco's signature. ⊠ *Plaza Santo Domingo el Antiguo s/n,* ☎ *925/222930.* ☑ *150 ptas.* ☉ *Mon.–Sat. 11–1:30 and 4–7, Sun. 4–7 (weekends only in winter).*

❻⓿ Santo Tomé. This is the home of El Greco's most famous painting, *The Burial of Count Orgaz.* If possible, arrive as soon as the building opens, as you may have to wait in line to get inside later on in the day, especially in summer. Adorned by an elegant Mudéjar tower, the chapel was specially built for its current purpose. The painting—the only El Greco to have been consistently admired over the centuries—portrays the benefactor of the church being buried with the posthumous assistance of St. Augustine and St. Stephen, who have miraculously appeared at the funeral to thank him for all the money he gave to religious institutions named after them. Though the count's burial took place in the 14th century, El Greco painted the onlookers in contemporary costumes and included people he knew; the boy in the foreground is one of El Greco's sons, and the sixth figure on the left is said to be the artist himself. ⊠ *Plaza del Conde 1,* ☎ *925/210209.* ☑ *150 ptas.* ☉ *Daily 10–1:45 and 3:30–5:45 (3:30–6:45 in summer).*

❻❷ Sinagoga del Tránsito (Tránsito Synagogue). Financed by Samuel Levi, this 14th-century rectangular structure is plain on the outside, but the inside walls are sumptuously covered with intricate Mudéjar decoration, as well as Hebraic inscriptions glorifying God, Peter the Cruel, and Levi himself. It is said that Levi imported cedars from Lebanon for the building's construction as did Solomon when he built the Temple in Jerusalem. Adjoining the main hall is the **Museo Sefardí** (Sephardic Museum), a small museum of Jewish culture in Spain. ⊠ *C. Samuel Levi s/n,* ☎ *925/223665.* ☑ *400 ptas., free Sun.* ☉ *Tues.–Sat. 10–1:45 and 4–5:45, Sun. 10–1:45.*

Dining and Lodging

$$$ ✕ **Asador Adolfo.** Only a few steps from the cathedral, but discreetly
★ hidden away and making no attempt to attract the tourist trade, this is unquestionably the best and most dignified restaurant in town. The

modern main entrance shields an old and intimate interior featuring in its principal dining room a wood-beam ceiling with extensive painted decoration from the 14th century. The emphasis is on freshness of produce and traditional Toledan dishes, but there is also much innovation. Especially tasty to start is the *tempura de flor de calabacín* (zucchini blossom tempura in a saffron sauce); a flavorful entrée is the *solomillo de cerdo* (pork loin with wild mushrooms and black truffles). Finish with a Toledan specialty, *delicias de mazapán* (marzipan), which is cooked here in a wooden oven and is the finest and lightest in the whole town. ⊠ *Granada 6 and Hombre de Palo 7,* ☎ *925/227321. Reservations essential. AE, DC, MC, V. No dinner Sun.*

$$ ✕ **Hierbabuena.** Here you can dine on an enclosed Moorish patio with plenty of natural light, at tables covered with crocheted tablecloths. The food is just as inviting as the setting, and the prices are surprisingly reasonable. The menu changes with the season; possibilities include artichokes stuffed with seafood and steak with blue-cheese sauce. ⊠ *Cristo de la Luz 9,* ☎ *925/223463. AE, DC, MC, V. No dinner Sun. Closed Mon.*

$–$$ ✕ **La Ria.** Down a tiny alley in front of Santo Tomé (☞ *above*), this little tapas bar serves generous helpings of fresh seafood. English is not spoken, but the linguistic effort is worth it. ⊠ *Callejón Bodegones 9,* ☎ *925/252532. No credit cards.*

$–$$ ✕ **Restaurant Maravilla.** With a quaint atmosphere and modestly priced menus, Maravilla is a great choice. Specialties include Toledan preparations of partridge or quail and a variety of seafood dishes. ⊠ *Plaza Barrio Rey 7,* ☎ *925/228582 or 925/228317. AE, DC, MC, V.*

$$–$$$ ✕⌸ **Hostal del Cardenal.** Built in the 18th century as a summer palace for Cardinal Lorenzana, this is a quiet and beautiful hotel whose light-colored rooms are decorated with old furniture. Some rooms overlook the hotel's enchanting wooded garden, which lies at the foot of the town's walls. From here it's hard to believe that the main road to Madrid is not far off. The restaurant has a longstanding reputation and is very popular with tourists; the setting is beautiful, and both the food and service are good. The dishes are mainly local, and in season you'll find delicious asparagus and strawberries from Aranjuez. ⊠ *Paseo Recaredo 24, 45004,* ☎ *925/224900,* ℻ *925/222991. 27 rooms. Restaurant. AE, DC, MC, V.*

$$$ ✕⌸ **Hotel Alfonso VI.** Smack in the middle of the historic district, this hotel offers great views of the city from its summer terrace. The rooms are modern, clean, and inviting; the restaurant is decorated in the ubiquitous Mudéjar style and serves delicious food. ⊠ *General Moscardó 2, 45001,* ☎ *925/222600,* ℻ *925/214458. 85 rooms. Restaurant. AE, MC, V.*

$$$$ ⌸ **Parador Nacional Conde de Orgaz.** This modern building on Toledo's outskirts blends well with its rural surroundings and has an unbeatable panorama of the town. The architecture and furnishings, emphasizing brick and wood, nod to the traditional Toledan style. ⊠ *Paseo Emperador s/n, 45001,* ☎ *925/221850,* ℻ *925/225166. 77 rooms. Pool. AE, DC, MC, V.*

$$$ ⌸ **Hotel Pintor El Greco.** Next door to the famous painter's house–museum, this friendly hotel occupies what was once a 17th-century bakery. Extensive renovation has resulted in a light and modern interior with some antique touches, such as exposed brick vaulting. ⊠ *Alamillos del Transito 13, 45002,* ☎ *925/214250,* ℻ *925/215819. 33 rooms. AE, DC, MC, V.*

Shopping

Toledo's province is the most renowned crafts center in Castile, if not all of Spain. Here, the Moors established **silverwork, damascene** (metalwork inlaid with gold or silver), **embroidery,** and **pottery** traditions that are still very much alive. Next to Toledo's church of San Juan de los Reyes is a turn-of-the-century art school that teaches these various crafts and helps to maintain standards. For cheaper pottery, you're better off stopping at the large roadside emporia on the outskirts of town, on the main road to Madrid. Better still, go to **Talavera la Reina,** 76 km (47 mi) west of Toledo, where most of this pottery is made. The finest embroidery in the province comes from **Oropesa** and **Lagartera.**

AROUND MADRID A TO Z

Arriving and Departing

By Plane

The only international airport in either Old or New Castile is Madrid's Barajas. Valladolid Airport has flights to Barcelona. For information on airlines serving Madrid, *see* Madrid A to Z *in* Chapter 2.

Getting Around

By Bus

Bus connections between Madrid and Castile are excellent. Two of the most popular services go to Toledo (1 hour) and Segovia (1½ hours); buses to the former leave every half hour from the **Estación del Sur** (⊠ C. Canaría 17, ☎ 91/468–4200), to the latter every hour from **La Sepulvedana** (⊠ Paseo de la Florida 11, ☎ 91/527–9537). Buses to Soria (3 hours) and Burgo de Osma (2½ hours) leave from **Continental Auto** (⊠ C. Alenza 20, ☎ 91/533–0400), while **Auto Res** (⊠ Plaza Conde de Casal 6, ☎ 91/551–7200) runs services to Cuenca (2 hours, 50 minutes) and Salamanca (3 hours). Services between the provincial towns are not as good as those to and from Madrid; if you're traveling between, say, Cuenca and Toledo, you will find it quicker to return to Madrid and make your way from there. Reservations are rarely necessary; if demand arises, additional buses are usually called into service.

By Car

A series of major roads with extensive stretches of divided highway— the N I, II, III, IV, and V—radiate from Madrid in every direction and make transport to the outlying towns easy. If possible, however, avoid returning to Madrid on these roads at the end of a weekend or on a public holiday. The side roads vary in quality and are rarely of the high standard that you find in, say, provincial France, but they constitute one of the great pleasures of traveling around the Castilian countryside by car—you are constantly coming across unexpected architectural delights and wild and spectacular vistas. Above all, you rarely come across other tourists.

By Train

All the main towns covered in this section are accessible by train from Madrid, and it's quite possible to visit each in separate day trips. There are commuter trains from Madrid to Segovia (2 hours), Alcalá de Henares (45 minutes), Guadalajara (1 hour), and Toledo (1½ hours). Train travel in Spain has improved in recent years, but it's still often faster to reach your destination by bus. Trains to Toledo depart from Madrid's **Atocha** station; trains to Salamanca depart from **Chamartín** station; and both stations serve Ávila, Segovia, El Escorial, and Sigüenza, although Chamartín may offer more frequent service to some. The one important town that can be reached only by train is Sigüenza. Check with **RENFE** for details (☎ 91/328–9020).

Contacts and Resources

Car Rental

It's often cheaper to rent cars in advance, while still at home, through international firms such as Hertz and Avis (☞ Car Rental *in* the Gold Guide). Spain's leading car-rental agency is **Atesa** (⊠ Infanta Mercedes 90, Madrid, ☎ 91/571–2145).

Fishing

The most common fish in Castile's rivers are trout, pike, black bass, and blue carp; among the main trout rivers are the Eresma, Alto Duero, Júcar, Jarama, Manzanares, Tajo, and Tormes. Madrid's **provincial office** (⊠ Princesa 3, ☎ 91/580–1653) has more information.

Golf

There are golf courses at Alcalá de Henares, Salamanca, and numerous smaller places immediately surrounding Madrid. For further information, contact the **Real Federación Española de Golf** (⊠ Capitán Haya 9, Madrid, 28020, ☎ 91/555–2682).

Guided Tours

Current information on city tours can be obtained from the local tourist offices, where you can also ask about hiring guides. You should be especially wary of local guides in Ávila and Toledo; they can be quite ruthless in trying to impose their services. If you join one, do not buy goods in the shops he takes you to; the prices are probably inflated, and the guide gets a kickback.

For a special art tour of Castile, including Salamanca, contact **Prospect Music & Art Tours Ltd.** (⊠ 10 Barley Mow Passage, Chiswick, London W4 4PH, ☎ 0181/995–2163). At the same address is by far the best of Great Britain's cultural-tour specialists, **Martin Randall Travel** (☎ 0181/994–6477), which offers an excellent five-day trip that includes Madrid and Toledo.

Visitor Information

The main provincial tourist office in **Madrid** is on the Plaza de España (⊠ Princesa 1, ☎ 91/541–2325). Useful information and excellent town plans can be obtained from the following local offices:

Alcalá de Henares (⊠ Callejón de Santa María, ☎ 91/889–2694), **Aranjuez** (⊠ Plaza San Antonio 9, ☎ 91/891–0427), **Ávila** (⊠ Plaza de la Catedral 4, ☎ 920/211387), **Ciudad Real** (⊠ Avda. Alarcos 21, ☎ 926/212925), **Ciudad Rodrigo** (⊠ Puerta de Amayuelas 5, ☎ 923/460561), **Cuenca** (⊠ Glorieta González Valencia 2, ☎ 969/178800), **Guadalajara** (⊠ Plaza Mayor 7, ☎ 949/211626), **Salamanca** (⊠ Casa de las Conchas, Rúa Mor s/n, ☎ 923/268571), **Segovia** (⊠ Plaza Mayor 10, ☎ 921/460334), **Sigüenza** (⊠ Plaza Mayor 1, ☎ 949/393251), **Soria** (⊠ Plaza Ramón y Cajal s/n, ☎ 975/212052), **Toledo** (⊠ Puerta de Bisagra s/n, ☎ 925/220843), **Valladolid** (⊠ Plaza de Zorrilla s/n, ☎ 983/351801), and **Zamora** (⊠ C. Santa Clara 20, ☎ 980/531845).

4 Barcelona and Northern Catalonia

Barcelona is one of Europe's most dynamic and artistic cities. From the medieval atmosphere of the Gothic Quarter's narrow alleys to the elegance of the Moderniste Eixample or the action-packed modern Olympic Village, Barcelona is on the move. Picasso, Miró, and Dalí have links to this vibrant city with its ever-stronger Catalan identity. After 40 years of repression through post–civil-war Franco dictatorship, Catalan language and culture have flourished since home rule was granted in 1975. Now this ancient romance language is heard in every street and is, along with Castilian Spanish, Barcelona's co-official language.

THE CAPITAL OF CATALONIA, 2,000-year-old Barcelona has long rivaled, even surpassed, Madrid in industrial muscle and business acumen. Though Madrid has revitalized its role as capital city, Barcelona has relinquished none of its power. After its comprehensive urban refurbishing prior to the 1992 Summer Olympics, Barcelona is coming into its own as one of Europe's most beautiful and modern cities. Few places can rival the narrow alleys of the Gothic Quarter for medieval atmosphere, or the boulevards in the Moderniste Eixample for elegance and distinction.

By George Semler

Barcelona enjoys a frenetically active cultural life and heritage. Perhaps most notably, it was the home of architect Antoni Gaudí (1852–1926), whose buildings are the most startling statements of Modernisme—a Spanish, and mainly Catalan, offshoot of Art Nouveau. Other leading Moderniste architects include Lluís Domènech i Muntaner and Josep Puig i Cadafalch. The painters Joan Miró (1893–1983), Salvador Dalí (1904–89), and Antoni Tàpies (born 1923) are also strongly identified with Catalonia. Pablo Picasso spent his formative years in Barcelona, and one of the city's treasures is a museum devoted to his works. Until recently the city boasted Spain's oldest and finest opera house, the Liceu (which burned down in 1994 and is being restored), and claims native Catalan musicians such as cellist Pablo (Pau, in Catalan) Casals (1876–1973), and opera singers Montserrat Caballé and Josep (José) Carreras. Barcelona's fashion industry is hard on the heels of those of Paris and Milan, and FC (Futbol Club) Barcelona, more a cultural phenomenon than a sports team, is arguably the world's most glamorous soccer club.

In 133 BC the Roman Empire annexed the city built by the Iberian tribe known as the Laietans and founded a colony they called Colonia Favencia Julia Augusta Paterna Barcino. In the 5th century, Barcelona became the Visigothic capital; the Moors invaded in the 8th century; and in 801, the Franks under Charlemagne captured Barcelona and made it their buffer zone at the edge of the Moors' Iberian empire. By 988, the autonomous Catalonian counties had gained independence from the Franks, and in 1137 they were united through marriage with the House of Aragon. In 1474, the marriage of Ferdinand of Aragon and Isabella of Castile brought Aragon and Catalonia into a united Spain. As the capital of Aragon's Mediterranean empire, Barcelona grew in importance between the 12th and the 14th centuries and began to falter only when maritime emphasis shifted to the Atlantic after 1492. Despite the establishment of Madrid as the seat of Spain's government in 1562, Catalonia continued to enjoy autonomous rights and privileges until 1714, when, in reprisal for having backed the Austrian Habsburg pretender to the Spanish throne, all institutions and expressions of Catalonian nationalism were suppressed by the triumphant Felip V of the French Bourbon dynasty. Not until the 19th century would Barcelona's industrial growth bring about a *Renaixença* (Renaissance) of nationalism and a cultural flowering that recalled the city's former opulence.

The tradition of Catalan independence nonetheless survived intact. Catalonia has revolted against Madrid's central authority on numerous occasions, and in particular during the Spanish civil war, when Barcelona was a Republican stronghold and a hotbed of anti-fascist sentiment. As a result, the Catalan identity and language were suppressed during the Franco dictatorship by such means as book burning, the renaming of streets and towns, and the banning of the Catalan language in schools and in the media. This repression had little lasting effect however, for the Catalans have jealously guarded their language and culture and generally think of themselves as Catalans first, Spaniards second.

Catalonian home rule was granted after Franco's death, in 1975, and Catalonia's parliament, the ancient Generalitat, was reinstated in 1980. Catalan is now heard on every street and eagerly promoted through free classes funded by the Generalitat. Street names are now in Catalan, and newspapers, radio stations, and a TV channel publish and broadcast in Catalan. The circular Catalan *sardana* is danced regularly all over town. The triumphant culmination of this rebirth was, of course, the staging of the Olympics in 1992—stadiums and pools were renovated, new harborside promenades created, and an entire set of train tracks moved to make way for the Olympic Village. Not content with this onetime project, Barcelona's last two mayors have presided over an urban renewal and the creation of postmodern structures that have made the city an architecture student's paradise.

Today Barcelona is a feast for all of the senses, though perhaps mainly the visual one. The pleasures of the palate, however, are not far behind; music prospers here; the air temperature is almost always about right, and even the fragrance of the Mediterranean occasionally overcomes urban fumes on the beach at Barceloneta or in the port.

Pleasures and Pastimes

Dining

The post-Franco renaissance of Catalan culture brought with it an important renewal of Catalan cuisine. A city where the best policy was once to look for Italian or French food or the odd faux-Castilian roast is now filled with exciting restaurants celebrating local produce from the sea as well as from inland and upland areas. Catalans are great lovers of fish, vegetables, rabbit, duck, lamb, game, and natural ingredients from the Pyrenees or the Mediterranean. The *mar i muntanya* (sea and mountain—that is, surf and turf), a recipe combining seafood with inland or highland products, is a standard specialty on most menus. The influence of nearby France seems to ensure finesse, while Iberian ebullience discourages pretense. The now-fashionable Mediterranean diet featuring "good" (anticholesterol) virgin olive oil, seafood, fibrous vegetables, onions, garlic, and red wine is nowhere better exemplified than in Catalonia. Catalan cuisine is wholesome and served in hearty portions. Spicy sauces are more prevalent here than elsewhere in Spain; you'll find *allioli,* for example—pure garlic and virgin olive oil (nothing else)— beaten to a mayonnaiselike sauce and used to accompany a wide variety of dishes, from rabbit to lamb to potatoes and vegetables. Typical entrées include *habas a la catalana* (a spicy broad-bean stew), *bullabesa* (fish soup-stew similar to the French bouillabaisse), and *espinacas a la catalana* (spinach cooked with oil, garlic, pine nuts, raisins, and bits of bacon). Bread is often doused with olive oil and spread with tomato to make *pa amb tomaquet,* delicious on its own or as an accompaniment to nearly anything. Read Colman Andrews's classic *Catalan Cuisine—Europe's Last Culinary Secret,* which lies on nearly every Catalan gourmet's nightstand, for a more detailed rundown of the products and practices of Catalan chefs.

Catalan wines from the nearby Penedès region, especially the local *méthode champenoise* (sparkling white wine known in Catalonia as *cava*), more than adequately accompany all regional cuisine.

Barcelona

Avda. Diagonal

Avda. de Pedralbes

Passeig de Manuel Girona

C. de les Escoles

Ronda del General Mitre

C. de Modolell

Via Augusta

Plaça Pius XII

Plaça de la Reina Maria Cristina

Plaça Prat de la Riba

C. de Sarria

Avda. de Sarria

C. de Calvet

C. de Muntaner

Via de Carles III

C. de Numància

Travessera de les Corts

Pl. de Francesc Macià

Avda. de Madrid

C. del Brasil

Gran

C. de Joan Güell

C. del Vallespir

C. de Berlin

Avda. de Josep Tarradellas

C. de Paris

C. de Villarroel

Avda

C. de Corsega

C. de Sants

Estació Sants

C. del Rossello

C. de Muntaner

C. d'Aribau

C. d'Antoni de Capmany

Pl. Països Catalans

Avda. de Roma

C. de Provença

Casanova

C. de Malle

C. de la Creu Coberta

C. de Valencia

C. de Calabria

C. de Viladomat

C. del Comte d'Urgell

C. de Villarroel

C. de

C. de Malle

C. d'Arago

Entença

Rocafort

C. del Comte Borrell

C. de

Casanova

Plaça d'Espanya

C. de Vilamari

C. de

la Diputació

Plaça Universita

Gran Via de les Corts Catalanes

Avda. Reina M. Cristina

C. de Sepulveda

Joaquin Costa

Plaça de Sant Jordi

Pl. de les Cascades

Avda. de Mistral

C. de Floridablanca

C. de

C. de Tamarit

Pg. de les Cascades

Avda. del Parallel

C. de Manso

Palau Nacional

C. de Lleida

C. de Magalhaes

C. de Blai

Rda. de Sant Pau

Carretes

Les Flores

C. de Hospit

C. de Sant Pau

C. la Unio

Jardins de Joan Maragall

Estadi Olimpic

Avda. de Miramar

C. Nou de la Rambl

KEY

Metro Stations

Railway Lines

Funicular

Teleferic

Camí dels Tres Pins

Pg. de Montjuic

Parc de Montjuïc

C. dels Mondials

Jardins de Miramar

Moll de Sant Bertrán

TORR DE JAUM

Castell de Montjuïc

TO TIBIDABO

Parc Güell

Parc del Guinardó

Plaça de Lesseps

Trav. de Dalt

C. de Sant Salvador

C. de les   Camèlies

Plaça Alfons el Savi

C. Gran de Gràcia

C. Menéndez Pelayo

C. de Verdi

C. de la Providència

C. de L'Escorial

C. de Pl. I Margall

Ronda del Guinardó

Travessera de Gràcia

Trav. de Gràcia

Diagonal

Plaça de Joan Carles I

C. de Còrsega

C. de Indústria

C. de Sardenya

Avda. de Gaudi

C. de Indústria

C. del Rosselló

C. de Bailén

Passeig de S. Joan

C. de Nápoles

C. de Sicília

C. de Marina

C. del Rosselló

C. de Provença

C. de Pau Claris

C. de Roger I'Lúria

C. de Roger de Flor

Temple Expiatiori de la Sagrada Familia

C. de Cartagena

Provença

Passeig de Gràcia

C. de Balmes

Rambla de Catalunya

C. de Valencia

C. d'Aragó

Avda. Diagonal

C. de Valencia

C. d'Aragó

Consell de Cent

C. de la Diputació

Plaça Tetuán

C. de Consell de Cent

C. del Bruc

C. de Girona

C. de Bailén

Plaça Tetuán

C. de Casp

P. de Carles I

Gran Via de   les Corts Catalanes

C. de Ribes

Pelai

Plaça de Catalunya

Pl. Urquinaona

C. d'Ausias   Marc

C. de Tànger

C. Sta. Anna

Ronda S. Pere

Arc del Triomf

Avda. de la Meridiana

C. de Sancho de Avila

La Rambla

Jonqueres

S. Pere Més Alt

Estació Norte Vilanova (Bus Station)

C. dels Almogàvers

Carme

Via Laietana

S. Pere Més Baix

C. Dels

Avda. de Carles I

C. de Pere IV

C. d'Alaba

C. de Pamplona

C. de Lutxana

Avda. Catedral

Passeig de Lluis Companys

Passeig Pujades

Avda. de la Meridiana

C. de Pujades

Pl. St. Jaume

C. Ferran

C. Princesa

Passeig del Born

C. del Comerç

Pg. Picasso

Passeig de Carles I

Avda. del Bogatell

C. de Llull

Plaça Reial

C. Ciutat

Parc de la Ciutadella

C. de Wellington

C. Ample

Pl. d'Antoni López

Estació França

Avda. d'Icària

Vila Olímpica

Pg. de Colom

Avda. d'Icària

Avda. Litoral Costat Muntanya

Parc de Mar

Rambla

Moll d'Espanya

Moll de Barceloneta

BARCELONETA

Passeig Marítim

Mediterranean Sea

0   450 yards

0   450 meters

CATEGORY	COST*
$$$$	over 7,000 ptas.
$$$	4,500–7,000 ptas.
$$	2,500–4,500 ptas.
$	under 2,500 ptas.

per person for a three-course meal, excluding drinks, service, and tax

Lodging

Barcelona's 1992 Olympic Games spawned a massive boom in hotel construction. New hotels shot up, and existing ones were renovated. The most spectacular new hotels are the Hotel Arts and the Hotel Rey Juan Carlos I, which joins (or possibly eclipses) the Princesa Sofía as the Barcelona luxury hotel nearest the airport. Room rates have increased at well above the rate of inflation in recent years, meaning that there are very few real bargains. Don't give up too easily, however, as most receptionists will become flexible about rates if they suspect you might leave based on price. Write or fax ahead asking for a discount; you may be pleasantly surprised.

Generally speaking, hotels in the Gothic Quarter and the Rambla are convenient for sightseeing and have plenty of Old World charm but, with some notable exceptions, are weaker on creature comforts. Those in the Eixample are generally set in late-19th-century to 1950s town houses, often Moderniste in design; all offer a choice of street or courtyard rooms, so be sure to specify when you book. The newest hotels, with the widest range of facilities and the least sense of being in Barcelona (or anywhere in particular), are toward the west, along the Diagonal. In general, reservations are a good idea, if only to make your bid for a good rate, but the Olympic explosion means that you can almost always find lodging with relative ease. Ask about weekend rates, which are often half-price.

CATEGORY	COST*
$$$$	over 20,000 ptas.
$$$	15,000–20,000 ptas.
$$	8,000–15,000 ptas.
$	under 8,000 ptas.

All prices are for a standard double room, excluding tax.

Modernisme

More than any other city in the world, Barcelona is filled with buildings and other works of the late-19th-century artistic and architectural movement known as Art Nouveau in France, *Jugendstil* in Germany, *sezessionstil* in Austria, *floreale* in Italy, *modernismo* in the rest of Spain, and Modernism in English-speaking countries. This movement was in many ways analogous to the 1960s "greening of America" in that it reflected a disillusionment with the fruits of technology and industry and a return to more natural shapes and aesthetic values. The curved line replaced the straight line; flowers and fruits and wild mushrooms were sculpted into facades. The pragmatic gave way to ornamental excess. Modernisme is everywhere in Barcelona, not only because it tapped into the playfulness of the Catalan artistic impulse (as seen in the works of Gaudí, Picasso, Miró, Dalí, and others) but because it coincided with Barcelona's late-19th-century industrial prosperity and an upsurge of nationalistic sentiment.

Museums

Barcelona's museums are abundant, dynamic, and constantly self-renewing. The Museu Picasso is probably the best known, but bear in mind that the city has better permanent collections of art. The best of these is the Romanesque exhibit at the Palau Nacional on Montjuïc.

Other less-discovered gems are the Thyssen-Bornemisza Collection at the Monestir de Pedralbes, above Sarrià, and the Catalan impressionists at the Museu d'Art Modern in the Ciutadella. The Fundació "la Caixa," at Passeig de Sant Joan 108, frequently offers excellent itinerant shows that have ranged from Kandinsky to William Blake. Gaudí's famous Pedrera house, on the Passeig de Gràcia, now has a superb permanent exhibit on the architect's life and work in addition to the frequent shows in Sala Gaudí. The new Centre de Cultura Contemporànea and Museu d'Art Contemporani, in the Raval area west of the Rambla, have shows and events of all kinds. Other museums with excellent displays are the Museu de la Ciencia in upper Barcelona, the Museu d'Història de la Ciutat in the Plaça del Rei, and the Museu d'Història de Catalunya in the Port Vell's Palau de Mar. As of 1997, there's even a Museum of Eroticism.

EXPLORING BARCELONA

Barcelona is made up of two main and contrasting parts. The old city lies between Plaça de Catalunya and the port. Above it is the grid-patterned extension, built after the city's third set of walls were torn down in 1860, known as the Eixample, where most of the Moderniste architecture is concentrated. Farther out are the former outlying towns Gràcia and Sarrià, the Pedralbes zone, and the Collserola hills behind the city. Ask your hotel or the tourist office about the Ruta del Modernisme, a new system of guides that takes you through some 50 Art Nouveau sites (☞ Guided Tours *in* Barcelona A–Z, *below*).

Numbers in the margin correspond to points of interest on the Barri Gòtic; La Rambla and the Raval; the Moderniste Eixample; Parc Güell, Tibidabo, and Pedralbes; Ciutadella and Barceloneta; and Montjuïc maps.

Great Itineraries

The Rambla, the Gothic Quarter, and all of old Barcelona hold constant surprises, even for longtime residents. Markets such as the Rambla's Boqueria, the Raval's Mercat de Sant Antoni, and the Els Encants flea market are always good browsing grounds, well seeded with cafés, bars, patios, and terraces for mid-itinerary breaks. You'll probably find here that the study of travel objectives is best balanced by the joys of aimless wandering. The air temperature is almost always just right, and occasionally the fragrance of the Mediterranean overcomes urban fumes on the beach at Barceloneta or in the port.

Three days would be sufficient to explore the Rambla and the Gothic Quarter, see the Sagrada Família and the main Moderniste sights, go to one or two of the most important museums, and perhaps take in a concert. Five days would allow a more thorough exploration of the same, as well as more museums and the chance to explore Barceloneta and the Collserola hills. A weeklong stay would give you time to learn the city's authentic rhythms and resources; check the daily papers for gallery openings and concerts; make a side trip to Sitges, Montserrat, or the Costa Brava; and approach a real understanding of what makes this the biggest and busiest city on the Mediterranean.

IF YOU HAVE 3 DAYS

Stroll the Rambla; then cut over to the **Catedral de la Seu** ① and walk around the Mons Taber, the high ground upon which the original Roman settlement was established and enclosed within Barcelona's first set of walls nearly 2,000 years ago. Detour through **Plaça del Rei** ③ before cutting back to **Plaça Sant Jaume** ⑦, where the Catalonian government, the Palau de la Generalitat, stands across the square from the *ajuntament* (city hall). From there it's a 10-minute walk to the **Museu Picasso** ⑤, from which another even shorter stroll leads past the church of **Santa Maria del Mar** ⑥ to Cal Pep, in Plaça de les Olles (for the best tapas in Barcelona), or to Set Portes for lunch or even dinner. Try to catch an evening concert at the **Palau de la Música** ㉛. Day two might be a Gaudí day: spend the morning at the **Temple Expiatori de la Sagrada Família** ㉔, midday at **Parc Güell** ㉖, and late afternoon walking past Casa Vicens, in Gràcia; La Pedrera and Casa Batlló, on Passeig de Gràcia; and the **Palau Güell** ⑪, just off the lower Rambla. On day three, take in the world's best Romanesque art collection at the **Museu Nacional d'Art de Catalunya** ㊸, in the Palau Nacional on Montjuïc, and perhaps wander Montjuïc's other important attractions, such as the **Fundació Miró** ㊷, the **Poble Espanyol** ㊺, and the Olympic facilities, especially Izosaki's superb Palau Sant Jordi and the restored Olympic Stadium. Take the cable car across the port for a late paella in **Barceloneta** ㊳.

IF YOU HAVE 5 DAYS

Walk the Rambla, the Boqueria market, Plaça del Pi, and the Barri Gòtic, including the **Catedral de la Seu** ① on the first day. The next day, take a few hours to see the **Museu Picasso** ⑤ and the church of **Santa Maria del Mar** ⑥. Walk through **Barceloneta** ㊳ and down to the **Olympic port** ㊴, or out onto the *rompeolas* (breakwaters) and back. On the third morning you can explore the Raval, to the west of the Rambla, and visit the new **Museu d'Art Contemporani** (MACB) ⑰ and **Centre de Cultura Contemporània** (CCCB) ⑱, as well as the medieval **Hospital de Sant Pau** ㉕ and Barcelona's oldest church, Sant Pau del Camp. If you have time, have a look at the **Museu Marítim** ⑩, the medieval shipyards, in the Reial Drassanes. In the afternoon you can take a guided tour of the **Palau de la Música** ㉛ and pick up tickets to a concert. The fourth day can be your Gaudí day, with the **Temple Expiatori de la Sagrada Família** ㉔ in the morning and **Parc Güell** ㉖ after lunch. In the late afternoon, walk down through Gràcia and see Gaudí's first house, Casa Vicens; farther down on Passeig de Gràcia you can walk past La Pedrera and Casa Batlló, in the heart of the city's grid-patterned Eixample, and another early Gaudí structure, the **Palau Güell** ⑪, just off the Rambla on Carrer Nou de la Rambla. Day five is a chance to explore Montjuïc: visit the **Museu Nacional d'Art de Catalunya** ㊸, in the Palacio Nacional; the **Fundació Miró** ㊷; the **Poble Espanyol** ㊺; and the Olympic facilities, the Palau Sant Jordi and the Estadio Olímpico. In the afternoon, take the cable car across the port and have an outdoor paella back in **Barceloneta** ㊳.

Barri Gòtic

This walk explores Barcelona's Gothic Quarter, a quiet warren of medieval buildings including the cathedral and the Picasso Museum. Parts of the Barri Gòtic and the Barri Xinès (or Barrio Chino), Barcelona's notorious red-light district, were significantly spruced up in preparation for the Olympic crowds. In the heart of the quarter, you'll come across squares freshly begot by the demolition of whole blocks and the planting of fully grown palms. Bag-snatching is not uncommon in these parts, so it's highly advisable not to carry one.

A Good Walk

A good walk through the Barri Gòtic could begin at **Catedral de la Seu** ① and move through and around the cathedral to the left to the **Museu Frederic Marès** ② (and its little terrace café, surrounded by Roman walls). Next, pass the patio of the Arxi de la Corona d'Aragó (Archives of the House of Aragon); then turn left again and down into **Plaça del Rei** ③.

As you leave Plaça del Rei, the **Museu d'Història de la Ciutat** ④ is on your left. Crossing Via Laetana, pass through the Plaça del Angel and walk down Carrer Princesa; this will take you to Carrer Montcada and a right turn to the **Museu Picasso** ⑤. As you continue down Carrer Montcada you'll pass some of Barcelona's most elegant medieval palaces before emerging into the Passeig del Born. Take a walk down to the Born itself, once one of Barcelona's major produce markets and now scheduled to be converted to a municipal library. Walk back to the church of **Santa Maria del Mar** ⑥, just past the Carrer Montcada end of the Passeig del Born. After spending some time inside, walk around the church's eastern (waterfront) side through the Fossar de les Moreres. A 10-minute walk up Carrer Argenteria and back across Via Laetana to Carrer Ferran will take you to the **Plaça Sant Jaume** ⑦, where the governments of Catalonia and Barcelona face each other in (at the moment) political discord. Try to arrange visits to these buildings, both of which are lavishly endowed with works of art. For a quick tour of Barcelona's *call* (from the Hebrew *qahal,* "meeting"), the medieval Jewish quarter, leave Plaça Sant Jaume on Carrer del Call, turn right on Sant Domènech del Call, and proceed 50 yards to what was once a synagogue on the corner of Carrer Fruita. Now turn left on Carrer Marlet down to the next corner of Arc de Sant Ramón del Call, where a stone plaque in Hebrew marks all that remains of the Jewish community that prospered here until the 1391 pogrom, directed primarily by agrarian revolutionaries. Go left back to Carrer del Call and out to Carrer Ferran via Carrer de la Boqueria and Volta del Remei. Finally, turn right on Carrer Ferran to **Plaça Reial** ⑧, one of Barcelona's few neoclassical squares.

TIMING

This walk covers some 2 km (1 mi) and, depending on stops, should take about three hours (including an hour in the Picasso Museum).

Sights to See

★ ❶ **Catedral de la Seu.** On Saturday afternoon and Sunday morning, Barcelona folk gather in the Plaça de la Seu to dance the *sardana,* a somewhat demure circular dance and a great symbol of Catalan pride. The magnificent Gothic cathedral was built between 1298 and 1450, with the spire and neo-Gothic facade added in 1892. Architects of Catalan Gothic churches strove to make the high altar visible to the entire congregation, hence the unusually wide central nave and slender side columns. Highlights are the beautifully carved choir stalls; Santa Eulàlia's tomb, in the crypt; the battle-scarred crucifix in the Lepanto Chapel; the intimate Santa Llucia chapel, in the front right corner; and the tall cloisters surrounding a tropical garden. ⊠ *Plaça de la Seu,* ☎ *93/315–2213.* ⊙ *Daily 7:45–1:30 and 4–7:45.*

Fossar de les Moreres (Cemetery of the Mulberry Trees). This low, marble monument stands in the open space along the eastern side of Santa Maria del Mar. It honors those defenders of Barcelona who gave their lives in the 1714 siege that ended the War of the Spanish Succession and established Felipe V on the Spanish throne. The inscription (EN EL FOSSAR DE LES MORERES NO S'HI ENTERRA CAP TRAIDOR, or IN THE CEMETERY OF THE MULBERRY TREES NO TRAITOR LIES) refers to the story of the graveyard keeper who refused to bury anyone who fought on the invading side, even when one of them turned out to be his son.

❹ **Museu d'Història de la Ciutat** (City History Museum). Here you can trace the evolution of Barcelona from its first Iberian settlement. Founded by a Carthaginian, Hamilcar Barca, in about 230 BC, the city soon passed into the hands of the Romans during the Punic Wars. It didn't expand much until the Middle Ages, when trading links with

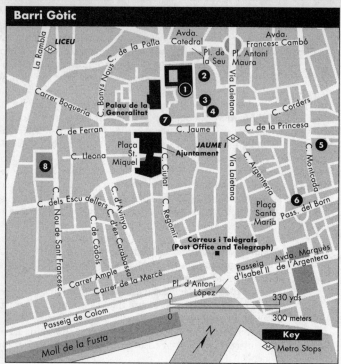

Genoa and Venice began its long and illustrious mercantile tradition. Look for the plans submitted for the 19th-century urban expansion, then called simply the Eixample (from *ensanche*, "widening" in Spanish), to see how different the city might have looked had Antoni Rovira Trias's radial plan not been blocked by cost-conscious bureaucrats in Madrid. Downstairs are some well-lighted Roman excavations. ⊠ *Palau Padellàs, Carrer del Veguer 2,* ☎ *93/315–1111.* ⊡ *600 ptas.* ⊙ *Tues.–Sat. 10–2 and 4–8, Sun. 10–2.*

OFF THE BEATEN PATH   **MUSEUM DEL CALÇAT** – Hunt down the tiny Shoe Museum, in a hidden corner of the Gothic Quarter between the cathedral and the Bishop's Palace. The collection includes a pair of clown's shoes and a pair worn by Pablo Casals. The tiny square, originally a graveyard, is just as interesting as the museum, with its bullet- and shrapnel-pocked walls and quiet fountain. ⊠ *Plaça de Sant Felip Neri,* ☎ *93/301-4533.* ⊡ *300 ptas.* ⊙ *Tues.-Sun. 11-2.*

② **Museu Frederic Marès** (Frederic Marès Museum). Here, off the left (north) side of the cathedral, you can browse for hours among the miscellany assembled by sculptor-collector Frederic Marès, which include everything from paintings and polychrome crucifixes to pipes and walking sticks. ⊠ *Plaça Sant Iu 5,* ☎ *93/310–5800.* ⊡ *350 ptas.* ⊙ *Tues.-Sun. 10–7:30.*

★ **⑤** **Museu Picasso** (Picasso Museum). The Picasso Museum is across Via Laietana, down Carrer de la Princesa—just to the right, on Carrer Montcada, from the Museu Frederic Marès. This narrow street contains some of Barcelona's most elegant medieval palaces, of which the museum occupies two, from the 15th century. Picasso spent many of his formative years in Barcelona, including his Blue and Rose periods (1901–06), and this collection—one of the world's best—is particularly strong on his early work rather than celebrated classics. Still, there is plenty here to warrant a visit, including childhood sketches, pictures from the beautiful Rose and Blue periods, and the famous 1950s Cubist variations on Velázquez's *Las Meninas*. If you're expecting black outlines and tortured lovers, you may be in for a beautiful and educational surprise. ⊠ *Carrer Montcada 15–19,* ☎ *93/319–6310.* ✆ *650 ptas.; ½ price Wed., free 1st Sun. of month.* ☉ *Tues.–Sat. 10–8, Sun. 10–3.*

Passeig del Born. The Passeig, once the site of medieval jousts, is at the end of Carrer Montcada, a long and narrow "square" lined with late-night cocktail bars and miniature restaurants with tiny spiral stairways and intimate corners.

❸ **Plaça del Rei.** This plaza is generally considered the oldest and most beautiful space in the Gothic Quarter. Upon Columbus's return from his first voyage to the New World, the Catholic Monarchs received him on the stairs fanning out here and in the Saló del Tinell, a magnificent banquet hall built in 1362. Other ancient buildings around the square are the Palau del Lloctinent (Lieutenant's Palace), the 14th-century chapel of Santa Àgata, and the Palau Padellàs.

❽ **Plaça Reial.** An elegant and symmetrical 19th-century arcaded square, the Plaça Reial is rimmed by yellow houses overlooking the wrought-iron Fountain of the Three Graces and lampposts designed by a young Gaudí in 1879. Sidewalk cafés line the entire square. In recent years the Plaça has earned a reputation for hosting drug pushers and the homeless, who occupy the benches on sunny days. The most colorful time here is Sunday morning, when crowds gather to sell and trade stamps and coins; at night it's a center of downtown nightlife. **Bar Glaciar,** on the uphill corner toward the Rambla, is a booming beer station for young internationals. **Tarantos, Jamboree,** and the **Barcelona Pipa Club** are all hot venues for jazz, flamenco, and rock.

❼ **Plaça Sant Jaume.** This central square behind the cathedral houses both Catalonia's and Barcelona's governments. The Plaça was built in the 1840s, but the two imposing buildings facing each other across it are much older. The 15th-century **ajuntament** (city hall) to the left has an impressive black-and-burnished-gold mural (1928) by Josep Maria Sert and the famous Saló de Cent, from which the Council of One Hundred ruled Barcelona between 1372 and 1714. You can wander into the courtyard, but to visit the interior you need to make arrangements with the office ahead of time. The **Palau de la Generalitat,** opposite, seat of the autonomous Catalan government, is an elegant 15th-century palace with a lovely courtyard and a second-floor patio with orange trees. The room whose windows you can see at the front is the Saló de Sant Jordi (St. George), named for Catalonia's dragon-slaying patron saint. Normally you can visit the Generalitat only on Día de Sant Jordi (St. George's Day), April 23; check with the *protocolo* (protocol office).

★ ❻ **Santa Maria del Mar.** Santa Maria del Mar, the most elegant of all Barcelona's churches, is on the Carrer Montcada end of Passeig del Born. Simple and spacious, it's something of an oddity in ornate and complex Moderniste Barcelona. The church was built from 1329 to 1383 in fulfillment of a vow made a century earlier by Jaume I to build a church for the Virgin of the Sailors. Its stark beauty is enhanced by a lovely rose window, soaring columns, and unusually wide vaulting. It's a fashionable place for concerts and weddings; if you happen by on a Saturday afternoon, you're bound to see a couple exchanging vows. ⊠ *Plaça de Santa Maria.* ☉ *Weekdays 9–12:30 and 5–8.*

La Rambla and the Raval

Barcelona's most famous promenade is a constant and colorful flood of humanity past flower stalls, bird vendors, mimes, musicians, newspaper kiosks, and outdoor cafés. Federico García Lorca called this street the only one in the world that he wished would never end; traffic plays second fiddle to the endless *paseo* (stroll) of both locals and visitors alike. The whole avenue is referred to as Las Ramblas (Les Rambles, in Catalan) or La Rambla, but each section has its own name: Rambla Santa Monica is at the southeastern or port end, Rambla de les Flors in the middle, and Rambla dels Estudis at the top leading down from Plaça de Catalunya.

A complete Rambla hike could begin at the Diagonal and continue down Rambla de Catalunya; through the Rambla proper, between Plaça de Catalunya and the Columbus monument; and across the port on the wooden Rambla de Mar boardwalk. El Raval is the area to the west of the Rambla; it was originally a slum stuck outside of Barcelona's second set of walls, which ran down the left side of the Rambla.

A Good Walk

Start on the Rambla opposite Plaça Reial and wander down the Rambla toward the sea, to the **Monument a Colom** ⑨ and the Rambla de Mar. As you move back to the Columbus monument, you may want to investigate the medieval **Drassanes Reiales** shipyards and **Museu Marítim** ⑩ as you start back up the Rambla. Gaudí's **Palau Güell** ⑪, on Carrer Nou de la Rambla, can be the next stop before you pass the **Gran Teatre del Liceu** ⑫ (which will probably still be under reconstruction). At the Miró mosaic at Pla de la Boqueria, cut right to the Plaça del Pi and the church of **Santa Maria del Pi** ⑬. Back on the Rambla, stroll through the **Boqueria** food market ⑭ and the **Palau de la Virreina** ⑮ exhibition center next door; then cut around to the lovely courtyards of the medieval **Antic Hospital de la Santa Creu** ⑯. Next, visit the new **Museu d'Art Contemporani** (MACB) ⑰ and the **Centre de Cultura Contemporània** (CCCB) ⑱, on Carrer Montalegre, before hooking back into the Rambla. On your return to the Rambla check out the various attractions in the **Port Vell** ⑲, especially the aquarium. Finish your walk along Carrer Tallers, ending up in **Plaça de Catalunya** ⑳.

TIMING

This walk covers about 2 km (1 mi). Allow three hours, including stops and visits.

Sights to See

⑯ **Antic Hospital de la Santa Creu.** Surrounded by a cluster of other 15th-century buildings, this medieval hospital is now home to a number of libraries and cultural and educational institutions. You can approach it from the back door of the Boqueria, or from either Carrer del Carme or Carrer Hospital. Particularly impressive and lovely is the courtyard of the Casa de Convalescència, with its Renaissance columns and scenes of the life of St. Paul portrayed in *azulejos* (ceramic tiles). ✉ *Carrer Hospital 54 and Carrer del Carme 45.*

Antigua Casa Figueres. This Moderniste grocery and pastry store on the corner of Petxina has a splendid mosaic facade and exquisite Art Nouveau fittings.

Barri Xinès. As you walk south from Plaça Reial toward the sea, Barcelona's notorious red-light district, the Barri Xinès (traditionally called the Barrio Chino in Castilian Spanish) is on your right. The Chinese never had much of a presence here; the name is a generic reference to foreigners of all kinds. The area is ill-famed for prostitutes, drug

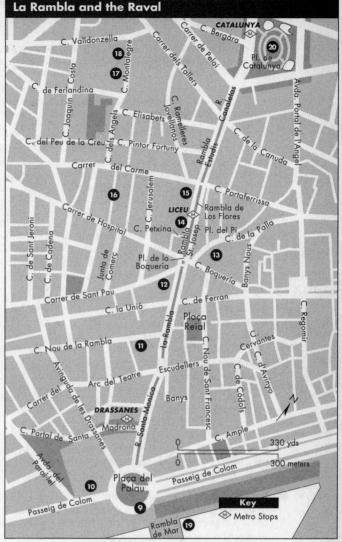

La Rambla and the Raval

pushers, and street thieves, but it's not as dangerous as it looks; in fact, the reinforced police presence here may even make it safer than other parts of the Gothic Quarter.

Boqueria. Barcelona's most spectacular food market, also known as the Mercat de Sant Josep, is an explosion of life and color complete with delicious coffee spots and **Pinotxo** (stand number 66–68), a little bar-bistro that has won acclaim as a gourmet sanctuary. Don't miss mushroom supplier and expert Petràs and his mad display of wild 'shrooms, herbs, nuts, and berries ("Fruits del Bosc"—Fruits of the Forest), at stand number 867–870. ⊠ *Rambla 91.*

Centre de Cultura Contemporànea de Barcelona (CCCB). This museum, lecture hall, concert hall, and exhibition space is worth checking out no matter what's on the schedule. Housed in the restored and renovated Casa de la Caritat, a former medieval convent and hospital, the CCCB now features a reflecting wall, in which you can see over the rooftops to Montjuïc and beyond. ✉ *Montalegre 5,* ☎ *93/412–0781.* 🎫 *350 ptas.–650 ptas.* ⊙ *Tues.–Fri. 11–2 and 4–8, Wed. and Sat. 11–8, Sun. 10–3.*

⑫ Gran Teatre del Liceu. Barcelona's once and future opera house is one of Europe's oldest and most beautiful. Long one of the city's most cherished cultural landmarks, the Liceu was gutted in early 1994 by a fire whose origins have aroused much speculation. Soprano Montserrat Caballé stood on the Rambla in tears as the beloved venue was consumed. The restoration is scheduled to be completed by early 1999; check for tours of undamaged rooms. ✉ *Carrer de Sant Pau 13 (at La Rambla).*

⑨ Monument a Colom (Columbus Monument). At the foot of the Rambla, take an elevator to the top of the Monument a Colom for a bird's-eye view over the city. (The entrance is on the harbor side.) 🎫 *375 ptas.* ⊙ *June 24–Sept. 24, daily 9–9; Sept. 25–June 23, Tues.–Sat. 10–2 and 4–8, Sun. 10–7.*

⑰ Museu d'Art Contemporani de Barcelona (Barcelona Museum of Contemporary Art). This 1992 building was designed by American architect Richard Meier and houses both a permanent collection and traveling exhibits. ✉ *Plaça dels Àngels,* ☎ *93/412–0810.* 🎫 *Tues. and Thurs.–Sun. 650 ptas.; ½ price Wed.* ⊙ *Tues.–Sat. 10–2 and 4–8, Sun. 10–2.*

⑩ Museu Marítim (Maritime Museum). The superb Museu Marítim is housed in the 13th-century **Drassanes Reials** (Royal Shipyards), to the right at the foot of the Rambla. It's full of ships, including a spectacular, life-size reconstructed galley; figureheads; nautical gear; and several early navigational charts. ✉ *Plaça Portal de la Pau 1.* 🎫 *850 ptas.; ½ price Wed., free 1st Sun. of month.* ⊙ *Tues.–Sat. 10–2 and 4–7, Sun. 10–2.*

⑮ Palau de la Virreina. The neoclassical Virreina Palace, built by a viceroy to Peru in 1778, is now a major exhibition center for paintings, photography, and historical items; find out what's on while you're here. The bookstore and municipal tourist office within are also useful stops. ✉ *Rambla de les Flors 99,* ☎ *93/301–7775.* ⊙ *Tues.–Sat. 10–2 and 4:30–9, Sun. 10–2, Mon. 4:30–9.*

★ ⑪ Palau Güell. Antoni Gaudí built this mansion in 1886–89 for his patron, a textile baron named Count Eusebi de Güell, and soon found himself in the international limelight. The prominent Catalan emblem between the parabolic entrance gates attests to the nationalist leanings that Gaudí shared with Güell. The facade is a dramatic foil for the treasure house inside, where spear-shape Art Nouveau columns frame the windows and prop up a series of minutely detailed wood ceilings. Some of Gaudí's early decorative chimneys garnish the roof. ✉ *Carrer/Nou de la Rambla 9.* 🎫 *500 ptas.; ½ price Wed., free 1st Sun. of month.* ⊙ *Tues.–Sat. 10–2 and 4–7, Sun. 10–2.*

⑳ Plaça de Catalunya. The Plaça de Catalunya is Barcelona's banking and transport center. It's at the head of the Rambla, marking the frontier between the new urbanization and the old city, between Plaça de Catalunya and the port.

⑲ Port. In the port beyond the Columbus monument—behind the ornate Duana, or former customs building, now headquarters for the Barcelona Port authority—is the **Rambla de Mar,** a sliding boardwalk (with drawbridge) that's taken up at night to allow boats in and out of the inner harbor. The Rambla de Mar extends out to the **Moll d'Espanya,** with its Maremagnum shopping center, IMAX theater, and new aquarium, a loop that can easily take a few hours to explore. Here you can board a Golondrina boat for a tour of the port or, from the Moll de Barcelona on the right, take a cable car to Montjüic or Barceloneta. Trasmediterranea passenger ferries leave for Italy and the Balearic Islands from the Moll de Barcelona. At the end of the quay is Barcelona's World Trade Center.

⑬ **Santa Maria del Pi** (St. Mary of the Pine). The adjoining **Plaça del Pi** and **Plaça de Sant Josep Oriol** are at once two of the Gothic Quarter's most bustling and most tranquil squares. The church of Santa Maria del Pi, like Santa Maria del Mar, is a fine example of Catalan Gothic architecture. Its gigantic rose window, which overlooks the diminutive square, is Barcelona's best.

The Moderniste Eixample

Above Plaça de Catalunya is the elegant checkerboard known as the Eixample. With the dismantling of the city walls in 1860, Barcelona embarked upon a vast expansion scheme fueled both by the return of rich colonials from America and by an influx of provincial aristocrats who had sold their estates after the debilitating second Carlist War (1847–49) (☞ Chronology *in* Chapter 16). The street grid was the work of urban planner Ildefons Cerdà; much of the building here was done at the height of Modernisme. The principal thoroughfares of the Eixample are Rambla de Catalunya and Passeig de Gràcia, where some of the city's most elegant shops and cafés are found.

A Good Walk

Starting in the **Plaça de Catalunya** ⑳, walk up Passeig de Gràcia until you reach the corner of Consell de Cent. Take a deep breath: you are about to enter the Bermuda Triangle of Moderniste architecture, the much-heralded **Manzana de la Discordia** ㉑. This is the "city block" or "apple" of discord (the pun only works in Spanish), where the three great figures of Barcelona's late-19th-century Moderniste (Art Nouveau) movement—Gaudí, Domènech i Muntaner, and Puig i Cadafalch— went hand to hand with three buildings and three very different styles. The Tàpies Foundation, with its rooftop *Chair and Cloud* sculpture by Antoni Tàpies himself, is just west, on Carrer Aragó. Gaudí's Casa Milà, known as La Pedrera, is three blocks farther up Passeig de Gràcia; after seeing it, hike or taxi to Gaudí's emblematic **Temple Expiatori de la Sagrada Família** ㉔. Finally, stroll over to Domènech i Muntaner's **Hospital de Sant Pau** ㉕.

TIMING

Depending on how many taxis you take, this is at least a three-hour walk. Add another two hours for a thorough exploration of the Sagrada Família.

Sights to See

★ ㉓ **Casa Milà.** Gaudí's Casa Milà, nicknamed La Pedrera (The Stone Quarry), has a remarkable, curving-stone facade that undulates around the corner of the block. When the building was unveiled, in 1905, local residents were not enthusiastic about the appearance of these cavelike balconies on their most fashionable street. Gaudí's rooftop chimney park is as spectacular as anything in Barcelona, especially in late afternoon, when the sunlight slants over the city into the Mediterranean. The Espai Gaudí (Gaudí Space), in the attic, has an excellent critical display of Gaudí's works, theories, and techniques. ⊠ *Passeig de Gràcia 92,* ☎ *93/484–5995.* ▣ *500 ptas.* ☉ *Guided visits Tues.–Sat. 10, 11, noon, 1, and 4.*

㉒ **Casa Montaner i Simó–Fundació Tàpies.** This former publishing house has been beautifully converted to hold the work of preeminent con-

The Moderniste Eixample

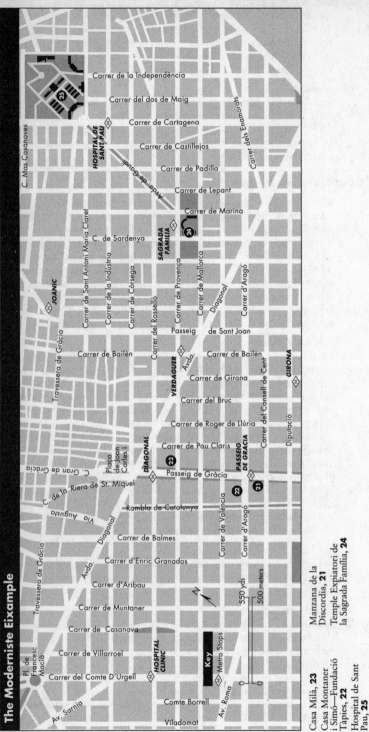

Carrer de la Independència

Carrer del dos de Maig

Carrer de Cartagena

Carrer de Castillejos

Carrer de Padilla

Carrer de Lepant

Carrer de Marina

C. Mas Casanoves

HOSPITAL DE SANT PAU

Avda. de Gaudí

Carrer dels Enamorats

C. de Sardenya

SAGRADA FAMILIA

Carrer de Sant Antoni Maria Claret

Carrer de la Indústria

Carrer de Còrsega

Carrer de Rosselló

Carrer de Provença

Carrer de Mallorca

Diagonal

Carrer d'Aragó

JOANIC

Travessera de Gràcia

Passeig de Sant Joan

Carrer de Bailèn

Carrer de Bailèn

Avda.

VERDAGUER

Carrer de Girona

GIRONA

Carrer del Bruc

Carrer de Roger de Llúria

Carrer del Consell de Cent

Carrer de Pau Claris

Diputació

DIAGONAL

Plaça de Joan Carles

23

PASSEIG DE GRACIA

Passeig de Gràcia

C. Gran de Gràcia

C. de la Riera de St. Miquel

22 21

Rambla de Catalunya

Via Augusta

Diagonal

Carrer de Balmes

Carrer de València

Carrer d'Aragó

Travessera de Gràcia

Carrer d'Enric Granados

Avda.

Carrer d'Aribau

Carrer de Muntaner

Carrer de Casanova

N

550 yds

500 meters

Carrer de Villarroel

HOSPITAL CLINIC

Key

Metro Stops

Pl. de Francesc Macià

Carrer del Comte D'Urgell

Comte Borrell

Av. Sarrià

Av. Roma

Viladomat

Casa Milà, **23**

Casa Montaner
i Simó—Fundació
Tàpies, **22**

Hospital de Sant
Pau, **25**

Manzana de la
Discordia, **21**

Temple Expiatori de
la Sagrada Família, **24**

temporary Catalan painter Antoni Tàpies, as well as frequent temporary exhibits. On top of the building is a tangle of metal entitled *Núvol i cadira* (*Cloud and Chair*). The airy, split-level Fundació Tàpies also has a bookstore that's strong on both Tàpies and Asian art. ⊠ *Carrer Aragó 255,* ☎ *93/487–0315.* ⊡ *600 ptas.* ☉ *Tues.–Sun. 11–8.*

㉕ **Hospital de Sant Pau.** The brick Hospital de Sant Pau is notable for its Mudéjar motifs and wards set among the gardens. ⊠ *Carrer Sant Antoni Maria Claret 167,* ☎ *93/291–9000.*

㉑ **Manzana de la Discòrdia.** The name is a pun on the word *mançana*, which means both "city block" and "apple," alluding to the architectural counterpoint on this block and to the classical myth of the Apple of Discord. The houses here are spectacular. The ornate Casa Lleó Morera (Number 35) was extensively rebuilt (1902–06) by Palau de la Música architect Domènech i Muntaner, and the Eusebi Arnau sculptures on the main floor are excellent. The pseudo-Gothic, pseudo-Flemish Casa Amatller (No. 41) is by Puig i Cadafalch. Next door is Gaudí's Casa Batlló, with a mottled facade that resembles nearly anything you want it to. Nationalist symbolism is at work here: the scaly roof line represents the dragon of evil impaled on St. George's cross, and the skulls and bones on the balconies are the dragon's victims. ⊠ *Passeig de Gràia 35, 41, and 43 (between Consell de Cent and Aragó).*

★ ㉔ **Temple Expiatori de la Sagrada Família** (Expiatory Temple of the Holy Family). Barcelona's most emblematic landmark, Antoni Gaudí's Sagrada Família is still under construction. Unfinished at his death, at age 74—Gaudí was run over by a tram and, unrecognized for several days, died in a pauper's ward in 1926—this striking and surreal creation causes consternation, wonder, howls of protest, shrieks of derision, and cries of rapture. Whatever your feelings, you can't deny that it occupies space in an exceptional and possibly unique manner. Gaudí envisaged three facades: Faith, Hope, and Charity, each with four towers collectively representing the 12 apostles. These, in turn, would be dwarfed by a giant central dome some 500 ft high, still unfinished (in fact, unbegun) today. Construction began again in 1940 but faltered due to confusion over Gaudí's plans; current controversy centers on sculptor Josep Maria Subirach's angular figures on the western facade, condemned by the city's intellectual elite as kitsch and the antithesis of Gaudí's lyrical style, and by religious extremists for depicting Christ in the nude. For 250 pesetas, an elevator can take you to the top of the east towers for a spectacular view, but the stairway, though narrow, steep, and often crowded, is a better way to get a feel for the building.

The crypt has a museum of Gaudí's scale models; photographs showing the progress of construction; and photographs of Gaudí's multitudinous funeral. The architect is buried here. ☎ *93/455–0247.* ⊡ *900 ptas.* ☉ *Nov.–Mar., daily 9–6; Apr.–June and Sept.–Oct., daily 9–7; July–Aug., daily 8 AM–9 PM.*

Upper Barcelona: Parc Güell, Tibidabo, Sarrià, and Pedralbes

A Good Walk

These rambles are spread across Barcelona's upper reaches. It's advisable to hop a cab to Güell Park and then to Güell Park and Sarrià; connecting the two on foot is a one- to two-hour hike from the back entrance of **Parc Güell** ㉖, across the Vallcarca viaduct, and up to Avenida del Tibidabo at Plaça John F. Kennedy. From there, the Passeig de Sant Gervasi leads over to Plaça de la Bonanova, where it becomes Passeig de la Bonanova to Plaça Sarrià. After you wander **Sarrià** ㉘, it's just a 20-minute walk to the **Monestir de Pedralbes** ㉙.

Parc Güell, Tibidabo, and Pedralbes

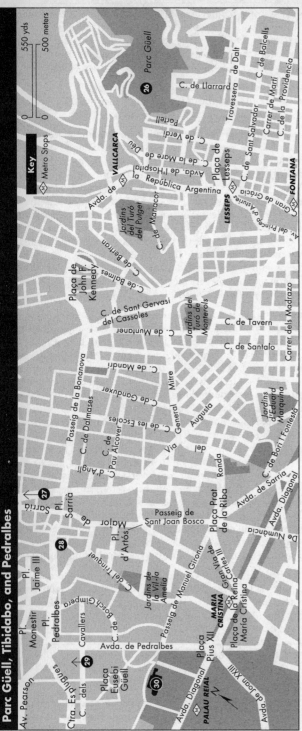

Key
Ⓜ Metro Stops

550 yds
500 meters

VALLCARCA

Parc Güell ㉖

C. de Llarrard

C. de Balcells

Carrer de Marf

C. de la Providencia

Travessera de Dalt

C. de Sant Salvador

C. de Verdi

C. de la Mare de Déu

C. de Portell

Avda. de l'Hospital

la República Argentina

Plaça de Lesseps

LESSEPS

Gran de Gràcia

FONTANA

Av. del Príncep d'Astúries

Avda. de Manacor

C. de Manacor

Jardins del Turó del Putget

Plaça de John F. Kennedy

C. de Balmes

C. de Bertran

C. de Sant Gervasi del Cassoles

Jardins del Turó de Monterols

C. de Tavern

C. de Muntaner

C. de Santalo

Carrer dels Madrazo

Passeig de la Bonanova

C. de Mandri

C. de Dalmases

C. de Ganduxer

Mitre

C. de les Escoles

General

Jardins d'Eduard Marquina

Via

Augusta

C. d'Anglí

C. de Pau Alcover

del

Ronda

C. de Bori I Fontestà

Plaça de Sarrià ㉗

Pl. de Sarrià

Major

Passeig de Sant Joan Bosco

Plaça Prat de la Riba

Avda. de Sarrià

Avda. Diagonal

De Numancia

Pl. d'Artós

Pl. Sarrià

C. del Tringuet

㉘

Pl. Pedralbes

Pl. Monestir

Pl. Jaime III

C. de Bosch i Gimpera

Jardins de la Vil·la Amèlia

Passeig de Manuel Girona

Gran Via de Carles III

MARIA CRISTINA

Plaça de la Reina Maria Cristina

Plaça Pius XII

Avda. de Pedralbes

Cavallers

Ctra. Esp

C. dels

Plugues

Plaça Eusebi Güell ㉙

Av. Pearson

Avda. Diagonal

Plaça Pius XII

PALAU REIAL

㉚

Avda. de Joan XXIII

N

Monestir de Pedralbes and Thyssen-Bornemisza Collection, **29**
Palau Reial de Pedralbes, **30**
Parc Güell, **26**
Sarrià, **28**
Tibidabo, **27**

TIMING

Allowing time for exploring Güell Park, Sarrià, and the Pedralbes Monastery and Thyssen-Bornemisza Collection, this is a five-hour outing that will necessarily end when the monastery closes at 2. Add another two hours if you want to go up to Tibidabo and the Collserola Tower.

Sights to See

㉙ Monestir de Pedralbes. Even without its Thyssen-Bornemisza Collection of Italian masters, this monastery is one of Barcelona's hidden treasures. Founded by Reina Elisenda for Clarist nuns in 1326, the convent has an unusual, three-story Gothic cloister, the finest in Barcelona, and its chapel has a beautiful stained-glass rose window and famous murals painted in 1346 by Ferrer Bassa, a Catalan much influenced by the Italian Renaissance. You can also visit the medieval living quarters. The monastery alone is one of Barcelona's delights, but the new **Thyssen-Bornemisza Collection,** installed in 1989 in what was once the dormitory of the nuns of the Order of St. Clare, sends it over the top. Surrounded by 14th-century windows and pointed arches, these canvases by Tiepolo, Tintoretto, Rubens, and Velázquez should not be missed. ⊠ *Baixada Monestir 9,* ☎ *93/203–9282.* ☞ *Monastery 350 ptas., Wed. 175 ptas., free 1st Sun. of month; monastery and cloister 350 ptas.; Thyssen-Bornemisza Collection 350 ptas.; combined ticket 650 ptas.* ☉ *Tues.–Sun. 10–2.*

OFF THE
BEATEN PATH

MUSEUM DE LA CIÈNCIA – Young scientific minds work overtime in the Science Museum, just below Tibidabo—many of its displays and activities are designed for children ages seven and up. ⊠ *Teodor Roviralta 55,* ☎ *93/212–6050.* ☞ *550 ptas.* ☉ *Tues.–Sun. 10–8. Metro: Avinguda de Tibidabo and Tramvía Blau halfway.*

㉚ Palau Reial de Pedralbes (Royal Palace of Pedralbes). Built in the 1920s for King Alfonso XII, this palace is now home to the **Ceramics Museum,** which takes in a wide sweep of Spanish ceramic art from the 14th to the 18th centuries. The influence of Moorish design techniques carefully documented. It's a 20-minute walk downhill from the monastery. ⊠ *Av. Diagonal 686,* ☎ *93/280–5024.* ☞ *550 ptas.; free 1st Sun. of month.* ☉ *Daily 10–3.*

㉖ Parc Güell. Güell Park is one of Gaudí's, and Barcelona's, most excellent resources. Whereas the Sagrada Família can be tiring in its massive energy and complexity, Parc Güell is light and playful, uplifting and restorative. Named after Gaudí's main patron, it was originally intended as a hillside garden suburb on the English model, but only two of the houses were ever built. It's an Art Nouveau extravaganza, with a mosaic pagoda, undulating benches, and large, multicolored lizards guarding a Moderniste grotto. ⊠ *Carrer d'Olot 3 (take metro to Lesseps; then walk 10 minutes uphill or catch Bus 24 to park entrance).* ☉ *Oct.–Mar., daily 10–6; Apr.–June, daily 10–7; July–Sept., daily 10–9.*

The **Gaudí Museum,** within Güell Park, occupies an Alice-in-Wonderland house in which Gaudí lived from 1906 to 1926. Exhibits include some of his eccentric furniture, decoration, and drawings. ⊠ *Parc Güell (up hill to right of main entrance),* ☎ *93/284–6446.* ☞ *450 ptas.* ☉ *Apr.–Oct., daily 10–2 and 4–7; Nov.–Mar., daily 10–2 and 4–6:30.*

OFF THE
BEATEN PATH

"EL BARÇA" – If you're in Barcelona between September and June, go see FC Barcelona play, preferably against Real Madrid (if you can get in). Games are generally played Saturday night or Sunday afternoon at

5, but there may be cup or international games during the week as well. Ask your hotel concierge how to get tickets, or call the club in advance. The massive Camp Nou stadium seats 130,000 and fills almost to capacity. A museum has an impressive array of trophies and a five-screen video showing memorable goals in the history of one of Europe's most colorful soccer clubs. ✉ *Arístides Maillol,* ☎ *93/330–9411.* ☒ *Museum 500 ptas.* ◷ *Oct.–Mar., Tues.–Fri. 10–1 and 4–6, weekends 10–1 and 3–6; Apr.–Sept., Mon.–Sat. 10–1 and 3–6.*

❷❽ **Sarrià.** This 1,000-year-old village was once a cluster of farms and country houses overlooking Barcelona from the hills; it's now a quiet enclave surrounded by the roaring metropolis. The main square, Plaça Sarrià, hosts an antiques and crafts market on Tuesday morning, *sardana* dances on Sunday morning, and Christmas fairs in season. The Romanesque church tower, lighted a bright ocher at night, looms overhead. Wander through the brick-and-steel **produce market,** behind and to the right of the church, and the tiny, flower-choked **Plaça Sant Gaietà,** behind the market. Cut through the Placeta del Roser, to the left of the church, to reach the elegant **town hall** in the Plaça de la Vila, noting the buxom bronze sculpture of Pomona, goddess of fruit, by famed Sarrià sculptor Josep Clarà (1878–1958). After peeking in to see the massive ceiling beams (and very reasonable set lunch menu) in the Vell Sarrià restaurant, at the corner of Major de Sarrià, go back and left of the town hall into tiny Carrer dels Paletes and back out to Major de Sarrià. Continue downhill through this (intermittently pedestrian-only) street to the bougainvillea- and honeysuckle-lined **Carrer Canet,** with its diminutive, cottagelike artisans' quarters. Turn right on Carrer Cornet i Mas and walk two blocks down to Carrer Jaime Piquet. A quick probe to the left will take you to No. 30, Barcelona's smallest and most perfect **Moderniste house,** with faux-medieval upper windows, wrought-iron grillwork, floral and fruited ornamentation, and organically curved and carved wooden doors. The next stop down Cornet i Mas is Sarrià's prettiest square, Plaça Sant Vicens, a leafy space ringed by old Sarrià houses and punctuated by a statue of the village patron saint. The café Can Pau is the local hangout, once a haven for authors such as Gabriel García Marquez and Mario Vargas Llosa, who lived in Sarrià in the '70s, on the cusp of their fame. It's a good place for coffee and a slice of tortilla. To get to the Monastir de Pedralbes from Plaça Sant Vicens, walk back up Mayor de Sarrià and through the market to the corner of Sagrat Cor and Ramon Miquel Planas. Turn left and walk straight west for 15 minutes.

Other Sarrià landmarks include the two **Foix** pastry stores, one on Plaça Sarrià 9–10 and the other on Major de Sarrià 57, above Bar Tomás. Both have excellent pastries, artisanal breads, produce, and cold *cava* and stay open until 9 PM on Sundays. The late J. V. Foix, son of the store's founders, was one of the great Catalan poets of the 20th century, a key player in keeping the Catalan language alive during the 40-year Franco regime. ✉ *Plaça Sarrià (take Bus 22 from the bottom of Avinguda de Tibidabo, or the FFCC train to Reina Elisenda).*

NEED A
BREAK?   **Bar Tomás,** just out on Major de Sarrià on the corner of Jaume Piquet, is a Barcelona institution, home of the finest potatoes in town. Order the famous *doble mixta* of potatoes with *allioli* and hot sauce. Draft beer (ask for a *caña*) is the de rigueur beverage.

❷❼ **Tibidabo.** Along with Montjuïc, Tibidabo is one of Barcelona's two major promontories. The views from this hill are legendary, really the most panoramic in Catalonia when the wind blows the smog out to sea. The shapes that distinguish Tibidabo from below turn out to be an unprepossessing, commercialized church; a vast radio mast; and the new, 850-ft communications tower, the Torre de Collserola. The exploitation is completed by a noisy amusement park. All in all, there's not much worth seeing here except the vista—particularly from the tower. Clear days are few and far between in fin-de-millennium Barcelona, but if you hit one, this excursion is worth considering. The restaurant **La Venta**, at the base of the funicular, is excellent and a fine place to sit in the sun in cool weather (the establishment traditionally provides straw sun hats). The bar **Mirablau** is also a popular hangout for evening drinks overlooking the lights of Barcelona. *Take the Tibidibo branch off the Sarrià subway; Buses 24 and 22 to Plaza Kennedy; or a taxi. At Avinguda Tibidabo, catch the Tramvía Blau, which connects with the funicular (☞ Getting Around, below) to the summit.*

Torre de Collserola. The Collserola Tower, which dwarfs Mt. Tibidabo, is a creation of Norman Foster, erected for the 1992 Olympics amid controversy over defacement of the traditional mountain skyline. The tower has a splendid panorama of the city when conditions allow. Take the funicular up to Tibidabo; from Plaza Tibidabo there is free transport to the tower. ⊠ *Av. de Vallvidrera*, ☎ *93/406–9354.* 🎟 *500 ptas.* ☻ *Wed.–Sun. and holidays 11–2:30, 3:30–8.*

Sant Pere, La Ribera, La Ciutadella, and Barceloneta

Barcelona's old textile neighborhood, around the church of Sant Pere, includes the flagship of the city's Moderniste architecture, the extraordinary Palau de la Música. The Barrio de la Ribera (waterfront), the Parc de la Ciutadella, and Barceloneta complete this walk along the periphery of what were once Barcelona's 13th-century walls.

A Good Walk

This neighborhood, or series of neighborhoods, lies generally to the left (north and east) of the Gothic Quarter. The area runs from the medieval Sant Pere textile district to the former waterfront, later silted and filled in to create La Barceloneta. Beginning in **Plaça de Catalunya** ⑳, it's no more than a 10-minute walk to the **Palau de la Música** ㉛, taking your first left off the Rambla. After inspecting the Palau (guided tours can be arranged on weekdays), continue along Carrer Sant Pere Més Alt to the Plaça Sant Pere on your way past the Sant Pere de les Puelles church and out to the **Arc del Triomf** ㉜, on Passeig de Sant Joan. From there, walk through the Parc de la Ciutadella and the Estació de França to the edge of the port, through **Barceloneta** ㊳, and along the beach to the **Port Olímpic** ㊴.

TIMING

Depending on the number of stops, this walk could take half a day. Count on at least three hours of actual walking time.

Sights to See

㉜ **Arc del Triomf.** This imposing, exposed-redbrick arch was built by Josep Vilaseca as the grand entrance for the 1888 Universal Exhibition.

㊳ **Barceloneta.** Once Barcelona's pungent fishing port and waterfront district, Barceloneta retains its colorful ambience. It's a pretty walk through narrow streets with lines of laundry snapping in the breeze overhead. Stop in Plaça de la Barceloneta and have a close look at the Baroque church of Sant Miquel del Port, with its somewhat outsized new sculpture of the saint in the alcove on the facade. Try the tapas bar on the sea side of the square.

Barcelona's beach, a little dusty and often crowded in summer, has improved much in recent years and can actually be used for swimming,

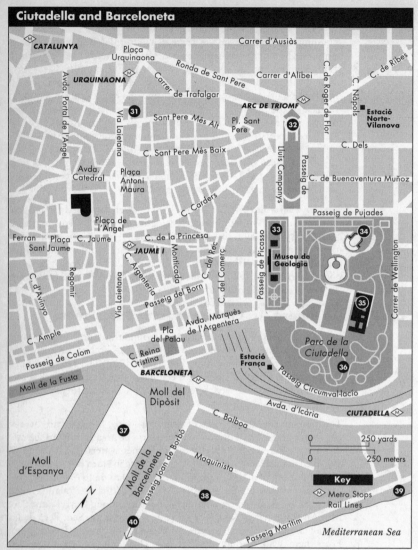

Ciutadella and Barceloneta

Arc del Triomf, **32**
Barceloneta, **38**
Castell dels Tres Dragons, **33**
Font de la Senyoreta Paraigua, **34**
Palau de la Ciutadella, **35**
Palau de la Música, **31**
Port Olímpic, **39**
Port Vell/Palau de Mar, **37**
Telefèric, **40**
Zoo, **36**

provided the winds and currents haven't created a backup of sewage. Take a close look at the water before you dive in.

NEED A
BREAK? **Can Manuel "la Puda,"** a friendly spot along Passeig Joan de Borbó, is a good choice for tasty and inexpensive paella in the sun. The nickname refers to the fragrance that used to emanate from this fishy district. ⊠ *Passeig Joan de Borbó 60–61,* ☎ *93/221–5013. AE, DC, MC, V. Closed Mon.*

③③ **Castell dels Tres Dragons** (Castle of the Three Dragons). Built by Domènech i Muntaner as the café for the 1888 Universal Exposition, this arresting building greets you as you enter the Ciutadella from Passeig Lluí Companys. It later became a workshop where Moderniste architects met to experiment with traditional crafts and to exchange ideas. It now holds the Museum of Zoology. ⊠ *Passeig Picasso 5,* ☎ *93/319–6912.* 🏛 *350 ptas.* ☉ *Tues.–Sun. 10–2.*

Estació de França. The elegantly restored Estació de França, Barcelona's main railroad station until about 1980 and still the stopping point for certain trains to and from France (notably the overnight *Talgo* to Paris), is outside the west gate of the Ciutadella. It's worth walking through to sense the Old World romance of Europe's traditional railroad system. ⊠ *Marquè de l'Argentera s/n,* ☎ *93/319–6416.*

NEED A
BREAK? You're just a step from Barcelona's best tapas at **Cal Pep** (⊠ Plaça de les Olles 8). Try the *gambitas* (baby shrimp) or *pulpo gallego* (octopus), and don't forget to order *pan de coca* (crunchy toast with oil and fresh tomato paste). Try not to give up if you have to wait for a while; they'll feed you wine in the meantime. It's fun and well worth it.

③④ **Font de la Senyoreta Paraigua** (Fountain of the Lady with the Umbrella). Escape the sights and sounds of the city by this fountain, its lake, and, behind it, the monumental *Cascada,* by Josep Fontserè, designed for the 1888 Universal Exhibition. The waterfall's rocks were the work of a young architecture student named Antoni Gaudí—his first public works, appropriately natural and organic, and certainly a hint of things to come.

Museu de Geologia. The Museum of Geology is next to the Castell dels Tres Dragons, not far from the beautiful Umbracle, the black slats of which help create jungle lighting for the museum's valuable collection of tropical plants. Barcelona's first public museum, it displays rocks, minerals, and fossils along with special exhibits on Catalonia and the rest of Spain. ⊠ *Parc de la Ciutadella,* ☎ *93/319–6895.* 🏛 *400 ptas.; free 1st Sun. of month.* ☉ *Tues.–Sun. 10–2.*

③⑤ **Palau de la Ciutadella** (Citadel Palace). This is the only surviving remnant of Felipe V's fortress, now shared by the Catalan parliament and the Museum of Modern Art. The palace's late-19th- and early 20th-century Catalan paintings and sculptures, by such artists as Isidro Nonell, Ramon Casas, and Marià Fortuny, form one of Barcelona's artistic treasures. A stroll through this collection makes it very clear that Catalonia's more famous artists—Gaudí, Picasso, Dalí, Miró—emerged not from nowhere but from an exceptionally rich artistic context. ⊠ *Plaça d'Armes, Parc de la Ciutadella,* ☎ *93/319–5728.* 🏛 *500 ptas.* ☉ *Tues.–Sat. 10–7, Sun. 10–2.*

Parc de la Ciutadella (Citadel Park). Once a fortress designed to consolidate Madrid's military occupation of Barcelona, the Ciutadella is now the city's main downtown park. The clearing dates from shortly after the War of the Spanish Succession, when Felipe V demolished some

2,000 houses in what was then the Barrio de la Ribera (waterfront neighborhood) to build a fortress and barracks for his soldiers and fields of fire for his artillery. The fortress walls were pulled down in 1868 and replaced by gardens laid out by Josep Fontserè. Within the park are a cluster of museums, the Catalan parliament, and a zoo.

★ ㉛ **Palau de la Música.** The Music Palace, on Carrer Amadeus Vives, is a flamboyant tour de force, designed by Domènech i Muntaner in 1908 and considered the flagship of Barcelona's Moderniste architecture. The tiny ticket booths in the richly embellished columns are, sadly, no longer in use. Try to attend a concert here, if only to see the interior, with its inverted, stained-glass cupola (☞ Nightlife and the Arts, *below*); otherwise, you can make an appointment to tour the hall on Tuesday, Thursday, or Saturday. ⊠ *Ticket office, Sant Francesc de Paula 2 (just off top of Via Laietana),* ☎ *93/268–1000.*

㊳ **Port Olímpic.** Choked with yachts, restaurants, and tapas bars of all kinds, the Olympic Port is just a mile up the beach, marked by the mammoth Frank Gehry goldfish sculpture in front of Barcelona's first real skyscraper, the Hotel Arts. The port rages on Friday and Saturday nights, especially in summer, with hundreds of young people of all nationalities circling and grazing until dawn.

㊲ **Port Vell.** From Pla del Palau, cross to the edge of the port, where the Moll d'Espanya, the Moll de la Fusta, and the Moll de Barceloneta meet. The modern wonders of the new Port Vell complex—the IMAX theater, aquarium, and Maremagnum shopping mall—loom seaward on the Moll d'Espanya. The Palau de Mar, with its five quayside terrace restaurants, stretches down along the Moll de Barceloneta. (Try Llevataps or, on the far corner, the Merendero de la Mari.) Take a stroll through the Museu de Historia de Catalunya (MHC) in the Palau de Mar for a purely Catalonian view of its national history. Along the Passeig Joan de Borbó are a dozen more traditional Barceloneta paella and seafood specialists.

Sant Pere de les Puelles (St. Peter of the Novices). One of the oldest medieval churches in Barcelona, this one has been destroyed and restored so many times that there is little left to see except the beautiful stained-glass window, which illuminates the stark interior. The word *Puelles* is from the Latin *puella* (girl)—the convent here was known for the beauty and nobility of its young women and was the setting for some of medieval Barcelona's most tragic stories of impossible love and romantic agony. ⊠ *Lluís El Piadós 1,* ☎ *93/268–0742.* ⊙ *Open for mass only.*

㊵ **Telefèric** (cable car). The cable car at the end of Passeig Joan de Borbócan takes you across to Montjuïc. Alternatively, you can walk to the end of the *rompeolas,* 3 km (1½ mi) out to sea, where you can catch a Golondrinas boat back into the port. ☎ *93/441–4820.* 🎫 *Cable car 850 ptas.* ⊙ *Oct.–June 21, weekends 11–2:45 and 4–7:30; June 22– Sept., daily 11:30–9.*

☾ ㊱ **Zoo.** Barcelona's first-rate zoo—the home of Snowflake, the world's only captive albino gorilla—occupies the whole bottom section of the park. There's a great reptile house, and a full complement of African animals. ⊠ *Parc de la Ciutadella,* ☎ *93/221–2506.* 🎫 *1,400 ptas.* ⊙ *Oct.–Apr., daily 10–6; May–Oct., daily 9:30–7:30.*

Montjuïc

Montjuïc, the hill to the south of town, is thought to have been named for the Jewish cemetery once located on its slopes, though an alternate explanation has it named for the Roman deity Jove, or Jupiter. The most dramatic approach is by way of the cross-harbor cable car from Barceloneta or from the mid-station in the port; but Montjuïc is normally accessed by taxi or Bus 61 (or on foot) from Plaça Espanya, or by the funicular that operates from the Paral.lel (Paral.lel metro stop on the green line).

A Good Walk

Walking from sight to sight on Montjuïc is possible but not recommended. You'll want fresh feet and backs to appreciate the sights here, especially the Romanesque art collection in the Palau Nacional and the Miró Foundation.

The *telefèric* drops you at the Jardins de Miramar, a 10-minute walk from the Plaça de Dante and the entrance to the amusement park. Rock-and-roll buffs may want to look up Chus Martínez, onetime colleague of Bill Haley and Eddie Cochrane, who runs the Bali restaurant here. Impromptu concerts for his guests are not unheard of. From here, another small cable car takes you up to the **Castell de Montjuïc** ㊶. From the bottom station, the **Fundació Miró** ㊷ is just a few minutes' walk, and beyond it is the Estadi Olímpic (Olympic Stadium). From there, on foot, cut straight down to the Palau Nacional and its **Museu Nacional d'Art de Catalunya** ㊸. From here, a wide stairway leads down toward Plaça de Espanya.

TIMING

With unhurried visits to the Miró Foundation and the Romanesque exhibit in the Palau Nacional, this is a four- to five-hour excursion. Have lunch afterward in the Poble Espanyol.

Sights to See

㊶ **Castell de Montjuïc.** Built in 1640 by rebels against Felipe IV, the castle has been stormed several times, most famously in 1705, by Lord Peterborough for Archduke Carlos of Austria. In 1808, during the Peninsular War, the castle was seized by the French under General Dufresne. Later, during an 1842 civil disturbance, Barcelona was bombed by a Spanish artillery battery from its heights. The moat has been made into attractive gardens, with one side given over to an archery range. The various terraces have panoramic views over the city and out to sea. The castle now functions as a military museum housing the weapons collection of early-20th-century sculptor Frederic Marès. ⊠ *Carretera de Montjuïc 66,* ☎ *93/329–8613.* ☜ *250 ptas.* ☉ *Oct.–Mar., Tues.– Sat. 10–2 and 4–7, Sun. 10–2; Apr.–Sept., Tues.–Sat. 10–2 and 4–7, Sun. 10–8.*

★ **Estadi Olímpic.** The Olympic Stadium was originally built for the Great Exhibition of 1929, with the idea that Barcelona would then host the 1936 Olympics (ultimately staged in Hitler's Berlin). After failing twice to win the nomination, Barcelona celebrated the attainment of its long-cherished goal by renovating the semiderelict stadium in time for 1992, providing seating for 70,000. Next door and just downhill stands the futuristic Palau Sant Jordi Sports Palace, designed by the Japanese architect Arata Isozaki. The structure has no pillars or beams to obstruct the view and was built from the roof down; that is, the roof was built first and then hydraulically lifted into place. ⊠ *Passeig Olímpic 17–19,* ☎ *93/426–2089.* ☉ *Weekdays 10–2 and 4–7, weekends 10–6.*

★ ㊷ **Fundació Miró.** The Miró Foundation was a gift from the artist Joan Miró to his native city and is one of Barcelona's most exciting contemporary-art galleries. The airy, white building was designed by Josep Lluís Sert and opened in 1975; an extension was added by Sert's pupil Jaume Freixa in 1988. Miró's unmistakably playful and colorful style,

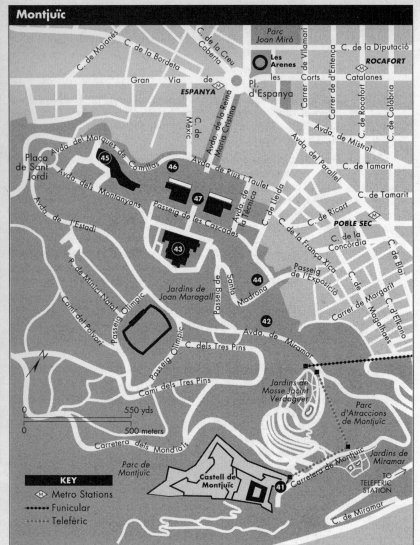

KEY

- Ⓜ Metro Stations
- ●••••• Funicular
- ••••••• Teleféric

Castell de
Montjuïc, **41**
Fundació Miró, **42**
Mies van der Rohe
Pavilion, **46**
Museu
Arqueològic, **44**

Museu
Nacional d'Art
de Catalunya, **43**
Plaça de les
Cascades, **47**
Poble Espanyol, **45**

BONUS MILES MAKE GREAT SOUVENIRS.

Earn Miles With Your MCI Card.

Take the MCI Card along on this trip and start earning miles for the next one. You'll earn frequent flyer miles on all your calls and save with the low rates you've come to expect from MCI. Before you know it, you'll be on your way to some other international destination.

Sign up for MCI by calling 1-800-FLY-FREE

Earn Frequent Flyer Miles.

AmericanAirlines
A'Advantage®

Continental Airlines
OnePass ▨▨.

▲ Delta Air Lines
SkyMiles®

NORTHWEST AIRLINES
WORLDPERKS®

▨ MILEAGE PLUS.
United Airlines

US AIRWAYS
DIVIDEND MILES

Is this a great time, or what? :-)

Easy To Call Home.

1. To use your MCI Card, just dial the WorldPhone access number of the country you're calling from.
2. Dial or give the operator your MCI Card number.
3. Dial or give the number you're calling.

# Austria (CC) ♦	022-903-012
# Belarus (CC)	
From Brest, Vitebsk, Grodno, Minsk	8-800-103
From Gomel and Mogilev regions	8-10-800-103
# Belgium (CC) ♦	0800-10012
# Bulgaria	00800-0001
# Croatia (CC) ★	0800-22-0112
# Czech Republic (CC) ♦	00-42-000112
# Denmark (CC) ♦	8001-0022
# Finland (CC) ♦	08001-102-80
# France (CC) ♦	0-800-99-0019
# Germany (CC)	0800-888-8000
# Greece (CC) ♦	00-800-1211
# Hungary (CC) ♦	00▼800-01411
# Iceland (CC) ♦	800-9002
# Ireland (CC)	1-800-55-1001
# Italy (CC) ♦	172-1022
# Kazakhstan (CC)	8-800-131-4321
# Liechtenstein (CC) ♦	0800-89-0222
# Luxembourg	0800-0112
# Monaco (CC) ♦	800-90-019
# Netherlands (CC) ♦	0800-022-9122
# Norway (CC) ♦	800-19912
# Poland (CC) ÷	00-800-111-21-22
# Portugal (CC) ÷	05-017-1234
Romania (CC) ÷	01-800-1800
# Russia (CC) ÷ ♦	
To call using ROSTELCOM ■	747-3322
For a Russian-speaking operator	747-3320
To call using SOVINTEL ■	960-2222
# San Marino (CC) ♦	172-1022
# Slovak Republic (CC)	00-421-00112
# Slovenia	080-8808
# Spain (CC)	900-99-0014
# Sweden (CC) ♦	020-795-922
# Switzerland (CC) ♦	0800-89-0222
# Turkey (CC) ♦	00-8001-1177
# Ukraine (CC) ÷	8▼10-013
# United Kingdom (CC)	
To call using BT ■	0800-89-0222
To call using C&W ■	0500-89-0222
# Vatican City (CC)	172-1022

CHASE

Flying to France on Friday? Get Francs from Chase on Thursday. Call Currency To Go at 935-9935 for overnight delivery.

CHASE
CURRENCY
TO GO
935-9935

Or pounds for London. Or Deutschmarks for Düsseldorf. Or any of 75 foreign currencies. Call **Chase Currency To Go**^{SM} **at 935-9935** in area codes 212, 718, 914, 516 and Rochester, N.Y.; all other area codes call 1-800-935-9935. We'll deliver directly to your door.* Overnight. And there are no exchange fees. Let Chase make your trip an easier one.

CHASE. The right relationship is everything.^{SM}

filled with Mediterranean light and humor, seems a perfect match for its surroundings, and the exhibits and retrospectives that open here tend to be progressive and provocative, from Moore to Mapplethorpe. Miró himself now rests in the cemetery on Montjuïc's southern slopes. During the Franco regime, which he strongly opposed, Miró first lived in self-imposed exile in Paris and in 1956 moved to Mallorca. When he died in 1983, the Catalans gave him a send-off amounting to a state funeral. ⊠ *Av. Miramar 71,* ☎ *93/329–1908.* ☒ *650 ptas.* ☉ *Tues.– Wed. and Fri.–Sat. 10–7, Thurs. 10–9:30, Sun. 10–2:30.*

㊻ Mies van der Rohe Pavilion. The reconstructed Mies van der Rohe Pavilion—the German contribution to the 1929 Universal Exhibition—has interlocking planes of white marble, green onyx, and glass. ⊠ *Av. Marquès de Comillas s/n,* ☎ *93/426–3772.* ☉ *Daily 10–6.*

㊹ Museu Arqueològic. Just downhill to the right of the Palau Nacional, the Museum of Archaeology holds important finds from the Greek ruins at Empúries, on the Costa Brava. These are shown alongside fascinating objects from, and explanations of, Megalithic Spain. ⊠ *Passeig Santa Madrona 39–41,* ☎ *93/423–2149.* ☒ *500 ptas.* ☉ *Tues.–Sat. 9:30– 1 and 4–7, Sun. 9:30–1.*

★ **㊸ Museu Nacional d'Art de Catalunya** (Catalonian National Museum of Art). This museum, housed in the imposing **Palau Nacional,** was built in 1929 and recently renovated by Gae Aulenti, architect of the Musée d'Orsay, in Paris. The Romanesque and Gothic frescoes and altarpieces here are simply staggering. Most were removed from small churches and chapels in the Pyrenees during the 1920s to ward off the threat of export by art dealers. When possible, the works are now being returned to their original homes or are being replicated, as with the famous *Pantocrator* fresco, a copy of which is now back in the church of Sant Climent de Taüll (☞ Chapter 6). The museum also contains works by El Greco, Velázquez, and Zurbarán. ⊠ *Mirador del Palau 6,* ☎ *93/423– 7199.* ☒ *900 ptas.; 500 ptas. for temporary exhibits only.* ☉ *Tues.– Wed. and Fri.–Sat. 10–7, Thurs. 10–9, Sun. 10–2:30.*

㊼ Plaça de les Cascades. Upon leaving the Mies van der Rohe Pavilion, you'll see the multicolored fountain in the Plaça de les Cascades. Stroll down the wide esplanade past the exhibition halls, used for Barcelona fairs and conventions, to the large and frenetic **Plaça d'Espanya.** Across the square is Les Arenes bullring, now used for theater and political rallies rather than bullfights. From here, you can take the metro or Bus 38 back to Plaça de Catalunya.

☙ **㊺ Poble Espanyol.** The Spanish Village was created for the 1929 Universal Exhibition. A tad too artificial to compete successfully with Montjuïc's other sights, it's a kind of Spain-in-a-bottle, with the local architectural styles of each province faithfully reproduced, enabling you to wander from the walls of Ávila to the wine cellars of Jerez. The liveliest time to come is at night, for a concert or flamenco show. ☒ *900 ptas.* ☉ *Mon. 9–8, Tues.–Thurs. 9–2, weekends 9–4.*

BARS AND CAFÉS

Barcelona may have more bars and cafés than inhabitants: colorful tapas emporiums; smart, trendy cafés; and a complete range of stylish, chic bars with rubrics ranging from *coctelerias* (cocktail bars) and *whiskerias* (often singles bars with professional escorts) to *xampanyerias* (champagne—actually *cava,* Catalan sparkling wine—bars). We suggest just a few. Most stay open until about 2:30 AM (☞ Nightlife and the Arts, *below,* for spots that close later).

Cafés

Café de l'Opera. Directly across from the Liceu, this high-ceiling Art Nouveau interior played host to opera goers and performers before the 1994 fire destroyed the theater. Central and de rigueur, it's a good bet if you're looking for someone; they're bound to pass through. ⊠ *Rambla 74,* ☎ *93/317–7585.* ⏰ *Daily 10 AM–2 AM.*

Cafe Paris. This popular spot is always a lively place to kill some time. Everyone from Prince Felipe, heir to the Spanish throne, to poet and pundit James Townsend Pi Sunyer can be spotted here in season. The tapas are excellent, the beer is cold, and the place is open 365 days a year from dawn to dawn. ⊠ *Calle Aribau 184, at Carrer Paris,* ☎ *93/209–8530.* ⏰ *Daily 6 AM–3 AM.*

Cafe Viena. The rectangular perimeter of this inside bar is always packed with local and international travellers in a party mood. It's a good place to meet until the reappearance of the traditional Zurich at the head of the Rambla. ⊠ *Rambla dels Estudis 115 ,* ☎ *93/349–9800.* ⏰ *Daily 8 AM–3 AM.*

Cafe Zurich. As this goes to press the Zurich is still out of commission as a result of the reconstruction of the block. However, this classic Rambla meeting point has been so important to Barcelona life that it's sure to reopen successfully. Stay tuned. ⊠ *Plaça Catalunya 1,* ☎ *no phone.* ⏰ *Daily 8 AM–3 AM.*

Els Quatre Gats. This is the café where Picasso staged his first exhibition and met the Modernistes. The restaurant serves respectable cuisine and snacks, such as different variations of *pa torrat* (slabs of country bread with tomato, olive oil, and anything from anchovies to cheese to cured ham or omelets). ⊠ *Montsió 3,* ☎ *93/302–4140.* ⏰ *Daily 8 AM–3 AM.*

Espai Barroc. This unusual "space" (*espai*), filled with Baroque decor and music, is in Carrer Montcada's most beautiful patio, the 15th-century Palau Dalmases, one of the many houses built by powerful Barcelona families between the 13th and 18th centuries. The stairway, decorated with bas-relief of the rape of Europa and Neptune's chariot, leads up to the Omnium Cultural, an institution for the study and exhibition of Catalonian history and culture. ⊠ *Carrer Montcada 20,* ☎ *93/310–0673.* ⏰ *Tues.–Sun. 4 PM–midnight.*

La Bodegueta. If you can find this dive (literally: it's a short drop below the level of the sidewalk), you'll also find a cozy and cluttered space with a dozen small tables, a few places at the marble counter, and lots of happy couples having coffee or beer, and maybe some ham or *tortilla española de patatas* (a typically Spanish, omeletlike potato-and-onion delicacy). ⊠ *Rambla de Catalunya 100,* ☎ *93/215–4894.* ⏰ *Mon.–Sat. 8 AM–2 AM, Sun. 7 PM–2 AM.*

Schilling. Near Plaça Reial, Schilling is always packed with young professionals, to the point where it's hard to get a table. It's a good place for coffee during the day and drinks and tapas at night. ⊠ *Ferran 23,* ☎ *93/317–6787.* ⏰ *Daily 10 AM–2:30 AM.*

Coctelerías

Almirall. This Moderniste bar in the Raval is quiet, dimly lit, and dominated by an Art Nouveau mirror and frame behind the marble bar. It's an evocative spot, romantic and mischievous. ⊠ *Joaquím Costa 33,* ☎ *93/302–4126.* ⏰ *Daily noon–2 AM.*

Boadas. This small, rather formal saloon near the top of the Rambla has become emblematic of the Barcelona *coctelería* concept, which usually entails a mixture of decorum and expensive mixed drinks amid wood and leather surroundings. ⊠ *Tallers 1,* ☎ *93/318–9592.* ☉ *Mon.–Sat. noon–2 AM.*

Dry Martini Bar. The eponymous specialty is the best bet here, if only to watch the ritual. This seems to be a popular hangout for mature romantics, husbands, and wives, though not necessarily each other's; it exudes a kind of genteel wickedness. ⊠ *Aribau 162,* ☎ *93/217–5072.* ☉ *Daily noon–2 AM.*

El Born. This former codfish emporium is now an intimate little haven for drinks, raclettes, and fondues. The marble cod basins in the entry and the spiral staircase up to the second floor are the quirkiest details, but everything here seems designed to charm and fascinate you in one way or another. ⊠ *Passeig del Born 26,* ☎ *93/319–5333.* ☉ *Daily 7 PM–2:30 AM.*

El Copetín. Right on Barcelona's best-known cocktail avenue, this bar has good cocktails and Irish coffee. It's dimly lit, and romantically decorated in a South Seas motif. ⊠ *Passeig del Born 19,* ☎ *93/317–7585.* ☉ *Daily 7 PM–3 AM.*

El Paraigua. Behind the *ajuntament,* this rather pricey bar serves cocktails in a stylish setting with classical music. ⊠ *Plaça Sant Miquel,* ☎ *93/217–3028.* ☉ *Daily 7 PM–1 AM.*

Miramelindo. The bar has a large selection of herbal liquors, fruit cocktails, pâtés, cheeses, and music, usually jazz. ⊠ *Passeig del Born 15,* ☎ *93/319–5376.* ☉ *Daily 8 PM–3 AM.*

Tapas Bars

Cal Pep. This lively hangout has Barcelona's best and freshest selection of tapas, served piping hot in a booming and boisterous ambience. ⊠ *Plaça de les Olles 8,* ☎ *93/319–6183.* ☉ *Mon. 8–midnight, Tues.–Sat. 1–4 and 8–midnight.*

Casa Tejada. The gregarious owner, Mr. Tejada, a former professional soccer player for FC Barcelona, seems to have a photographic memory for everyone who has ever snapped a tapa in his saloon. Though a little out of the way, Casa Tejada is handy to the boiling music-bar scene on nearby Marià Cubí. ⊠ *Tenor Viñas 3,* ☎ *93/200–7341.* ☉ *Daily 6 AM–2 AM.*

El Irati. This boisterous Basque bar between Plaça del Pi and the Rambla has only one drawback: it's hard to get into. While this is a clear sign of quality, the narrow shape of the place can be a problem at peak hours. Try to beat the crowds by coming at 1 PM or at 7:30 PM. The excellent tapas can be washed down with *txakolí* (young, white Basque wine). ⊠ *Cardenal Casañas 17,* ☎ *93/302–3084.* ☉ *Tues.–Sun. noon–midnight.*

Euskal Etxea. Euskal Etxea is the best of the three Basque bars in or near the Gothic Quarter. Try a *txakolí.* The tapas and canapés will speak for themselves. A restaurant and a Basque cultural circle round out this social oasis. ⊠ *Placeta de Montcada 13,* ☎ *93/310–2185.* ☉ *Tues.–Sat. 8:30 AM–midnight.*

La Palma. Behind the *ajuntament,* toward the post office, is this cozy café reminiscent of a Paris bistro, with marble tables, tapas to graze on, and newspapers to read. ⊠ *Palma Sant Just 7,* ☎ *93/315–0656.* ☉ *Daily 7 AM–3 PM and 7 PM–10 PM.*

Xampanyerias

El Xampanyet. Just down the street from the Picasso Museum, hanging *botas* (leather wineskins) announce one of Barcelona's liveliest *xampanyerias,* stuffed to the gills most of the time. The house *cava,* cider, and *pan con tomate* (bread with tomato and olive oil) are served on marble-top tables surrounded by barrels and walls decorated with *azulejos* (tiles) and fading yellow paint. ⊠ *Montcada 22,* ☎ *93/319–7003.* ⊙ *Tues.–Sun. 8:30–4 and 6:30–midnight.*

La Cava del Palau. Very handy for the Palau de la Música, this champagne bar serves a wide selection of *cavas,* wines, and cocktails, along with cheeses, pâtés, smoked fish, and caviar, on a series of stepped balconies adorned with shiny *azulejos.* ⊠ *Verdaguer i Callis 10,* ☎ *93/310–0938.* ⊙ *Mon.–Sat. 7 PM–2:30 AM.*

BEACHES

Barcelona beaches have improved and proliferated. Starting at the southern end is the Platja (beach) de Sant Sebastià, recently declared a nudist enclave, followed by the beaches of La Barceloneta, Passeig Marítim, Port Olímpic, Nova Icaria, Bogatell, and, at the northern tip, the Mar Bella. Topless bathing is the rule.

North of the City

North of Barcelona, the first beaches are Montgat, Ocata, Vilasar de Mar, Arenys de Mar, Canet and Sant Pol de Mar, all accessible by train from the RENFE station in Plaça Catalunya. Sant Pol is the pick, with a clean beach, a lovely old town, and Sant Pau, one of Catalonia's top restaurants. The farther north you go, toward the Costa Brava, the better the beaches.

South of the City

Ten kilometers (6 miles) south is the popular day resort Castelldefels, with a series of handy and happening beachside restaurants and bars and a long, sandy beach for sunning and bathing. Sitges, another 25 minutes south, has better sand and clearer water.

DINING

Barcelona restaurants are so many and so exciting that keeping up with them is a lifetime project. Don't be daunted if the selection seems overwhelming. Stick with local produce and local cuisine: roast suckling pig, for example, a Castilian specialty, will nearly always be better in Castile, where the best and freshest piglets prevail. Here, look instead for *mar i muntanya* (surf and turf) specialties such as rabbit and prawns, or dark meat with fruits or sweets, as in duck with pears. *Menús del día* (menus of the day) are good values, though they vary in quality and are generally served only at lunchtime. Restaurants usually serve lunch 1–4 and dinner 9–11. Some places, notably Botafumeiro and Set Portes, serve continuously from 1 PM to 1 AM, a convenience for travelers with jetlag or early flights to catch. Tipping, though common, is not required; 10% is perfectly acceptable.

$$$$ ✕ **Beltxenea.** Long one of Barcelona's top restaurants, Beltxenea retains an atmosphere of privacy in its elegant dining rooms. In summer you can dine outside in the formal garden. Chef Miguel Ezcurra's Basque cuisine is exquisite. A specialty is *merluza con kokotxas y almejas* (hake simmered in stock with clams and barbels). The house wines are excellent. ⊠ *Mallorca 275,* ☎ *93/215–3024. Reservations essential. AE, DC, MC, V. Closed Sun. and Aug. No lunch Sat.*

$$$$ ✕ **Botafumeiro.** Barcelona's finest shellfish restaurant serves continu-
★ ously from 1 PM to 1 AM on Gràcia's main thoroughfare. The mood is
maritime, with white tablecloths and pale varnished-wood paneling,
and the fleet of waiters will impress you with their soldierly white outfits and lightning-fast service. The main culinary attraction is the
mariscos Botafumeiro (myriad plates of shellfish that arrive one after
the other). Costs can mount quickly; try the half-rations at the bar if
you're on a budget. ⊠ *Gran de Gràcia 81,* ☎ *93/218–4230. AE, DC,
MC, V. Closed Mon. No dinner Sun.*

$$$$ ✕ **El Racó de Can Fabes.** Santi Santamaria's master class in Mediter-
★ ranean cuisine is well worth the 45-minute train ride (or 30-minute drive)
north of Barcelona to Sant Celoni. Ranked as one of Spain's top three
gourmet restaurants (along with El Bullí in Roses and Arzak in San
Sebastián), this sumptuous display of good taste and even better tastes
is a must for anyone interested in fine dining. Catch any train bound
for France from the RENFE station on Passeig de Gràcia. ⊠ *Sant Joan
6,* ☎ *93/867–2851. AE, DC, MC, V. Closed Sun. night and Mon. Jan.
27–Feb. 10 and June 23–July 7.*

$$$$ ✕ **Jean Luc Figueras.** Jean Luc Figueras's former restaurants (Eldorado
★ Petit, Azulete) shot instantly to the top of all known gourmet lists, and
this one continued the tradition by earning a Michelin star in its first
year. Charmingly installed in the Gràcia town house that was once
Cristóbal Balenciaga's studio, this exceptional spot makes everyone's
short list of Barcelona's best restaurants. Try the *lubina amb tripes de
bacalao i botifarra* (sea bass with cod tripe and sausage). ⊠ *C. Santa
Teresa 10,* ☎ *93/415–2877. Reservations essential. AE, DC, MC, V.
Closed Sun. No lunch Sat.*

$$$$ ✕ **Neichel.** Hailing from Alsace-Lorraine, chef Jean-Louis Neichel is
not bashful about his reputation as he explains such French delicacies
as the *ensalada de gambas al sésamo con puerros* (shrimp in sesame-
seed sauce with leeks). Prices fluctuate widely depending on your
choice. The setting is the ground floor of a Pedralbes apartment block,
mundane modernity compared with the cooking. ⊠ *C. Bertran i
Rozpide 16 bis, off Av. Pedralbes,* ☎ *93/203–8408. Reservations essential. AE, DC, MC, V. Closed Sun., Jan. 1–6, Holy Week, and Aug.
No lunch Sat.*

$$$$ ✕ **Passadis del Pep.** Hidden away through a tiny passageway off the
Pla del Palau, this lively bistro serves a rapid-fire succession of delicious seafood tapas and wine as soon you appear. Sometime late in the
proceedings you may be asked to make a decision about your main
course, usually a fish of one kind or another. As long as you do not
choose *bogavante* (lobster), criminally expensive in Spain, everything
will be fine. ⊠ *Pla del Palau 2,* ☎ *93/310–1021. AE, DC, MC, V. Closed
Sun. and last 2 wks of Aug.*

$$$$ ✕ **Sant Pau.** Carme Ruscalleda's place in Sant Pol de Mar is a spec-
★ tacular 40-minute train ride along the beach from Plaça Catalunya's
RENFE station (look for the Calella train north), and the train drops
you right at her door. It's one of Barcelona's best gourmet excursions.
Increasingly hailed as one of Catalonia's top culinary artists, Ruscalleda whips up a taster's menu that you won't soon forget—follow
her suggestions and those of her husband, Toni. ⊠ *Nou 10, Sant Pol
de Mar,* ☎ *93/760–0662. AE, DC, MC, V. Closed Mon. April 1–17
and Nov. 3–20. No dinner Sun.*

$$$ ✕ **Can Gaig.** This traditional Barcelona eating house is close to per-
fect in design, decor, *and* dining. Known for its market-fresh ingredi-
ents and traditional yet innovative fare, the menu balances seafood and
upland specialties, game, and domestic raw materials. Try the roast par-
tridge with Iberian bacon. ⊠ *Passeig de Maragall 402,* ☎ *93/429–1017,*

Barcelona Dining and Lodging

Parc Güell

9

7
ant Elíes

Plaça de
Lesseps

Trav. de Dalt

C. de Sant Salvador

C. de les   Camèlies

C. de la Providència

Plaça Alfons
el Savi

Ronda del
Guinardó

13

C. de l'Escorial

C. de Pi i Margall

Augusta

C. Menéndez Pelayo

Verdi

C. de

10

Avda. de Gaudí

C. a Aribau

C. Tuset

Travessera de Gràcia

Avda. Diagonal

Via

8

Travessera de Gràcia

C. de Sardenya

C. de Marina

Plaça
de Joan
Carles I

12

C. de Còrcega

11

C. de Indústria

C. de Bailén

C. de S. Joan

57

C. del Rosselló

15 **14**

16 **17** **18**

Rambla de Catalunya

C. de Pau Claris

C. de Roger Itúria

Passeig de S. Joan

C. de Provença

C. de Mallorca

Temple
Expiatori de
la Sagrada
Família

C. de Sardenya

Avda. de Gaudí

19 **20** **21**

Pg. de
Gràcia

C. de Valencia

C. d'Aragó

C. de Roger de Flor

Avda. Diagonal

C. de Napoles

C. de Sicília

C. de Sardenya

Passeig de Carles I

C. de Balmes

Consell de Cent

22

C. de la Diputació
Gran Vía de les
Corts Catalanes

C. de Bailén

Plaça
Tetuán

C. de Girona

C. de Casp

C. de
Ribes

Plaça
Universitat

23

26

24   **i** **25**

Pl.
Urquinaona

C. del Bruc

Ronda
Universitat

Pelai

C. dels Tallers

Pl. de
Catalunya

Ronda S. Pere

27

Jonqueres

S. Pere Més Alt

Arc del
Triomf

Estació Vilanova-Norte
(Bus Station)

Avda. de la Meridiana

28

29 **36**

del Carme

35

Porteferrissa

40

Via Laietana

S. Pere Més Baix

39

C. Dels

Passeig de
Lluís Companys

Passeig de Carles I

Avda. de la Meridiana

31 **32**

33

37

Avda. Catedral

Catedral

C. Ciutat

Passeig
Pujadas

C. de Wellington

41

37

Pl. St. Jaume

Pl. de l'Angel

C. de Picasso

43

44

38

C. Ferran

46 **47**

C. Princesa

C. del Comerç

Pg. Picasso

Parc de la
Ciutadella

45

Passeig del Born

51 **49**

Plaça Reial

50

Passeig
Isabel II

48

Avda. M. de
l'Argentera

52

Pl.

i **Estació**
Franca

KEY

i

C. Ample

Portal
de la
Pau

Pg. de Colom d'Antoni
López

Moll de la Fusta

Avda. d'Icària

Metro Stations
Railway Lines
Funicular
Teleféric
i **Tourist Information**

53

54

TORRE
DE
JAUME I

Moll
d'Espanya

Passeig D. Joan
de Borbó

BARCELONETA

0   450 yards

0   450 meters

55

FAX *93/429–7002. Reservations essential. AE, DC, MC, V. Closed Mon., holiday evenings, and Aug.*

$$$ ✕ **Can Isidre.** This small restaurant just inside the Raval from Avinguda del Paral.lel has a longtime following among Barcelona's artistic elite. Pictures and engravings, some original, by Dalí and other prominent artists line the walls. The traditional Catalan cooking draws on the nearby Boqueria's fresh produce and has a slight French accent—the homemade foie gras is superb. Come and go by cab at night; the area between Can Isidre and the Rambla is risky. ✉ *Les Flors 12,* ☎ *93/441–1139. Reservations essential. AE, MC, V. Closed Sun., Holy Week, and mid-July–mid-Aug.*

$$$ ✕ **Casa Leopoldo.** Hidden away in the dark Raval (literally, "slum"), this excellent *casa* serves some of the finest seafood and Catalan fare in Barcelona. Try to approach by taxi or on foot from Carrer Hospital in order to avoid the dangerous-looking (though not, in fact, very dangerous) Barrio Chino. ✉ *Sant Rafael 24,* ☎ *93/441–3014. AE, DC, MC, V. Closed Mon.*

$$$ ✕ **El Asador de Aranda.** Few restaurants can compete with this setting—a large, detached redbrick castle above the Avenida Tibidabo metro station. The dining room is large and airy, with a terra-cotta floor and traditional Castilian furnishings. The traditional Castilian cooking has won high praise ever since the restaurant opened in 1988. Try *pimientos de piquillo* (hot spicy peppers) and then *chorizo de la olla* (chorizo stew). ✉ *Av. Tibidabo 31,* ☎ *93/417–0115. AE, DC, MC, V. No dinner Sun.*

$$$ ✕ **El Racò d'en Freixa.** Chef Ramó Freixa, one of Barcelona's up-and-coming culinary lights, is taking founding father José María's work to another level. His clever reinterpretations of traditional recipes, all made with high-quality raw ingredients, have qualified the younger Freixa's work as *cuina d'autor* (designer cuisine). Try the pig's feet with quail in a garlic-and-parsley gratin. ✉ *Sant Elíes 22,* ☎ *93/209–7559. AE, DC, MC, V. Closed Sun. dinner, Mon., Holy Week, and Aug.*

$$$ ✕ **El Tragaluz.** *Tragaluz* means skylight—literally, "light swallower"—and is an excellent choice if you're still on a design high from Vinçón, Bd (Barcelona design) (☞ *Shopping, below*), or Gaudí's Pedrera. El Tragaluz is a sensory feast, with a glass roof that opens to the stars and slides back in good weather. The chairs, lamps, and fittings, designed by Javier Mariscal (creator of 1992 Olympic mascot Cobi) all reflect Barcelona's ongoing passion for playful shapes and concepts. ✉ *Passatge de la Concepció 5,* ☎ *93/487–0196. Reservations advised. AE, DC, MC, V. Closed Jan 5. No lunch Mon.*

$$$ ✕ **Jaume de Provença.** People come here because they've heard about the chef, Jaume Bargués. Dip into his haute-cuisine repertoire for *lenguado relleno de setas* (sole stuffed with mushrooms) or *lubina* (sea bass) soufflé. In the Hospital Clinic part of the Eixample, the restaurant is decorated in modern black and bottle green. ✉ *Provença 88,* ☎ *93/430–0029. Reservations essential. AE, DC, MC. Closed Mon. and Aug. No dinner Sun.*

$$$ ✕ **La Bona Cuina.** When the Madolell family converted their antiques business into a restaurant, in the late 1960s, it soon gained respect for its neo-Baroque elegance, intimacy, and nouvelle Catalan cuisine. Fresh fish is the house specialty; try the *bacalao à la Cuineta* (cod with spinach, raisins, pine nuts, and white sauce). The location, overlooking the apse of the cathedral, is memorable. ✉ *Pietat 12,* ☎ *93/268–2394. Reservations not accepted. AE, DC, MC, V. Closed Tues.*

$$$ ✕ **Quo Vadis.** Just off the Rambla, near the Boqueria market, a shiny gray facade camouflages one of Barcelona's most respected restaurants. A succession of small dining rooms decorated in grays and greens provides an atmosphere of sleek intimacy. The much-praised cuisine in-

cludes *hígado de ganso con ciruelas* (fried goose liver with prunes). ⊠ *Carme 7, ☎ 93/317–7447. AE, DC, MC, V. Closed Sun.*

$$$ ✕ **Reial Club Marítim.** For sunset or harbor views, excellent maritime fare, and a sense of remove from the city, try Barcelona's yacht club, El Marítim, just around the harbor through Barceloneta. Make tracks for the shellfish paella, *rodaballo* (turbots), *lubina* (sea bass), or *dorado* (sea bream). Ask for the freshest fish they have and you won't be disappointed. ⊠ *Moll d'Espanya, ☎ 93/221–7143. Reservations advised. AE, DC, MC, V. Closed Mon.*

$$$ ✕ **Set Portes.** These "Seven Doors" near the waterfront hide a high-
★ ceiling dining room, black-and-white marble floor, and mirrors aplenty. Going strong since 1836, this festive and elegant restaurant serves continuously from 1 PM to 1 AM, seven days a week. The cooking is Catalan, and the portions are enormous. Specialties are paella *de peix* (fish) and *sarsuela Set Portes* (seafood casserole). ⊠ *Passeig Isabel II 14, ☎ 93/319–3033. AE, DC, MC, V.*

$$$ ✕ **Talaia Mar.** Generally understood as the finest restaurant in the Olympic Port, this bright spot has wonderful views of the Mediterranean and fresh produce from it as well. The taster's menu is a bargain and a good way to see and sample the chef's best work for little more than a regular meal would cost. ⊠ *Marina 16, ☎ 93/221–9090. Reservations advised. AE, MC, V.*

$$$ ✕ **Tram-Tram.** At the end of the old tram line just uphill from the vil-
★ lage of Sarrià, Isidre Soler and his wife, Reyes, have put together one of Barcelona's finest and most original new culinary opportunities. Try the *menú de gustación* (tasting menu) and you might be lucky enough to get the marinated tuna salad, cod medallions, and the venison filet mignons, among other tasty creations. Perfectly sized portions and the graceful setting—especially in or near the garden out back—keep locals coming back. Reservations are a good idea, but Reyes can almost always invent a table. ⊠ *Major de Sarrià 121, ☎ 93/204–8518. AE, MC, V. Closed Sun. and Dec. 24–Jan. 6.*

$$–$$$ ✕ **Los Caracoles.** Just below Plaça Reial, a wall of roasting chickens announces one of Barcelona's most famous tourist haunts, a colorful spot with both excellent dining and a cosmopolitan atmosphere. A mere walk through the kitchen into the restaurant is exciting enough to inspire a feeding frenzy. The walls are thickly hung with photos of bull-fighters and visiting celebrities, and at night you're likely to be serenaded at your table. House specialties are Castilian roasts, fresh Mediterranean fish dishes, and, of course, *caracoles* (snails). It's open 365 days a year, with continuous service from 1 PM to midnight. ⊠ *Escudellers 14, ☎ 93/302–3185. AE, DC, MC, V.*

$$ ✕ **Bilbao.** Located at the corner of Venus and Perill, this boisterous
★ bistro is known for top value. Its excellent Catalan menu focuses on simple, popular recipes. The overhanging balcony seems to place all diners on stage, and things get fun and foolish quickly. Early dining is recommended for both lunch and dinner, as it gets crowded later on. ⊠ *Carrer de Perill 33, ☎ 93/458–9624. No credit cards. Closed Sun.*

$$ ✕ **Brasserie Flo.** Opened in 1982 by a group of Frenchmen, this used to be a textiles factory. You dine in a large, elegantly restored warehouse with arched vaulting, steel columns, and wood paneling all just a block from the Palau de la Música. The menu is an exciting combination of French and Catalan dishes. Try the freshly made foie gras and *choucroute*. ⊠ *Jonqueres 10, ☎ 93/319–3102. AE, DC, MC, V.*

$$ ✕ **Café de l'Acadèmia.** With wicker chairs and stone walls, this place is sophisticated-rustic, frequented by politicians from the nearby Generalitat. Classical music forms the background, and the excellent cuisine makes it more than a mere café. ⊠ *Lledó 1, ☎ 93/319–8253. ◷ Daily 9–4 and 9–11:30.*

$ ✕ **Agut.** Wood paneling surmounted by white walls, on which hang 1950s
★ canvases, forms the setting for the mostly Catalan crowd in this homey
restaurant in the lower reaches of the Gothic Quarter. Agut was founded
in 1924, and its popularity has never waned—not least because the hearty
Catalan fare offers fantastic value. In season (September–May), try the
pato silvestre agridulce (sweet-and-sour wild duck). There's a good selection of wine, but no frills such as coffee or liqueur. ⊠ *Gignàs 16,* ☎
93/315–1709. AE, MC, V. Closed Mon. and July. No dinner Sun.

$ ✕ **Egipte.** Hidden away behind the Boqueria market, Egipte has be-
come more and more popular over the last few years, especially with
a young set. The traditional Catalan home cooking, featuring such favorites as *favas a la catalana* (broad beans stewed with sausage), em-
anates from an overstretched but resourceful kitchen, and the results
can be uneven. Nonetheless, the many-tiered dining rooms, with marble-
top tables and Egyptian motifs, continue to draw a lively and sophisticated crowd. The best time to come is lunchtime, when the *menú del
día* is a great value. There are sister branches at Jerusalem 3 and Rambla 79. ⊠ *Jerusalem 12,* ☎ *93/317–7480. Reservations not accepted.
AE, DC, MC, V. Closed Sun.*

$ ✕ **El Glop.** Noisy, hectic, and full of jolly diners from all over Barcelona,
El Glop has specials like *calçotades* (giant spring onions baked in a clay
oven) and *asados* (barbecued meats). House wine arrives in a *porró*
(*porrón*, in Spanish; unless you're practiced at pouring wine into your
mouth from some distance, save your blushes—and clothes—by using
the wider opening and a glass). Bright and simply furnished, the restaurant is a few blocks north of Plaça del Sol, in Gràcia. ⊠ *Sant Lluís 24,*
☎ *93/213–7058. MC, V. Closed Mon.*

$ ✕ **La Fonda.** This is one of three Camós-family restaurants that offer
top value for your peseta. The other two locations are in nearby Plaça
Reial: **Les Quinze Nits** (⊠ Plaça Reial 6) and **Hostal de Rita** (⊠ Carrer Arago 279), near the corner of Arago and Pau Claris. Be early (1
for lunch, 8 for dinner); reservations are not accepted, and long lines
tend to form. The food is traditional Catalan, and the decor is a tasteful mixture of modern and rustic design. ⊠ *Escudellers 10,* ☎ *93/301–
7515. AE, DC, MC, V.*

$ ✕ **La Tramoia.** This surprising new place at the corner of Rambla de
Catalunya and Gran Via gives marvelous tastes at low prices in a
lively, boisterous atmosphere. Try the onion soup or the *gambas al ajillo*
(shrimp cooked in garlic and olive oil) and the *allioli*. Tramoia is Catalan for "backstage" as well as for "swindle," or the intrigue behind a
deal; here you see the chef behind glass. ⊠ *Rambla de Catalunya 15,*
☎ *93/412–3634.* ☉ *Daily 1 PM–4:30 PM and 8 PM–1 AM.*

$ ✕ **Sopeta Una.** Dining in this cozy, minuscule restaurant, with old-
fashioned, earthy decor and an intimate ambience, is more like eating
in someone's house. Try the *cors de carxofes* (artichoke hearts), and
for dessert, don't miss the traditional Catalan *música,* if it's on the
menu—a plate of raisins, almonds, and dried fruit served with a glass
of Muscatel. ⊠ *Verdaguer i Callis 6,* ☎ *93/319–6131. AE, V. Closed
Sun. and Aug.*

LODGING

Barcelona's hotel selection is, like the restaurant list, vast. The downtown hotels, such as the Ritz, the Claris, the Condes de Barcelona, and
the Colón, probably best combine comfort with a sense of where you
are, while the sybaritic new palaces, like the Arts, the Rey Juan Carlos I, the Hilton, and the Princesa Sofía, cater more to business travelers seeking familiar surroundings and luxury rather than geography.
Meanwhile, the smaller hotels, such as the Jardí and the España, are

less than half as expensive and more representative of the life of the city.

$$$$ ⊞ **Avenida Palace.** At the bottom of the Eixample, between the Rambla de Catalunya and Passeig de Gràcia, this hotel conveys elegance and antiquated style despite dating from only 1952. The lobby is wonderfully ornate, with curving staircases leading off in many directions. Everything is patterned, from the carpets to the plasterwork, a style largely echoed in the bedrooms, although some have been modernized and the wallpaper tamed. If you want contemporary minimalism, stay elsewhere. ⊠ *Gran Via 605–607, 08007,* ☎ *93/301–9600,* FAX *93/318–1234. 160 rooms. Restaurant, bar, health club. AE, DC, MC, V.*

$$$$ ⊞ **Condes de Barcelona.** This is one of the city's most popular hotels—
★ reserve well in advance. The stunning, pentagonal lobby features a marble floor and the original columns and courtyard from the 1891 building. The most modern rooms have Jacuzzis and terraces overlooking interior gardens. An affiliated fitness club around the corner offers golf, squash, and swimming. ⊠ *Passeig de Gràcia 75, 08008,* ☎ *93/488–2200,* FAX *93/487–1442. 183 rooms. Restaurant, bar, parking. AE, DC, MC, V.*

$$$$ ⊞ **Fira Palace.** This relatively new hotel (open since the 1992 Olympics) has established itself among Barcelona's finest business and convention havens. Close to Barcelona's Convention Palace, the hotel also offers easy access to Montjuïc and its attractions. Impeccably modern, it's a solid choice for generic creature comfort rather than local color. ⊠ *Av. Rius i Taulet 1, 08004,* ☎ *93/426–2223,* FAX *93/424–8679. 260 rooms, 16 suites. Restaurant, piano bar, pool, health club, parking. AE, DC, MC, V.*

$$$$ ⊞ **Hotel Arts.** This luxurious Ritz-Carlton monolith overlooks Barcelona from the new Olympic Port, providing unique views of the Mediterranean, the city, and the mountains behind. A short taxi ride from the center of the city, the hotel is virtually a world of its own, with three restaurants (one specializing in Californian cuisine), an outdoor pool, and the beach. ⊠ *C. de la Marina 19–21, 08005,* ☎ *93/221–1000,* FAX *93/221–1070. 399 rooms and 56 suites. 3 restaurants, bar, pool, beauty salon, beach, parking. AE, DC, MC, V.*

$$$$ ⊞ **Hotel Claris.** Widely considered Barcelona's best hotel, the Claris is a fascinating melange of design and tradition. The rooms come in 60 different layouts, all furnished in classical, 18th-century English style, with lots of wood and marble. On site are a Japanese water garden, a first-rate restaurant, and a rooftop pool, all near the center of Barcelona. ⊠ *Carrer Pau Claris 150,* ☎ *93/487–6262,* FAX *93/215–7970. 106 rooms and 18 suites. Restaurant, bar, pool. AE, DC, MC, V.*

$$$$ ⊞ **Le Meridien.** The English-owned and -managed Le Meridien vies with the Rivoli Ramblas (☞ *below*) as the premier hotel in the Rambla area. Bedrooms are light, spacious, and decorated in pastels. The hotel hosts such music types as Michael Jackson and is very popular with businesspeople; fax machines and computers in your room are available on request. A room overlooking the Rambla is worth the extra noise. ⊠ *Rambla 111, 08002,* ☎ *93/318–6200,* FAX *93/301–7776. 209 rooms. Restaurant, bar, parking. AE, DC, MC, V.*

$$$$ ⊞ **Princesa Sofia.** Long considered Barcelona's foremost modern hotel despite its slightly out-of-the-way location on Avinguda Diagonal, this towering high-rise offers a wide range of facilities and everything from shops to three different restaurants, including one of the city's finest, Le Gourmet, and the 19th-floor Top City, with breathtaking views. The modern bedrooms are ultracomfortable and decorated in soft colors. ⊠ *Plaça Pius XII 4, 08028,* ☎ *93/330–7111,* FAX *93/411–2106. 505 rooms. 3 restaurants, bar, indoor and outdoor pools, beauty salon, sauna, health club, parking. AE, DC, MC, V.*

$$$$ ▥ **Rey Juan Carlos I–Conrad International.** This modern skyscraper towering over the western end of Barcelona's Avinguda Diagonal is an exciting commercial complex as well as a luxury hotel. Here you can buy or rent jewelry, furs, art, fashions, flowers, caviar, and even limousines. The lush garden, which includes a pond with swans, has an Olympic-size swimming pool; the green expanses of Barcelona's finest in-town country club, El Polo, spread luxuriantly out beyond. There are two restaurants: Chez Vous serves French cuisine, and Café Polo has a sumptuous buffet as well as an American bar. ✉ *Av. Diagonal 661–671, 08028,* ☏ *93/448–0808,* FAX *93/448–0607. 375 rooms, 40 suites. 2 restaurants (3 in summer), bar, pool, beauty salon, spa, paddle tennis, tennis courts, meeting rooms. AE, DC, MC, V.*

$$$$ ▥ **Ritz.** Founded in 1919 by Caesar Ritz, this grande dame of Barcelona
★ hotels, formerly the Hotel Ritz, changed ownership and name in 1996. Extensive refurbishment has restored it to its former splendor. The imperial entrance lobby is awe-inspiring; the rooms contain Regency furniture, and some have Roman baths and mosaics. As for the price, you can almost double that of the nearest competitor. Service is generally excellent. ✉ *Gran Via 668, 08010,* ☏ *93/318–5200,* FAX *93/318–0148. 158 rooms. Restaurant, bar. AE, DC, MC, V.*

$$$ ▥ **Alexandra.** Behind a reconstructed Eixample facade, everything here is slick and contemporary. The rooms are spacious and attractively furnished with dark-wood chairs, and those that face inward have thatch screens on the balconies for privacy. From the airy, marble hall up, the Alexandra is perfectly suited to modern martini sippers. ✉ *Mallorca 251, 08008,* ☏ *93/487–0505,* FAX *93/488–0258. 81 rooms. Restaurant, bar, parking. AE, DC, MC, V.*

$$$ ▥ **Calderón.** Ideally placed on Rambla's chic and leafy Rambla Catalunya, this modern high-rise has a range of facilities normally found only in hotels farther out of town. Public rooms are huge, with cool, white-marble floors, and the bedrooms follow suit. Aim for one of the higher rooms, from which the views from sea to mountains and over the city are breathtaking. ✉ *Rambla de Catalunya 26, 08007,* ☏ *93/ 301–0000. 264 rooms. Restaurant, piano bar, indoor and outdoor pools, health club, squash, free parking. AE, DC, MC, V.*

$$$ ▥ **Colón.** This cozy, old town house has a unique charm and intimacy
★ reminiscent of an English country inn—and it lays claim to the sightseer's ideal location. The rooms are comfortable and tastefully furnished. The ones in the back are, if anything, noisier, as there is no longer any auto traffic on the front side, and the church bells are equally audible all over the neighborhood—so by all means try to get a room with a view of the cathedral. The Colón was a great favorite of Joan Miró, and for comfort, ambience, and location it's very possibly the best place in Barcelona. ✉ *Av. Catedral 7, 08002,* ☏ *93/301–1404,* FAX *93/317– 2915. 147 rooms. Restaurant, bar. AE, DC, MC, V.*

$$$ ▥ **Gallery.** This modern hotel in the upper part of the Eixample, just below the Diagona, offers impeccable comfort and service and a central location for middle and upper Barcelona. In the other direction, it's only 30 minutes' walk from the waterfront. Aptly named, and built primarily of glass and steel, the hotel is near Barcelona's prime art-gallery district, a few blocks away on Consell de Cien. ✉ *Roselló 249, 08008,* ☏ *93/415–9911,* FAX *93/415–9184. 110 rooms, 5 suites. Bar, cafeteria. AE, DC, MC, V.*

$$$ ▥ **Gran Derby.** Every bedroom in this modern Eixample hotel has its own sitting room, and each is decorated with modern, black-and-white tile floors, plain light-colored walls, and coral bedspreads. Some have an extra bedroom, making them ideal for families. Only the location is less than ideal; for sightseeing purposes, it's a bit out of the way, just below Plaça Francesc Macià. ✉ *Loreto 28, 08029,* ☏ *93/*

322–3215, FAX *93/419–6820. 44 rooms. Bar, café, parking. AE, DC, MC, V.*

$$$ ⚑ **Majestic.** With an unbeatable location on the city's most stylish boulevard and a great rooftop pool, the Majestic is a near-perfect place to stay. The different combinations of wallpaper, pastels, and vintage furniture in the rooms and the mirrors, leather sofas, and marble in the reception area all suit the place well. The building is part Eixample town house and part modern extension, so bear this in mind when booking your room. ✉ *Passeig de Gràcia 70, 08008,* ☎ *93/488–1717,* FAX *93/488–1880. 335 rooms. Restaurant, bar, pool, health club, free parking. AE, DC, MC, V.*

$$$ ⚑ **Rivoli Ramblas.** Behind the upper-Rambla facade lies imaginative, slick, modern decor with marble floors. Bedrooms are elegant, and the roof-terrace bar has panoramic views. ✉ *Rambla 128, 08002,* ☎ *93/ 302–6643,* FAX *93/317–5053. 87 rooms. Restaurant, spa, health club. AE, DC, MC, V.*

$$
★ ⚑ **España.** They've modernized the already-large bedrooms here—the best and quietest overlook the bright, interior patio—and now this erstwhile budget hotel is a winner, even if the stunning public rooms are still the main draw. The highlight is the Moderniste ground floor, designed by Domènech i Muntaner: a superbly sculpted hearth by Eusebi Arnau, elaborate woodwork, and a mermaid-populated Ramón Casas mural in the breakfast room. Try to see this lovely concentration of Art Nouveau, even if you only stop in for a meal. ✉ *Sant Pau 9–11, 08001,* ☎ *93/318–1758,* FAX *93/317–1134. 76 rooms. Restaurant, breakfast room, cafeteria. AE, DC, MC, V.*

$$ ⚑ **Gran Via.** Architecture is the attraction at this grand 19th-century town house, located near the main tourist office. The original chapel has been preserved, and you can have breakfast in a hall of mirrors, climb an elaborate Moderniste staircase, and make calls from Belle Epoque phone booths. The rooms have plain alcoved walls, bottle-green carpets, and Regency-style furniture; those overlooking Gran Via itself have better views but are quite noisy. ✉ *Gran Via 642, 08007,* ☎ *93/318–1900,* FAX *93/318–9997. 53 rooms. Breakfast room, parking. AE, DC, MC, V.*

$$ ⚑ **Montecarlo.** The Rambla entrance takes you through an enticing marble hall, and upstairs you come to a sumptuous reception room with a dark-wood Moderniste ceiling. The rooms are modern, bright, and functional; ask for a view of the Rambla if you don't mind a bit of noise. ✉ *Rambla 124, 08002,* ☎ *93/412–0404,* FAX *93/318–7323. 76 rooms. Bar, cafeteria, parking. AE, DC, MC, V.*

$$ ⚑ **Nouvel.** Centrally located just below Plaça de Catalunya, this hotel blends white marble, etched glass, elaborate plasterwork, and carved, dark woodwork in its handsome Art Nouveau interior. The rooms have pristine marble floors, firm beds, and smart bathrooms. The narrow street is pedestrian-only and therefore quiet, but views are nonexistent. ✉ *Santa Anna 18–20, 08002,* ☎ *93/301–8274,* FAX *93/301–8370. 74 rooms. Breakfast room. AE, MC, V.*

$$ ⚑ **Oriente.** Down toward the seamier end of the Rambla, Barcelona's oldest hotel has nonetheless retained some style and charm. Ornate public rooms and glowing chandeliers recall a bygone era. The only drawback is the somewhat functional decor of the bedrooms, some of which have an extra bed for families. Located just below the Liceu Opera House, it's popular with businesspeople. ✉ *Rambla 45–47, 08002,* ☎ *93/302–2558,* FAX *93/412–3819. 142 rooms. Restaurant, bar. AE, DC, MC, V.*

$$ ⚑ **Regente.** The Moderniste decor and copious stained glass lend style and charm to this smallish hotel. The public rooms have been renovated over the last two years and are carpeted in many different patterns. The bedrooms, fortunately, are elegantly restrained; the verdant roof terrace (with a pool) and the prime position on the Rambla de Catalunya seal the positive verdict. ⊠ *Rambla de Catalunya 76, 08008,* ☏ *93/487–5989,* ℻ *93/487–3227. 78 rooms. Restaurant, bar, pool. AE, DC, MC, V.*

$$ ▦ **Rialto.** This hotel seems to have taken a leaf from the paradors' book with its subdued pine floors, white walls, and walnut doors. The rooms (ask for an interior one if you fancy a quiet night) echo this look, with heavy furniture set against light walls. There's a vaulted bar in the basement and a modern, mirrored *salón* off the lobby. ⊠ *Ferran 42, 08002,* ☏ *93/318–5212,* ℻ *93/310–4081. 140 rooms. Bar, cafeteria. AE, DC, MC, V.*

$$ ▦ **San Agustín.** Just off the Rambla in the leafy square of the same name, the San Agustín has long been a favorite with musicians performing at the Liceu Opera House. Rooms are small but pleasantly modern, with plenty of fresh wood and clean lines. ⊠ *Plaça de San Agustí 3, 08001,* ☏ *93/318–1708,* ℻ *93/317–2928. 77 rooms. Bar, cafetería. AE, DC, MC, V.*

$$ ▦ **Suizo.** The last of the Gargallo hotels lacks the spacious corridors of the Rialto, but its public rooms are preferable, with elegant, modern seating in front, either near the reception area or one floor up, and good views over the noisy square. The bedrooms have bright walls and wood or tile floors. ⊠ *Plaça del Àngel 12, 08002,* ☏ *93/315–0461,* ℻ *93/310–4081. 50 rooms. Restaurant, bar, cafeteria. AE, DC, MC, V.*

$ ▦ **Continental.** This comfortable hotel, with canopied balconies, stands at the top of the Rambla, just below Plaça de Catalunya. Space is tight, but the rooms manage to accommodate large, firm beds. It's high enough over the Rambla to escape street noise, so ask for a room overlooking Barcelona's most emblematic street. George Orwell stayed here with his wife in 1937 after recovering from a throat wound—so it's a good place to read *Homage to Catalonia.* ⊠ *Rambla 138, 08002,* ☏ *93/301–2508,* ℻ *93/302–7360. 35 rooms. Breakfast room. AE, DC, MC, V.*

$ ▦ **Jardí.** Perched over the traffic-free and charming Plaça del Pi and Plaça Sant Josep Oriol, this hotel's newly renovated rooms have modern pine furniture, white walls, and small but new bathrooms. Exterior rooms are the prettiest, but they can be noisy in summer. The in-house breakfast is excellent, but the alfresco tables at the Bar del Pi, downstairs, are ideal in summer. All in all, it's a great value. Caveat: the quietest rooms are four flights up, and there is no elevator. ⊠ *Plaça Sant Josep Oriol 1, 08002,* ☏ *93/301–5900,* ℻ *93/318–3664. 40 rooms. Breakfast room. AE, DC, MC, V.*

$ ▦ **Paseo de Gràcia.** Formerly a hostel, the Paseo de Gràcia has soft-color bedrooms with plain, good-quality carpets and sturdy wooden furniture. Add to this the location, on the handsomest of the Eixample's boulevards, and you have an excellent budget option if you want to stay uptown. Some of the rooms, though not necessarily the newest, have balconies with views west over the city and the Collserola hills beyond. ⊠ *Passeig de Gràcia 102, 08008,* ☏ *93/215–5828,* ℻ *93/ 215–3724. 33 rooms. Bar, breakfast room. AE, DC, MC, V.*

$ ▦ **Peninsular.** Built for the 1890 Universal Exposition, this hotel in the
★ Barri Xines features a coral-marble lobby and an appealing interior courtyard painted white and pale green and splashed with hanging plants. The bedrooms have tile floors, good showers, and firm beds. Look at a few before choosing, because each is different—some look onto the street, some into the courtyard. ⊠ *Sant Pau 34, 08001,* ☏ *93/302–3138,* ℻ *93/302–3138. 100 rooms, 80 with bath. Breakfast room. MC, V.*

NIGHTLIFE AND THE ARTS

Barcelona has wide-ranging arts and nightlife scenes that start early and never quite stop. To find out what's on, look in newspapers or the weekly *Guía Del Ocio,* available at newsstands all over town. *Activitats* is a monthly list of cultural events, published by the *ajuntament* and available from its information office in Palau de la Virreina (✉ Rambla 99).

The Arts

Concerts

Catalans are great music lovers. Barcelona's main concert hall is the **Palau de la Música** (✉ Sant Francesc de Paula 2, ☎ 93/268–1000), whose ticket office is open weekdays 11–1 and 5–8, Saturday 5–8 only. Sunday-morning concerts, at 11, are a popular tradition. Tickets range from 1,000 to 15,000 pesetas and are best purchased well in advance. Performances run September–June. Check the music listings in *El País,* Spain's daily newspaper, for concerts around town. Watch especially for the *Solistas del OBC,* a series of free performances held in the town hall's opulent Saló de Cent—this is world-class chamber music in an incomparable setting. In June and July, the city's annual summer music festival brings a long series of concerts. In late September, the **International Music Festival** forms part of the feast of Nostra Senyora de la Mercè (Our Lady of Mercy), Barcelona's patron saint.

Dance

L'Espai de Dansa i Música de la Generalitat de Catalunya—generally listed as **L'Espai,** or the Space (✉ Travessera de Gràcia 63, ☎ 93/414–3133)—was opened by the Catalonian government in February 1992 and is now Barcelona's prime venue for ballet, modern dance, and various musical offerings. **El Mercat de les Flors** (✉ Lleida 59, ☎ 93/426–1875) near Plaça de Espanya, is the more traditional setting for modern dance and theater.

Film

Though some foreign films are dubbed, more and more movies are shown in their original language. Look for listings marked *v.o.* (*versión original*). The **Icaria Yelmo** (✉ Salvador Espriu 61, near Carles I metro stop) movie theater complex in the Olympic Port now has the most ample selection of films in English. The **Filmoteca** (✉ Av. Sarrià 33, ☎ 93/430–5007) shows three films daily in *v.o.,* often English. The **Verdi** (✉ Verdi 32, Gràcia), **Arkadin** (✉ Travessera de Gràcia 103, near Gràcia train stop), the **Rex** (✉ Gran Via 463), **Casablanca** (✉ Passeig de Gràcia 115), and **Renoir Les Corts** (✉ Eugeni d'Ors 12) tend to have recent releases in *v. o.*

Flamenco

Barcelona is not richly endowed with flamenco haunts, as Catalans consider flamenco—like bullfighting—a foreign import from Andalusia. **El Patio Andaluz** (✉ Aribau 242, ☎ 93/209–3378) has flamenco shows twice nightly (10 and midnight) and audience participation in the karaoke section upstairs. **El Cordobés** (✉ Rambla 35, ☎ 93/317–6653) is the most popular club with tour groups. Other options include **El Tablao de Carmen** (✉ Poble Espanyol, ☎ 93/325–6895) and **Los Tarantos** (✉ Plaça Reial 17, ☎ 93/318–3067).

Opera

Barcelona's opulent and beloved **Gran Teatre del Liceu** was gutted by flames in early 1994 and will probably not be restored until early 1999. The box office remains open at San Pau 1 (☎ 93/317–4142); operas and musical events will be staged at the **Palau Sant Jordi** sports hall, on Montjuïc; the **Palacio Nacional,** above Plaza España; and the **Palau de la Música.** Some of the Liceu's most spectacular halls and rooms were unharmed by the fire, and you may be able to tour some of these during the restoration (☞ La Rambla and the Raval *in* Exploring Barcelona, *above*).

Theater

Most plays are performed in Catalan, though some are performed in Spanish. Barcelona is well known for avant-garde theater, and for troupes that specialize in mime and special effects (**La Fura dels Baus, Els Joglars, Els Comediants**). An international mime festival is held most years, as is the **Festival de Títeres** (Puppet Festival).

The best-known modern theaters are the **Teatre Lliure** (✉ Montseny 47, Gràcia, ☎ 93/218–9251), **Mercat de les Flors** (✉ Lleida 59, ☎ 93/318–8599), **Teatre Romea** (✉ Hospital 51, ☎ 93/317–7189), **Teatre Tívoli** (✉ Casp 10, ☎ 93/412–2063), and **Teatre Poliorama** (✉ Rambla Estudios 115, ☎ 93/317–7599), all of which stage a dynamic variety of classical, contemporary, and experimental theater.

Many of the older theaters specializing in big musicals are along the Paral.lel. These include **Apolo** (✉ Paral.lel 56, ☎ 93/241–9007) and **Victòria** (✉ Paral.lel 6769, ☎ 93/441–3979). In July and August, an open-air summer theater festival brings plays, music, and dance to the **Teatre Grec** (Greek Theater) on Montjuïc (✉ Rambla 99, ☎ 93/316–2700), as well as other venues.

Nightlife

Cabaret

Drop in at the venerable **Bodega Bohemia** (✉ Lancaster 2, ☎ 93/302–5061), where a variety of singers perform to an upright piano, or the minuscule **Bar Pastis** (✉ Santa Mònica 4, ☎ 93/318–7980), where the habitués form the cabaret and a phonograph plays Edith Piaf.

Arnau (✉ Paral.lel 60, ☎ 93/242–2804) is an old-time music hall that's still going strong. The richly decorated **Belle Epoque** (✉ Muntaner 246, ☎ 93/209–7711) stages the most sophisticated shows in town.

Casinos

The **Gran Casino de Barcelona** (☎ 93/893–3666), 42 km (26 mi) south in Sant Pere de Ribes, near Sitges, also has a dance hall and some excellent international shows in a 19th-century setting. Rumors of an imminent Gran Casino in the Olympic Port, under the Hotel Arts, persist, so inquire once you get here: you may be a mere elevator ride away from Las Vegas. The only other casinos in Catalonia are in **Lloret del Mar** (☎ 972/366512) and **Perelada** (☎ 972/538125), both in Girona province, up the coast from Barcelona.

Jazz Clubs

Try **La Cova del Drac** (✉ Vallmajor 33, ☎ 93/200–7032) or the Gothic Quarter's **Harlem Jazz Club** (✉ Comtessa Sobradiel 8, ☎ 93/310–0755), which is small but puts on atmospheric bands. **Barcelona Pipa Club** (✉ Plaça Reial 3, ☎ 93/302–4732) is another hot jazz club, located above **Glaciar** in the southwest corner of Plaça Reial. **Jamboree-Jazz & Dance-Club** (✉ Plaça Reial 17, ☎ 93/301–7564) is a center for jazz, rock, and flamenco. **La Boîte** (✉ Diagonal 477, ☎ 93/419–5950) has an eclectic musical menu, as do **Luz de Gas** (✉ Muntaner 246, ☎ 93/209–7711) and **Luna Mora** (✉ Next to the Hotel Arts, in the Olympic Port, ☎ 93–221–6161), offering everything from country blues to soul. The Palau de la Música holds an **international jazz festival** in November, and nearby Terrassa has its own jazz festival in March. The bustling **Blue Note** (☎ 93/225–8003), in the Port Vell's Maremagnum shopping complex, draws a mixture of young and not-so-young nocturnals to musical events and Wednesday-night buffets. Food and drinks are served until dawn, and credit cards are accepted.

Late-Night Bars

Bar musical is Spanish for any bar with music loud enough to drown out conversation. The pick of these are **Universal** (✉ Marià Cubí 182–184, ☎ 93/200–7470), **Mas i Mas** (✉ Marià Cubí 199, ☎ 93/209–4502), and **Nick Havanna** (✉ Rosselló 208, ☎ 93/215–6591). **L'Ovella Negra** (✉ Sitjàs 5, ☎ 93/317–1087) is the top student tavern. **Glaciar** (✉ Plaça Reial 13, ☎ 93/302–1163) is *the* spot for young out-of-towners.

For a more laid-back scene, with high ceilings, billiards, tapas, and hundreds of students, visit the popular **Velodrom** (✉ Muntaner 211–213, ☎ 93/230–6022), just below Diagonal. Two blocks away is the intriguing *barmuseo* (bar-cum-museum) **La Fira** (✉ Provença 171, ☎ 93/323–7271). Downtown, deep in the Barrio Chino, try the **London Bar** (✉ Nou de la Rambla 34, ☎ 93/302–3102), an Art Nouveau circus haunt with a trapeze suspended above the bar. Don't miss **Bar Almirall** (✉ Joaquin Costa 33, ☎ 93/412–1535) or **Bar Muy Buenas** (✉ Carme 63, ☎ 93/442–5053).

Nightclubs and Discos

Barcelona is currently so hot that it's hard to keep track of the nightspots of the moment. Most clubs have a discretionary cover charge and like to inflict it on foreigners, so dress up and be prepared to talk your way past the bouncer. Any story can work; for example, you own a chain of nightclubs and are on a world tour. Don't expect much to happen until 1:30 or 2.

Tops for some time now is the prisonesque **Otto Zutz** (✉ Lincoln 15, ☎ 93/238–0722), just off Via Augusta. **Club Fellini** (✉ Marqués de l'Argentera s/n, ☎ 93/319–5356), in the Estació de França, is a new hot spot, and **Fibra Optica** (✉ Beethoven 9, ☎ 93/209–5281) and the nearly classic **Up and Down** (✉ Numancia 179, ☎ 93/280–2922), pronounced "Pen-*dow*," are both anything but calm. **Bikini** (✉ Deu i Mata 105, at Entença, ☎ 93/322–0005) will present you with a queue on particularly festive Saturday nights. **Oliver y Hardy** (✉ Diagonal 593, ☎ 93/419–3181), next to the Barcelona Hilton, is more popular with the older set (i.e., you won't stand out if you're over 35); **La Tierra** (✉ Aribau 230, ☎ 93/200–7346) and **El Otro** (✉ Valencia 166, ☎ 93/323–6759) also accept postgraduates with open arms. **Zeleste** (✉ Almogavers 122, ☎ 93/309–1204) is another standard hangout, particularly popular with jazz and rock buffs. **La Boîte** (✉ Diagonal 477, ☎ 93/419–5950) has live music and a nice balance of civilization and insanity.

For an old-fashioned *sala de baile* (dance hall) with a big band playing tangos, head to **La Paloma** (✉ Tigre 27, ☎ 93/301–6897); the kitschy 1950s decor creates a peculiar atmosphere that's great fun.

OUTDOOR ACTIVITIES AND SPORTS

Golf

Barcelona is ringed by some excellent golf courses. Call ahead to reserve tee times.

Around Barcelona

Reial Club de Golf El Prat (✉ El Prat de Llobregat, 08820 , ☎ 93/379–0278), 36 holes. Note: the greens fee at El Prat is 24,000 ptas. **Club de**

Golf de Sant Cugat (✉ Sant Cugat del Vallès, 08190 , ☎ 93/674–3958), 18 holes. **Club de Golf Vallromanes** (✉ Vallromanes, 08188, ☎ 93/568–0362), 18 holes. **Club de Golf Terramar** (✉ Sitges, 08870, ☎ 93/894–0580), 18 holes.

Farther Afield
Club de Golf Costa Brava (✉ La Masía, Santa Cristina d'Aro, 17246, ☎ 972/837150), 18 holes. **Club de Golf Pals** (✉ Platja de Pals, Pals, 17256, ☎ 972/637009), 18 holes.

Health Clubs

Catalans are becoming increasingly keen on fitness. You'll see gyms everywhere; for specifics, look in the *Páginas Amarillas/Pàgines Grogues* (*Yellow Pages*) under "Gimnasios/Gimnasis." We can recommend the new and exciting **Crack,** which has a gym, a sauna, a pool, six squash courts, and paddle tennis. ✉ *Pasaje Domingo 7,* ☎ *93/215–2755.* ✉ *Day membership 1,750 ptas.; small supplement for courts.*

Hiking

You may not have come to Barcelona with the idea of heading for the hills, but the **Collserola** hills behind the city offer well-marked trails, fresh air, and lovely views. Take the Sabadell or Terrassa FFCC train from Plaça de Catalunya and get off at the Baixador de Vallvidrera. The nearby information center can supply you with maps of this surprising mountain woodland just 20 minutes from downtown.

Swimming

Indoor
Try the **Club Natació Barceloneta** (✉ Passeig Marítim, ☎ 93/309–3412) or the **Piscines Pau Negre Can Toda** (✉ Ramiro de Maetzu, ☎ 93/213–4344). Each charges 500 pesetas.

Outdoor
Uphill from Parc Güell is the **Parc de la Creueta del Coll** (✉ Castell-terçol, ☎ 93/416–2625), which has a huge outdoor swimming pool. The fee is 500 pesetas.

Tennis

The cheapest place to play tennis is the **Complejo Deportivo Can Caralleu** (Can Caralleu Sports Complex), above Pedralbes, a 30-minute walk uphill from the Reina Elisenda subway stop (FFCC de la Generalitat). ☎ *93/203–7874.* ✉ *Daytime 1,250 ptas. per hr, nighttime 1,450 ptas. per hr.* ☉ *Daily 8 AM–11 PM.*

Alternatively, try the upscale **Club Vall Parc.** ✉ *Carretera de la Rabassada 79,* ☎ *93/212–6789.* ✉ *Daytime 2,500 ptas. per hr, nighttime 3,100 ptas. per hr.* ☉ *Daily 8–midnight.*

SHOPPING

Shopping Districts

Barcelona's prime shopping districts are the Passeig de Gràcia, Rambla de Catalunya, and Avinguda Diagonal up to Carrer Ganduxer. Farther out on the Diagonal is shopping colossus **L'Illa,** which includes **FNAC, Marks & Spencer,** and plenty of other consumer temptations. The **Maremagum** mall, in Port Vell, is another shopping option. For small boutiques, try **Carrer Tuset,** north of Diagonal. For more affordable, more old-fashioned, typically Spanish-style shops, prowl the area between the Rambla and Via Laietana, especially around **Carrer Ferran.** The area surrounding **Plaça del Pi,** from the Boqueria to Carrer Portaferrissa and Carrer de la Canuda, has fashionable boutiques and jewelry and gift shops. Most shops are open Monday–Saturday 9–1:30 and 5–8, but some close in the afternoon. Virtually all close on Sunday.

Specialty Stores

Antiques

Carrer de la Palla and Carrer Banys Nous, in the Gothic Quarter, are lined with antiques shops full of maps, books, paintings, and furniture. An **antiques market** is held every Thursday from 10 to 8, in front of the cathedral. The **Centre d'Antiquaris** (✉ Passeig de Gràcia 57) contains 75 antiques stores. Try **Gothsland** (✉ Consell de Cent 331) for Moderniste design.

Art

Many of Barcelona's art galleries are along Carrer Consell de Cent (and around the corner on Rambla de Catalunya) between Passeig de Gràcia and Carrer Balmes, including **Galeria Joan Prats** (Rambla de Catalunya 54), **Sala Dalmau** (Consell de Cent 347), and **Sala Rovira** (Rambla de Catalunya 62). The nearby **Joan Gaspart Gallery** (Plaça Letamendi 1) is another player. Carrer Petritxol, which leads down into Plaça del Pi (☞ La Rambla and the Raval *in* Exploring Barcelona, *above*), is also lined with art galleries, most notably the dean of Barcelona art galleries, **Sala Parès.** Carrer Montcada has **Galeria Maeght** and others, and the Passeig del Born is worth checking out. **Galeria Verena Hofer** is around the corner on Plaça Comercial, across from the Born; and the ticking **Metrònom** is on nearby Carrer Fussina. Near Plaça del Pi, several art galleries command attention along Carrer de la Palla, particularly **Sala d'Art Artur Ramón** (Carrer de la Palla 23). Important spaces for itinerant exhibitions include **Fundació Caixa de Catalunya–La Pedrera** (Provença 261–265), **Fundació La Caixa–Centre Cultural** (Passeig Sant Joan 108), **Sala El Vienès-Casa Fuster** (Passeig de Gràcia 132), and **La Virreina** (Rambla 99).

Boutiques and Fashion

If you are after fashion and jewelry, you've come to the right place. Barcelona makes all the headlines on Spain's booming fashion front. **El Bulevard Rosa** (✉ Passeig de Gràcia 53–55) is a collection of boutiques that stock the very latest outfits. Others are on Avinguda Diagonal between Passeig de Gràcia and Carrer Ganduxer. **Adolfo Domínguez,** one of Spain's top designers, is at Passeig de Gràcia 35 and Diagonal 570; **Toni Miró**'s two **Groc** shops, with the latest looks for men, women, and children, are at Muntaner 385 and Rambla de Catalunya 100. **David Valls,** at Valencia 235, represents new and young Barcelona fashion design, and **May Day** carries clothing, footwear, and accessories from the cutting edge. **Joaquim Berao,** a top jewelry designer, is at Roselló 277.

Ceramics

Itaca (✉ Ferrán 26, ☎ 93/301–3044) has a good selection of ceramic plates, bowls, and inspired objects of all kinds, including pottery from Talavera de la Reina and La Bisbal. **Art Escudellers** (✉ Calle Escudellers 5, ☎ 93/412–6801) carries ceramics from all over Spain, with more than 140 different artists represented. The big department stores are also worth checking. For Lladró, try **Pla de l'Os** (✉ Boqueria 3, ☎ 93/301–4088), just off the Rambla.

Department Stores

The ubiquitous **El Corte Inglés** has four locations: Plaça de Catalunya 14, Porta de l'Angel 19–21, Avinguda Francesc Macià 58, and Diagonal 617 (Metro: Maria Cristina). **Marks & Spencer** is in the shopping mall L'Illa, at Diagonal 545, along with a full array of stores from **Benetton** to **Zara.**

Design and Interiors

At Passeig de Gràcia 102 is **Gimeno,** whose elegant displays range from unusual suitcases to the latest in furniture design. **Vinçon,** a couple of doors down at No. 96, is equally chic; some 50 years old, it has steadily expanded through a rambling Moderniste house that was once the home of Moderniste poet-artist Santiago Rusiñol and the studio of his colleague, the painter Ramón Casas. It stocks everything from Filofaxes to handsome kitchenware. **Bd** (Barcelona design), at Carrer Mallorca 291–293, is another spectacular design store in another Moderniste gem, Doménech i Muntaner's Casa Thomas.

Food and Flea Markets

The **Boqueria** market, on the Rambla between Carrer del Carme and Carrer de Hospital, is Barcelona's most colorful and bustling food market and the oldest of its kind in Europe. It's open Monday–Saturday and is most active before 3 PM. **Els Encants,** Barcelona's biggest flea market, is held Monday, Wednesday, Friday, and Saturday 8–7, at the end of Dos de Maig, on Plaça de les Glòries (Metro: Glòries, red line). The **Sant Antoni** market, at the end of Ronda Sant Antoni, is an old-fashioned food and clothes market that's best on Sunday. On Thursdays, a natural produce market (honeys, cheeses) fills **Plaça del Pi** with interesting tastes and aromas.

SIDE TRIPS

Numbers in the margin correspond to points of interest on the Side Trips from Barcelona map.

Montserrat

48 *50 km (30 mi) west of Barcelona.*

A nearly obligatory side trip from Barcelona is the shrine of La Moreneta, the Black Virgin of Montserrat, high in the mountains of the Serra de Montserrat. These weird, saw-toothed peaks have given rise to countless legends: here St. Peter left a statue of the Virgin Mary carved by St. Luke, Parsifal found the Holy Grail, and Wagner sought inspiration for his opera. A monastery has stood on this site since the early Middle Ages, though the present 19th-century building replaced the rubble left by Napoleon's troops in 1812. Montserrat is a world-famous shrine and one of Catalonia's spiritual sanctuaries. Honeymooning couples flock here by the thousand seeking La Moreneta's blessing on their marriages, and twice a year, on April 27 and September 8, the diminutive statue of Montserrat's Black Virgin becomes the object of one of Spain's greatest pilgrimages.

Follow the A2/A7 *autopista* on the new upper ring road (Ronda de Dalt) or from the western end of Diagonal as far as Salida (Exit) 25 to Martorell. Bypass this industrial center and follow signs to Montserrat. You can also take a train from the Plaça Espanya metro station to Montserrat, or a guided tour with Pullmantur or Julià.

Only the basilica and museum are regularly open to the public. The **basilica** is dark and ornate, its blackness pierced by the glow of hundreds of votive lamps. Above the high altar stands the famous poly-

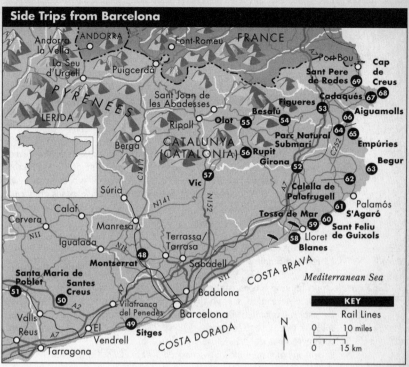

Side Trips from Barcelona

chrome statue of the Virgin and Child to which the faithful can pay their respects by way of a separate door. ☎ *93/835–0251.* ☉ *Daily 6–10:30 and noon–6:30.*

The monastery's **museum** has two sections: the Secció Antiga (open Tuesday–Saturday 10:30–2) contains Old Masters, among them paintings by El Greco, Correggio, and Caravaggio, and the amassed gifts to the Virgin; the Secció Moderna (open Tuesday–Saturday 3–6) concentrates on recent Catalan painters.

Montserrat is as memorable for its setting as for its religious treasures, so be sure to explore these strange, pink hills. The vast monastic complex is dwarfed by the grandeur of the jagged peaks, and the crests are dotted with hermitages. The hermitage of **Sant Joan** can be reached by funicular. The views over the mountains to the Mediterranean and, on a clear day, to the Pyrenees are breathtaking, and the rugged, boulder-strewn setting makes for dramatic walks and hikes.

Sitges, Santes Creus, and Poblet

This trio of attractions to the south and west of Barcelona can be seen comfortably in a day. Sitges is the prettiest and most popular resort in Barcelona's immediate environs, flaunting an excellent beach, a picturesque old quarter, and some interesting Moderniste bits. It's also one of Europe's premier gay resorts. The Cistercian monasteries west of here are characterized by monolithic Romanesque architecture and beautiful cloisters.

Head southwest along Gran Via or Passeig Colom to the freeway that passes the airport on its way to Castelldefels. From here, the new freeway and tunnels will get you to Sitges in 20–30 minutes. From Sitges, drive inland toward Vilafranca del Penedès and the A7 freeway. The A2 (Lleida) leads to the monasteries.

Regular trains leave Sants and Passeig de Gràcia for Sitges; the ride takes half an hour. From Sitges, trains go to L'Espluga de Francolí, 4 km (2½ mi) from Poblet (Lleida line). For Poblet, stay with the train to Tarragona and catch a bus to the monastery (⊠ Autotransports Perelada, ☎ 973/202058).

Sitges
49 *43 km (27 mi) south of Barcelona.*

Head for the museums here. The most interesting is the **Cau-Ferrat,** founded by the artist Russinyol and containing some of his own paintings together with two El Grecos. Connoisseurs of wrought iron will love the beautiful collection of *cruces terminales,* crosses that once marked town boundaries. ⊠ *Fonollar s/n,* ☎ *93/894–0364.* ☑ *250 ptas.; free Sun.* ☉ *Tues.–Sun. 9:30–2.*

NEED A BREAK?	Linger over excellent seafood in a nonpareil sea-view setting at **Vivero.** ⊠ *Passeig Balmins s/n,* ☎ *93/894–2149. Closed Tues. Dec.–May.*

En Route   Upon leaving Sitges, make straight for the A2 *autopista* by way of Vilafranca del Penedès. If you're a wine buff, you may want to stop here to taste the excellent Penedès wine; you can tour and sip at the **Bodega Miguel Torres** (⊠ Comercio 22, ☎ 93/890–0100). There's an interesting **Museu del Vi** (Wine Museum) in the Royal Palace, with descriptions of winemaking history. ☑ *500 ptas.* ☉ *Tues.–Sun. 10–2 and 4–7.*

Santes Creus
50 *95 km (59 mi) west of Barcelona.*

Santes Creus, founded in 1157, is the first of the monasteries you'll come upon as A2 branches west into the province of Lleida. Three austere aisles and an unusual 14th-century apse combine with the newly restored cloisters and the courtyard of the royal palace. ☎ 977/638329. ☑ *450 ptas.* ☉ *Oct.–Mar., daily 10–1 and 3–6; Apr.–Sept., daily 10–1 and 3–7.*

Montblanc is at Exit 9 off A2, its ancient gates too narrow for cars. A walk through its tiny streets reveals Gothic churches with intricate stained-glass windows, a 16th-century hospital, and medieval mansions.

Santa Maria de Poblet
51 *8 km (5 mi) west of Santes Creus.*

This splendid Cistercian foundation at the foot of the Prades Mountains is one of the great masterpieces of Spanish monastic architecture. The cloister is a stunning combination of lightness and size; on sunny days the shadows on the yellow sandstone are extraordinary. Founded in 1150 by Ramón Berenguer IV in gratitude for the Christian Reconquest, the monastery first housed a dozen Cistercians from Narbonne. Later, the Crown of Aragon used Santa Maria de Poblet for religious retreats and burials. The building was damaged in an 1836 anticlerical revolt, and monks of the reformed Cistercian Order have managed the difficult task of restoration since 1940. Today, monks and novices again pray before the splendid retable over the tombs of Aragonese rulers, restored to their former glory by sculptor Frederic Marés; sleep in the cold, barren dormitory; and eat frugal meals in the stark refectory. You can join them if you'd like; 18 very comfortable rooms are available (for men only). Call Padre Benito (☎ 977/870089) to arrange a stay of up to 15 days within the stones and silence of one of Catalonia's gems. 🎫 *600 ptas.* ⏲ *Guided tour daily 10–12:30 and 3–6 (until 5:30 Oct.–Mar.).*

Girona and Northern Catalonia

The ancient city of Girona, often ignored by visitors who bolt from its airport to the resorts of the Costa Brava, is an easy and worthwhile day trip from Barcelona. Much of the city's charm comes from its narrow medieval streets—with frequent stairways, as required by the steep terrain. Historic buildings here include the cathedral, which dominates the city from the top of 90 steps; Arab baths; and an antique and charming Jewish quarter.

Northern Catalonia boasts the green rolling hills of the Ampurdan, the Alberes mountain range at the eastern tip of the Pyrenees, and the rugged Costa Brava. Sprinkled across the landscape are charming *masías* (farmhouses) whose austere, grayish or pinkish staggered stone rooftops and ubiquitous square towers make them look like fortresses. Churches dignify the villages, and even the tiniest of these has its own arcaded square and *rambla* where villagers take their evening *paseo.*

Girona

52 *97 km (60 mi) northeast of Barcelona.*

Park in the Plaça Independencia and find your way to the tourist office at Rambla Llibertat 1. Then head to the old quarter, across the River Onyar, past Girona's best-known view: the orange waterfront houses, their windows draped with a colorful array of drying laundry, reflected in the waters of the Onyar. Use the cathedral's huge Baroque facade as a guide up through the labyrinth of streets.

At the base of the 90 steps, go left through the Sobreportes gate to the **Banys Arabs** (Arab Baths). Built by Morisco craftsmen in the late 12th century, long after Girona's Islamic occupation (795–1015) had ended, the baths are both Romanesque and Moorish in design. 🎫 *375 ptas.* ⏲ *May–Sept., Tues.–Sat. 10–2 and 4–7, Sun. 10–2; Oct.–Apr., Tues.–Sun. 10–1.*

Across the River Galligants is the church of **Sant Pere** (Holy Father), finished in 1131 and notable for its octagonal Romanesque belfry and the finely detailed capitals atop the columns in the cloister. Next door is the **Museu Arqueològic** (Museum of Archaeology), which documents the region's history since Paleolithic times. 🎫 *Free.* ⏲ *Church and museum daily 10–1 and 4:30–7.*

The stepped Passeig Arquaeològic runs below the walls of the Old City. From there, climb through the Jardins de la Francesa to the highest ramparts. From here you have a good view of the 11th-century **Romanesque Tower of Charlemagne,** the oldest part of the cathedral.

To see the inside of Girona's **cathedral,** designed by Guillem Bofill in 1416, complete the loop around it. The cathedral is famous for its immense, uncluttered Gothic nave, which at 75 ft is the widest in the world and the epitome of the spatial goals of Catalan Gothic architects. The **museum** contains the famous *Tapis de la Creació* (*Tapestry of the Creation*) and a 10th-century copy of Beatus's manuscript *Commentary on the Apocalypse.* 🎫 *375 ptas.* ⏲ *Oct.–June, daily 9:30–1:15 and 3:30–7; July–Sept., daily 9:30–7.*

Next door to the cathedral is **Palau Episcopal** (Bishop's Palace), which houses the **Museu d'Art,** a good mix of Romanesque, Catalan Gothic, and modern art. 🎫 *Free with ticket for Arab Baths (☞ above).* ⏲ *Tues.–Sat. 10–7, Sun. 10–1.*

Upon leaving Plaça dels Apòstols along Carrer Claveria, turn right down Carrer Lluis Batlle i Prats. Plunge right down the tiny Carrer Sant Llorenç, formerly the cramped and squalid center of the 13th-century *Call*, or Jewish quarter. Halfway down on the left is the small **Bonastruc Ça-porta,** a museum of Jewish history, open Tuesday–Saturday 10–2 and 4–7 and Sunday 10–2, and the **Pati dels Rabís** (Rabbis' Courtyard).

DINING AND LODGING

$$$$ ✕ **Albereda.** Excellent Ampurdan cuisine is served in a bright, if somewhat subdued, setting. Try the *galleta con langostinos glaceada* (zucchini bisque with prawns). ⊠ *C. Albereda 7 bis,* ☎ 972/226002. *AE, DC, MC. Closed Sun.*

$$–$$$ ✕ **Cal Ros.** This historic place was once a haunt of Girona intellectuals. *Arroz a la cazuela,* similar to a paella but cooked in a deeper pan, is a specialty, particularly *arroz de perdiz a la cazuela con alcachofas y butifarra negra* (rice and partridge with artichokes and black sausage). ⊠ *C. Cort Reial 9,* ☎ 972/217379. *MC, V. Closed Sun. evening, Mon.*

$$–$$$ ✕ **Penyora.** Here you'll find both good local fare and, if you order from the prix-fixe menu, a bargain. ⊠ *C. Nou del Teatre 3,* ☎ 972/218948. *AE, DC, MC. Closed Tues.*

$$–$$$ ▥ **Ultonia.** This central hotel is decorated with attractive wooden tables, paneling, and cupboards. ⊠ *Gran Via Jaume I 22, 08002,* ☎ 972/203850, ﬀ 972/203334. *45 rooms. Coffee shop. AE, DC, MC, V.*

Figueres

➅➂ *37 km (23 mi) north of Girona.*

Figueres, a bustling country town and the capital of the Alt Empordà (Upper Ampurdan), is 37 km (23 mi) north of Girona on the A7 *autopista.* Walk along the **Figueres Rambla,** scene of the *passeig (paseo* in Castilian; the constitutional midday or evening stroll), and visit the **Museu Dalí,** a spectacular homage to a unique artist. The museum is installed in a former theater next to the bizarre, ocher-color Torre Galatea, where Dalí lived until his death in 1989. The remarkable Dalí collection includes a vintage Cadillac with ivy-cloaked passengers whom you can water for 25 pesetas. Dalí himself is entombed beneath the museum. ▦ *Oct.–May 650 ptas., June–Sept. 1,000 ptas.* ⊘ *Oct.–May, Tues.–Sun. 10:30–5:30; June–Sept., Tues.–Sun. 9–7:15.*

OFF THE   **AMPURDAN UPLANDS –** For a trip into the Ampurdan uplands, take the
BEATEN PATH   N II 10 km (6 mi) north of Figueres and turn west on Gi 502. Work your
                 way 13 km (8 mi) west to the village of Maçanet de Cabrenys. From
                 there, follow signs to the Santuari de les Salines, where you'll find a
                 chapel and a tiny restaurant open in summer. Above Salines is one of
                 the greatest beech forests in the Pyrenees. The new road from Maçanet
                 goes to the village of Tapis and on to Coustouges.

DINING AND LODGING

$$$ ✕ **Ampurdan.** Hailed as the birthplace of modern Catalan cuisine, this restaurant 1½ km (1 mi) north of Figueres on the N II serves hearty portions of superb French, Catalan, and Spanish cooking in a simple setting. Try one of the fish mousses. ⊠ *Carretera N II,* ☎ 972/500562. *AE, DC, MC, V.*

$$ ✕▥ **Hotel Duran.** A well-known hotel and restaurant, the Duran is open every day of the year. Try the *lentilles amb morro de vadella* (lentils with calf snout) or the *mandonguilles amb sepia al estil Anna* (meatballs and cuttlefish), a *mar i muntunya* (surf and turf) specialty of the house. ⊠ *C. Lasauca 5, 17600,* ☎ 972/501250. *65 rooms. AE, MC, V.*

Besalú

54 *34 km (21 mi) north of Girona.*

Besalú, once the capital of a feudal county as part of Charlemagne's 8th- and 9th-century Spanish March, is 25 km (15 mi) west of Figueres on C260. This ancient town's most emblematic feature is its **fortified bridge,** with crenellated battlements. Also, main sights are its two **churches,** Sant Vicenç and Sant Pere, and the ruins of the convent of **Santa Maria** on the hill above town. The tourist office is in the arcaded Plaça de la Llibertat and can provide current opening hours for Sant Pere as well as keys to the *migwe,* the unusual **Jewish baths** discovered in the 1960s.

The town of **Castellfollit de la Roca** perches on its prowlike basalt cliff over the Fluvià River 16 km (10 mi) west of Besalu.

Olot

55 *55 km (34 mi) northwest of Girona.*

Olot, the capital of the Garrotxa, is just 5 km (3 mi) from Castellfollit de la Roca. Famous for its 19th-century school of landscape painters, Olot has several excellent Art Nouveau buildings, including one with a facade by Domènech i Muntaner. The **Museu Comarcal de la Garrotxa** (County Museum of La Garrotxa) holds an important assemblage of Moderniste art and design as well as sculptures by Miquel Blai, creator of the long-tressed maidens who support the balconies along Olot's main boulevard. ⊠ *Carrer Hospici 8,* ☎ *972/279130.* ⊠ *450 ptas.* ☉ *Mon. and Wed.–Sat. 10–1 and 4–7, Sun. 10–1:30.*

The villages of **Vall d'En Bas** lie south of Olot off Route A153. A new freeway cuts across this countryside to Vic, but you'll miss a lot by taking it. The twisting old road will lead you through rich farmland past farmhouses characterized by dark wooden balconies bedecked with bright flowers. Turn off for **Sant Privat d'En Bas** and **Els Hostalets d'En Bas.**

DINING AND LODGING

$$$ ✗ **Restaurante Ramón.** Ramón is so exclusive that he adamantly refused to be in this book, so please don't let him see it. Olot's gourmet alcove par excellence, Restaurante Ramón is the opposite of rustic: sleek, modern, international, and refined. Samples of the *cuina de la terra* (home cooking of regional specialties) include *patata de Olot* (potato stuffed with veal) and *cassoleta de judias amb xoriç* (white haricot beans with sausage). ⊠ *Plaça Clarà 10,* ☎ *972/261001. Reservations essential. AE, DC, MC, V. Closed Thurs.*

$ ⊞ **Hotel La Perla.** Known for its friendly, family ambience, this hotel is always Olot's first to fill up. On the edge of town toward the Vic Road, it's walking distance from two parks. ⊠ *Avda. Santa Coloma 97, 17800,* ☎ *972/262326,* ℻ *972/270774. 30 rooms, 30 apartments. Restaurant, bar. MC, V.*

Rupit

56 *97 km (60 mi) north of Barcelona.*

Rupit is a spectacular stop for its medieval houses and its cuisine, the highlight of which is beef-stuffed potatoes. Built into a rocky promontory over a stream in the rugged Collsacabra region, Rupit (about halfway from Olot to Vic) has some of the most aesthetically perfect stone houses in Catalonia, some of which were reproduced for Barcelona's Poble Espanyol.

$$ ✕ **El Repòs.** Hanging over the river that runs through Rupit, this restaurant serves the best meat-stuffed potatoes around. Ordering a meal is easy: just learn the word *patata*. Other specialties include duck and lamb. ✉ *C. Barbacana 1,* ☎ *93/856–5000. MC, V.*

Vic

57 *66 km (41 mi) north of Barcelona.*

Known for its conservatism and Catalan nationalism, Vic rests on a 1,600-ft plateau at the confluence of two rivers and serves as the area's commercial, industrial, and agricultural hub. Vic's wide **Plaça Major,** surrounded by Gothic arcades and well supplied with bars and cafés, perfectly expresses the city's personality. Vic's religiosity is demonstrated by its 35 churches, of which the largely neoclassical **cathedral** is the foremost. The 11th-century Romanesque tower, El Cloquer, built by the Abbot Oliva, and the powerful modern murals painted twice by Josep Maria Sert (first in 1930 and again after fire damage in 1945) are the cathedral's high points. Next door, the **Museu Episcopal** (Bishop's Museum) houses a fine collection of religious art and relics. ☞ *450 ptas.* ☉ *Mon.–Sat. 10–1 and 4–7, Sun. 10–1:30.*

DINING

$$ ✕ **Ca l'U.** Translated as "The One," Ca l'U is in fact *the* place in Vic for hearty local cuisine with a minimum of pretense and expense. Try the *llangostinos i llenguado* (prawns and sole) or the regional standard, *botifarra i mongetas* (sausage and beans). ✉ *Plaça Santa Teresa 4–5,* ☎ *93/886–3504. MC, V. Closed Mon. No dinner Sun.*

LODGING

$$$ 🏨 **Parador de Vic.** This quietly charming parador, also known as the Parador del Bac de Sau, is 14 km (8½ mi) northeast of town off the Roda de Ter road past the village of Tavernoles. The views take in a stunning mountain and nearly lunar landscape over the Sau Reservoir. ✉ *Carretera Vic Roda de Ter, 08500,* ☎ *93/8887311. 36 rooms. Coffee shop, pool, tennis court. MC, V.*

Girona and Northern Catalonia Essentials

ARRIVING AND DEPARTING

By Bus: Sarfa (✉ Estació Norte–Vilanova Calle Alí Bei 80, ☎ 93/265–1158) has buses every 1½ hours to Girona, Figueres, and Cadaqués. For Vic try **Segalés** (Fabra i Puig Metro stop, ☎ 93/231–2756), and for Ripoll call **Teisa** (✉ Pau Claris 118, ☎ 93/488–2837).

By Car: Barcelona is now completely surrounded by a new network of *rondas,* or ring roads, with quick access from every corner of the city. Look for signs for these *rondas;* then follow signs to France (Francia), Girona, and the A7 *autopista,* which goes all the way to France. Leave the *autopista* at Salida (Exit) 7 for Girona. The 100-km (62-mi) ride to Girona takes about one hour.

By Train: Trains leave **Sants** and **Passeig de Gràcia** every 1½ hours for Girona, Figueres, and Port Bou. Some trains for northern Catalonia and France also leave from the França Station. For Vic and Ripoll, catch a Puigcerdà train (every hour or two) from Sants or Plaça de Catalunya.

GUIDED TOURS

Trenes Turísticos de RENFE (☎ 93/490–0202) operates guided tours to Girona by train May through September, leaving Sants at 10 AM and returning at 7:30 PM. It also runs train tours to Vic and Ripoll, leaving Sants at 9 AM and returning at 8:40 PM. The cost for each is 1,500 pesetas. Call RENFE to confirm.

The Costa Brava

The Costa Brava (Wild Coast) is a rocky stretch of shoreline that begins at Blanes and continues north through 135 km (84 mi) of coves and beaches to the French border at Port Bou. This tour concentrates on selected pockets—Tossa, Cap de Begur, Cadaqués—where the rocky terrain has discouraged the worst excesses of real-estate speculation. Here, on a good day, the luminous blue of the sea still contrasts with red-brown headlands and cliffs; the distant lights of fishing boats reflect on wine-color waters at dusk; and umbrella pines escort you to the fringes of secluded *calas* (coves) and sandy, white beaches.

Exploring the Costa Brava

58 The closest Costa Brava beaches to Barcelona are at **Blanes,** where, between May and October, launches (✉ Crucetours, ☎ 972/314969) can take you to Cala de Sant Francesc or the double beach at Santa Cristina.

59 The next stop north from Blanes along the coast road is **Tossa de Mar,** christened "blue paradise" by painter Marc Chagall, who summered here in 1934. The only Chagall painting in Spain is in Tossa's Museu Municipal (Municipal Museum, ☎ 972/340709, ✉ 350 ptas., ☉ Tues.–Sun. 10–1, 5–8). Tossa's walled medieval town and pristine beaches are both among Catalonia's best.

60 **Sant Feliu de Guixols** comes next after Tossa de Mar, after 23 km (15 mi) of hairpin curves over hidden inlets. Tiny turnouts or parking spots on this route nearly always lead to intimate coves with stone stairways winding down from the road. Visit Sant Feliu's two fine beaches, church and monastery, Sunday market, and lovely Passeig del Mar.

61 **S'Agaró,** one of the Costa Brava's most elegant clusters of villas and seaside mansions, is just 3 km (2 mi) north of Sant Feliu. The 30-minute walk along the sea wall from La Gavina to Sa Conca beach is a delight.

62 Up the coast from S'Agaró, a road leads east to **Llafranc,** a small port with quiet waterfront hotels and restaurants, and forks right to **Calella de Palafrugell,** a pretty fishing village known for its July Habaneras (Catalan-Cuban sea chanties inspired by the Spanish-American War) festival. Just south is the panoramic promontory **Cap Roig,** with views of the barren Formigues (Ants) Isles and a fine botanical garden that you can tour with a guide for 450 ptas. March–December, daily 9–9. The left fork drops down to **Tamariu,** one of the Costa's prettiest inlet towns. A climb over the bluff leads down to the parador at **Aiguablava,** a modern eyesore overlooking magnificent cliffs and crags.

63 From **Begur,** the next town north of Aiguablava, you can go east through the *calas* or take the more inland route past the rose-color stone houses and ramparts of the restored medieval town of **Pals.** Nearby **Peratallada** is another medieval town with fortress, castle, tower, palace, and well-preserved walls. North of Pals there are signs for Ullastret, an Iberian village dating from the 5th century BC. **L'Estartit** is

64 the jumping-off point for spectacular **Parc Natural Submarí** (Underwater Natural Park), at the Medes Isles, famous for diving and for underwater photography.

65 The Greco-Roman ruins at **Empúries** are Catalonia's most important archaeological site. This port, complete with breakwater, is considered one of the most monumental ancient engineering feats on the Iberian Peninsula. As the Greek's original point of arrival in Spain, Empúries was also where the Olympic Flame entered Spain for Barcelona's 1992 Olympic Games.

66 The **Aiguamolls** (Marshlands), an important nature reserve filled with migratory waterfowl from all over Europe, lies mainly around **Castelló d'Empúries**, but the main information center is at El Cortalet, on the road in from Sant Pere Pescador. Follow the road from Empúries, crossing the Fluvià River at Sant Pere Pescador, and proceed north through the wetlands to Castelló. From Castelló d'Empúries, a series of roadways and footpaths traverse the marshes, the latter well marked on the maps available at the information center.

67 **Cadaqués,** Spain's easternmost town, still has the whitewashed charm that made this fishing village into an international artists' haunt in the early 20th century. The Marítim is the central hangout both day and night; after dark, you might also enjoy the Jardí, across the square. Salvador Dalí's house (now a museum) still stands at Portlligat, a 30-minute walk north of town.

The **Museu Perrot-Moore,** in the old town, has an important collection of graphic arts dating from the 15th to the 20th centuries, including works by Dalí. ☜ *400 ptas.* ⊙ *June 15–Oct. 15, daily 5–9.*

You can now visit the **Casa Museu Salvador Dalí,** a site long associated with Dalí's summer frolics with everyone from poets such as Federico García Lorca and Paul Eluard (whose wife, Gala, became Dalí's muse and spouse) to filmmaker Luis Buñuel. Filled with bits and pieces of the surrealist's daily life, it's an important point in the "Dalí triangle," completed by the castle at Púbol and the Museu Dalí, in Figueres. ⊠ *Port Lligat (3-km walk from town center, along beach),* ☎ *972/ 258063.* ☜ *1,200 ptas.* ⊙ *Tues.–Sun. 10:30–5:30*

The **Castillo Pubol,** Dalí's former castle-home, is now the resting place of Gala, his perennial model and mate. It's a chance to wander through yet more Dalí-esque landscape: lush gardens, fountains decorated with Wagner (the couple's favorite composer) masks, distinctive elephants with giraffe's legs and clawed feet. Two lions and a giraffe stand guard near Gala's tomb. ⊠ *Rte. 255 toward La Bisbal, 15 km (9 mi) east of A7's exit 6,* ☎ *972/511800.* ☜ *600 ptas.* ⊙ *Daily mid-March–June, 10:30–5:30, July–Sept., 10:30–7:30. Closed Oct.–mid-March.*

68 **Cap de Creus,** just north of Cadaqués, Spain's easternmost point, is a fundamental pilgrimage, if only for the symbolic geographical rush. The hike out to the lighthouse—through rosemary, thyme, and the salt air of the Mediterranean—is unforgettable. The Pyrenees officially end (or rise) here. New Year's Day finds mobs of revelers here awaiting the first emergence of the "new" sun from the Mediterranean.

69 The monastery of **Sant Pere de Rodes,** 7 km (4.3 mi) by car, plus a 20-minute walk, above the pretty fishing village El Port de la Selva, is the last and one of the most spectacular sites on the Costa Brava. Built in the 10th and early 11th centuries by Benedictine monks—and sacked and plundered repeatedly since—this Romanesque monolith commands a breathtaking panorama of the Pyrenees, the Empordà plain, the sweeping curve of the Bay of Roses, and Cap de Creus. (Topping off the grand trek across the Pyrenees, the Cap de Creus is a 6-hour walk away on the well-marked GR11 trail.)

Dining and Lodging

AIGUABLAVA

$$ ☷ **Parador de la Costa Brava.** This modern parador stands on a promontory overlooking sheer cliffs and surging seas. The service is impeccable. ⊠ *Parador Nacional Aiguablava, 17255, Begur, Girona,* ☎ *972/622162,* FAX *972/622166. 87 rooms. Restaurant, minibars, pool. AE, DC, MC, V.*

CADAQUÉS

$$$$ ✗ **El Bullí.** This famous restaurant is one of the top three or four in
★ Spain. It's located in Cala Montjoi, near Roses, 7 km (4½ mi) from
Cadaqués by sea or footpath and 22 km (14 mi) by car. Chef Fernando
Adrià will astound and delight your palate with his 12-course taster's
menu. ✉ *Cala Montjoi, Roses, Girona,* ☎ *972/150457. AE, DC, MC,
V. Closed Mon.–Tues.*

$$ ✗ **Can Pelayo.** This tiny, family-run restaurant serves the best fish in
town. It's hidden behind Plaça Port Alguer, a few minutes' walk south
of the town center ✉ *Carrer Nou 11,* ☎ *972/258356. MC, V. Closed
weekdays Oct.–May.*

$$–$$$ ✗▥ **Hotel Rocamar.** Rocamar has modern rooms with splendid views,
excellent service, and first-rate cuisine with no gourmet pretensions.
✉ *C. Doctor Bartomeus s/n, 17488 Cadaqués, Girona,* ☎ *972/258150,*
FAX *972/258650. 70 rooms. Restaurant, bar, indoor pool, tennis court.
AE, DC, MC, V.*

$$ ▥ **Hotel LlanéPetit.** This intimate little inn is just below the Rocamar
at beach level. It's charming, slightly less expensive, and has a very
Mediterranean air. ✉ *C. Doctor Bartomeus 37, 17488 Cadaqués,
Girona,* ☎ *972/258050,* FAX *972/258778. 37 rooms. Bar, breakfast room.
AE, DC, MC, V.*

CAP DE CREUS

$$ ✗▥ **Bar Cap de Creus.** Right next to the Cap de Creus lighthouse, this
restaurant commands spectacular views. The cuisine is simple and
good, and proprietor Chris Little rents three apartments (four beds each)
upstairs. ✉ *Cap de Creus s/n, 17488 Cadaqués, Girona,* ☎ *972/
159271. MC, V. Closed Mon.–Thurs. Oct.–June.*

PALAFRUGELL

$$ ✗ **Cypsele.** This restaurant serves such local fare as *es niu,* an explosive combination of game fowl, fish tripe, pork meatballs, and cuttle-
fish, stewed in a rich sauce. ✉ *C. Ancha 22,* ☎ *972/199005. MC, V.*

PERETALLADA

$$ ✗ **Can Bonay.** The fine local cuisine includes duck with turnips and
pig's feet with snails. The look is rustic, but the quality is first-rate. ✉
Plaça Espanya 4, ☎ *972/634034. MC, V.*

S'AGARÓ

$$$$ ▥ **El Hostal de la Gavina.** At the eastern corner of Sant Pol beach, this
hotel is a superb display of design and cuisine founded in 1932 by Josep
Ensesa, who invented S'Agaró itself. The Gavina offers complete com-
fort, superb dining, and tennis, golf, and riding nearby. ✉ *Plaça de la
Rosaleda s/n, 17248,* ☎ *972/321100,* FAX *972/321573. Restaurant. AE,
DC, MC, V.*

TAMARIU

$$ ✗ **Royal.** This sunny, beachside spot serves fisherman-style creations
of superb freshness and quality. The *suquet* (fish cooked slowly to create
its own juice, or *suc*) is especially commendable. ✉ *Passeig de Mar 9,*
☎ *972/620041. MC, V.*

TOSSA DE MAR

$$–$$$ ▥ **Hotel Mar Menuda.** This modern hideaway on the Costa Brava of-
fers as much peace and quiet—*and* as many varieties of water sports—
as you can possibly handle. Equipment and instruction are available
for windsurfing, sailing, swimming, and scuba diving. The hotel terrace overlooks the coast and the town of Tossa de Mar, with a medieval
castle and an old quarter full of cobbled streets. ✉ *Playa Mar Menuda*

s/n, 17320 Tossa de Mar, Girona, ☎ *972/341000,* ℻ *972/340087. 40 rooms, 10 suites. Restaurant, pool, tennis court. AE, DC, MC, V. Closed Nov. 1–Dec. 27.*

Costa Brava Essentials

ARRIVING AND DEPARTING

By Bus: Buses to Blanes, Lloret, Sant Feliu de Guixols, Platja d'Aro, Palamos, Begur, Roses, and Cadaqués are operated by **Sarfa** (⊠ Estació de Norte-Vilanova, C. Ali-Bei 80, ☎ 93/265–1158; Metro Arc de Triomf).

By Car: From Barcelona, the fastest way to the Costa Brava is to start up the A7 *autopista* as if to Girona and take Salida (Exit) 10 for Blanes. Coastal traffic can be slow and frustrating, and the roads tortuous.

By Train: A local train pokes along the coast to Blanes from Sants and Passeig de Gràcia or from Plaça Catalunya.

GUIDED TOURS

Between June 1 and September 31, Julià and Pullmantur run coach and cruise tours to Empúries, L'Estartit, the Medes Isles underwater park, and the medieval town of Pals. The Medes Isles stop includes lunch, swimming, and underwater exploration. Buses leave Barcelona at 9 and return at 6. The price per person is 10,500 pesetas with lunch, 8,250 pesetas without.

BARCELONA A TO Z

Arriving and Departing

By Bus

Barcelona has no central bus station, but most buses to Spanish destinations operate from the **Estació Norte Vilanova** (⊠ End of Av. Vilanova, a couple of blocks east of Arc de Triomf, ☎ 93/245–2528). Most international buses arrive at and depart from the **Estació Autobuses de Sants** (⊠ Carrer Viriato, next to Sants train station, ☎ 93/490–4000). Scores of independent companies operate from depots dispersed throughout town (☞ Excursions *in* Guided Tours, *below*).

By Car

Don't be intimidated by either driving or parking here. You can usually find a legal and safe parking place on the street, and underground public parking is increasingly plentiful.

By Plane

All international and domestic flights arrive at the spectacular glass, steel, and marble **El Prat de Llobregat** airport, 14 km (8½ mi) south of Barcelona, just off the main highway to Castelldefels and Sitges. For information on arrival and departure times, call Iberia at the airport (☎ 93/401–3131, 93/401–3535, or 93/301–3993; 93/302–7656 for international reservations and confirmations).The only airlines with direct flights from the United States to Barcelona are TWA and Delta.

Check first to see if your hotel provides a free shuttle service; otherwise, you can high-tail it into town via train, bus, taxi, or rental car.

BETWEEN THE AIRPORT AND DOWNTOWN

By Bus. The Aerobus leaves the airport for Plaça de Catalunya every 15 minutes (6 AM–11 PM) on weekdays and every 30 minutes (6:30 AM–10:50 PM) on weekends. From Plaça de Catalunya, it leaves for the airport every 15 minutes (5:30 AM–10:05 PM) on weekdays and every 30 minutes (6:30 AM–10:50 PM) on weekends. The fare is 500 pesetas.

By Car. Follow signs to the Centre Ciutat and you'll enter the city along Gran Via. For the port area, follow signs for the Ronda Litoral. The journey to the center of town can take anywhere from 15 to 45 minutes depending on traffic. Allow 15 minutes before 7:30 in the morning or after 9 at night.

By Taxi. Cab fare from the airport into town is 2,500–3,000 pesetas.

By Train. The train leaves the airport every 30 minutes between 6:12 AM and 10:13 PM. This train stops first at the Sants-Estació, then at Plaça de Catalunya, later at the Arc de Trionf, and finally at Clot. Trains going to the airport begin at 6 AM from the Clot station, stopping at the Arc de Trionf at 6:05 AM, Plaça de Catalunya at 6:08 AM, and Sants at 6:13 AM. The fare is 350 pesetas on weekdays, 375 pesetas on weekends and holidays.

By Train

Almost all long-distance and international trains arrive and depart from the **Sants-Estació** (⊠ Plaça dels Països Catalans s/n, ☎ 93/490–0202). En route to or from Sants, some trains stop at another station on **Passeig de Gràcia** (⊠ At Aragó, ☎ 93/490–0202). The Passeig de Gràcia station is often a good way to avoid the long lines that form at Sants during holidays. The **Estació de França** (⊠ Avda. Marques Argentera s/n, ☎ 93/319–3200), near the port, handles certain long-distance trains within Spain, some international trains, and particularly trains to and from France.

Getting Around

Modern Barcelona, above the Plaça de Catalunya, is built on a grid system, though there's no coordinated numbering system. The old town, from the Plaça de Catalunya to the port, is a labyrinth of narrow streets, and you'll need a good street map to get around it. Most sightseeing can be done on foot—you won't have any choice in the Barri Gòtic—but you'll need to use the metro or buses to link sightseeing areas. The Dia T1 is valid for one day of unlimited travel on all subway, bus, and FFCC lines. For general information on public transport, call 93/412–0000. Maps showing bus and metro routes are available free from booths in Plaça de Catalunya.

By Boat

Golondrinas harbor boats make short trips from the Portal de la Pau, near the Columbus Monument. The fare is 500 pesetas for a 30-minute trip. Departures are spring and summer (Holy Week through Sept.), daily 11–7; fall and winter, weekends and holidays only, 11–5. It's closed December 16–January 2. For information call ☎ 93/442–3106.

By Bus

City buses run daily from 5:30 AM to 11:30 PM. The fare is 145 pesetas (155 pesetas Sunday and holidays); for multiple journeys purchase a Targeta T1, which buys you 10 rides for 800 pesetas (like the metro's T2, plus buses). Route maps are displayed at bus stops. Note that those with a red band always stop at a central square—Catalunya, Universitat, or Urquinaona—and blue indicates a night bus. From June 12 to October 12 the **Bus Turístic** (9:30–7:30 every 30 minutes) runs on a circuit that passes all the important sights. A day's ticket, which you can buy on the bus, costs 1,300 pesetas (850 pesetas half day) and also covers the fare for the Tramvía Blau, funicular, and Montjuïc cable car across the port. The ride starts at Plaça de Catalunya.

By Cable Car and Funicular

The Montjuïc Funicular is a cog railroad that runs from the junction of Avinguda Paral.lel and Nou de la Rambla to the Miramar Amusement Park on Montjuïc (Metro: Paral.lel). It operates weekends and holidays 11 AM–8 PM in winter, and daily 11 AM–9:30 PM in summer; the fare is 145 pesetas. A *teleféric* then takes you from the amusement park up to Montjuïc Castle. In winter the *teleféric* runs weekends and holidays 11–2:45 and 4–7:30; in summer, daily 11:30–9. The fare is 375 pesetas.

A Transbordador Aeri Harbor Cable Car runs between Miramar and Montjuïc across the harbor to Torre de Jaume I on Barcelona's *moll* (quay), and on to Torre de Sant Sebastià, at the end of Passeig Joan de Borbó in Barceloneta. You can board at either stage. The fare is 850 pesetas (1,000 pesetas round-trip), and the car runs October–June, weekdays noon–5:45, weekends noon–6:15, and July–September, daily 11–9.

To reach the summit of Tibidabo, take the metro to Àvinguda de Tibidabo, then the Tramvía Blau (275 pesetas one-way) to Peu del Funicular, and finally the Tibidabo Funicular (375 pesetas one-way) from there to the Tibidabo fairground. It runs every 30 minutes, 7:05 AM–9:35 PM ascending, 7:25 AM–9:55 PM descending.

By Metro

The subway is the fastest, cheapest, and easiest way to get around Barcelona. You pay a flat fare of 135 pesetas no matter how far you travel, but it's more economical to buy a Targeta T2 (valid for metro and FFCC Generalitat trains, Tramvía Blau [blue tram], and the Montjuïc Funicular; ☞ *above*), which costs 700 pesetas for 10 rides. The system runs 5 AM–11 PM (until 1 AM on weekends and holidays).

By Taxi

Taxis are black and yellow and show a green light when available for hire. The meter starts at 325 pesetas (which lasts for six minutes), and there are supplements for luggage, night travel, Sundays and holidays, rides from a station or to the airport, and for going to or from the bullring or a football match. There are cab stands all over town, and you can also hail cabs on the street. Make sure the driver turns on the meter. To call a cab, try ☎ 93/387–1000, 93/490–2222, or 93/357–7755, 24 hours a day.

Guided Tours

Excursions

These are run by **Julià Tours** and **Pullmantur** and are booked as outlined below. The most popular trips are full or half-day tours to Montserrat and day trips to the Costa Brava resorts, including a cruise to the Medes Isles.

Orientation

Urban sightseeing tours are run by **Julià Tours** (⊠ Ronda Universitat 5, ☎ 93/317–6454) and **Pullmantur** (⊠ Gran Via 635, ☎ 93/318–5195).Tours leave from these offices, but you may be able to arrange a pick-up at your hotel. Prices are 4,600 pesetas for a half day and 11,750 pesetas for a full day, including lunch.

Personal Guides

Contact **City Guides Barcelona** (☎ 93/412–0674), the **Barcelona Guide Bureau** (☎ 93/268–2422), or the **Asociación Profesional de Informadores Turísticos** (93/319–8416) for a list of English-speaking guides.

Special-Interest and Walking Tours

La Ruta del Modernismo (The Modernism Route), created by Barcelona's *ajuntament* (town hall), connects some 50 key sites in the city's rich endowment of Art Nouveau architecture. Everything from Gaudí's first lamppost to the colossal Sagrada Família to the odd Moderniste phar-

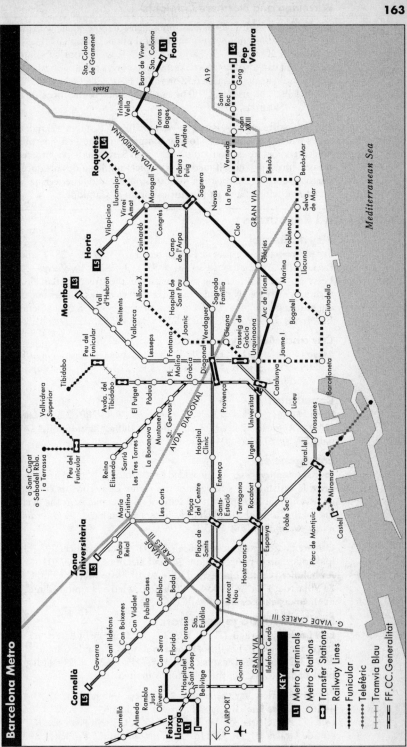

Barcelona Metro

macy or bakery shows up in this comprehensive route, along with guided visits of buildings not open to the general public. Palau Güell (⊠ Carrer Nou de Rambla 3–5, ☎ 93/317–3974) is the tour's "kilometer zero." You can also buy the ticket, which covers admission to all sites on the walk, at the Casa Lleó Morera (⊠ Passeig de Gràcia 35, ☎ 93/488–0139). The price is 1,500 pesetas for adults. Both offices are open Monday–Saturday 10–7.

The bookstore in the Palau de la Virreina (⊠ La Rambla 99) rents cassettes whose walking tours follow footprints painted on sidewalks—different colors for different tours—through Barcelona's most interesting areas. The do-it-yourself method is to pick up the guides produced by the tourist office, *Discovering Romanesque Art* and *Discovering Modernist Art,* which have art itineraries for all of Catalonia.

Contacts and Resources

Bicycle Rental
Try **Bicitram** (⊠ Marquès de l'Argentera 15, ☎ 93/792–2841) and **Los Filicletos** (⊠ Passeig de Picasso 38, ☎ 93/319–7811). **Un Menys**—"One Less," in Catalan, meaning one less car on the streets of Barcelona—organizes increasingly popular outings that tack drinks, dinner, and dancing onto a gentle bike ride for a total price of about 5,000 pesetas. ⊠ *Esparteria 3,* ☎ *93/268–2105,* 𝔽𝔸𝕏 *93/319–4298. AE, DC, MC, V.*

Car and Motorcycle Rental
Atesa (⊠ Balmes 141, ☎ 93/237–8140), **Avis** (⊠ Casanova 209, ☎ 93/209–9533), **Hertz** (⊠ Tuset 10, ☎ 93/217–3248), and **Vanguard** (cars and motorcycles; ⊠ Londres 31, ☎ 93/439–3880).

Consulates
United States (⊠ Passeig Reina Elisenda 23, ☎ 93/280–2227), **Canada** (⊠ Via Augusta 125, ☎ 93/209–0634), **United Kingdom** (⊠ Diagonal 477, ☎ 93/419–9044).

Emergencies
Tourist Attention, a service provided by the local police department, will provide assistance if you've been the victim of a crime, need medical or psychological help, or need temporary documents in the event of loss of the originals. English interpreters are on hand. ⊠ *Guardia Urbana, Ramblas 43,* ☎ *93/301–9060.*

Other emergency services: **Police** (☎ 091 national police; 092 municipal police; main police station: ⊠ Via Laietana 43, ☎ 93/301–6666). **Ambulance** (Creu Roja, ☎ 93/300–2020). **Hospital** (Hospital Clinic: ⊠ Villarroel 170; ☎ 93/454–6000/7000; Metro Hospital Clinic, blue line). **Emergency doctors** (☎ 061).

English-Language Bookstores
BCN Books (⊠ Aragó 277, ☎ 93/487–3455) is one of Barcelona's top stores for books in English. **El Corte Inglés** (⊠ Plaça de Catalunya 14, ☎ 93/302–1212; ⊠ Diagonal 617, ☎ 93/419–2828) sells English guidebooks and novels, but the selection is limited.

For more variety, try the **English Bookshop** (Entença 63, ☎ 93/425–4466), **Jaimes Bookshop** (⊠ Passeig de Gràcia 64, ☎ 93/215–3626), **Laie** (⊠ Pau Claris 85, ☎ 93/318–1357), **Libreria Francesa** (⊠ Passeig de Gràcia 91, ☎ 93/215–1417), **Come In** (⊠ Provença 203, ☎ 93/253–1204), or **Llibreria Bosch** (⊠ Ronda Universitat 11, ☎ 93/317–5308; ⊠ Roselló 24, ☎ 93/321–3341). The bookstore at the **Palau de la Virreina** (⊠ La Rambla 99, ☎ 93/301–7775) has good books on art, design, and Barcelona in general.

Late-Night Pharmacies

Look on the door of any pharmacy or in any local newspaper under "Farmacias de Guardia" for the addresses of those open late at night or 24 hours. Alternately, dial 010.

Travel Agencies

American Express (✉ Rosselló 257, at Passeig de Gràcia, ☎ 93/217–0070), **Iberia** (✉ Diputació 258, at Passeig de Gràcia, ☎ 93/401–3381; ✉ Plaça de Espanya, ☎ 93/325–7358), **WagonsLits Cook** (✉ Passeig de Gràcia 8, ☎ 93/317–5500), and **Bestours** (✉ Diputación 241, ☎ 93/487–8580).

Visitor Information

Tourist offices dealing primarily with Barcelona are at the **Centre d'Informació Turistic de Barcelona** (✉ Plaça de Catalunya 17, lower level, ☎ 93/304–3135, FAX 93/304–3155; ⊙ daily 9–9); **Sants-Estació,** open daily 8–8; **Estació França,** open daily 8–8; **Palau de Congressos** (✉ Av. María Cristina s/n), open daily 10–8 during trade fairs and congresses only; **ajuntament** (✉ Plaça Sant Jaume), open June 24–September, weekdays 9–8 and Saturday 8:30–2:30; and **Palau de la Virreina** (✉ La Rambla 99), open Monday–Saturday 9–9 and Sunday 10–2.

Offices with information about Catalonia and the rest of Spain are at **El Prat Airport** (☎ 93/478–4704), open Monday–Saturday 9:30–8 and Sunday 9:30–3, and **Centre d'Informació Turística** (✉ Palau Robert, Passeig de Gràcia 107 [at Diagonal], ☎ 93/238–4000), open Monday–Saturday 10–7. For general information and referrals in English, dial 010.

In summer (July 24–September 15), **tourist information aides** patrol the Gothic Quarter and Ramblas area 9 AM–9 PM; they travel in pairs and are recognizable by their uniforms of red shirts, white trousers or skirts, and badges.

5 Portrait of Madrid and Barcelona

Spanish Food and Wine

SPANISH FOOD AND WINE

THE CUISINE of Spain is among the most varied and sophisticated in Europe. Favored by a wealth of natural produce almost unrivaled, Spain has traditionally been an agricultural country, famous since ancient times for its extensive wheat fields, vineyards, and olive groves and for pig and cattle raising. A recent medical report has even concluded that the Spaniards eat more healthily than any other Western nation, largely because they insist on fresh produce and avoid canned and convenience foods.

The geographic variety of the peninsula accounts, of course, for the extremely varied nature of Spain's produce. For instance, the snowcapped mountains of the Sierra Nevada have Nordic cultures on their upper slopes, while those lower down yield tropical fruits unique to Europe, such as custard apples. And with both an Atlantic and a Mediterranean coastline, Spain boasts an exceptional range of fish and seafood.

Another major influence on Spanish cuisine has been the 7½ centuries of Moorish presence here. The Moors gave Iberian cooking an exotic quality by using new ingredients, such as saffron, almonds, and peppers; they introduced the art of making sweets and pastries; and they created refreshing dishes such as *ajo blanco* (a cold almond-based soup) that are still popular today. One of the world's pioneering gastronomes was Ziryab, an Arab who worked in 10th-century Córdoba and brought to Europe the new Arab fashion for eating a regular sequence of dishes, beginning with soup and ending with dessert.

Whether inherited from the Moors or not, Spaniards' love of food stretches back at least several centuries. A famous poem by the 16th-century Sevillian writer Baltasar del Alcázar expresses this feeling:

There are three things
That hold my heart Love's captive
My fair Inés, cured ham,
And aubergines and cheese

When traveling around their country, Spaniards often seem to prefer hunting down local gastronomic specialties to visiting museums and monuments. They tend to assume that foreigners do not share their passion for food—both because so many tourists are unadventurous in their tastes, and because they refuse to adapt to Spain's idiosyncratic eating times and traditions. You're more likely to find outstanding food in a dirty village bar where olive stones and shrimp heads are spat out onto the floor than in many luxurious urban restaurants; the Spaniards aren't as snobbish about eating as, say, the French are. But if you decide to have lunch before 2 PM or dine before 10, the only restaurants you'll find open are probably those that cater to bland international tastes.

The most Spanish of culinary traditions is undoubtedly that of the tapa (bar snack). Many people who dismiss Spanish food as unimaginative will make an exception of the tapa, without realizing that these snacks are miniature versions of classic dishes served in restaurants or in Spanish homes. The tradition originated in Andalusia, where a combination of heat and poverty made it impractical to sit down to a heavy meal in a restaurant. Today tapas are generally taken as appetizers before lunch or supper, but in the south they are still often regarded as a meal in themselves. Eating tapas allows you to sample the variety of Spanish food and also prevents you from getting too drunk, especially if you decide to go on a *tapeo*, the Spanish equivalent of a bar crawl. In some of the more old-fashioned bars, you are automatically served a tapa of the barman's choice when you order a drink. Having to choose a tapa yourself is not always easy, for the barman often recites at great speed a seemingly interminable list. The timid, baffled tourist usually ends up pointing to some familiar tapa that's standing on the counter.

THE SPANIARDS' predilection for tasting small quantities of many dishes also shows up in restaurants, where they normally share food and order dishes *para picar* (to nibble at).

A selection of *raciones* (larger versions of tapas) makes a popular starter for those dining in a group.

Soups in Spain tend not to be smooth and creamy, as they are in France, but watery, highly spiced, and very garlicky. One of the most common hot soups is a *sopa de ajo* (garlic soup), which consists of water, oil, garlic, paprika, stale bread, and cured ham. This is far more appetizing than it sounds, as is the famous gazpacho, a cold blend of water, bread, garlic, tomatoes, and peppers. Most people today make gazpacho in a blender, but it's best when prepared by hand in a terra-cotta mortar, the ingredients slowly pounded with a pestle. There are several variations on gazpacho, including *salmorejo,* which comes from Córdoba and has a denser texture. Particularly good is the *ajo blanco,* the basis of which is almonds rather than tomatoes; served always with peeled muscatel grapes or slices of honeydew melon, this dish encapsulates the Moorish custom of combining sweet and savory flavors.

The Spanish egg dish best known abroad is the *tortilla* (not the same as the Mexican tortilla—here it's an omelette of onions and potatoes), which is generally eaten cold. *Huevos flamencos* ("Gypsy eggs") is a traditional Sevillian dish now found in all parts of Spain, consisting of eggs fried in a terra-cotta dish with cured ham, tomatoes, and a selection of green vegetables. The exact ingredients vary as much as Gypsy cooking itself, which tends cleverly to incorporate whatever is at hand.

The Spaniards—and the Andalusians and Galicians in particular—are known for consuming vast quantities of fish and seafood. Some of the finest seafood washes up in western Andalusia and in Galicia, the former being renowned for shrimp, prawns, and crayfish, the latter for oysters, lobsters, and crabs, and the much sought-after (if revolting-looking) *percebes* (goose barnacles). Another specialty of the Galician coast is scallops chopped up with breadcrumbs, onions, parsley, and peppers and served in their shells (the same shells that Christian pilgrims wear on their way to Santiago de Compostela). *Changurro,* a stuffed king crab, is a specialty of the Basque country, where you'll also find one of Spain's most interesting fish dishes, *bacalao al pil-pil* (cod fried in garlic and covered in a green sauce made from the gelatin of the fish). A fish dish now common all over Spain is *trucha a la Navarra* (trout wrapped in pieces of bacon). In Andalusia most fish is deep-fried in batter—which is why the place is sometimes disparagingly called the "land of the fried fish" by outsiders. In fact, you need considerable art, as well as spanking-fresh fish, to be able to fry the fish as well as Andalusians do, and to and achieve the requisite texture of crispness on the outside and succulence inside. The *chancetes* (whitebait) and *sardinas* (sardines) are especially good in Málaga, and you should try the *salmonetes* (red mullet) and *acedías* (miniature sole) along the Cádiz coast. *Adobo,* also delicious, is fried fish marinated in wine.

THE COLD MEATS and sausage products of Spain are renowned—in particular, the cured hams of Trevélez and Jabugo, the *chorizo* (spicy paprika sausage), and the *morcilla* (blood sausages) of Granada and Burgos, the latter sometimes incorporating nuts. Meat, when served hot, is usually unaccompanied by a sauce or vegetables and presented rare. The great meat-eating center of Spain is Castile, which is famous for its *cochinillo* (suckling pig), a specialty of Segovia, and *cordero* (lamb), both of which are roasted in wood or clay ovens. The most sophisticated and elaborate poultry dishes in Spain are prepared in the Catalan district of Girona and include chicken with lobster and turkey stuffed with raisins, pine nuts, and *butifarras* (spicy Catalan sausages).

Fish, meat, and seafood come together in *paella,* a saffron-flavored rice dish that many consider the most typical of Spanish dishes. Paella originated in Valencia and, in fact, dates no earlier than the late 19th century. The one Spanish dish that can truly claim to be the most national and traditional is the meat stew referred to by Madrileños as *cocido,* by Andalusians as *potaje,* and by Catalans as *escudella.* Despite the slight regional variations, the three basic ingredients remain the same—meats, legumes, and vegetables. The dish is usually served in three courses, beginning with the broth in which everything is cooked and finishing with the meats, which Spaniards sometimes shred and mix together on their plates to form what they call *pringa.*

The range and quality of Spanish cheeses is impressive, but most of them are little-known and can be bought only in the area where they're made. The hard cheeses of La Mancha are best well matured—a good *Manchego viejo* is almost the equal of an Italian Parmesan. If you can find it, try *Cabrales,* an exquisite sheep's cheese that is rather like a melting Roquefort.

SPANIARDS DO not usually finish a meal with a dessert. They tend to bake the many almond- and honey-based sweets and pastries of Moorish derivation, such as *polvorones,* only around Christmas or Easter. Ever since St. Teresa devised *yemas* (candied egg yolks), Spanish convents have specialized in all kinds of sweet products. The yemas were once distributed free to the poor, but their production has now become a profitable industry for the nuns. The correct procedure for buying anything from a convent is to ring the bell and then address the nun (who is often hidden behind a rotating drum) with the words *Ave María Purísima.* You can then proceed to order your yemas, *bizcochos* (sponge biscuits), *tocinos de cielo* (an excellent variant of crème caramel), or whatever else appears on the list pinned up in the convent's entrance hall.

Spain claims to be more extensively covered with vineyards than is any other country in the world. Until recently, foreigners have considered the quality of Spanish wines barely equal to the quantity; Spanish "plonk" was thought suitable only for parties where people would be too drunk to notice. The Spaniards themselves, as unpretentious in their drinking as in their eating habits, did not help matters by washing wine down with *gaseosa* (carbonated lemonade) and buying wine from great barrels simply marked *tinto* (red) or *blanco* (white), along with a figure indicating the alcohol content. Recently, increased tourism has led to the enormous promotion of Spanish wines, which are now very much in fashion. Villages with excellent wine that has yet to be commercialized do still exist.

The cheap variety of Spanish wines comes mainly from Valdepeñas, in the middle of the dreary plains of La Mancha, Spain's largest wine-growing area. On the other end of the scale are the celebrated red wines of La Rioja, which have a full-bodied, woody flavor thanks to having matured for up to eight years in casks made of American oak (the oldest and best of these wines are labeled *Reserva*). This aging technique was introduced by French vintners from Bordeaux and Burgundy, who moved to the Rioja in the 19th century, hoping to escape the phylloxera epidemic that was destroying the vines in their own country. Curiously, however, there are few places today in France where wine is aged as long as it is here. Among the better Riojas are those of Imperial, Marqués de Murrieta, and Marqués de Riscal. Marqués de Riscal, in fact, has recently moved into the nearby Rueda district, where it has marketed one of Spain's most distinguished white wines. Catalonia specializes in sparkling white wines (the most renowned being Codorniu and Freixenet), and produces Spain's greatest variety of wines overall.

THE ONE Spanish wine that has always been popular with foreigners is sherry. The English have dominated the sherry trade in Jerez de la Frontera since the 16th century, and most of the famous labels are foreign (Domecq, Harvey, and Sandeman, for instance). The classic dry sherry is the *fino; amontillado* is deeper in color and taste, and *oloroso* is really a sweet dessert wine. Another fortified Andalusian wine is Manzanilla, which is made in the delightful coastal town of Sanlúcar de Barrameda and depends for its production on the cool sea breezes there. This wine, with a faint tang of the sea, does not travel well, and there are even those who believe that it tastes better in the lower part of Sanlúcar than in the upper town. Sherry and Manzanilla are generally thought of as aperitif wines, and indeed they are the ideal accompaniment to tapas; to eat a Sanlúcar prawn with a glass of Manzanilla is many Spaniards' idea of paradise. Spaniards tend also to drink sherry and Manzanilla when sitting down to a meal, a custom that has yet to catch on outside the country. In England, sherry still has the genteel associations of an Oxford college, but the Spaniards have a more robust attitude toward it. You'll probably never think of sherry in the same way again if you attend Seville's *Feria de Abril,* where more sherry and Manzanilla are reputedly drunk in a week than in the whole of Spain the rest of the year. Incidentally, Manzanilla has a reputation for not creating a hangover, and some make the dubious claim that it is an excellent cure for gout.

Some of Spain's finest brandies, such as Osborne, Terry, Duque de Alba, and Carlos III, also come from Jerez. Málaga has a sweet dessert wine that enjoyed a vogue with the English in the 19th century (look for the label Scholtz). *Aguardientes* (aquavits) are manufactured throughout Spain, with the most famous brands coming from Chinchón, near Madrid. A sweet and popular liquor called Ponche Caballero comes in a silver-coated bottle that looks like an amateur explosive. Sangria, which many tourists enjoy, should consist of fruits, wine, brandy, and Cointreau but is usually served as a watered-down combination of wine and lemonade with the odd piece of orange thrown in. If you *really* want to look like a tourist, try drinking wine from a *porrón,* a glass vessel from which you pour the wine into your mouth from a distance of at least one foot. A raincoat is recommended.

You are truly initiated into Spanish ways after your first night spent drinking until dawn. Ideally, you'll follow this experience by a snack of *churros* (doughnut fritters) dipped into hot chocolate; the more hardened souls will order a morning glass of aguardiente. After a few hours' sleep, you'll have a proper breakfast (around 11 o'clock) consisting of toast rubbed in garlic or covered in *manteca colorada* (spicy pig's fat). Soon it will be time for the midday tapas—and so a typical Spanish day continues.

—Michael Jacobs

INDEX

WHEREVER YOU TRAVEL, *H*ELP IS NEVER FAR AWAY.

From planning your trip to providing travel assistance along the way, American Express® Travel Service Offices are always there to help you do more.

Madrid and Barcelona

American Express Travel Service
Plaza de las Cortes 2
Madrid
(34) (91) 3225445

American Express Travel Service
Paseo de Gracia 101
Corner Rosellon
Barcelona
(34) (93) 2170070

do more AMERICAN EXPRESS
Travel